WHEN BAD MEN COMBINE

THE STAR ROUTE SCANDAL AND THE TWILIGHT OF GILDED AGE POLITICS

SHAWN FRANCIS PETERS

LOUISIANA STATE UNIVERSITY PRESS

BATON ROUGE

Published by Louisiana State University Press
lsupress.org

Designer: Barbara Neely Bourgoyne
Typeface: Whitman

Cover illustration: "On the Trail of Corruption," chromolithograph by
Joseph F. Keppler, printed in Puck, May 4, 1881.

Cataloging-in-Publication Data are available at the Library of Congress.

ISBN 978-0-8071-7900-0 (cloth)
ISBN 978-0-8071-7961-1 (epub)
ISBN 978-0-8071-7962-8 (pdf)

When bad men combine, the good must associate; else they will fall,
one by one, an unpitied sacrifice in a contemptible struggle.

—EDMUND BURKE, "Thoughts on the Cause of the Present Discontents" (1770)

CONTENTS

Illustrations follow page 96

PREFACE
Fraud at Its Finest

Chances are, you do not know much, if anything, about the subject of this book. These days, few people do.

The Star Route scandal, which roiled American politics in the 1870s and 1880s, has received scant attention from scholars of American political history for the past 150 years. To my knowledge, no one has ever written a book about it previously, and it has been the subject of only a handful of peer-reviewed scholarly articles, the most prominent of which was published in the venerable *Mississippi Valley Historical Review* almost ninety years ago (in 1935). Someone earlier penned a fine master's thesis about it at the University of Wisconsin–Madison. (This was all the way back in 1918.) The most recent study of note to focus on the subject at any length was a doctoral dissertation completed in 1980. Most of this scattered and fairly obscure scholarly activity took place before I was born in the mid-1960s. If you want to learn about the topic, you really have to do some digging—and, even then, you might not turn up very much.

When I first started looking into the Star Route affair, I was puzzled by the almost total lack of attention it had received from historians and political scientists. After all, here was a gripping story of political corruption that embroiled some of the most prominent men in the United States (including four presidents, several cabinet officers, and many members of Congress) and captured the nation's attention for more than a decade. Year after year in the 1870s and 1880s, stories recounting the sordid details of the scandal were routinely featured in newspapers across the country. Politicians in both major parties repeatedly invoked the Star Route uproar to assail their partisan enemies and, more substantively, to make a case for reforming the nation's civil-service system. In short, in its time, the Star Route scandal was a major political event, not a mere footnote.

So why has no one really paid close attention to this significant and compelling story for the last century and a half? As the contemporary saying goes, it's complicated—very, very complicated.

The tumult over the mishandling of Star Routes, which reached its height with two spectacular criminal trials in Washington, DC, in 1882 and 1883, centered on the manipulation of postal-delivery contracts by cunning entrepreneurs and their accomplices within the federal Post Office Department (what we now know as the U.S. Postal Service). No one ever really knew how many mail contractors or government officials were involved, or how much they fleeced from the federal government by inflating the value of the contracts at issue. Our best guess is that the main group of Star Route culprits—often called a "ring" or "combination"—illegally siphoned off at least $400,000 (the equivalent of about $11 million in 2021), but some estimates put the overall actual figure of the government's losses at closer to $4 million (over $100 million today). Likewise, it was hard to know how many postal routes were affected by these rampant frauds. That federal politicians and bureaucrats were involved in Star Route contracting swindles (either by taking bribes and kickbacks themselves or by simply looking the other way when others cheated) was one of the worst-keep secrets in Washington, but the case was so sprawling that no one ever seemed to know its exact boundaries.

The two lengthy Star Route trials clarified things, but only somewhat. The federal government's case was, to put it kindly, a mess, and both juries almost certainly were compromised by bribery. A subsequent congressional investigation of this prosecution—incredibly, the *seventh* such inquiry that examined the Star Route frauds over a period of about a dozen years—amounted to little more than a glorified exercise in finger-pointing. Despite the best efforts of a phalanx of attorneys, investigators, journalists, and politicians, it seemed that no one ever really got to the bottom of what had actually happened with the dubious postal contracts.

Aside from the sheer complexity of the story, there was also the matter of its timing. The controversy over the mishandling of Star Route contracts began during the presidency of Ulysses Grant and continued through the tenure of his successor, Rutherford Hayes. It probably reached its peak just as James

Garfield was taking office as president in 1881. To his credit, Garfield gave the matter his full attention and agonized over how it should be addressed by his administration, but he was shot, and later died, just a few months after being sworn into office. Chester Arthur succeeded him as president and, somewhat awkwardly, inherited the case. The misadventure thus lasted over four presidential administrations, making it difficult to neatly categorize in a chronological sense.

All of which is to say that I now understand why no one before me has ever endeavored to write a book about the Star Route scandal. It is a hard story to tell.

It is, however, a tale well worth telling. Individuals involved in untangling the mystery of the Star Route affair understood its import and rarely shied away from underscoring its seriousness and significance. In 1883, Attorney General Benjamin Brewster privately told William Chandler, the well-connected secretary of the Navy, about "these complicated and infamous cases, in which a body of scoundrels defy the whole judicial power of the Government, after they have abused great public trusts." Brewster, who was part of the team that prosecuted the Star Route case before becoming attorney general in 1881, spoke for many when he asserted that the frauds "brought the public service into shame and scandal, and robbed the public Treasury of millions of money collected from the people and dedicated by law to a function of government of the greatest general necessity."[1]

Brewster's biographer, Eugene Coleman Savidge, agreed with his assessment of the Star Route swindle and the epic legal battle that it precipitated. Writing in 1891, Savidge claimed: "The famous Star Route trials are without parallel in American history. . . . Not only did they involve grave legal questions, the recovery of fabulous sums of money, and the punishment of an army of evil-doers, but they struck deeply and relentlessly into the deepest influences surrounding our body politic." Savidge marveled that the frauds— and the federal government's bungling efforts to prosecute those implicated in perpetrating them—had such profound political consequences for the nation in the post-Reconstruction era. "They involved the political control of the United States Senate, the financial policy of a great government, the peace of two Presidents, one Presidential candidate, and two distinguished cabinets," he observed. "They drew tears and the wringing of hands from the very Senate chamber, charged with heaviness an atmosphere to resound to the sharp crack of the assassin's pistol, and injected a Democratic interregnum into the long rule of the Republican party." And for Savidge, the Star Route cases were more than just grubby political affairs. "They display the quaintest medley of influences and motives—vanity, ambition, revenge, avarice, fear—and yield an indescribable aroma of the underlying strata of Washington life," he wrote. "There is symbolized a range of motives as wide as destiny itself."[2]

Henry Adams, the great nineteenth-century man of letters and a keen observer of American political life, followed the Star Route case closely from his home in Washington. He wrote that the real-life misdeeds of the scandal's principal actors were more lurid than anything found in the often shocking realist novels of Honoré Balzac and William Makepeace Thackeray. A reformer, Adams believed that the scandal, and the government's clumsy response to it, represented everything that had gone wrong with American politics in the years after the Civil War.[3]

Adams was a great friend of Wayne MacVeagh, who, as Brewster's predecessor as attorney general, had helped get the federal government's postal-corruption prosecution underway in 1881. MacVeagh, too, was stunned by the frauds as he reviewed the evidence that had been compiled by government investigators. "These revelations these papers make would indeed seem to us most extraordinary but that we have grown familiar with such things," he wrote to Postmaster General Thomas James. "Mark Twain, I am sure, would never have invented them."[4]

Most contemporaneous evaluations of the Star Route affair failed to match the soaring rhetoric found in Savidge's analysis or the literary bent of Adams and MacVeagh. In the 1870s and 1880s, press coverage of the postal frauds was as hyperbolic and cynical as it was pervasive. Typical headlines termed the corrupt scheme "Fraud at Its Finest" and the "Slickest of Swindles." Even before the first Star Route trial laid bare all of the squalid the details of the alleged bid-rigging conspiracy, the *Chicago Daily Inter Ocean* argued, "Never has so despicable a scheme of robbery been conceived in such wanton disregard of public right and decency, and pushed forward to success more brazenly."[5]

The trials themselves—both of them marathon proceedings marked by intrigue and bombast—also seemed extraordinary to observers in the press. With the nation seemingly hanging on their every word, some of the best lawyers in the country matched wits and expounded upon weighty matters of law, ethics, and politics. "The Star route trials are in some particulars unprecedented in the history of the country," the New York *Sun* observed. Not that the proceedings really satisfied anyone. After they had ended, the *New York Times* lamented that "the long trials ended in a flagrant and scandalous miscarriage of justice." As often happens in messy political-corruption cases, there was no neat, clean triumph of justice and the rule of law over rascality and greed.[6]

This book represents a modest effort to finally untangle this important but long-forgotten history. Doing so provides a glimpse into a uniquely tumultuous period in American political history. In the 1870s and 1880s, both major parties—and American society in general—grappled with the end of Reconstruction and the untidy business of creating a new political and social order. Following the many twists and turns of the Star Route case allows us to examine how modern politics emerged, in fits and starts, from the enormous upheaval wrought by the Civil War.

One important change came in the nature of government itself. A dizzying and seemingly nonstop series of scandals plagued American politics in the 1870s. What has been dubbed by historian Mark Wahlgren Summers as "the era of good stealings" featured the infamous "Salary Grab" of 1873, the New York Custom House imbroglio, the Crédit Mobilier scandal, and the excesses of the Whiskey Ring, all of them involving federal officials who abused their positions in order to enrich themselves. The Star Route case was, in some respects, the final straw for those who believed that the time had come for a system grounded in avarice and political patronage to be replaced by one based on professional competence and merit. It was no coincidence that the landmark Pendleton Civil Service Act was signed into law by President Arthur in the middle of the second Star Route trial in 1883.[7]

The Star Route prosecution also demonstrated how political and professional rivalries and allegiances can complicate the pursuit of justice in a political-corruption case. The prosecution was formally launched in 1881 by a Republican administration that found itself in the uncomfortable position of investigating the alleged wrongdoing of two men, Tom Brady and Stephen Dorsey, who had rendered important—and almost certainly nefarious— services to the party in the previous two presidential elections, both of which the Republicans had won by razor-thin margins. (Brady had aided the Hayes campaign in Florida in 1876, while Dorsey had performed crucial work in Indiana for the Garfield campaign in 1880.) Successive Republican administrations never could shake the accusation that they were not genuinely committed to prosecuting men who had, to some degree, helped make the administrations possible through underhanded campaign tactics. These efforts were rendered all the more difficult by the prosecutors themselves, a mismatched set of attorneys who bickered constantly and routinely accused one another of wrongdoing—often with good reason.

A further complication was the assassination of President Garfield in 1881. Garfield lingered near death and then succumbed just as the federal government's efforts in the Star Route case got underway. The prosecution fell into the lap of his overmatched successor, Chester Arthur, a machine politician who never had shown much enthusiasm for ferreting out corruption and promoting reform. (Indeed, Arthur himself seemed to personify the disreputable "spoils system" loathed by so many Americans.) To the surprise of many, Arthur did not scuttle the case in order to protect his fellow Republican Stalwarts, but his administration's faltering handling of it ultimately helped pave the way for the party's failures at the ballot box in 1882 and 1884.

It is also important to note the possible connections between the Star Route affair and Garfield's assassination, links that have heretofore never been fully appreciated by scholars of this period. The president's killer, Charles Guiteau, clearly was inflamed by the toxic political atmosphere that swirled around Garfield in the first months of his administration. At a bare minimum, the bitter controversy over the postal-corruption case—which was fed not only by partisan charges leveled at Republicans by Democrats but also by intense intraparty squabbling between competing Republican factions—helped create the poisonous political environment that inspired the deranged Guiteau. Some people, in fact, have gone a step further and suggested a direct link between the Star Route case and Guiteau. In a thinly veiled novelization of the assassin's life, his sister claimed, *"Yes, the 'Star Route' business killed Garfield!"* Other observers also raised questions about how the president's death might have been connected to the Star Route case, among them special prosecutor William Cook, who, just days before the shooting, had warned Garfield that he might be in danger. Exploring these possible links to the president's murder can add to our appreciation of the complex, if not confounding, legacy of the Star Route case.[8]

A few caveats are necessary before we jump into recounting this labyrinthine story.

First, in a strict sense, it might be a bit of a misnomer to refer to the Star Route "case" in the singular. In fact, myriad postal-corruption cases came to light all over the United States in the later part of the nineteenth century. For the sake of simplicity, however, I will generally focus on the federal government's attempt to prosecute the combination associated with two prominent Republican political figures: Stephen Dorsey, who served a term as a senator from Arkansas from 1873 to 1879, and Tom Brady, who served as second assistant postmaster general in the late 1870s. Their case was the one that attracted by far the most public attention at the time, and it was representative of the other frauds that were rumored to have taken place.

Likewise, I will use the term "Star Route trials" to refer to the two most prominent trials of individuals connected to the frauds. These occurred in Washington, DC, in 1882 and 1883. There were several other civil and criminal cases involving the allegedly suspect handling of Star Route contracts, but none achieved the notoriety of the pair of legal proceedings at the center of this book.

The terms "Dorsey ring" or "Dorsey combination" appear frequently in the text. In general, these terms refer to the core group of men who were tried together by the federal government for conspiracy in 1882 and 1883. They were

- The aforementioned Stephen Dorsey and Tom Brady;
- John Dorsey, the senator's brother;
- Montfort Rerdell, a longtime associate of Stephen Dorsey's who served the senator as a sort of jack-of-all-trades;
- Harvey Vaile, a successful businessman from Independence, Missouri, who engaged in Star Route contracting;
- John Miner, a Star Route contractor; and
- William Turner, a clerk in the Contract Division of the Post Office.

John Peck's fate is illustrative of how confusing the story of the Star Route frauds could be. Peck, Stephen Dorsey's brother-in-law and sometime business associate, was put on trial with the rest of the Dorsey combination in 1882—this despite the fact that he already had died from tuberculosis. (Prosecutors apparently refused to believe until after the trial started that Peck had passed away.)

The cast of characters in this story is vast. For the sake of brevity and clarity—and perhaps also the reader's sanity—I have not attempted to examine the backgrounds and activities of everyone connected to the principal

Star Route case. A number of men (Albert Boone, James Bosler, and Monroe Salisbury in particular) appear on the fringes of this story and possibly merit deeper study, but including much about them here might have resulted in an even more expansive account. (See the "Dramatis Personae" section that follows for a handy guide of individuals discussed in the text.)

I have also tried to simplify, to the extent possible, my discussion of the actual Star Routes themselves. As I note in the text, at one point there were hundreds of individual Star Routes covering hundreds of thousands of miles in the West, Southwest, and Pacific Northwest. In the pages that follow, I will mostly concern myself with the nineteen routes contracted by the Dorsey combination that were at issue in the main fraud trials of 1882 and 1883.

The men and women who delivered mail on Star Routes in the nineteenth century often were forced to traverse rocky and treacherous backcountry trails, many of them stretching for long distances over unfamiliar terrain. The legal saga at the heart of this book—which has, in a narrative sense, its own fair share of precarious twists and turns—begins with an examination of how and why those far-flung postal routes came into being and how a few crafty individuals tried to make some fast money from their operation.

DRAMATIS PERSONAE

Chester A. Arthur	Twenty-first president of the United States (1881–85)
Bradley Barlow	Postal-contract speculator; congressman from Vermont (1879–81)
James G. Blaine	Senator from Maine (1876–81); secretary of state (1881 and 1889–92); leading Republican Half-Breed
George Bliss	Federal prosecutor in Dorsey ring Star Route case
Albert Boone	Postal-contract speculator associated with Dorsey ring
James Bosler	Banker and business associate of Stephen Dorsey
Thomas J. Brady	Second assistant postmaster general of the United States (1876–81); defendant in Star Route trials
Benjamin Brewster	Attorney general of the United States (1881–85)
Richard Carpenter	Defense attorney in Star Route trials
Jefferson Chandler	Defense attorney in Star Route trials
Powell Clayton	Governor of (1868–71) and senator from (1871–77) Arkansas

Charles Cole	Defense attorney in first Star Route trial; law partner of prosecutor William Cook
Roscoe Conkling	Senator from New York (1867–81); leading Republican Stalwart
William Cook	Star Route special prosecutor in Dorsey ring Star Route case
George Corkhill	District attorney of Washington, DC
Walter Smith Cox	Associate justice of the Supreme Court of the District of Columbia (1879–99)
John Crane	Foreman of jury in second Star Route trial
John Creswell	Postmaster general of the United States (1869–74)
William Dickson	Foreman of jury in first Star Route trial
John Dorsey	Defendant in Star Route trials; brother of Stephen Dorsey
Stephen Dorsey	Senator from Arkansas (1873–79); defendant in Star Route trials; brother of John Dorsey
George Edmunds	Senator from Vermont (1866–91); chair of Senate Judiciary Committee
Stephen Elkins	New Mexico territorial delegate to Congress (1873–77); postal-contract speculator
John French	Chief clerk in the Contract Division of the Post Office under Tom Brady
James A. Garfield	Twentieth president of the United States (1881)
Albert Gibson	New York *Sun* reporter; later, federal prosecutor in Dorsey ring Star Route case
Charles Guiteau	Assassin of President Garfield, executed in 1882
Mornay D. Helm	Federal government printer; editor of *Washington Evening Critic*
Solomon Henkle	Defense attorney in Star Route trials
Charles Henry	Marshal of the District of Columbia
Lemon Galpin Hine	Defense attorney in Star Route trials

Timothy Howe	Postmaster general of the United States (1881–83)
Robert Green Ingersoll	Defense attorney in Star Route trials
Thomas James	Postmaster general of the United States (1881)
Marshall Jewell	Postmaster general of the United States (1874–76); chair of the Republican National Committee (1880–83)
William Pitt Kellogg	Louisiana politician tried in 1884 for receiving bribe from postal contractor
William Ker	Federal prosecutor in Dorsey ring Star Route case
Fred Lilley	Post Office auditor implicated in Star Route frauds
William Lilley	Father of Fred; attacked by Stephen Dorsey in 1883
Isaac Wayne MacVeagh	Attorney general of the United States (1881)
Joseph McKibbin	Postal-route speculator; wrote early newspaper exposé of Star Route frauds
John McSweeney	Defense attorney in first Star Route trial
Richard Merrick	Federal prosecutor in Dorsey ring Star Route case
George Miller	Washington police officer fired for tampering with jury in first Star Route trial
John Miner	Member of Dorsey ring; defendant in Star Route trials
Oliver Morton	Senator from Indiana (1867–77); patron of Tom Brady
John Peck	Member of Dorsey ring; died before first Star Route trial
George Pendleton	Senator from Ohio (1879–85); author of Pendleton Civil Service Act
Montfort Rerdell	Member of Dorsey ring; defendant in Star Route trials
John Sanderson	Postal-contract speculator; his indictment was thrown out before first Star Route trial
George Spencer	Senator from Alabama (1868–79)

William Springer	Congressman from Illinois (1875–95); chair of Star Route investigative committee (1884)
Enoch Totten	Defense attorney in first Star Route trial
William Turner	Clerk in Post Office's Contract Division; defendant in first Star Route trial
James Tyner	Postmaster general of the United States (1876–77); first assistant postmaster (1877–81)
Harvey M. Vaile	Member of Dorsey ring; defendant in Star Route trials
John Walsh	Banker tied to Kellogg bribery case and other Star Route frauds
Arthur Williams	Defense attorney in Star Route trials
Jeremiah Wilson	Defense attorney in Star Route trials
Patrick Henry Woodward	Government Star Route investigator
Andrew Wylie	Associate justice of the Supreme Court of the District of Columbia (1863–85); presided over Star Route trials

WHEN BAD MEN COMBINE

CELERITY, CERTAINTY, AND SECURITY
The Post Office Conquers the West, 1789–1878

In an age of same-day shipping, instantaneous global communication, and regular attacks on the competency of the U.S. Postal Service, it might be difficult to fully appreciate the critical role played by what we now deride as "snail mail" in the development of the United States in the nineteenth century. As the country expanded and emerged as an economic juggernaut, the regular delivery of letters and parcels was essential to a breathtaking expansion of commerce, settlement, and culture. The mails were a lubricant that kept the new nation's engine humming.

With language in the Constitution empowering Congress to "establish post offices and post roads," the federal Post Office Department was created in 1792. It provided mail service throughout the nascent United States, which at that point were all clustered along the Eastern Seaboard. By 1800, there were 903 post offices and more than 20,000 miles of post roads (roads designated for the transportation of mail) in the westward-expanding country. The number of post offices grew to 8,450 by 1830, at which point the United States boasted 74 post offices for every 100,000 inhabitants. (The comparable figure for France was 4.)[1]

Even in these early stages, there were concerns that the Post Office would become a hotbed of patronage, waste, and outright fraud. The federal government was still relatively small, and its increasingly far-flung postal operations were sure to tantalize politicians who were looking for lucrative—and perhaps illicit—ways to reward their political allies and relatives, if not themselves. "I view it as a source of boundless patronage to the executive, jobbing to members of Congress and their friends, and a boundless abyss of public money," a worried Vice President Thomas Jefferson wrote of the Post Office to James Madison in 1798.[2]

In 1844, a reappraisal of the Post Office's mission came at the behest of Congress, which appointed a commission to evaluate its goals and inherent value. The U.S. Postal Commission found that reliable mail delivery provided an essential function in the nation's budding democratic system and overall political economy. Its report stated, "The United States Postal Service was created to render the citizen worthy, by proper knowledge and enlightenment, of his important privileges as a sovereign constituent of his government; to diffuse enlightenment and social improvement and national fellowship, elevating our people in the scale of civilization and bringing them together in patriotic affection." Indispensable in myriad ways to the growing nation, mail service needed to be reliable as well as cheap and accessible for ordinary citizens, according to the commission. For the nation to flourish, common people had to be able to send letters and parcels at minimal expense, and this service had to be dependable.[3]

Congress responded to this lofty call by instituting a series of reforms, among them a reduction of postage costs and the authorization, in 1847, of postage stamps. (Before then, a letter's postage was paid for by the recipient.) At roughly the same time, the price and distance were decoupled in postage charges; it would no longer cost more to send mail farther. The result was a boom in the public's already surging use of the mails: between 1844 and 1851, the annual number of letters sent in the United States more than doubled, increasing from 38 million to 83 million. The volume of mail further swelled when, in 1863, Congress established a blanket postage rate of three cents for all letters, whatever their origin or destination.[4]

After the Civil War, mail was increasingly destined for the western regions of the country, where millions of Americans flocked in an effort to find economic opportunity and social mobility. At the war's end, there were a total 2,084 post offices located west of Kansas City, Missouri. In 1889, there were 10,777 post offices in that area, a five-fold increase over roughly twenty-five years.[5]

The nation's breakneck westward expansion in the middle decades of the nineteenth century posed some formidable challenges for mail delivery. The United States added millions of square miles of territory with the annexation of Texas (1845), the Oregon Treaty (1846), and the Treaty of Guadalupe Hidalgo

(1848), in which the United States seized the northern third of Mexico. "All of this new territory came with new challenges for the Post Office Department," scholar Cameron Blevins observed. "How was it going to transport the mail across millions of acres of land, much of it occupied and controlled by Native people? What kind of service should it offer, and how much was it willing to pay for that service?"[6]

New settlements in places like the Dakota, Colorado, and Arizona Territories, for instance, were widely scattered and not easily served by rail or steamboat, conveyances that often carried the mail over long distances. Moreover, in a period of booms and busts, communities in these remote areas often sprouted up—then vanished—almost overnight. Finally, restive Native American populations, still not reconciled to being pushed off their lands by white settlers, often targeted travelers. In these rough and fluctuating conditions, the Post Office itself lacked the wherewithal to provide reliable mail delivery at a reasonable cost.

Mining areas in the West presented a particular challenge for mail delivery in the nineteenth century. "At best the mines were hundreds of miles away from the larger centers of settled life," historian Frederic Logan Paxson wrote in 1922. "The transitory character of the mining camp made it possible for a city of ten thousand inhabitants to appear within a single month and to disappear as rapidly. The mining communities demanded a mail service sufficiently elastic to keep up with their shiftings from place to place." In the West, mail service had to respond to what Paxson called "the sudden and unexpected demands of a shifting population." (For all of its outsized role in the mythology of the West, the Pony Express played only a relatively brief and inconsequential part in this service, going bankrupt in the fall of 1861 after eighteen months of operation.)[7]

Initially, the federal government paid stagecoach proprietors to handle mail deliveries in these isolated areas. What emerged after 1845 was a makeshift web of postal routes operated by a variety of private contractors. Service on these "Star Routes"—so named because they were denoted in Post Office records by three asterisks, indicating certainty, celerity, and security—was carried out by horse, stagecoach, and wagon after a contractor won the rights to one through a process of competitive bidding. Bidders were awarded multiyear contracts after pledging to deliver the mail between two points a particular number of times per week and at a particular speed. Adjustments to contracts could be made if the Star Route operators were able to demonstrate that routes required faster or more frequent mail delivery.[8]

To be sure, Star Route contracts reflected some of the considerable legitimate costs involved for the stage companies and individuals who carried the mail in the West. Blevins, in his excellent history of the Post Office's role in facilitating the nation's westward expasion, explained the many daunting challenges these contractors faced. "Horses, mules, and oxen required loads of hay and grain, along with barns and stables to house the animals and their feed," the historian noted. "A firm then had to hire new route agents, drivers, and hostlers and arrange for their room and board at hotels and way stations. Once a stage firm had set up the route, it required constant infusions of capital to cover salaries, repairs and maintenance, rent for buildings, room and board, feed and supplies, and local taxes and road tolls."[9] Yet the elasticity of Star Route contracts meant that they could be easily manipulated to reflect costs that were exaggerated or wholly imaginary. Newspapers, politicians, and, finally, federal prosecutors alleged that contracts repeatedly were changed in such a manner to enrich favored contractors and their accomplices in the Post Office rather than to provide better mail service.

The work on Star Routes was not for the faint of heart. In a memoir recounting his childhood, Carl Anderson described the bedraggled appearance of the carriers who had delivered mail to his hometown post office. (Door-to-door mail delivery began in 1863, but for many years, it was typically only available in large urban areas.) "Mostly the carriers came on horseback, the mail locked in government saddle bags," wrote Anderson, whose father had served as the town's postmaster. "These were very often covered with mud and it was a messy job. The easiest way to handle them was to sit in a chair with the saddle-bags across the lap. Mud—fresh and dried—horse hair, horse; sweat—you can imagine what it would do to clothing."[10]

Throughout a difficult winter, a contractor named Stringer was unable to traverse the Big Horn Mountains and make the challenging sixty-five-mile trip from Buffalo to Ten Sleep in Wyoming Territory. When he thought the weather finally had broken in the early spring, he set out from Buffalo on a saddlehorse, with the accumulated mail being carried on four pack mules. Stringer made it twenty-five miles before the conditions deteriorated and forced him to continue his journey on snowshoes, temporarily leaving his mail and stock at an emergency cabin. When one of the snowshoes broke, he trudged twelve miles to his own ranch to regroup. "He was five days getting to it," according to an admiring account. "Most of the way he crawled on his hands and knees. With hunger and exhaustion he was all but dead." Stringer recuperated, fixed his snowshoe, and then backtracked to recover the stock and mail he had briefly abandoned. Stringer then resumed his journey to Ten Sleep; it took another week of arduous travel before he arrived.[11]

In the late nineteenth century, Mary Fields, known as "Stagecoach Mary," earned renown as the first Black female Star Route mail carrier. Fields, a former slave, delivered mail between Cascade, Montana, and St. Peter's Mission, where a group of Ursuline nuns operated a school. As she carried the mail on the ten-mile route, the intrepid Fields was known to have a .38-caliber Smith & Wesson revolver under her apron for use to ward off brigands and wild animals. Attackers approached Fields at their peril. The film star Gary Cooper, who was born in Montana, told *Ebony* magazine in 1959 that Fields "could whip any two men in the territory" and "had a fondness for hard liquor that was matched only by her capacity to put it away."[12]

In places like Henry County, Missouri, the weekly arrival of Star Route mail carriers "was almost a gala day at the country post office," in the words of one account. When the carrier was due to arrive in a remote settlement, people came from miles around and squeezed themselves so tightly into the post office that "often the mail would have to be taken in through a window, or, like Peter's revelation from heaven, let down through the roof." The postmaster would read out the names of mail recipients, and those who were lucky enough to hear their names called would press through the throng to collect their mail. It was a social event that helped create a sense of community in a sparsely settled area.[13]

The Post Office required certain guarantees from the daring entrepreneurs who bid on Star Route contracts. Applicants needed to have two sureties (or bondsmen) sign their applications, and the good faith of these guarantors had to be assured by a local postmaster. These formalities, designed in part to suppress brazen speculation, did not scare off many bidders, as Star Routes had the potential to be incredibly valuable. "Properly handled," one study later noted, "those contracts would be worth a mint."[14]

And there was no shortage of these potentially profitable contracts to be had. By the end of the 1880 fiscal year, the Post Office had contracted for mail service on more than 9,200 Star Routes, which could be found in every state and territory and covered a total of 215,480 miles. The longest and most lucrative routes were in the sparsely populated areas of the Trans-Mississippi West. For instance, the Post Office originally contracted the Star Route between Fort Worth, Texas, and Yuma, Arizona—a distance of 1,560 miles—for $154,000 per year. Shorter routes in more settled areas were worth far less. The Post Office paid all of $278.44 annually for services on the twenty-six-mile Star Route between Rockport and College Springs, Missouri.[15]

By 1893, there were in operation in the United States 17,000 Star Routes covering a total of 240,000 miles. Annual travel over them by mail carriers was said to total a staggering 100,000,000 miles (roughly the distance between the earth and the sun).[16]

The second assistant postmaster general of the United States controlled this sprawling system. In his 1893 overview of the duties of the office, Marshall Henry Cushing, the private secretary to Postmaster General John Wanamaker, remarked on "the almost immeasurable diversity and magnitude of the affairs with which it has to deal." This broad purview included railroad mail routes, steamboat mail routes, mail messenger routes, regulation wagon routes, special routes, and Star Routes. Cushing observed that the second assistant postmaster, in order to properly control this broad domain, needed "to be familiar with the laws under which all of this business is to be distributed, to provide rules stringent enough to hold all these contractors to the faithful performance of their obligations, to do the labor of hand and brain required merely for the record of these transactions, to inspect the service with method and dispatch, to investigate complaints, and to have the hardihood honestly to invite them." It was a multifaceted role—also a powerful one.[17]

The second assistant postmaster's handling of Star Route contracts involved a wide variety of interrelated activities. His duties included establishing schedules for the proposed routes, advertising the opening of bidding, awarding contracts to the lowest bidders, and adjusting contracts if delivery schedules on routes needed to be tweaked. In this work, the second assistant postmaster enjoyed a great deal of latitude. There were few hard-and-fast regulations governing how the incumbent was to handle Star Route contracts beyond some vague provisions mandating that he show due regard for the productiveness of routes.[18]

With few regulations in place, the second assistant postmaster could exercise enormous discretion when it came to adjusting the contracts. Because Star Routes often traversed remote and largely unknown territories, it was understood that the service schedules formalized in contracts often were no better than educated guesses. As a result, formal agreements frequently were amended after contractors had begun operating routes. Changing a Star Route contract to reflect an increased number of delivery trips was a relatively straightforward process involving a pro rata calculation based on the original value of the contract. But a more complex formula was used when a contractor informed the second assistant postmaster that a faster schedule (what was known as expedition of service) was needed on a route. This calculation factored in the number of men and animals necessary to carry out the more rapid service.[19]

According to Sharon K. Lowry's careful study of the central figure in the Star Route scandal, Stephen Dorsey, "the system under which Star Routes operated opened a number of avenues for mail contract speculation." Speculators often intentionally offered low bids on Star Routes in the hope that they later would be able to convince the second assistant postmaster to increase their value. If this happened (and it often did), subcontractors could be employed to perform the actual work on the routes, and the speculator could still turn a profit—without doing much more than simply low-bidding on a contract and then haggling with the Post Office.[20]

Speculators could make enormous sums if they successfully bid upon and then subcontracted multiple Star Routes. Perhaps the most successful of these was Bradley Barlow, a gumptious businessman and sometime politician from Vermont. An active and influential figure, Barlow began to speculate in Star Route contracts before the Civil War, during the administration of President James Buchanan. By 1874, he was contracting more than $1.2 million worth of routes. At that point, Barlow was collecting about 80 percent of all the monies appropriated by the Post Office for Star Routes.[21]

Some observers wondered whether Barlow and other Star Route contractors owed their success to something other than sheer grit and entrepreneurial spirit. Investigators later reviewed increases approved for all Star Routes early in 1877 by the second assistant postmaster. They found that a disproportionate share of them wound up in the hands of three speculators, one being the ambitious Barlow. The increases awarded to Barlow alone in this brief period totaled over $100,000, a figure that surpassed the total amount of increases granted (for some 8,000 routes) by the Post Office over a similar period the previous year.[22]

Barlow's success was grounded in several interrelated corrupt practices that plagued Star Route contracting throughout the post-Reconstruction era. Ideally, the competitive bidding process would have driven down costs by pitting bona fide prospective contractors against one another: to secure a contract on a given route, they would have to offer the lowest possible legitimate bid for a Star Route and then execute the contract at that price. Yet large, organized groups of bidders (or combinations) realized that they could easily manipulate this process by working together and driving out legitimate, ethical competitors. Many times, a phony (or straw) bid would be offered with the understanding that the contractor had no intention of ever fulfilling it at such a low price. After he won the contract from the Post Office, the straw bidder would simply allow himself to be declared a failing contractor and permit another contractor to take over the route at an inflated price approved after the second assistant postmaster general determined that increased service was required on the route. The surety requirement was supposed to guard against this kind of manipulation, but it was widely known that many bids were backed only by so-called straw bonds (that is, worthless guarantees). Such was Barlow's prowess in this realm that he was known as the king of the straw-bid contractors.[23]

A later study by a federal prosecutor offered a bleak overall assessment of this debased system. According to his report, the methods of the Post Office in handling Star Route contracts "promoted wastefulness, facilitated corruption, enabled a few contractors, with the assistance of high officers and subordinates, to wrongfully obtain vast sums of money from the Treasury, and generally brought the department into dishonor and bad repute throughout the land." The Star Routes became synonymous with graft.[24]

Corruption was manifest during John L. Routt's tenure as second assistant postmaster general, which began in 1871. Like many federal bureaucrats in this era, Routt owed his position to his loyalty to the Republican Party rather than to any particular interest or competence in performing his job duties. One history of the period mentioned that he became notorious for his love of "receiving barrels of oranges, boxes of cigars, cases of wine and mineral water, and other gifts and favors from mail contractors." It was said that he eventually handed over most of his duties to his chief clerk, a man who spent much of his time selling life-insurance policies to mail contractors rather than attempting to regulate them. (None of this seemed to harm Routt's reputation: he later served two terms as governor of Colorado and one as mayor of Denver.)[25]

The corruption of the Star Route service began as early as the 1860s, but "by the end of the 1870s, the situation had devolved into a full-fledged institutional crisis," according to one account. At that point, Tom Brady held the position of second assistant postmaster general. Brady's name, as much as any other, would be associated with the scandal, as he was widely believed to have received innumerable kickbacks for altering Star Route contracts and forgiving fines.[26]

Thomas Jefferson Brady was born in Muncie, Indiana, in 1839. His family was a prominent one in the fledgling city: in 1865, his father, John Brady, was chosen as the first mayor of Muncie under its new city charter. Brady graduated from Asbury College (now DePauw University) and then embarked on a teaching career before studying law. He was admitted to the bar in 1860 but put his legal career on hold in order to defend the Union during the Civil War. He served in several of Indiana's infantry regiments and fought in the Battle of Pea Ridge, the Battle of Port Gibson, the Siege of Vicksburg, and the storming of Fort Anderson, North Carolina. Brady rose to the rank of colonel before the war ended in 1865. (Later in life, he often would be referred to as "General Brady," a reference to the brevet rank he was awarded for meritorious service after the war's conclusion.)[27]

Brady achieved his greatest success in the Civil War in December 1863 while leading troops as the colonel of the 117th Indiana Infantry. In what was later described as "one of the most daring and brilliant achievements of the [Union] campaign in East Tennessee," Brady's troops looked to be boxed in at Clinch Mountain Gap by forces commanded by James Longstreet, the eminent Confederate lieutenant general. Brady, realizing that his men were in danger of being annihilated, determined that he had but one option. "I adopted the only alternative left me—to retreat," he later wrote. "The night was dark and cold, our route pathless and very rough, while the enemy was on either side of us, his pickets extending far upon the sides of the mountain, but all were impressed with the danger attending the movement and marched in silence." Staying cool in a potentially calamitous situation, Brady shepherded his men to safety, calmly leading them "through dangerous bypaths and down precipices that would appall the heart of an Alpine tourist, to a place of safety," according to one admiring account.[28]

Brady's role in the capture of Fort Anderson indirectly—and quite unintentionally—connected him to President Abraham Lincoln's assassination in April 1865. After the Confederate force there had been subdued, one of Brady's men snatched the garrison flag flown at the fort, and eventually, it came into Brady's possession. Brady and others decided that this trophy should be presented to Indiana governor Oliver Morton, who was a great friend of Lincoln's, at a ceremony at the National Hotel in Washington. The president himself was not originally scheduled to attend the festivities, but he changed his plans at the last minute and was present to see the flag handed over to Morton. The switch in Lincoln's itinerary foiled a kidnapping plot that had been hatched by John Wilkes Booth and five coconspirators, who had hoped to grab the president as he traveled to his original destination and then exchange him for Confederate prisoners. After their kidnapping plan miscarried, Booth and his compatriots—apparently by coincidence—repaired to the National Hotel, where they saw Morton receive the Confederate garrison flag captured by Brady's men. To make matters worse, they heard Lincoln praise the contributions to the war effort made by Black soldiers. The ceremony left Booth visibly outraged, and some historians have speculated that it was the moment at which he resolved to kill the president rather than simply kidnap him.[29]

Brady returned to Indiana after the Civil War and resumed his legal practice. He also became a newspaperman, purchasing the *Muncie Times* in 1868. A statewide biographical compendium published in 1880 gushed over Brady's work with the *Times*, saying that he "so enlarged and improved [the newspaper], both mechanically and intellectually, that it soon became the leading Republican journal in central Eastern Indiana. In fact, his connection with the *Times* may be considered an epoch in journalism in Eastern Indiana."[30]

In 1870, Oliver Morton, who had moved on to the Senate after his stint as Indiana's governor, recommended Brady to President Ulysses Grant for the position of U.S. consul to St. Thomas in the Danish West Indies (now the U.S. Virgin Islands). Brady was "a gallant soldier, an editor and well qualified for the position," he wrote to the president. This endorsement from Morton, a prominent Republican senator, was enough for the president, and Brady got the post. Brady's growing political connections were evident not only in Morton's initial endorsement for consular role but also in the senator's sanctioning of his ongoing political activities in the continental United States. A year into his posting in the Caribbean, the senator wrote to Grant again and said that Brady would need to return home for a period of leave "to render important political service" to Republicans in Indiana.[31]

While in the Caribbean, Brady monitored developments in nearby Santo Domingo (as the Dominican Republic was then known) for the Grant administration, which was hoping to annex the island. He dutifully supported Grant's plan, reporting that the idea of annexation was popular among those living in Santo Domingo. "The unanimity of sentiment among the people in favor of annexation continues," he wrote in a public letter in February 1871, and "the better class of the island are almost unanimously in favor of it, anticipating renewed life and prosperity as a result." Despite Brady's efforts, the plan ultimately failed, with the Senate failing to ratify the treaty that the Grant administration had negotiated with Dominican president Buenaventura Báez.[32]

Brady returned home again to Indiana in 1874 to chair the Republican Party's state central committee. Like any canny Republican, he "waved the bloody shirt" (as the saying went), invoking the southern Democrats' violent rebellion during the Civil War and their ongoing resistance to Reconstruction in states like Louisiana and Arkansas. "I desire to call your attention to the horrible scenes of violence and bloodshed transpiring in the South," he wrote in a letter distributed to newspaper editors throughout the state, "and suggest that you give them as great prominence in your paper from [this] time until after the election."[33]

This effort caused a stir, although not perhaps for the reasons Brady had intended. Newspapers sympathetic to the Democrats wondered why he was concerning himself with political matters in the Hoosier State when he should have been worrying about his government post in the Caribbean. "What on earth is he doing here in Indiana?" the *Indiana State Sentinel* asked. "Why isn't he off attending to his official duties as United States consul to the Island of St. Thomas? What business has he drawing his salary as a servant of the people and spending his time in the performance of the labors of a party hack?" (For good measure, the newspaper scoffed at Brady's reference to southern violence, dismissing it as a "stale trick.") Another newspaper quipped that Brady "doubtless finds it more congenial to be running an Indiana campaign than to be sitting on a barren slope of that much exposed island sucking a sugar cane and waiting for the honey-scented evening breeze from the Caribbean sea."[34]

Brady's private correspondence during the 1874 campaign was even more explicit and strident in its condemnation of the Democrats. Hoping to whip up enthusiasm among Republican precinct committeemen before the election, Brady warned them in an anxious letter, "upon the result of this campaign depends the future of Republicanism in this state, the election of a United States Senator, the cause of temperance, of equal rights for all men, and of national honor." Failure for their party, he cautioned, would ensure "the success of the most disreputable pack of demagogues who ever strove for power, banded together in the name of Democracy, and representing all that is evil in society and the prejudices born of ignorance and hatred."[35]

In July 1875, Brady returned to the United States for good to serve as supervisor of internal revenue for Ohio and Indiana. When he took over the position, there were "rumors of frauds of the most gigantic character at Cincinnati and other points in his jurisdiction," according to one account. (These charges related to Whiskey Ring bribery schemes, which involved tangled connections between corrupt internal revenue agents, distillers, rectifiers, gaugers, and storekeepers.) Brady's investigation yielded little. This seemed to harm his reputation, and a rumored promotion to become the federal commissioner of internal revenue never materialized. Instead, he was transferred to the revenue district encompassing Kentucky, Tennessee, Alabama, Mississippi, and Louisiana.[36]

Unflattering accounts of Brady's work for the internal revenue bureau, and his connections with Senator Morton, emerged over time. According to a gossipy book anonymously published in 1885, "It is said that Morton possessed many attributes of the astute politician, but certain it is that he was a poor judge of men. Perhaps no man in American politics ever surrounded himself with so many third-rate men as Morton," who would "fix his mind upon making something out of a third-rate man, and would at once boost him into high positions, and hold him there until he had filled his depleted exchequer." Prominent among the ranks of Morton's unprincipled henchmen was Brady, who was derisively described in the book as "that sweet-scented adventurer."[37]

As always, Brady complemented his government work with efforts on behalf of his party and his political patron Morton, who aspired for the presidency. When the Republicans held their convention in Cincinnati in 1876, he tried to rally support for the senator by touting Indiana's key role in the upcoming election. "I say to you without prejudice, as goes Ohio and Indiana, so goes the Union," he told a reporter. The other leading Republican candidates—principally James Blaine of Maine and Senator Roscoe Conkling of New York—simply would not be able to attract voters in these key states,

Brady argued. Morton, with his "immense personal popularity" in Indiana, would be the obvious compromise choice, with Ohioan Rutherford B. Hayes as his running mate. Morton ultimately faltered at the convention, but Brady was not completely off the mark: Hayes wound up at the top of the Republican ticket that year.[38]

A loyal Republican, Brady worked diligently for the ticket as a fund-raiser and all-around fixer. His skills in the latter realm were on full display after voting ended and the election still hung in the balance. With the final results in Florida unclear, operatives from both parties, including Brady, descended upon the state in hopes of influencing the final count there. It was said that President Grant sent Brady to Florida to help ensure that state elections officials would make an honest count of the votes—provided, of course, that the result did not favor Samuel Tilden, the Democratic candidate. One commentator reported that Brady went to Florida with a coterie of federal employees and "bearing also a sum of money for immediate use" in swaying the election in favor of the Republican ticket. His efforts were successful: Hayes eventually was awarded Florida's crucial electoral votes and thereby won the presidency.[39]

A House of Representatives special committee later was established to investigate alleged frauds committed by both parties as the 1876 election hung in the balance in Florida. That body took a long, hard look at Brady's efforts on behalf of the Hayes campaign in the Sunshine State. Called upon to testify at the congressional inquiry, Brady explained that he had gone to Florida after Interior Secretary Zachariah Chandler relayed a request for assistance from President Grant. "I went down there," he stated of his work in Florida, "to see a fair count." To help ensure that this equitable tabulation of votes took place without undue interference from the Democrats, he had taken $2,000 with him when he traveled to Tallahassee, the state capital.[40]

At the time of his Florida mission, Brady had recently been appointed to a new job in the federal government, second assistant postmaster general. Democrats on the House committee wanted to know why he had reported back on his efforts on behalf of Hayes in Florida to his boss in his federal department, Postmaster General James Noble Tyner. Did it not appear that the two men had been engaged in partisan political activities on behalf of the Republicans while they had been drawing pay from the Post Office? Brady offered an innocent—if not entirely plausible—explanation, stating in his testimony that he had gone to Florida "as a personal matter entirely. I telegraphed to [Tyner] simply as I would to a friend. . . . I had a request, not instructions, from Mr. Tyner to keep him posted as to what was going on in Tallahassee, and I tried to do it."[41]

The House committee was particularly interested in the flurry of "cipher telegraphic dispatches"—coded telegrams—that representatives from both parties had sent to various recipients to report on their activities in Florida during the aftermath of the 1876 election. This reliance on subterfuge seemed to suggest that something underhanded had taken place as the competing campaigns jockeyed to influence the final vote count. Brady had sent several of these suspicious messages himself, using a cipher system to communicate with Tyner, who had been referred to as "John Wing."

Brady's own telegrams to Tyner were less controversial than the coded messages from Democrats that he had accumulated and later publicized. Although the details of his activities were somewhat murky, Brady somehow had come into possession of a cache of telegrams sent by forces working on behalf of Tilden. According to his later testimony, Brady had decided to keep the telegrams as souvenirs or "relics" before determining to send them anonymously to Whitelaw Reid, the editor of the *New-York Tribune*, who had them decoded and then published (much to the embarrassment of the Democrats). He sheepishly told Congress that he had sent the telegrams to Reid because "it looked as if there was an immense amount of latent rascality there" that needed to be exposed in the press.[42]

At least in part as a reward for his yeoman's work on behalf of the Republican Party, Brady was appointed second assistant postmaster general in 1876. He owed this job to Senator Morton and to Tyner, a former congressman from Indiana who had become postmaster general that year. Given Brady's well-known history as a political operative, not everyone applauded the move. "It is the intention of the Republicans to make use of the Post Office Department for political purposes," one Texas newspaper groused, "and it is handy to have such men . . . as Brady in charge to enable them to realize all the advantages that are to be derived from the postal service."[43]

Brady's broad responsibilities in his new role included oversight of the nation's numerous Star Routes. According to an admiring biographical piece, Brady believed that establishing and maintaining effective mail routes in remote areas was essential to cultivating settlement and boosting economic development. "Brady took the ground that the enterprising pioneers who left behind them most of the comforts and all of the luxuries of the older states, and who penetrated the wild of the far West for the purpose of founding new homes for themselves and their descendants, and who were building up new commonwealths, were entitled to the very best mail facilities the department could give them," the item claimed. This would be a recurring defense of Brady's controversial activities as second assistant postmaster general: in his official duties, he was devoted to helping common folk and promoting progress, not obsessed with committing fraud and amassing great personal wealth.[44]

After he decamped for Washington, Brady maintained a formidable reputation in Indiana. He stopped in Indianapolis and Muncie, his home town, in the summer of 1878 and, by several accounts, received a hero's welcome. A newspaper reported that his reception in both cities "partook very much of the character of an ovation."[45]

Other accounts of Brady's tenure in office were less salutary. A later annual report of the postmaster general insisted that Brady had repeatedly violated the letter and the spirit of the law by amending Star Route contracts in a manner that benefited contractors—and enriched himself. An 1879 newspaper article bearing the damning headline "The Post Office as a Political Machine" singled out Tyner and Brady for using their federal roles for political and personal gain. It called Brady cunning and asserted that he "knows all about the methods of straw bidding and other devices of pet contractors."[46]

Brady's conspicuous affluence fueled speculation that he had used his various government positions to line his pockets. He earned about $3,500 annually in his position as second assistant postmaster general, but in 1879, he was reported to be worth a whopping $5.5 million. It was said that he had "made a million dollars in stock speculation" in the years after he joined the Post Office. In 1879, he reportedly bought $300,000 worth of stock in a telephone company; a year later, he purchased a controlling interest in a Washington newspaper, the National Republican. This did not seem to be the bleak financial profile of a penurious public servant.[47]

Brady's bank account swelled at least in part because of his deep and long-standing ties to Theodore Vail, a communications innovator and entrepreneur who would serve two terms as president of American Telephone & Telegraph. He was Vail's "old friend and backer," according to the latter's biographer, and the two men entered into several extraordinarily remunerative business partnerships over the years, including the aforementioned telephone venture.[48]

Brady's newfound wealth was a staple of political gossip back in his home state. "General Brady is a very wealthy man now," the *Terre Haute Weekly Gazette* noted. "He was quite a poor man when he went to Washington." The newspaper jibed that Brady probably would claim—implausibly—that he owed his sudden riches to his "very economical wife."[49]

If one salacious book is to be believed, Brady and his lieutenants in the Post Office enjoyed "hilarious old times" as they were engaging in fraud and "abstracting lucre from the Federal Treasury. Not only did they enjoy fine dinners, costly wines and cigars, but they also had attached to their establishments fast horses and fast women." According to this account, Brady and his compatriots operated out of a well-appointed private room in the Post Office Department. From there, they concocted plots to bribe and manipulate members of Congress into protecting their various fraudulent schemes. "This room was used by the members of the ring during the day, and was apportioned out by hours. Sometimes a mistake was made, and two officials would attempt to enter it at the same hour, when a few oaths would be indulged in, but matters would generally assume their equilibrium without more damage than a little smoke," the book asserted. "It was in this room where the pretty 'lady' lobbyists usually assembled to get their instructions from Brady & Co. It was there they were told just how many blandishments to bestow on this or that congressman. A Senator or a member whose vote was indispensable, and whose opposition would do harm, would have to be placated at any cost, even if it became necessary for a pretty Treasury girl to carry him to Baltimore and insure him a nice time." According to this tell-all account, "Money, women, and wine were the strong levers they employed to pry open the doors of the Treasury, and the success which attended their efforts has long since become known to every household in the land."[50]

CHAPTER FIRST IN
THE HISTORY OF PLUNDER
Early Accusations and Investigations, 1872–1878

In the early 1870s, long before Tom Brady joined the Post Office as second assistant postmaster general, newspapers in New York and Washington, DC, began to publish alarming reports about irregularities in Star Route services and contracting. Colonel Joseph Chambers McKibbin was one of the first to sound an alarm, offering a lengthy diatribe on the subject in the pages of the *Washington Daily Patriot* early in January 1872. His caustic story, brimming with outrage and invective, would set the tone for press coverage of the Star Route scandal over the next decade.

A former member of Congress from California and a decorated Civil War veteran, McKibbin possessed plenty of firsthand knowledge of the vagaries of the Star Routes, as he was himself a mail contractor. Armed with inside information about how Star Routes were bid upon, awarded, and then operated, he authored a report in the *Patriot* that was nothing short of incendiary. Writing what he called "chapter first in the history of plunder," he decried the "monstrous robberies" that were endemic in the sprawling federal postal system. A member of Congress, summarizing the gist of the accusations, later said that McKibbin had leveled "grave charges against the management of the [Post Office] in letting mail contracts in the West and South."[1]

McKibbin was among the first to publicly outline the general contours of the Star Route frauds. The swindle, he asserted, was grounded in a system of "straw or fraudulent bids." In this scam, a group (or ring) of ostensibly independent mail contractors would arrange for one of their number to submit a preposterously low bid to the Post Office to operate a mail route in some remote and godforsaken part of the West or South—for instance, from Missoula in Montana Territory to Walla Walla in Washington Territory. By law, the contract would be awarded to this low bidder, but he never had any intention of operating the route at a bargain price. Rather, he would intentionally default on the contract, forcing the Post Office (again by law) to deem him a failing contractor and award the contract to the next-lowest bidder, who was another member of the ring. A series of defaults would result in the contract being awarded to a member of the ring at a grossly inflated price. The spoils of the fraud would be divided among the ring members, who might also use their funds to bribe Post Office officials to turn a blind eye to the swindle and forgive any fines that had been leveled. Contractors outside the ring could be bribed or coerced into either participating in the scam or simply abandoning their own bids.[2]

And the "manifest fraud," as McKibbin termed it, did not end once the straw bidders finally started delivering the mail. The cheating contractors often sought to amend their agreements with the Post Office by arguing that they were providing mail delivery more quickly, or more frequently, between two points than had been stipulated originally. They also produced reams of petitions and affidavits allegedly signed by residents of distant towns who were now demanding more frequent mail service. Quicker mail delivery, provided more often, allowed an unprincipled contractor to demand heftier payments from the Post Office.[3]

The straw-bid legerdemain was deplorable, and not only because of the sheer amount of graft involved. Quite often, improved services promised in renegotiated Star Route contracts existed on paper only; the mail actually might not get delivered more rapidly after a contractor received additional payments to speed things up. Delayed and inefficient mail routes harmed people in small, isolated towns in the Great Plains and West who relied on the mail to conduct business, communicate with friends and family, and generally stay connected to the outside world.

Colonel McKibbin insisted that no less an authority than John Creswell, the postmaster general, countenanced this fraudulent system. He asserted in the *Patriot* that the straw-bidders were "friends of Mr. Creswell, and are to be seen at all times in his office." These brazen crooks "daily take him by the hand, and they might congratulate each other on each new piece of successful villainy." With Creswell in their corner, they had nothing to fear.[4]

The stench of corruption suffused the Post Office, according to McKibbin.

Speaking for all those who were dismayed that the straw bidders had been given such free reign to defraud the federal government, he asserted, "We believe, from Mr. Creswell himself down to the local postmasters, that rottenness and corruption permeate the whole Department." Given the scope and severity of the problems in the Post Office, he wrote, there was only one possible solution: a thorough congressional investigation that would expose the Star Route racket in its entirety.[5]

To be sure, even before a congressional inquiry got underway, many members of Congress already were aware of how frauds were being perpetrated in connection to the Star Routes. As Alabama senator George Spencer later said, "It was sort of an open secret. It was in the air." Even if the details were sketchy, everyone seemed to know that there was something questionable, if not downright illegal, about how Star Route contracts were being handled by the Post Office.[6]

Over time, Spencer developed a clearer idea of how Star Route contractors conspired with Post Office insiders to grossly inflate the value of their contracts. He later explained it in testimony before the House of Representatives.

> The plan was this: These contracts were originally let at very low rates, with a long schedule of time. They were principally once-a-week service, with not more than two or three miles, or perhaps two miles and a half, an hour. Then the service was increased from once-a-week to three-times-a-week, or to seven-times-a-week, and then the schedule of time was increased to four, five, or six miles an hour, and one route that was let originally for $2,700 was afterwards expedited and increased up to, if my recollection serves me right, as high as $52,000.[7]

There were kickbacks involved as well, according to Spencer. From what the senator had heard, contractors were expected to return roughly one-third of whatever money they gained through expedition to the key postal official who facilitated the scam. "It was supposed to go," Spencer later said, "to the second assistant postmaster general." At the height of the Star Route scandal in the late 1870s, this key post was occupied by Tom Brady, the well-connected Republican political operative.[8]

Although people like Senator Spencer knew the general outlines of the Star Route grift, outsiders had a hard time really understanding every nuance and detail. It was often difficult, for instance, to determine which individuals were in fact bidding on, and then operating, the various Star Routes. Proxies were used to obscure the identities of those involved and thereby shield them from any potential criminal or civil liability. Albert Gibson, who reported on the frauds for the New York *Sun* and then worked for the federal government to prosecute the swindlers, later said, "I will state . . . that you cannot tell who is the real party in interest as it appears upon the books. Gentlemen who are engaged in carrying the mails do not always bid in their own name, and the contracts are not always in their own names. . . . A man may have half a dozen people who bid and the contracts are made of course in the name of the accepted bidder." This system of obfuscation helped shield wrongdoers from civil or criminal liability.[9]

Anyone who wanted to get to the bottom of the Star Route frauds thus faced some daunting challenges, among them the fact that many of those implicated were connected to prominent politicians in both major parties. Still, McKibbin's spectacular charges were serious enough to gain the attention of the Committee on Post Offices and Postal Roads in the House of Representatives. A few weeks after his claims appeared in print in 1872, the committee hauled before it the *Daily Patriot*'s managing editor, O. K. Harris, and McKibbin himself to explain the genesis of the story.

As the investigation got underway, other newspapers in the nation's capital cast doubt on McKibbin's claims. The *Evening Star* claimed that they amounted to little more than sour grapes, sniffing, "It may be stated that he is a disappointed mail contractor, and this may account for his charges against Mr. Creswell." There also were accusations that McKibbin, a Democrat, had politically partisan motives in attacking Creswell, a Republican who had been appointed postmaster general in 1869 by President Grant. Such was the partisan rancor surrounding the charges that a Republican in the House, citing the former congressman's role in publicizing the alleged corruption in the Post Office, called him "the Mephistopheles who gives life and direction to every scene in this blackmailing drama." In attacking Creswell, the Democrats were "desiring political capital even at the expense of justice and right."[10]

For his part, an indignant McKibbin decried the accusation that partisanship had motivated him to expose the straw-bid swindle in the pages of the *Patriot*. Livid over having his motives questioned, he insisted that his only intention had been to share proof that the Post Office had become a sinkhole of corruption. "In the publication that I made," he later told Congress, "I published every fact that I was aware of in connection with the Post-Office Department that I thought would show what I believed to exist, to wit, fraud and corruption from one end to the other."[11]

With Republicans in control of the chamber, the claims lodged by Mc-Kibbin failed to gain much traction in the House of Representatives. Not surprisingly, the Committee on Post Offices and Postal Roads cleared Creswell, the Republican postmaster general, of any wrongdoing. Democrats, just as predictably, issued a minority report excoriating Creswell; they later claimed that tens of thousands of dollars in bribes had helped quell the investigation. With that, the story of the Star Route frauds went away—but only briefly.[12]

In 1874, a group of Democrats in the House—their ranks included Representatives John King Luttrell of California and William Henry Stone of Missouri—attempted to revive McKibben's charges and launch another investigation into misdeeds in the Post Office relating to Star Route contracting. The effort went nowhere, in large part because the Republicans who still controlled the House had little interest in further embarrassing the already embattled Grant administration. To make matters worse, Luttrell and Stone apparently were not particularly adept in presenting their accusations.[13]

Although Congress temporarily lost interest in the scandal, the media did not. Then as now, sensational stories featuring corrupt politicians in league with unscrupulous businessmen were a surefire way to sell newspapers. As long as they captured the interest of readers, breathless stories detailing how the Star Routes were being exploited, and by whom, continued to appear in print.

Hoping to rekindle public interest in the Star Route scandal, the New York Sun, a newspaper with unmistakable Democratic leanings, "undertook the work of bringing to grief the men who had defied the Congressional investigations" and "exposing the frauds in the Post Office Department," as it later declared. Attorney and journalist Albert Gibson—who would later play a controversial role in the government's prosecution of Star Route tricksters—spearheaded this effort by penning a series of articles on how contractors had colluded with one another and more than a few Post Office officials to pilfer hundreds of thousands of dollars from the federal government. The Sun's editorials on the scandal ended with the same call to action: "Turn the rascals out."[14]

Then and later, there was much speculation as to what had prompted the *Sun* to pursue the Star Route story so tenaciously. George Bliss, who later worked with Gibson on prosecuting the postal-fraud cases in court, believed that Democrat Samuel Tilden, the politically ambitious governor of New York, bankrolled the *Sun*'s investigation in order to uncover information that could be used against Republicans in a presidential campaign. (He would in fact be the Democrats' nominee in 1876, eventually losing to Hayes.) "At some time or other," Bliss later told Congress, "Mr. Tilden became so far interested in the matter that he furnished money to enable that investigation to be quietly pursued." A Stalwart Republican, Bliss believed that partisan motives—not some noble commitment to public service—underlay the newspaper's devotion to the story.[15]

Thanks in part to the *Sun*'s persistence, a turning point for the Star Route investigations came in 1875, when Democrats seized control of the House of Representatives for the first time since the Civil War. Democrats now held a comfortable majority in the lower chamber, which meant that they could use its myriad committees and subcommittees to investigate the alleged misdeeds of the Grant administration. No longer run by sympathetic Republicans, the Committee on Post Offices and Postal Roads took a fresh—and much more critical—look at reports of frauds in Star Route contracts, as did the powerful Ways and Means Committee.

The latter body conducted a lengthy investigation. Early in 1876, it issued a scathing report detailing how rings of straw bidders, using a "sham method of obtaining contracts," had defrauded the government of millions of dollars. Creswell, who had resigned from his position as postmaster general in June 1874, was singled out for particularly harsh criticism. The committee's report argued that his testimony, along with the ample evidence presented by other witnesses, "suggests either collusion between the [Post Office] Department and wrong-doers, or else a criminal negligence or a gross incompetency in the apprehension and discharge of the duties of the office" of postmaster general.[16]

While concluding that Marshall Jewell, the current postmaster general, had not directly engaged in corrupt practices related to the straw-bid racket, the Ways and Means Committee nevertheless declared that he had not been aggressive enough in bringing to justice the crooks who had benefited from the corrupt bidding system. The report complained that Jewell, "for political or other reasons," had failed to mount "an investigation into the condition of his predecessor's administration—such as would have been incident to the prosecution of the guilty clerks" in the Post Office who had facilitated the frauds.[17]

The Ways and Means Committee's investigation was followed, early in 1876, by another inquiry by the Committee on Post Offices and Postal Roads. To the delight of Democrats, there were more damaging revelations about the workings of straw-bid chicanery and how the Post Office, under Republican control, had covered it up. The committee heard startling testimony from Bradley Barlow, who detailed how he and his fellow postal contractors had conspired with officials in the Post Office and "robbed the government of several million dollars," as the New York *Sun* reported. Barlow's testimony included a claim that, in 1872, he had paid approximately $40,000 to a Washington, DC, attorney named William H. Farrar for the purpose of killing the congressional investigation sparked by McKibbin's provocative article in the *Washington Patriot*.[18]

By this point, the public had grown accustomed to stories of corruption in the Grant administration. Several alleged rings had been—or were in the process of being—exposed, among them the notorious Whiskey Ring, in which whiskey makers colluded with federal officials in a massive tax-evasion scam, and a corrupt circle of officeholders who exploited the operations of the New York Custom House for personal gain. Several members of Grant's cabinet were implicated in other scandals, including Interior Secretary Columbus Delano, Attorney General George Williams, and Secretary of War William Belknap. (Facing impeachment, Belknap resigned from the cabinet. He was impeached by the House of Representatives anyway and later tried by the Senate, which narrowly acquitted him.) The Star Route frauds were, in comparison, relatively prosaic, apparently involving some postal clerks and a few hardscrabble mail contractors from the hinterlands.

But the Post Office scandal simply would not go away. With Tilden leading the ticket, the Democrats lost the 1876 presidential election and faced another four years with a Republican (this time Hayes) still occupying the White House. But remaining in control of the House of Representatives and eager to embarrass the opposition, Democrats in 1878 mounted yet another investigation into the allegedly widespread rigging of Star Route contracts.

This inquiry represented a watershed in the scandal because it marked the first time that members of Congress themselves were seriously linked with fraudulent bids and payoffs of Post Office officials. At least initially, it was unclear which party benefited from these revelations, as both Democrats and Republicans seemed to have tried to enrich themselves in various ways through bogus Star Route contracts. The apparently bipartisan nature of the double-dealing made Congress wary of probing it in earnest. No one could predict which party would be more chagrined by what would be uncovered.

As usual, the New York *Sun* helped lead the charge. In a series of articles published in the first months of 1878, the newspaper delved into the minutiae of the Star Route contracts and revealed how bidders apparently had worked with a variety of officials in Washington to fatten their postal contracts. The *Sun*'s exposés at this point were noteworthy because they were not limited to the alleged corruption of minor government officials. The newspaper now suggested that current and former members of Congress were involved in the Star Route frauds.

In a story headlined "A Contractor's Bonanza," the *Sun* focused on four suspiciously lucrative Star Routes. For all of these, contractors had profited from enormous increases in pay because of alleged changes in delivery that had expedited the speed and frequency of mail delivery. Through a series of increases, one route (from Mesilla, New Mexico, to San Diego, California) netted contractors $559,097, an immense sum at that time. The *Sun* reported that these increases were made on the recommendation of Stephen B. Elkins, who was then New Mexico Territory's at-large delegate to Congress. The paper pulled no punches with Elkins, describing him as having been notoriously associated with several rings of disreputable postal-contract speculators.[19]

In another explosive story, the *Sun* trumpeted in a headline, "Are There Senators in the Post Office Ring?" The accompanying editorial criticized three members of the upper chamber of Congress—Stephen Dorsey of Arkansas, William Henry Barnum of Connecticut, and John P. Jones of Nevada—for having served as sureties, or guarantors, of some specious bonds issued by a Star Route contractor named John Chidester. It pointed out that the senators were barred by law from entering into such agreements with individuals holding federal contracts.[20]

In themselves, these were not necessarily dramatic charges. It seemed unlikely that there would have been much of a fuss made over a few senators exercising poor judgment in guaranteeing some bonds. What made the bond story so intriguing was that it involved, as the *Sun* gleefully noted, "an alliance between a carpet-bagger [Dorsey], a Radical Republican [Jones], and the acting chair of the Democratic National Committee [Barnum]." The trio's political sympathies spanned a significant portion of the political spectrum.[21]

Politically speaking, these were prominent and extremely strange bed-fellows. Barnum, a distant cousin of the famed showman P. T. Barnum, had served as chair of the Democratic National Committee since 1877. Dorsey had been a member of the Republican National Committee since 1876 and was on his way to becoming its secretary in 1880. For his part, Jones was a fantasti-cally wealthy man who had earned a fortune from mining the Comstock Lode, a lucrative silver deposit in Nevada. The three senators were influential poli-ticians in the capital, not backbenchers who made easy targets.

It was Dorsey who probably faced the most peril as House Democrats be-gan to zero in on apparent irregularities in the awarding of two dozen postal contracts in Arkansas, the state he had represented in the Senate since 1873. "Carpetbagger" was a pejorative term used to describe politically and econom-ically opportunistic northerners who descended on the South during Recon-struction. (It was said that these cunning newcomers carried their possessions in cheap luggage rendered from carpet fabric.) In terms of his background and character, Dorsey certainly fit the carpetbagger stereotype. No one ever described him as being a great statesman or a noble public servant.

A native of Vermont, Dorsey had moved to Ohio as a teenager. Years later, the story was told of how the plucky young man from New England had ar-rived, eager and wide-eyed, in the town of Oberlin and then attempted to make his way in the world. According to this tale, Dorsey stepped off the train without having any contacts in town and somehow made his way to a board-inghouse operated by a man named Chauncey Wack, an establishment known around town simply as "Wack's." Unbeknown to Dorsey, the boardinghouse had a poor reputation in Oberlin (the quirky Wack had famously opposed the rescue of a fugitive slave in the area in 1858), and this made it difficult for him to find work or make friends. Undaunted, Dorsey persevered and gradually gained acceptance in the town. He found work as a painter and soon was seen diligently plying his trade all over Oberlin. Dorsey also courted Wack's daughter, Helen, and they eventually married. Townspeople, impressed by his work ethic and character, eventually warmed to him.[22]

The Civil War interrupted Dorsey's schooling at Oberlin College. He left school to enlist in the 42nd Ohio Infantry Regiment, which was then under the command of a colonel named James A. Garfield. (Garfield would rise to the rank of major general in the Union army and eventually would be elected president—with Dorsey's help—in 1880.) Dorsey served capably under Garfield and several other military commanders, including another future president, Lieutenant General Ulysses Grant, as well as Major General William Rosecrans. Before the war ended, he earned the rank of colonel and saw combat in several battles, including Shiloh, Stone River, and Chickamauga.[23]

After the war, Dorsey tried to secure a position with the Treasury Department. When that effort failed, he settled in Sandusky, Ohio, a bustling manufacturing and trading hub located on Lake Erie. He found his footing as a partner in a manufacturing firm, which he subsequently gained a controlling interest in and then merged with the Sandusky Tool and Iron Company. Dorsey showed so much ability as the superintendent of the company's plant that he was hired away by the fledgling Arkansas Central Railway. Arriving in Arkansas early in 1871—it is not known whether he carried with him the proverbial carpetbag—he wasted little time in lining up various types of state and local assistance for the railroad, which proposed to lay tracks between Helena, Arkansas, and Little Rock, the state capital. Several spurs to other communities were planned as well.

The railroad brought with it the promise of economic development, and Dorsey's efforts earned him broad praise—until he began to dabble in politics. After he purchased a controlling interest in a Republican newspaper, the previously congenial Democratic press began to question Dorsey's methods of securing public funding for the railroad as well as his overall aims in coming to Arkansas from Ohio in the first place.

Late in 1872, Dorsey emerged as a candidate to replace Republican Benjamin Franklin Rice, whose term in the U.S. Senate was set to expire the following year. Having moved to the state scarcely a year earlier, Dorsey was open to charges of being a carpetbagger, but the fact that he was so recently arrived actually worked to his advantage in that he had not yet created very many longstanding enemies or gotten mired too deeply in any noteworthy political scandals. As the *Arkansas Gazette* put it, "if he has stolen anything, stuffed any ballot-boxes, or been a party to any such conduct, or in any manner aided or abetted in oppressing the people, we have not heard of it." The Democrats put forward Augustus Hill Garland. Republican Thomas Bowen then gave way to Dorsey, who bested Garland by a vote of 87 to 11 in the state assembly.

(There would not be direct election of U.S. senators until the ratification of the Seventeenth Amendment in 1913.)[24]

Dorsey's election to the Senate was greeted with mixed reviews. Some newspapers responded favorably, including the *Little Rock Morning Republican,* which noted, "He is a man of broad and comprehensive views and undoubted ability, while his consistency as a Republican and his moral character are above reproach." Many saw his quick rise to prominence as being emblematic of the can-do spirit of the nation as a whole.[25]

Others, however, were less enthusiastic about Dorsey's meteoric rise, pointing to his roots in Vermont and Ohio as well as his alleged crookedness in running the Arkansas Central. The *Helena World,* an Arkansas paper that was sympathetic to Democrats, called Dorsey little more than "an iron-monger [from] Ohio" who had "been in our state only about two years all told." The paper further complained that he had lined his own pockets while building a substandard railroad. (To cut costs, Dorsey—without advertising the fact beforehand—had built it on a narrow gauge, which limited the type and volume of rail traffic it could handle.) "He is unknown to the people of Arkansas. He came here to promote his railroad interests," the *World* observed. "He obtained state, county and city aid, under the most solemn pledges. By trickery, hocus-pocus, and legerdemain, the gauge of the road was changed from standard to narrow gauge, as adopted. Today we have a wheelbarrow road from Helena westward, costing nothing in comparison with the one he professed to come here to construct." There were also credible and oft-repeated charges that Dorsey had secured his election by bribing state lawmakers.[26]

Almost immediately, ongoing political turmoil in Arkansas threatened to overshadow Dorsey's tenure in the Senate. The so-called Brooks-Baxter War pitted two factions of Arkansas Republicans against one another: the more conservative "minstrels" (because their leader had once appeared in a minstrel show) and the more radical "brindletails" (their leader was said to possess a voice like a brindle-tail bull). In an election marred by accusations of widespread fraud and intimidation on both sides, the minstrel Elisha Baxter defeated the brindletail Joseph Brooks for the governorship in 1872. The Brooks faction, believing that Baxter's election would signal the end of reform in the state, refused to concede defeat, leading to a prolonged fight in the courts, pitched battles in the streets that eventually claimed at least two hundred casualties, and federal intervention by the Grant administration. A fragile and muddled truce was reached in 1874, with voters adopting a new state constitution and the Democrat Garland winning the reconstituted governorship.[27]

Dorsey could not avoid getting enmeshed in the Brooks-Baxter War, although it was sometimes difficult to determine which side he favored or why. He apparently supported Baxter initially, but it was rumored that he eventually backed the defeated Brooks, at least in part because Baxter opposed a measure widely known as the "Railroad Steal Bill," which would have netted a number of railroads, among them the Arkansas Central (in which Dorsey still maintained a financial stake), millions of dollars. Baxter's eventual alliance with the Democrats, who were rising to preeminence in the state, signaled doom for the political career of Dorsey in Arkansas. There was simply no way that the state legislature would reelect the Republican when his term ended.

Not that Dorsey was much of a senator anyway. An otherwise sympathetic biographer would later write that his career in the upper chamber was "singularly unspectacular" and "unimpressive." He authored few significant pieces of legislation and missed nearly 60 percent of the votes taken during his first four years in office. Dorsey "apparently did not take his senatorial duties seriously," the biographer concluded, and he spent much of his time in Washington wheeling and dealing outside the Senate chambers. A newspaper maintained that he was "simply a nonentity" who proved to be "of little use either to his friends or to his party."[28]

Dorsey apparently did not make much of an impression on those who observed the Senate chamber. The pioneering female journalist Mary Clemmer Ames, in an account from early in Dorsey's Senate tenure, expressed admiration for his rise from humble origins but dismissed him as a "stoutly-built and rather fleshy young man standing by the cloak-room door, with straight, jet-black hair, jet-black eyes, and not distinguished features."[29]

Some within the party viewed Dorsey as being scarcely better than the Democratic opposition. Congressman James Blaine's bid for the Republicans' presidential nomination in 1876 was damaged by the emergence of what became known as "the Mulligan letters," which purported to show that he had been involved in some questionable dealings involving the sale of Arkansas railroad bonds. Blaine always believed that Dorsey—seeking revenge for his support of a congressional report that had helped Democrats gain political control in Arkansas—was behind the scandal. James Garfield, then an Ohio congressman, noted in his journal that Blaine had told him that Dorsey and

Roscoe Conkling, Blaine's bitter enemy, engineered the release of the letters as part of a "plot . . . to injure his presidential prospects." The episode would leave Blaine distrustful of Dorsey. Several years later, he would describe his fellow Republican as being part of a "whole nest of unclean birds who wish to go in for loot and booty."[30]

Even in a golden age of political corruption, Dorsey's notoriously questionable ethics stood out. His apparent willingness to trade votes and influence for cash was a staple of gossip in the capital during the 1870s. It was said that his Senate vote could be bought, "often not for a very high price."[31]

When the House investigation of postal contracts got underway in 1878, Dorsey and his defenders complained that the accusations of fraud against him were grounded in some intraparty squabbling over political patronage with Powell Clayton, the former Arkansas governor and fellow Republican who had served as the state's other U.S. senator until March 1877. It was said that Clayton and a member of his inner circle, an attorney and former judge named "Poker Jack" McClure, had cooked up the claims in order to exact revenge for Dorsey's purported role in the removal of a federal internal-revenue collector in Arkansas. Smarting from the demise of their ally, Clayton and McClure allegedly wanted to secure the removal of Little Rock postmaster Ozra Amander Hadley, a former acting governor of the state and supporter of Dorsey.[32]

Whatever their politically tangled origins, the sensational charges against Dorsey received prominent attention throughout the country in the spring of 1878. A *New York Times* headline blared "Mail Contract Fraud Discovered— Senator Dorsey Said to Be Implicated." The most critical press reports openly accused him of having engaged in wrongdoing, with one paper asserting that the senator appeared to have been involved in "transactions of a doubtful, not to say criminal, character." Such was the prominence of the budding scandal that even the *Evening Star,* a Washington newspaper that generally sympathized with him, found itself forced to report on "Senator Dorsey and Those Mail Contracts." He was fast becoming the public face of the Star Route tumult.[33]

Dorsey apparently had not been involved in postal-contract bidding for very long. Late in 1877, John Peck, his brother-in-law, approached the senator and said he hoped to set himself up as a mail contractor. As one of Dorsey's attorneys, John McSweeney, later told the story in court, the senator hardly could say no to Peck; the man was like a brother to him and was suffering from consumption (tuberculosis). Still, Dorsey tried to caution him against getting involved in operating Star Routes in the West, warning that it could be a costly and nightmarishly complicated endeavor. There were physical dangers as well, given Peck's fragile condition and the presence of potentially hostile Native Americans in many parts of the region. "I tell you," Dorsey reportedly said, "don't do it." He thought it was simply too risky.[34]

But Peck persisted, telling the skeptical Dorsey that he possessed "genius enough to manage this thing." He argued that he could maintain his health and safety while also making some money by contracting with the Post Office for some mail routes. The senator, unwilling to turn his back on a family member and friend, finally relented. "Well," Dorsey said, "if this is the game, I won't desert you." Despite his reservations, he would help Peck.[35]

Thus prompted, Dorsey approached an established mail contractor named Albert E. Boone for help late in 1877. Boone did not boast a reputation for probity. In 1914, Warren G. Harding (then senator-elect from Ohio) described him as "a typical promoter, as strong in the faith as he was short in finances." Always on the make, Boone—seeing an opportunity to cultivate a valuable connection in Dorsey—agreed to help Peck. In return, the senator apparently offered to assist him in various ways with his own postal-contract bids, which were sure to involve Peck somewhere along the line, possibly as a subcontractor. Dorsey took it upon himself to print and send out (using his congressional franking privileges) some 5,000 circulars asking postmasters for information that would help Boone in several of his contract bids. Once the circulars were sent back to the senator in Washington, Boone dispatched bidding proposals to postmasters in Arkansas who were allied with Dorsey. Accompanying these proposals was a letter from Dorsey himself asking for help in securing bondsmen for these bids. The senator also reached out to some of his moneyed friends to back Boone. Thus did John P. Jones, the wealthy Republican senator from Nevada, and DeWitt Clinton Wheeler, New York City's influential police commissioner, become bondsmen on behalf of a postal contractor they almost certainly had never met.[36]

These were ethically suspect moves for a sitting U.S. senator, but Dorsey might have already been looking forward to life after office. In the fallout of the Brooks-Baxter War, Democrats began a long period of ascendancy in state politics with the election of Augustus Hill Garland as governor in 1874, and it seemed extremely unlikely that lawmakers in Arkansas would select Dorsey when he came up for reelection in the state assembly in 1878. (Predictably, they would in fact elect a Democrat, attorney James D. Walker, to replace him.)

With Dorsey's time in the Senate apparently winding down, the Arkansas Star Route bidding scheme began to take shape late in 1877, when a group of men allied with Peck arrived in Washington to assist Boone. Their number included John Dorsey, the senator's brother. John Dorsey had known Peck for several years through their family ties, and the two men had often discussed the possibility of getting involved in, and profiting from, mail contracts. John Miner, a man who had long known Stephen Dorsey, also joined the group in Washington. His connection to the senator dated back to the time Dorsey had spent in Ohio prior to his move to Arkansas in 1871: Miner had served as a director of the Sandusky Tool Company when Dorsey had been the superintendent of its plant.[37]

The nascent firm came to be known as Miner, Peck, and Company. To keep their roles hidden, John Dorsey and Boone were silent partners. Stephen Dorsey had no ostensible role in the enterprise, but it became clear over time that he would play an integral role in keeping it afloat by bringing to bear the resources and connections at his disposal as a senator. He also was the nexus of the group: not all of the men involved in the bidding scheme knew each other very well, but they all had some connection to the Arkansas senator. He would later be likened to the hub of a wheel, with the other men in the combination radiating outward from him in the manner of spokes.

The new firm wasted no time in getting into the postal-contract business. Over the winter of 1877–78, it bid on more than one thousand Star Route contracts. Much of the work on the bids had to be done without Peck, who was in New Mexico and attempting to recover from a bout of tuberculosis. To help fill the void, Stephen Dorsey recruited his clerk, Montfort Rerdell. He would do much of the administrative work for the combination.[38]

Rerdell was born in Montgomery County, Alabama, in 1841. It would be an understatement to say that his early life was difficult. "My parents both died within two hours of each other when I was two months old," he later said. "Till eleven years of age I lived with my grandmother in Richmond County, Georgia. At her death I was employed in different stores in Augusta, Georgia, till I was fourteen, when I returned to Alabama to hunt for an uncle whom I never was able to find." The gritty Rerdell eventually found employment on a steamship before serving in the Georgia Volunteers during the Civil War. Captured when Union forces led by Major General William Tecumseh Sherman overtook Savannah, Rerdell pledged his allegiance to the United States and quickly found a role working under Logan Holt Roots in the Union army's quartermaster corps.[39]

Following Roots westward, Rerdell eventually wound up in Arkansas after the war ended. Probably through his connections to Roots (who owned a plantation in the area and would be elected to Congress in 1868), Rerdell became the clerk of the board of registration for Prairie County. He was elected sheriff of Van Buren County in 1868.[40]

Rerdell's tenure as sheriff came at a time of intense political turmoil in Arkansas, with competing factions battling for control of the state. Rerdell sometimes found himself squarely in the middle of these fights, most notably in the spring of 1874, when he and county supervisor William Stobaugh were attacked by a group of several dozen armed men as they attempted to travel to Little Rock. Stobaugh was shot and killed, but Rerdell was able to escape on horseback. After riding at breakneck pace for six miles, he eventually was able to elude his attackers by scrambling into some rugged terrain. "It was a narrow escape for the sheriff," according to one newspaper report, and a "dastardly assassination" of Stobaugh.[41]

Rerdell was targeted because he, like many in Arkansas, apparently got caught up in the Brooks-Baxter War, which roiled the state in 1874. He seemed to have backed Baxter initially but then switched his allegiance to Brooks (in the manner of Stephen Dorsey). After changing sides, he admitted that, as a Baxterite, he had played a part in rigging elections in Van Buren County in 1872. "There were many irregularities in the conduct of the election," he later admitted to a state investigative committee, "and some ballots stuffed." He divulged that he himself was elected sheriff that year "by the fraudulent conduct of myself and others."[42]

After nearly becoming a casualty in the Brooks-Baxter War, Rerdell moved to the Kansas City, Missouri, area. He soon fell on hard times. "I there engaged in milling and speculating," he later said of his time in Missouri. "In the next twelve months, I lost over $60,000 and became a bankrupt." Broke and at loose ends, Rerdell turned to Stephen Dorsey for help. He had supported the latter's bid for the Senate in 1873, "when my efforts contributed largely to his success," as he later put it. Dorsey returned the favor and found Rerdell a clerkship in the District of Columbia's municipal government. (At the time, Dorsey chaired the Senate's District of Columbia Committee.) Beholden to Dorsey, Rerdell also volunteered to work as the senator's private secretary.[43]

As the postal-contracting combination came together, Rerdell brought with him a degree of relevant experience that some of the other men lacked, having been a mail contractor in Arkansas after the Civil War. Just as importantly, he was a steadfast supporter of Dorsey and a beneficiary of the senator's political patronage. Loyal and industrious, he seemed like a natural to bring on board. The new enterprise would need a hard worker who was not afraid of getting his hands dirty.

Working feverishly at the last minute to shore up the paperwork required to file their bids on time with the Post Office, the men—minus the sickly and absent Peck—got together on the third floor of Stephen Dorsey's home at 1121 I Street NW in Washington. (These were the temporary quarters of Miner, who was lodging with his Arkansas friend.) While his brother and his partners filled out bidding forms, the senator dropped in occasionally to monitor their progress and offer his input. With his help, the firm ultimately was awarded contracts on 134 of its bids for Star Route contracts.[44]

It was not long before rumors and accusations about the firm's bids began to surface in public. There was, for instance, the matter of Peck's signature (notarized by Boone) on the bids. As Peck had been battling tuberculosis in New Mexico at the time the bids were prepared, the signatures almost certainly were forgeries. Moreover, bondsmen in Arkansas had been secured before the actual bidders were named, which appeared to flout the whole idea of having someone acting as a surety. How could an individual vouch for a bidder who had not been named yet?

Had these been the only accusations floating around, it is unlikely that anyone would have paid much attention to the Star Route bids submitted by Miner, Peck, and Company. It was the role in them allegedly played by a U.S. senator that really raised eyebrows. Stephen Dorsey appeared to have violated federal law by asking postmasters (in writing, no less) to secure bondsmen before the names of bidders on Star Route contracts had been specified. And given the positions held in the firm by his brother (John Dorsey), his brother-in-law (Peck), his private secretary (Rerdell), and his longtime associate from Ohio and Arkansas (Miner), it was widely assumed that Senator Dorsey had some kind of hidden financial stake in the Star Route bids submitted by the group.[45]

In March 1878, spurred by the claims made against Senator Dorsey and the firm so closely tied to him, the House Committee on Post Offices and Postal Roads opened yet another inquiry (the fifth congressional probe since 1872) into postal contract bid-rigging. If the hearings were not the stuff of high drama, they did expose some apparent irregularities in how Miner, Peck, and Company had pursued Star Route contracts in Arkansas. A Little Rock attorney named William Wallace Wilshire testified that he had been approached by Ozra Amander Hadley, the city's postmaster, to sign on as a surety for about fifty blank bids. According to the lawyer, Hadley had claimed that the request for bondsmen was made by Stephen Dorsey, but Wilshire reported to Congress that he never had been in direct communication about the matter with the senator.[46]

Albert Boone also testified before the committee. Hoping to downplay Dorsey's role in the affair, Boone said that he, not the senator, had contacted postmasters in Arkansas in an effort to find bondsmen for his firm's bids. He also dismissed the idea that there was anything crooked about seeking sureties without providing the bidders' names or even the amount of their bids. These were routine practices, Boone said, measures by which contractors sought to protect themselves from competitors. Nothing untoward had happened.[47]

Senator Dorsey, who was regularly being pilloried in the press, did not wait to be subpoenaed by the committee. In an unusually defiant gesture for a member of Congress suspected of having committed fraud, he approached the panel and demanded the opportunity to testify under oath. As his attorney later paraphrased it (undoubtedly with some degree of dramatic embellishment), Dorsey rapped on the door of the room in which the House committee was meeting and bellowed: "Sirs, I have been waiting these many days expecting, in common fairness, that you would ask me, under oath, to say something about these allegations. You have not sent for me, but I have come, and am here. Swear me in." He had nothing to hide and wanted to be heard.[48]

Physically, the pudgy Dorsey did not cut an imposing figure. But what he lacked in stature, he made up for in bravado. In his testimony before the House committee, Dorsey loudly proclaimed his innocence and dismissed the charges leveled against him as being utterly baseless. He castigated its members for not having immediately come to him with their concerns about the Arkansas postal bids, as he could have explained everything quickly and saved them the trouble of holding hearings. "I have rendered each and every one of my friends and constituents who have asked me all the legitimate assistance that lay in my power to advance their lawful interests," Dorsey sputtered, "and it need not have required an investigation by a congressional committee to ascertain this fact."[49]

The senator was emphatic in stating that he had done nothing wrong and did not have any financial stake in the questionable Star Route bids. He even went so far as to assert that his efforts had resulted in *savings* for taxpayers, as the bids in question had reduced costs on several postal routes. (It was unclear how he could claim credit for economical bids with which he had no involvement.) "Senator Dorsey denied unqualifiedly and positively that he had any interest, remote, contingent, or possible, in any mail contracts, in the past present or future," the *Evening Star* in Washington reported. "He denied he had given any assistance to Peck, Miner, and the other contractors, for any reward or hope of reward, and notified the committee that he should perform the same service at any time that he was called upon."[50]

As J. Martin Klotsche noted in his careful study of the Star Route furor, the 1878 House inquiry did not suffer from a want of potentially incriminating evidence. What it lacked was political will from either side of the aisle to follow through. Neither party wanted to risk implicating one of its own simply to take down an opponent. For Democrats, Republican carpetbagger Dorsey represented a tempting target, but any effort to oust him was sure to invite an attack on someone in their own ranks, such as Senator Barnum, who also had been implicated in the Post Office imbroglio. "The prevailing opinion seemed to be," according to Klotsche, "that the Democrats could not afford to sacrifice Barnum in order to punish Dorsey." In the end, with members of both parties sensing that they might be at risk, "a considerable group of persons felt that Congress was not sincere in its desire to probe these cases." Political expediency prevailed, and the investigation petered out.[51]

President Hayes distanced himself from the persistent scandal, claiming that he had directed his subordinates to look into any irregularities in Star Route contracting that had been brought to his attention. He further insisted that it had been up to Congress, not the executive branch, to mount a thorough investigation if it suspected wrongdoing by the likes of Tom Brady and Dorsey. Hayes later wrote in his diary:

Congress is always ready to investigate charges against the officers of an Administration. Their means are ample and their powers great. I had no means to take testimony or compel witnesses to testify. I called the attention of [appropriate Post Office authorities] to the matter. They said all was correct on the face of things. I directed them to afford every possible facility to the congressional committees of investigation. The result of some months of active and angry controversy was that both branches of the Democratic Congress sustained the inculpated officer, General Brady. I had no relations with him. I found him in place when I became President, with a good reputation as a capable and faithful officer.[52]

In another diary entry, Hayes complained, "Enemies blame me for not discovering the fraud and putting a stop to it." He argued that he did in fact mandate closer regulation of Star Routes when he learned that contractors might be bilking the government. And besides, the repeated inquiries conducted by Congress always came to nothing. "The investigation was in the hands of Congress," Hayes wrote. "They sustained Brady." As far as the president was concerned, his hands were clean.[53]

Others were less sure. The journalist and attorney Albert Gibson, in his study of Republican corruption in this period, noted that Brady "was continued in office and protected by Hayes notwithstanding the most serious charges [that] were repeatedly made against him in connection with the Star Route mail contracts." Although "it was during the Hayes administration that the gigantic Star Route frauds were perpetrated," Brady was not removed from office until Hayes's successor, James Garfield, took office in the early months of 1881. "Sufficient evidence to have put honest men on inquiry was made public at a much earlier date, but Brady was protected." Gibson suggested that Brady had been safeguarded because he had helped fix the vote for Hayes in Florida in 1876.[54]

THE CYNICISM OF THIS

Stephen Dorsey and His Ring, 1878–1881

Its principals having survived the House of Representatives investigation relatively unscathed, Miner, Peck, and Company set about fulfilling its postal contracts in the summer of 1878. To that end, Montfort Rerdell obtained a month-long leave of absence from his federal post with the Senate's District of Columbia Committee. This was a relatively straightforward matter, as that body was still overseen by his political patron, Stephen Dorsey. The Arkansas senator provided Rerdell with letters of introduction as the latter traveled to Dakota Territory to set up operations on one of the thirty Star Routes that John Dorsey had successfully bid upon. At the same time, Stephen Dorsey's financial stake in the firm deepened: he endorsed four promissory notes over to the contractors, taking as security drafts against the future earnings on dozens of Star Route contracts.[1]

In the new venture, Senator Dorsey surrounded himself with men he knew well and trusted, like John Peck, his brother-in-law. An active Republican who had been a delegate to the party's 1876 national convention in Cincinnati, Peck had worked closely with the senator for several years and had served a stint as a director of the Arkansas Central Railway, which Dorsey had run. Peck's previous business ventures had shown him to be a shrewd, if not ruthless, businessman. During the Reconstruction era, the state of Arkansas sought to raise revenue by leasing convicts to private contractors, who essentially ran for-profit prisons fueled by inmate labor. Peck and a silent partner, Zebulon Ward, entered into a ten-year agreement with the state that allowed them to lease convicts from Arkansas' prisons. The duo profited from a brutal and corrupt system that exploited prisoners, most of whom were Black men and former slaves.[2]

Peck's various business ventures suffered, however, as his health faltered. As his company began its operations, Peck contracted tuberculosis and sought treatment in New Mexico (most likely because Dorsey owned an enormous ranch there). Distant and infirm, he was unable to give much attention to the new enterprise.

Miner, Peck, and Company was slow in executing its far-flung postal contracts. Miner's personal attorney, Lemon Galpin Hine, later explained that the firm was somewhat overwhelmed, never having expected the Post Office to accept so many of its bids. "As you must all know, parties who bid will make, say, a thousand bids and perhaps get one contract in thirty or forty or fifty. The average is not one in fifty," Hine noted. "Mr. Miner thought if he could get four or five contracts out West he could superintend them, ride around there and look after them, and his health would be improved." (Miner, like Peck, claimed to be suffering from a prolonged illness during this period.) All told, the men in the firm submitted roughly 475 bids. To their astonishment, 134 of them were accepted by the Post Office, "a five or six times greater number than was expected," Hine stated. No one anticipated that their bids would be so successful.[3]

The firm was staggered by the prospect of running so many postal routes over so much territory. Miner alone took on responsibility for those in northern Colorado, Utah, Nevada, California, Oregon, Washington Territory, Idaho, and Montana, "a region of country that in extent would amaze the most sanguine," according to Hine. Miner made an earnest effort to figure out how to deliver the mail in a timely fashion along his far-flung routes but, according to his lawyer, was so "confused and amazed at having so many proposals accepted [that] he hardly knew what to do."[4]

Miner felt that he was obligated, both ethically and legally, to fulfill his many postal contracts. Hine later explained that his client "was bound in honor under his bid, to do precisely what he had undertaken to do." In April 1878, Miner traveled from Washington to his home in Sandusky, Ohio, to secure additional capital and begin the process of finding subcontractors— hearty and enterprising individuals who would actually deliver the mail—for his dozens of routes. By the time he returned to the nation's capital on July 23, Miner believed that he had managed to "let every one of the routes in his region of country; that is, he had made contracts with persons to carry the mail over every one of the routes; some at a considerable loss, some at a considerable gain," according to his attorney. Overall, he felt that he stood to make a tidy profit.[5]

But even before he returned to Washington, Miner began to hear rumblings that all was not well with the execution of his postal contracts. "He heard on his way," Hine later stated, "rumors that some of those parties with whom he had made contracts had failed to put the routes into operation." A bungling subcontractor failed to provide any service on eight postal routes. Two routes in Nebraska and another pair in Utah also were failures. By the time he reached the nation's capital, Miner learned that his subcontractors had failed on as many as eighteen of his routes. His attorney later insisted that the blame for the flopped routes did not rest with Miner, as "he had done everything that a mortal man could do" to ensure their success. The real fault lay with his incompetent and perhaps unscrupulous subcontractors.[6]

Among members of the firm, Miner's struggles were not unique, and this represented no small threat to the partnership. In July 1878, Albert Boone learned from Second Assistant Postmaster General Tom Brady that Miner, Peck, and Company would be officially declared failing contractors if they did not get down to business and put into service numerous contracted routes by the middle of August. Boone knew that defaulting in such a manner would be disastrous for the postal-contracting concern. It would result in the partnership's current contracts being voided, and the contractors would be barred from bidding on any others in the future. Furthermore, their bondsmen (who had been recruited in murky circumstances) would be liable for the full amount of their roughly thirty bonds.[7]

As he had done in the past, Boone turned to Stephen Dorsey for help. Feeling that the firm's future hung in the balance, he asked the senator for money to help get its postal routes up and running. Dorsey demurred; he was strapped for cash and simply did not have any money to lend. He informed Boone that finding another partner might be the best way to infuse cash into the already struggling partnership.[8]

Boone, worried that the partnership was headed toward insolvency, resolved to cut his losses and sold Miner his interest in the firm. Miner then decided to take Dorsey's advice to heart and find another partner who could help stabilize the floundering enterprise and take over some of its failing routes. Apparently armed with power of attorney from Peck and John Dorsey, he turned to an experienced postal contractor named Harvey Merrick Vaile and offered him a deal: if Vaile could advance money to revive the postal failing routes, he could have a one-third stake in the partnership. Vaile accepted, and in August, the firm was rechristened Vaile, Miner, and Company.

Partnering with Vaile was a canny move. Born in Vermont in 1831, he eventually made his way to Kentucky and earned a law degree from the University of Louisville. After moving to the Kansas City area in the late 1850s, Vaile practiced law, made some shrewd investments, and bravely dabbled in Republican politics in a region that was not known for its cordial political discourse. It was later said that his authorship of some blunt newspaper editorials backing Lincoln's 1860 candidacy for president forced him to flee angry mobs on several occasions.[9]

Vaile amassed a fortune in the 1860s and 1870s, in part through shrewd Star Route contracting. His cash cow was the lengthy—and therefore tremendously profitable—route between Independence, Missouri, and Santa Fe, New Mexico. As he accumulated wealth through his legal practice and mail contracting, Vaile acquired status and property in Independence. "Vaile owned orchards, vineyards, farm land, sheep, dairy cows, and cattle," in the words of one recounting. He "lived as if he was the wealthiest man in the city!"[10]

The centerpiece of Vaile's empire was a magnificent home in Independence. Designed by the Kansas City architect Asa Beebe Cross, the massive Second Empire–style home was said to have been inspired by an opulent house that Vaile and his wife had seen on a visit to Normandy. It featured thirty-one rooms, ornate furnishings imported from Europe, nine marble fireplaces, and three chandeliers that originally had been designed for the White House. A breathless 1882 *Kansas City Times* article called it a *"masion d'or"*—mansion of gold—and asserted that it was "the most princely house and the most comfortable home in the entire west."[11]

Miner was elated to hand off some of his failing routes to the stable and prosperous Vaile, but the arrival of the new partner fundamentally altered the finances of the firm. Vaile's assumption of postal subcontracts (at full price) on routes initially awarded to Peck and John Dorsey meant that those two men would see no profit from those routes, as they might have if Vaile had simply subcontracted from them for a lower rate. (From the perspective of the men who bid on postal routes, this was the whole point of the practice of subcontracting: they could reap the difference between what the Post Office awarded them for the contract and what they paid out to subcontractors to do the actual work on the routes.) Furthermore, Vaile's assumption of the routes essentially nullified the value of the drafts that Senator Dorsey held as security for the notes he had earlier endorsed.[12]

A series of rows—verbal and otherwise—ensued when Dorsey returned to Washington late in 1878 from a trip to his New Mexico ranch and learned what Miner and Vaile had done. The senator's notes were past due when he came back to the capital, and the drafts he had been holding as security were now basically worthless. He thus believed, not without reason, that the reorganization of the firm had jeopardized his credit. Dorsey also was displeased that his brother John and brother-in-law Peck had been cut out of dozens of potentially money-spinning postal contracts. The senator was so incensed by the new partner's apparent chicanery that "a violent quarrel erupted when he met Vaile for the first time," according to one account. The two men apparently came to blows over how the reorganization had been handled.[13]

Vaile tried to make amends, or at least appeared to do so initially. He consented to paying John Dorsey and Peck for their interest in the contracts they initially had won from the Post Office. Vaile also reached a settlement with Stephen Dorsey, agreeing to reimburse him for the money he had advanced to the contractors and to pay his outstanding notes. At this point (December 1878), John Dorsey and Peck had dissociated themselves from the firm, but Rerdell had remained, performing clerical tasks on the routes and representing the firm at the Post Office.[14]

Matters remained unsettled early in 1879, as Vaile was slow to repay Peck and the Dorseys the money owed to them. Stephen Dorsey's frustrations bubbled over on March 4, 1879, the day after his Senate term expired. Now freed from the constraints of public office, he wrote to Second Assistant Postmaster Brady to complain that Vaile's Star Route subcontracts were invalid, having been made without approval of his brother or Peck. Dorsey demanded that Brady void Vaile's subcontracts by April 1 of that year.[15]

Faced with the prospect of losing dozens of potentially profitable routes, Vaile and Miner negotiated yet another reorganization of the postal contracts with Stephen Dorsey. At this point, all 134 of the routes originally awarded to Boone, John Dorsey, and Miner were parceled out to Vaile (40 percent), Miner (30 percent), and Stephen Dorsey, who would be acting on behalf of his brother and Peck (30 percent). There were other financial arrangements made as well. Using proceeds from the routes now under his control, Dorsey agreed to pay his brother John and Peck for their interest in the contracts they had originally won (something Vaile never had done) and to compensate himself for most of the debt that Miner and Vaile owed him. His payments to Peck and his brother amounted to $10,000 each.[16]

Once this settlement had been reached, there was no chance that Vaile and Miner would continue to work with Stephen Dorsey, who they now regarded as a sharp. They teamed up to form Vaile, Miner, and Company, while Dorsey paired with a Pennsylvania banker named James Bosler. Dorsey was not interested in the grubby work of running the postal routes he had taken over and left that task to Bosler, who actually had practical experience in government contracting. The two reached an agreement whereby they would share profits from the routes and provide repayment to Dorsey for money he had earlier paid to his brother and Peck. The new partners secured clerical assistance from Rerdell, who had abandoned Miner and Vaile.[17]

With this new arrangement in place, Stephen Dorsey largely turned his attention to other matters. He apparently was happy to leave Bosler and Rerdell in control of operations on the routes and wait for the profits that would allow him to recoup the money he had invested. He focused on his vast ranch in New Mexico and speculation in silver mines in Colorado as well as the upcoming presidential election in 1880. Compared to the grave business of keeping a Democrat out of the White House, the Star Routes were a trifling concern.[18]

While Dorsey moved on, his former associates in the postal-contract game squabbled among themselves. After Rerdell left the employ of Miner and Vaile, he bickered with the two men over pay. Claiming he was owed over $300 in wages, Rerdell filed a civil suit late in May 1879. They eventually reached a settlement (Rerdell got $200), but not before Vaile suggested in a court filing that Dorsey, his public statements to the contrary notwithstanding, had been involved in postal contracts while he had served in the Senate.[19]

Alleged irregularities in Star Route contracts garnered national headlines yet again late in 1879, when it became known that appropriations for the routes were in danger of running out. Congress had appropriated $5.9 million (the equivalent of roughly $150 million in 2021) for routes for the 1879–80 fiscal year, but the Post Office was slated to have spent almost two-thirds of funding by the midway point (January 1, 1880). Brady, who oversaw the Star Routes, wrote to Postmaster General David Key in December 1879 to propose that he turn to Congress and ask for a supplemental appropriation of almost

$2 million to cover the potential shortfall. He explained that the overruns were the result of Congress having approved two thousand additional routes after the initial appropriation had been made. Key agreed and in turn wrote to both the House of Representatives and the Senate, stating that "the business interests of the country would be promoted by [the] prompt and favorable action of Congress" in approving the supplemental funds for the Star Routes. If those monies were not forthcoming, it was possible that mail deliveries would stop in remote locations throughout the West.[20]

The *New York Times* made much of the potential shortfall in Star Route funds and suggested that it was due in no small part to the profligate (if not simply corrupt) workings of the Post Office. The second assistant postmaster general was subjected to especially sharp criticism, with the newspaper bemoaning "Brady's peculiar methods" of handling increased payments for several routes. The *Times* further noted that increases on all routes tended to be approved when Key was traveling and Brady was acting postmaster general. This seemed to suggest that Brady was tweaking Star Rout contracts when his boss was not present to provide more robust oversight.[21]

Brady's request for additional funding for Star Routes (the equivalent of more than $40 million in 2021) created an uproar in Congress and the press. The New York *Sun* pointed out that the costs of the additional routes approved by Congress only amounted to $400,000 and that "raising the old service of ring contractors," who were adept at cheating the Post Office, had created most of the need for additional funds.[22]

On January 12, 1880, the House Appropriations Committee launched an investigation into fraud and cost overruns in the Star Routes. (Depending on how one counted, this marked the sixth congressional investigation of the matter.) Many newspapers with Democratic leanings expressed confidence in the inquiry, which was being conducted by a subcommittee led by Representative Joseph Blackburn, a hard-bitten Kentucky Democrat who had made a name for himself as a skilled trial lawyer. Sympathetic editorialists proclaimed that the dogged Blackburn would root out corruption without regard for individuals' political affiliations. They failed to mention that the inquiry was seen by Democrats as a means of embarrassing Republicans in the run-up to the November presidential election.

A subcommittee of the House Appropriations Committee, under the chairmanship of Blackburn, began its Star Route hearings on January 12. Wasting no time, the subcommittee called Tom Brady as its first witness. The second assistant postmaster general did his best to justify the ballooning Star Route budget and the need for a substantial additional appropriation. Since 1876, he said, Congress had approved thousands of new postal routes covering more than 14 million miles. With so many new routes being contracted, there were bound to be a few administrative and budgetary hiccups. No one could have foreseen the shortfall.

In high dudgeon, Brady bristled at the idea that any fraud had been committed. Everything relating to Star Route contracting had been done by the book. "The action of the department has been thus far in strict conformity with the law, and will continue to be," he declared. "In every case of additional service, compensation therefore has been regulated and fixed by and according to the terms" of federal law, "and every allowance for any increase of expedition in carrying the mails" had been authorized by law. Brady himself certainly had done nothing wrong in merely following Post Office regulations and helping provide faster mail service in remote parts of the country.[23]

These protestations of innocence seemed to have little effect on Blackburn and his skeptical subcommittee colleagues, whose number included James Henderson Blount, a Democrat from Georgia. They quizzed Brady on the specifics of several routes where there had been substantial increases for expedition. Among them were Number 40101, a notoriously suspicious route running from Santa Fe to Prescott, Arizona, that would often draw the attention of reporters, investigators, and, eventually, federal prosecutors. Brady came under fire for sweetened contracts, such as those granted to Miner, Peck, and John Dorsey. The second assistant postmaster general had nearly sextupled annual payments on a dozen of their routes, increasing the aggregate yearly payment from $44,666 to $262,373.[24]

As he discussed various routes where costs had skyrocketed, Brady was forced to admit that his initial estimates for the costs of Star Route services had been too low.

"Then, to that extent, you misled Congress," Blount stated, suggesting that Brady had known all along that he would need to come back to Congress later for more money to fund Star Route services.

"The appropriation was made a year ago," Brady replied, "when things were very different."[25]

At one point in the proceedings, Brady was called upon to explain how and why a few large groups of bidders seemed to dominate the Star Route contracts. "It seems to me . . . that so far as fairness in receiving bids is concerned," he insisted, "the safeguards are perfect, and no contractor can have an advantage over the other." But, Brady noted, larger and more experienced firms had some inherent advantages over their smaller and greener potential competitors: they could more accurately assess which routes might be profitable, absorb losses on routes that performed poorly, and employ small armies of subcontractors to do the actual work of delivering the mail.[26]

The postal contractors who testified before the Ways and Means subcommittee explained that some of the additional costs for the Star Routes simply resulted from the hardships they faced in carrying the mail. M. T. Patrick was asked if he had been given any military protection to help ward off Native Americans and brigands. "Not any," the clearly rankled Patrick said. Receiving no help from the government, he and his colleagues were forced to spend a fair amount of money to defend themselves against attacks and ensure that the mail was delivered safely. It had never occurred to him that he would need to factor in such costs when he bid on Star Routes.[27]

Other contractors faced tougher questions about the increased costs they claimed after bidding on their contracts. John Miner, who was part of the Dorsey combination, was quizzed about a request for an expedition he had made on Route 35051, which connected the towns of Bismarck and Tongue River in Dakota Territory. Members of the subcommittee asked him to explain a letter he had written to Brady on September 20, 1878. Asking for increased payments for the route, Miner had stated: "The number of men and animals necessary to carry the mails on route 35051, Bismarck to Tongue River, three times a week, is 12 men and 13 animals. The number of men and animals necessary to carry said mails on a reduced schedule of 65 hours is 150 men and 150 animals." In his testimony, Miner clarified that he had not meant to suggest that there would be more trips on the route. He had simply meant that the speed of each trip would be reduced from 104 to 65 hours. The additional funds were needed, he elaborated, because "it requires a large number of men to open the road, to build bridges, and all that sort of thing, which on a long schedule of time would not be required." Faster service required costly infrastructure.[28]

Members of the subcommittee were incredulous over this self-serving explanation. When he had bid on the 250-mile route in Dakota Territory, Miner had said it would require 13 animals covering 19 miles each per day. Yet in his letter to Brady, Miner had stated that the route would require 150 animals covering a little under 2 miles per day—a dramatic change from the initial terms of the contract. When asked to account for the discrepancies, Miner waxed philosophical, saying that they were attributable to the difference "between a man's foresight and his hindsight."[29]

This explanation, though clever, failed to impress members of the appropriations subcommittee, dour men who suspected that Miner (with Brady's help) had defrauded the federal government. The magnitude of the proposed change in the Dakota Territory contract—many more animals traveling far fewer miles each per day—made them wonder if Miner actually knew the details of the operations of Route 35051.[30]

"What number of animals have you employed on that route at this time?" he was asked.

"I cannot tell," Miner admitted.

"Can you tell us the highest number of animals you ever had employed on it at any time?"

"I have not any actual knowledge on that point."

"You do not know much about this route, do you?"

"Very little," Miner conceded. "I am not the practical man in it."[31]

In its report on the Star Route irregularities, the House Ways and Means subcommittee rebuked Second Assistant Postmaster General Brady for having made "arbitrary allowances of vast sums of money" that benefited particular contractors, all "without any commensurate advantages to the country" in terms of the actual services being provided. It found that his administration of Star Route contracts allowed combinations of mail contractors to cheat the government by demanding additional payments for services that provided no real benefit. The Dorsey combination was held out as an example of a system infected with rampant corruption.[32]

Brady took a drubbing in the press as well. The New York *Sun* carped that the country had been defrauded by an organized conspiracy that had Brady serving as "its head and front in the Post Office Department." The *New York Times* offered another characteristically unfavorable assessment. "The history of this affair is extremely discreditable to the Post Office Department, and shows an inefficiency and laxness of administration which cannot be too soon remedied," the newspaper stated.

> It does more than this, for the facts indicate a way of doing business which is wasteful of the public money, reckless of official responsibility, and indifferent to the requirements of law to a degree for which corruption is the most natural and logical explanation. In numerous instances, contractors have favored at the expense of the Treasury, in violation of the spirit, if not the letter, of the law, and it requires a child-like confidence in the purity of the postal officers to suppose that their extravagant and utterly useless squandering of public money has been permitted from simple carelessness. At the very best, Brady, as the man most directly implicated, can only escape condemnation for dishonest conspiracy with the contractors to defraud the Treasury by pleading a lack of capacity which renders him wholly unfit for his place.[33]

Throughout the subcommittee's hearings, Brady insisted that he had done nothing inappropriate in granting, and then sweetening, Star Route contracts. He also boasted that in asking for an additional appropriation, he had the backing of numerous members of Congress on both sides of the aisle, many of whom were reluctant to see cutbacks in postal service that might harm their districts. And in fact, despite all of the damning testimony relating to questionable practices in Post Office contracting, the full House of Representatives ultimately passed a deficiency appropriation bill to cover the Star Route contracts, although the amount was less than what Brady had asked for initially ($1.1 million). The money came with caveats limiting future pay increases for expedited service on the routes and cautioning that the provision of the additional funds by Congress was in no way intended "to affect the validity or legality of acts or omissions of any officer of the United States or to affect any proceedings therefore." The government, in other words, was leaving its options open in case it wanted to file criminal charges stemming from improprieties in Star Route contracting.[34]

The passage of the deficiency appropriation measure, coming as it did during an investigation of why it was even necessary in the first place, disturbed more than one observer. That the House of Representatives had seen fit to "appropriate money blindly for jobbers," as one newspaper fumed, led to widespread accusations that contractors had paid congressmen to vote for the bill. One House member asserted that more than a dozen of his colleagues had essentially sold their votes to mail contractors, and few people doubted his claim.[35]

It was rumored that Stephen Dorsey resorted to a cunning subterfuge to ensure that the deficiency appropriation would pass. According to one author at the time, when it appeared that the measure was a half-dozen votes shorts of passage, Dorsey made contact with several key lawmakers and promised them that funds from his Star Route combination would be used to support their respective candidates for the Republican nomination for president, which was to be decided at the party's upcoming convention in Chicago. Thanks to the promise of these riches, the bill eventually "went through the House with a rush, so potent was the proffered offer of Star service gold," as described by the writer. When Dorsey then withheld the promised money, the aggrieved politicians—having been shortchanged in a corrupt bargain—were powerless to publicly complain. They could not very well go to the press and gripe that Dorsey had not paid off their bribes.[36]

At the Republican convention, held in Chicago's cavernous Interstate Exposition Building, Dorsey and other members of the party's Stalwart faction, led by Senator Conkling, backed former president Grant for an unprecedented third term. When the convention deadlocked, the delegates chose a compromise candidate to lead the party's ticket in the 1880 election. James Garfield, a genial congressman from Ohio, was deemed acceptable by the party's warring—and, after thirty-five fruitless ballots, exhausted—factions. As a consolation to the Stalwarts, Dorsey was then appointed as secretary of the party's national committee, where he would work under the nominal supervision of Marshall Jewell, the chair. A later study of the Republican Party during the Gilded Age depicted Dorsey in this moment as being a "flamboyant political operator with many shadowy connections. . . . Nearly everyone distrusted him, but no one—not even Jewell, who immediately clashed with him—doubted that he was, as [Whitelaw] Reid described him, 'a man of admirable executive qualities and great force.'"[37]

Refusing to sulk over Grant's defeat at the convention, Dorsey soon set about helping Garfield prevail over the Democratic candidate, Winfield Scott Hancock, in the general election. He focused his efforts on New York as well as Indiana, which was widely viewed as being essential to Garfield's chances of prevailing.[38] Part of the Hoosier State's importance stemmed from its quirky voting schedule. One of the few remaining "October states," it held two separate fall elections in 1880: one on October 12 for governor, and another on November 2 for president. It was thought that a strong showing by Republicans in the earlier contest would give them momentum heading into the main event the following month.[39]

Dorsey realized that his political future might hinge on the outcome in Indiana. Speaking of his aspirations, he said, "I have sense enough to know that if I want anything, the way to get it is to show myself entitled to it by the management of the canvass." A good result in that key state would put him in good stead with the incoming Republican administration, if there was one.[40]

Failure, however, might mean the end of his political career. When he prepared to set out for Indiana from New York City, he joked with Chester Arthur, the party's nominee for vice president, "General, if I don't succeed, I shall never come back here again." He explained that if the Republicans lost the election, he could spend his retirement at his ranch in New Mexico. Arthur, knowing that he also would not be able to recover from a defeat in the campaign, replied, "Let me know [if you go back to the ranch] where there would be room enough for me."[41]

The campaign proved to be a monumental challenge. Late in July 1880, Dorsey despaired that the Garfield election effort was in disarray; very little had been done since the convention had chosen him as the party's nominee. "We are about where we were the day we organized," he noted. "No money has been raised, nor general organization effected." To that end, Dorsey arranged a meeting of the Republican National Committee in New York in early August. Although the main purpose of the gathering was not accomplished—a sullen Conkling, who had backed Grant at the convention, stayed away and did not make peace with Garfield—the candidate's trip from Ohio was a success overall and helped breathe life into the moribund campaign.[42]

In Indiana, "Dorsey was told to do 'whatever it takes,' given four hundred thousand dollars to do it, and to work out of sight," as one of his biographers later wrote. "It was argued that Dorsey would only be using the same dirty tricks that the Democrats were using. For two months, Dorsey was busy undercover everywhere in Indiana." (It was widely reported that the $400,000 put at Dorsey's disposal came in the form of sacks of $2 "greenbacks" that could be easily distributed to prospective voters.) Republicans were particularly worried that Democrats would illegally import out-of-state voters to support Hancock at the Indiana polls. To stop this practice, Dorsey hired agents from the Pinkerton Detective Agency to watch polling locations and monitor arrivals in railroad stations. Detectives and party operatives also were on alert for qualified voters who might attempt to cast ballots twice. Dorsey wrote that the Republicans expected "Democratic leaders to perpetrate every species of fraud" to steal votes from Garfield. It was widely known that Republicans were engaging in similarly underhanded tactics, probably under Dorsey's aegis, but this was viewed as being standard practice during an election season. An Indianapolis attorney named W. P. Fishback later alleged that Dorsey had disbursed tens of thousands of dollars "to be used in buying votes, hiring repeaters, bribing election officials to stuff the ballot-boxes and falsify election returns."[43]

For the most part, Republicans winked at Dorsey's transgressions on the campaign trail. The *Nation* quoted one party wag as saying, "It would not have done to send anyone out to carry Indiana who was loaded up with the Ten Commandments."[44]

Dorsey's exploits in Indiana were recounted by the humorist David Ross Locke, who wrote a column under the pseudonym Petroleum Vesuvius Nasby for many years in the *Toledo Blade*. In one column, the fictional Nasby recalled in his signature colloquial idiom how he had met with some Democrats in Kentucky and discussed a favorite topic, "Republikin corrupshun." "I [said] that it is charged that Stephen W. Dorsey, in 1880, when Garfield wuz the Republikin candidate, and Hancock the Dimekratic, went into the state uv Injeany and corruptly bought up venal voters at $2 a head, wich kerried the state for Garfield," Nasby recalled. "'Sich infamus corrupshen,' I continnered, 'wuz enuff to make the very blood bile in the vanes of every Dimekrat.'" To Nasby's dismay, the assembled "Dimekrats" had cheered Dorsey's largesse and expressed hope that he would attempt to buy *their* votes in the next election cycle.[45]

Garfield wisely did not sully himself with the dirty work of his presidential campaign, but the man at the top of the Republican ticket was aware of the importance of Dorsey's efforts on his behalf in Indiana and offered him praise and encouragement. At one point, the candidate received word that Dorsey was thinking about walking away from his indispensable role in the campaign because he was being denied sufficient money and personnel in the Hoosier State. Garfield, realizing that he desperately needed Dorsey (and Indiana), wrote to him: "Don't relax any grip anywhere. . . . I rely greatly on your calm equipoise which has shown itself so often and so well hitherto." Dorsey remained in his role.[46]

Not everyone viewed Dorsey's partisan political activities favorably. Eager to portray their opponents in a negative light, Democrats openly wondered how the senator's campaign work in Indiana was being funded. Was the Garfield campaign awash in cash because of the ethically questionable handling of Star Route contracts by various prominent Republicans, most notably Second Assistant Postmaster Brady and Dorsey himself? After all, the Republicans involved in the Whiskey Ring scandal during the Grant administration had used their ill-gotten gains to fund campaigns in the past. Maybe they were pulling a similar trick in 1880 with plundered Star Route money.

Dorsey and his army of Republican partisans prevailed in Indiana, with Garfield winning the state by a margin of just over 6,000 votes. The state's fifteen electoral votes helped propel Garfield to a narrow victory over Hancock in the Electoral College. The victorious—and grateful—candidate wrote to Dorsey that his crucial work in Indiana had "vindicated itself and silenced all cavillers."[47]

Through his productive efforts in Indiana, Dorsey made a favorable impression upon Garfield, and the president-elect consulted with him about political matters after the election. In December 1880, Garfield wrote in his journal of Dorsey, "He is a man of great ability and with strong and decisive views of the merits of men." He turned to the former senator, a Stalwart, in the interregnum between the election and his inauguration to act as intermediary with the ever-unhappy Roscoe Conkling, who was predictably upset over the president-elect's handling of cabinet appointments. At one point, Dorsey privately reported to Garfield that Conkling had expressed a sincere "desire to be his friend" and work together for the good of the party. "I cannot convey to you the manner, earnestness and power with which this explanation was made," he wrote, eager to shore up the standing of Conkling, his Stalwart ally. "It was intense in the highest degree." (As later events would show, this was wishful thinking on Dorsey's part; internecine battles between Conkling and Garfield would overshadow the early days of the new administration.)[48]

It was a measure of Dorsey's standing with the president-elect that he continued to offer unsolicited, and quite blunt, political advice to Garfield during this period. Ever-loyal to Conkling, he expressed dismay over the prospect of

James Blaine, Conkling's great rival, gaining influence after his appointment as secretary of state. (Everyone knew that Blaine was furiously lobbying to prevent any of Conkling's New York allies from joining him in the cabinet.) "No President has even done a wiser thing than you have done in placing Mr. Blaine at the head of your cabinet," Dorsey wrote. "And not ever has done or could do so unwise a thing as to permit him to have a hand in selecting the other members of your cabinet or in any degree to control it after it is selected."[49]

Dorsey's efforts in the 1880 campaign were recognized by his party a few months after the election with a lavish dinner at Delmonico's, the fabled New York restaurant. In February 1881, more than one hundred social, political, and business leaders turned out for the sumptuous event, among them such luminaries as Thurlow Weed, John Jacob Astor III, J. Pierpont Morgan, and the clergyman Henry Ward Beecher. Garfield was not on hand, but former president Grant was present, and he escorted Dorsey's wife, Helen, into the dining room for a dinner that the *New York Times* called "one of the finest which Delmonico has ever furnished."[50]

Grant's laudatory remarks on this occasion underscored the importance of Dorsey's work for the victorious Garfield campaign. "We have assembled this evening to do honor to a gentleman, who, we think, has contributed more than any one man in bringing about the result that we all hoped for, and now feel so grateful for at the last presidential election," the former president said of Dorsey. "To his skill, his executive ability, we are largely, if not wholly, indebted for the result which was attained there [in Indiana]."[51]

Vice President–elect Arthur also offered fulsome praise for Dorsey at the Delmonico's dinner. He told the gathering that the grateful Republicans had come together that evening "to do honor to Senator Dorsey, to express our appreciation of his great services in the last campaign . . . and also to express our great regard and esteem for him personally." It was undeniable, Arthur said, that "Mr. Dorsey, with his matchless skill, cool head, and wonderful courage, was able to save Indiana"—and, by extension, the nation as a whole.[52]

Apparently in a playful mood, Arthur also alluded to Dorsey's ethically dubious tactics in securing the vote for the Republican ticket in Indiana. With a twinkle in his eye, he told the dinner guests: "I don't think we had better go into the minute secrets of the campaign, so far as I know them, because I see reporters present, who are taking it down. . . . Indiana was really, I suppose, a Democratic state. It had always been put down in the book as a state that might be carried by close and careful and perfect organization and a great deal of. . . ." When Arthur paused, someone in the audience helpfully cried out "soap!" (then a popular slang term for money). The impromptu comment elicited guffaws from the crowd, as everyone knew that Dorsey had indeed spent considerable amounts of cash to win the day for the Republicans in Indiana.[53]

Arthur sat next to the guest of honor during the dinner. It was, a biographer later wrote, "Senator Stephen W. Dorsey's finest hour."[54]

Not everyone was impressed by Dorsey's triumphal Delmonico's dinner, however. James Rood Doolittle, who had served Wisconsin in the Senate during the Civil War, fulminated about the event in a June 1884 letter to former Indiana governor (and future vice president) Thomas Hendricks. Doolittle stated that the hundreds of thousands of dollars "stolen from the Star Route thieves under Dorsey was spent to buy votes in Indiana in 1880." Worse than this bit of chicanery was "the fact that Arthur, the present President of the United States, without blushing, at a public dinner, when an ex-president sat by his side, openly, as it honors were being given to some great conquering hero, boasted of the achievement of carrying Indiana by wholesale bribery, as if it were a great victory." The dinner demonstrated to Doolittle that the Republicans simply had no shame about their embrace of corrupt practices.[55]

James Blaine, who rarely missed an opportunity to impugn Stalwarts, saw the Delmonico's dinner as a cunning ploy by Dorsey to position himself to have influence over the incoming administration's operation of Star Routes. "I am afraid the true intent and meaning of the Dorsey dinner in New York was to enable him to make demands of the administration which will in the end modestly center in the second assistant postmaster generalship," he wrote to Garfield, "through which channel, in my judgment, there are cunning preparations being made by a small cabal to steal half a million a year during your administration." Blaine recognized the potential perils of Garfield allowing himself to become entangled with Dorsey. "I again beg you to keep yourself free from all possible commitments as to the minor cabinet," he cautioned, "which in the P.O.D. [Post Office Department] is even more important than the major."[56]

Like Blaine, William Chandler saw myriad warning signs in the post-election celebration of Dorsey. In a letter to Garfield, the influential Republican deplored the sheer brazenness of the Delmonico's dinner, expressing his disgust at "the gross want of sense, propriety and taste which prepared a public celebration and glorification of the use of money to carry elections. It was more than a mistake; it was a gross outrage on the Republican Party and an unblushing proclamation of its shame, the effect of which, if not repudiated, will be great for evil during the next four years." He went on to warn the president-elect of the dangers that lay ahead because of the long-simmering postal-corruption scandal:

> The evidently desired sequel of all this apotheosis of corruption is to be the plunder of the government to reward those who boast that they did the deed. The "Star Service" is the grand prize which is to nourish them and to furnish the scandals of the next presidential fight. They are willing to have a cabinet nominally honest; but the lesser cabinet—the Assistant Secretaries and the Assistant Postmaster General, it would be unreasonable to refuse to a band of disinterested patriots who, as Mr. Beecher, speaking at the deification of corruption, said of Dorsey, have done their work in a manner "almost sublime." They may well expect to name the cabinet, select the assistants and get annual incomes from their influence with them![57]

(In his sanctimonious messages to Garfield, Chandler failed to mention that Republicans had facilitated the work of an accused Star Route thief, Tom Brady, in helping secure Hayes's dubious victory in Florida in the 1876 election.)[58]

Garfield himself professed to be baffled by the dinner and what it might mean for his party or his presidency. Not long after he received troubling reports about the Delmonico's episode from Blaine and Chandler, he wrote that it was a "curious affair, whose whole significance I do not yet understand."[59]

PROBE THIS ULCER TO THE BOTTOM

President Garfield Takes Action, Spring 1881

Around the time that Republicans were gathering at Delmonico's in New York to honor Stephen Dorsey's wily contributions to the successful 1880 presidential campaign, President-elect James Garfield was assembling his cabinet. This is a delicate task for any incoming president, but Garfield, hoping to keep a divided Republican Party together, faced an especially difficult challenge. He not only hoped to appoint men who would be loyal to him and would dutifully support the policies of his administration but also had to maintain the fragile truce that existed between the party's warring Stalwart and Half-Breed factions, which were led by two famously cunning and difficult-to-please men, James Blaine and Roscoe Conkling. Garfield needed to somehow reconcile a variety of potentially competing interests even before he was sworn into office.

For the role of postmaster general, Garfield considered Thomas Lemuel James, a former newspaperman who had been serving as the postmaster of New York City. James had performed capably in that difficult role, instituting some much needed reforms while keeping the peace with Conkling's powerful and patronage-hungry Stalwart political machine. There was some hope among members of the incoming administration that he might perform a similar balancing act on the national stage.[1]

The improvements implemented by James in New York had included setting up examinations for job applicants that would distinguish those who were well qualified from those who were merely politically well connected. He also had enlarged the city's carrier system and substantially increased the number of daily mail deliveries. James was said to have introduced a simple dictum to guide the operations of New York City's postal system: "A letter must be kept in motion; it must not lie dormant at any branch office!"[2]

Although he was a Stalwart and closely allied with Conkling, James held a strong belief that promoting partisan political interests came second to serving the public. He wrote to George William Curtis, an advocate for civil-service reform, "The Post Office is a business institution and should be run as such, and it is my deliberate judgement that I and my subordinates can do more for the party of our choice by giving the people of our city a good and efficient postal service than by controlling primaries and dictating nominations." Such an approach later earned him praise from one historian as an "exceptionally fine head" of the New York City post office.[3]

James actually had been offered the postmaster general post a year earlier by Garfield's predecessor, President Hayes, but he had declined after being warned off by the powerful Conkling. The senator had told him in a letter not to take the position "at the tail-end of this administration," as he most likely would have to give up the job after a new president took office in 1881. Conkling had assured him, "There will be a better time to take the office."

Garfield wavered in offering the position to James, fearing that his ties to Conkling and Arthur (under whom he had worked in the New York Custom House) might be problematic. Whitelaw Reid, the editor of the *New-York Tribune,* had been impressed by James's reforms in New York and intervened on his behalf, arranging a clandestine meeting with the president-elect. Garfield wanted to know that James would give "full and first support" to the administration and not continue to serve Conkling. After James offered his reassurances, Garfield tendered him the position.[4]

With Garfield's offer in hand, James again went to Conkling, hoping this time to get his blessing for taking the Post Office position. But the senator snickered when James said that he would be named to Garfield's cabinet.

"Do you expect to be secretary of the treasury?" Conkling said, the sarcasm in his voice unmistakable. Both knew that a man of James's modest standing would not be offered such a coveted position in the administration.

Hurt by the joke, James replied that he would be heading the Post Office rather than the Treasury.

"The Treasury is the only place in Garfield's cabinet that New York can afford to accept," Conkling told him. If the state would only be allotted one spot in the cabinet, it would have to be a plum like Treasury, a department with enormous influence and patronage—patronage that of course would be controlled by Conkling and his Stalwart allies. The Post Office was, in comparison, a backwater and not worthy of consideration.

"I am not a candidate for that post," James told him, undoubtedly thinking back to Conkling's earlier promise that a more propitious time to take the office would come along one day. "But I am a candidate for the Post Office Department, and I have come here to ask your support."

Conkling again dismissed the idea. "The Treasury is the only post New York can accept," he declared.[5]

James, sensing that Garfield's offer probably represented his last chance to serve in a cabinet, defied Conkling and took the Post Office position anyway. Thomas Connery, the editor of the *New York Herald*, praised the move. He later called James "one of the most earnest, sincere, and useful of Conkling's associates" in New York. "All the world knows how splendidly James administered the New York post office, what valuable reforms and improvements he had introduced; and how the American people confidently predicted his promotion to a higher field of action. For James to be made postmaster general was the most natural and logical outcome of distinguished services covering many years."[6]

In taking the postmaster generalship, James became embroiled in a complicated row that threatened to derail Garfield's presidency almost as soon as it began. Conkling was infuriated by Garfield's reluctance to consult with him over appointments, his anger reaching its apogee when the president attempted to name Judge William H. Robertson as collector of the Port of New York. Conkling believed that Garfield had gone back on both tradition and a specific promise in failing to consult with him and New York's other senator, Thomas C. Platt, before attempting to fill this patronage-rich post (once held by Arthur, Conkling's Stalwart ally and now Garfield's vice president).

In a move calculated to demonstrate their strength, Conkling and Platt both resigned their Senate seats in protest over the Robertson nomination, thinking they would be swiftly reelected and given a mandate to oppose Garfield. The tactic, however, backfired in stunning fashion: weary of Conkling's arrogant maneuvering, Empire State lawmakers elected two other men (Elbridge Lapham and Warner Miller) to fill their seats. With Platt and Conkling no longer voicing opposition in the Senate, Robertson's nomination to the

New York Custom House post was confirmed. The entire episode was a fiasco for Republicans, and it deepened an already serious rift between their Stalwart and Half-Breed factions.

Being caught in the middle of such bitter internecine battles did not seem to affect James's sunny disposition. He was known to be an affable and unpretentious man who seemingly had a good word for everyone he met, whatever his or her station in life. An acquaintance once told the story of meeting James while riding uptown on an elevated train in New York. James shook hands with the friend and the man's companion, who was a visitor from England, and then easily settled into a broad-ranging conversation with them that covered everything from theater and politics to the weather. The friend eventually introduced James to the Englishman by saying, "Let me present to you the postmaster general of the United States." The visitor was cowed by being in the presence of a member of the cabinet and bowed his head.

"This is not a joke, is it?" the Englishman inquired after James had exited the car. "That was really one of your cabinet ministers, or whatever you call them?" The visitor, who was acquainted with august and stuffy statesmen in his native land, simply could not believe that such a friendly and plainspoken man was the leader of a major department of the federal government.[7]

As he took office in Washington as postmaster general, James, having been alerted to the matter by former Alabama senator George Spencer and others, already was aware of the magnitude of the alleged Star Route frauds and the necessity of making a comprehensive investigation of them as soon as possible. He knew that, after festering for many years, the scandal had to be addressed in a forthright manner by the new administration. James later said that he had become concerned after speaking with Spencer and "other well-informed gentlemen. It was their belief that millions of dollars had been wasted on unnecessary 'star' service—service much of which was never performed and which was procured by improper means." These men helped convince James that, as he later put it, "an honest, thorough investigation would render practicable retrenchments without detriment to the service, which would not only make the Post Office Department self-sustaining, but would yield a respectable revenue to the Treasury."[8]

At the time, the new postmaster general expressed his feelings in a letter to Thurlow Weed, the prominent New York Republican and newspaper publisher. "Rest assured I shall do my whole duty in the matter of the Star

Route swindlers," James assured him. "It is a hard task, but it shall be pushed fearlessly, regardless of whom it may involve."[9]

James's views on the need to mount an impartial investigation of the Star Route frauds were unconcealed, and this made his appointment as postmaster general unpopular among those in Washington who had been linked to the scandal. He later said that because of his determination to ferret out the truth of this matter, "bitter opposition to my appointment to a Cabinet position . . . developed in certain quarters." Many people feared that he would be kicking a political hornets' nest if he conducted an impartial inquiry.[10]

No one opposed James's appointment more vociferously than Stephen Dorsey, the former senator from Arkansas. The two men had a contentious history, having locked horns on several occasions while James had served as New York City's postmaster. During Garfield's bid for the presidency the previous year, for instance, James had resisted Dorsey's demand that all post-office clerks demonstrate their political loyalty by donating to the Republican campaign. Furthermore, he had ignored the ex-senator's request to certify bondsmen on some Star Route bidding forms. Dorsey, incensed at the prospect of this foe winding up in the cabinet, wrote to Garfield, "I am opposed to James' appointment because he is not fit for this great place and he is the merest tool of scheming men in this state [New York]." In another letter, he sounded almost desperate to stop the designation of James, telling the president-elect: "I would no more speak of him or recognize him than I would the vilest wretch I ever knew or saw. I beg you not to do it."[11]

Jockeying to head off James's appointment, Dorsey pushed Garfield to select New Yorker Charles Folger for the cabinet. If the president-elect chose him for attorney general or secretary of the Treasury, New Yorkers could not lay claim to another cabinet seat—and that of course meant that James could not be appointed to lead the Post Office (and possibly spearhead an investigation of Dorsey). But Folger's bid for the cabinet failed (it somehow fell victim to meddling from both Conkling *and* Blaine, no small feat), and James got the Post Office role.[12]

Dorsey made no secret of the fact that he also detested the incoming attorney general, Wayne MacVeagh. A Pennsylvanian who had graduated from Yale and briefly served in the Union army during the Civil War, MacVeagh had enjoyed a successful legal and diplomatic career. In the early 1870s, he had served as the U.S. ambassador to the Ottoman Empire, and, in 1877, he had garnered attention for his efforts to resolve political tensions in Louisiana. The MacVeagh commission had managed to broker a compromise in which Democrats there dropped their opposition to Hayes's election in return for the withdrawal of federal troops from the state.[13]

Henry Adams, the vaunted nineteenth-century writer, once wrote that MacVeagh was "a man of extraordinary ability and character; the only man in American politics who says what he thinks, and thinks honestly." This candor impressed Adams (the two men were longtime friends and exchanged numerous warm letters over the years), but it often rankled MacVeagh's fellow Republicans, many of whom regarded him as a prig. MacVeagh apparently quit his ambassadorial post in Turkey because, as one observer later put it, "the Grant administration disgusted him," and in 1871, he became a leader in the party's reform wing, which would oppose Grant's 1876 bid for a third term as president. Such was his commitment to reform that in Pennsylvania, Mac-Veagh waged a lengthy battle with the machine of the political boss and Grant loyalist Simon Cameron—this despite the fact that he had married Cameron's daughter, Virginia.[14]

In an address delivered in 1886 at Yale Law School's commencement ceremonies, MacVeagh would underscore the essential role played by attorneys in ensuring good government and thereby supporting democracy. He would tell the crop of soon-to-be lawyers: "The best way of developing a patriotic spirit is by helping to make and keep all the ministries of the state pure and beneficent. No class of citizens can do more to enable [us] to realize this high ideal of good government than the lawyers of the country."[15]

Blaine recognized the value of appointing a man of such ability and rectitude to the cabinet. "There is no other stone in your hand that will kill so many political dogs with one throw," he wrote to Garfield of MacVeagh. "I guess you'd better fire it."[16]

Stephen Dorsey, fearing that one such projectile might be headed in his direction, implored Garfield not to consider either MacVeagh or James for positions in the cabinet. According to a biographer, Dorsey's reaction to their appointments "can only be described as panic." Not without reason, he concluded that reform-minded cabinet members might expose him for his role in Star Route irregularities and then have him prosecuted. When Garfield ignored his importunings and prepared to name James as postmaster general,

Dorsey dispatched an unhinged and pleading letter to the president. Begging him to reconsider, the former senator played his ace in the hole: he reminded the president of his pivotal role in securing the election for the Republican ticket in the previous fall.[17]

"I am tired of this blathering talk about MacVeagh to go into the cabinet from Pennsylvania and James from New York," Dorsey wrote to Garfield. "Such detestable rot should be smoked out at once, and you ought to do it in some public way."[18]

Garfield stood firm, however, and both James and MacVeagh joined his cabinet. Dorsey never got over it. Describing the genesis of the government's Star Route prosecution, he later bitterly recalled that "at the beginning of General Garfield's administration, two members of his cabinet [James and MacVeagh], whose personal hostility to me had grown out of my active opposition to their appointment to the positions they held, led them to seize upon the old Star Route scandal and use it as a weapon to break down my influence with the administration."[19]

Garfield probably learned about the postal frauds from a variety of sources close to or within his administration. Some information apparently reached him—in a roundabout way—from Samuel Tilden, the failed Democratic nominee for president in 1876. In preparing for another run for the White House in 1880, Tilden had asked attorney Charles McLean to accumulate evidence about Star Route cozenage, which he had planned to use to embarrass whoever the Republicans nominated. He ultimately had been beaten out for the nomination by Winfield Hancock, and the materials had not been fully used in the ensuing campaign by the Democrats. But MacLean made their existence known to his law partner, Henry Knox, who had a long acquaintance with Garfield. As the Ohioan prepared to take office early in 1881, MacLean allowed Knox to approach the president-elect with the startling information he had accumulated about the manipulation of Star Route contracts.[20]

Around the time of his appointment as postmaster general, James had two conversations with Garfield about the Star Route frauds. The president asked him what he knew about them and how he had gained that information. James admitted that his knowledge "was derived from the newspapers, from the investigations which had taken place, and from hearsay," as he later put it. Already realizing the seriousness of the allegations that were swirling around the

Post Office, mail contractors, and their allies in Congress, Garfield acknowledged that his administration would need to mount a serious investigation; he could not imagine starting off his presidency by engaging in a cover-up. According to James, Garfield used an agricultural metaphor to describe the task at hand: "He . . . said that from what he kept hearing, he was afraid there was something very wrong in the [Post Office] Department itself; that if so, he expected me to find it out, and then put the plow into the beam, and after that to subsoil it." In short, the president wanted James to initiate a deep and comprehensive inquiry, and to do so as quickly as possible.[21]

On March 9, 1881, just after he had been sworn in as postmaster general, James met again with Garfield, and the Star Route swindle was a main topic of conversation. The president "said he was satisfied that there had been willful waste of public money and gross corruption" involving "unnecessary and extravagant service" in dozens of the postal routes, as James later put it. A concerned Garfield directed him to investigate irregularities in Star Route bidding and contracting. The new president's charge to James was clear: he was "to pursue the investigation until there were no more facts to ascertain." Furthermore, "if the inquiry should disclose that any person or persons had been guilty of corruption or fraud, that person or those persons must be handed over to the Department of Justice" for prosecution.[22]

James summoned David Parker, the Post Office's chief investigator, and discussed how the investigation should proceed. "I wish to have the matter quietly but thoroughly investigated," he explained, "and suggest that we assign this task to P. H. Woodward." Parker agreed, thinking Woodward, a man of great tact and discretion, would be perfect for the delicate job.[23]

Patrick Henry Woodward had formerly served as chief special agent in the Post Office Department. Later described by the postmaster general as "a man of character and integrity," Woodward already was generally familiar with the Star Route scams and had exposed several straw-bidding rings a few years earlier. When James told the president that he wanted to place the investigation in Woodward's capable hands, Garfield agreed.[24]

After attending Harvard Law School, Woodward had practiced law in Connecticut and then worked briefly as a reporter for the *Hartford Courant*. He had left journalism in 1865 to join the Post Office, eventually rising to the rank of chief special agent. Woodward became such an expert on mail-related crimes that he wrote a seminal history of the Post Office's secret service. Woodward, an apolitical authority in postal crimes, was in many ways a natural choice to spearhead the government's investigation into possible chicanery in the awarding of Star Route contracts.[25]

Woodward and James soon met in New York City to discuss the incipient investigation and the possibility that Woodward could lead it as a confidential agent of the Post Office Department. From the outset, James said that he wanted the inquiry to attract as little attention as possible. "He desired that the investigation should be conducted in a way to develop the facts quietly," Woodward later said of the postmaster general, "without causing scandal." Woodward took the assignment and set about the laborious process of gathering information to determine if Star Route contractors and Post Office officials had illegally enriched themselves.[26]

Woodward's contributions to the case would be considerable. "I think without Mr. Woodward, these cases never would have been instituted," Benjamin Brewster, MacVeagh's successor as attorney general, later said. "I think he was, to use one word, invaluable." This was especially true for the attorneys who ultimately would prosecute the Star Route case in court. "I do not think there was a fact in the case they did not acquire from him," Brewster said of Woodward.[27]

By his own later admission, Woodward was not completely up to speed with the Star Route imbroglio when he took over the investigation in April 1881. "When recalled by Mr. James," he later said, "I had been out of the service a number of years, and having no expectation of re-entering it had given, during the interval, little attention to postal matters." Luckily for Woodward, there were plenty of men who were willing and eager to provide him with information about the fraudulent postal-contracting scheme.[28]

Early on, George Spencer, the former Republican senator from Alabama, was instrumental in getting Woodward's investigation up and running. A few months previously, Spencer had encountered journalist Albert Gibson in New York City. Gibson's work for the New York *Sun* had been crucial in keeping Star Route corruption in the public eye during the 1870s, and he was keen to see the incoming Garfield administration take the scandal seriously. To that end, he had told Spencer that he would be willing to share some of the detailed and damning research he had compiled while working for the *Sun*. According to Gibson, the materials would show how contractors, colluding with unscrupulous Post Office officials like Tom Brady, had bilked the government by rigging rate increases for improved services on their postal routes. "He told me of a table of 93 routes that he had complied, showing how much the increase of service had been, how much expedition there had been, and how much pay the contractors were getting at that time," Spencer later said. "It was a very valuable compilation," one that could save "a great deal of labor" for anyone looking to mount a full-scale investigation of the postal frauds.[29]

Gibson's revelations came as no surprise to Spencer. After leaving the Senate in 1879, he had spent some time in Nevada, "and in his travels on the frontiers had learned much about the star mail service" and the irregularities that plagued it, according to the account of Woodward. Spencer had become aware of several bid-rigging plots and reported them to postal authorities.[30]

Although he would prove famously reluctant to testify in court about his knowledge of the Star Route frauds, at this point, the former senator was willing to share what he knew, provided that his name was not connected with the investigation. Spencer informed Post Office officials that he "did not want to play the role of informer before the country"—that is, he did not want to be known as a snitch. Such were his concerns on this score that he discussed them directly with President Garfield, who assured him that he would be able to remain anonymous. "I received from him a pledge that any information I should give him on this subject should be strictly confidential," Spencer later said of the president, "and that my name should not be connected with it."[31]

To be sure, Spencer had been no pillar of rectitude during his time in public office. In the words of one later study, "His tenure in Congress is remembered for corruption and abuses of office, including embezzlement, vote tampering, and political patronage that earned him the epithet of 'carpetbagger.'" Spencer's ignominious reputation might have had something to do with Garfield not wanting to publicize his role in aiding the Star Route investigation.[32]

Acting behind the scenes, Spencer arranged a meeting between the newspaperman Gibson and the investigator Woodward. According to Spencer, Gibson first provided Woodward with a general idea of his work in probing the Star Route frauds, then followed up by furnishing extensive documentation showing how the schemes had been working. Gibson later said that he provided "quite a mass of stuff, being tabulated statements of a number of routes, from which a table of 93 routes had been made up, giving, in each case, the date of the contract, the original pay, and the subsequent increases for expedition and increased trips." Given the complexity and scope of the alleged offenses, such materials were invaluable to Woodward, helping him make sense of how mail contractors had been able to use pledges of expedited services to increase the value of contracts that initially had been worth relatively little.[33]

As he labored to set the federal Star Route investigation into motion, Woodward quickly realized that Gibson, who probably knew more about the postal contract double-dealing than anyone, might be a godsend. The newspaperman "possessed a minute knowledge of the inner history of the frauds," as he later put it, and was armed with reams of documents that would provide direct evidence of how crooked postal contractors had fleeced the government. Woodward asked if Gibson would be interested in joining the investigation in a formal capacity. The journalist recently had ended his tenure with the *Sun* and was eager to find work, but he doubted that he would pass muster with the incoming Republican administration. Everyone knew that he was a staunch Democrat.

And Gibson was not just any Democrat. He had actively worked for the Tilden (1876) and Hancock (1880) presidential efforts, assisting in the preparation of the party's mammoth and unabashedly partisan *Campaign Text Book*, which provided an exhaustive catalog of Republican corruption. During both campaigns, these tomes were sent out to Democrats across the country, with the instruction to disseminate far and wide their charges of Republican wrongdoing. It was the party's bible for vituperative partisan attacks on the opposition.

Denunciations of the Republicans' alleged mishandling of, and complicity in, the Star Route frauds were a central feature of both editions of the Democrats' campaign book. Passages that were almost certainly penned by Gibson for the 1880 version proclaimed, among other things: "During the long years of Republican administration, every department of the government has grown corrupt. The mismanagement, maladministration, profligacy and corruption of the Post Office Department is, and has been, if possible, worse than that of any other department of the public service." Evidence proved "beyond the shadow of doubt," the *Text Book* asserted, that "a ring of contractors for what is known as the Star Route mail service controlled the department" during the tenures of Postmasters General John Creswell, Marshall Jewell, and James Noble Tyner. The book singled out prominent Republican Stephen Dorsey as one of those who had bribed their way into influence and then benefited handsomely. In fact, an entire section of the 1880 *Text Book* was devoted to exposing "Senator Dorsey's rake."[34]

This kind of invective was nothing new for Gibson; he had condemned graft and fraud in the Grant and Hayes administrations for many years. One of his great journalistic coups for the *Sun* had been uncovering the massive Crédit Mobilier bribery scandal, which had implicated numerous Republican politicians, including Massachusetts congressman Oakes Ames. The tenacious Gibson had made a career of exposing such egregious breaches of the public's trust by elected officials.[35]

Woodward, believing that Gibson was uniquely qualified to help with the investigation, championed him with Postmaster General James and Attorney General MacVeagh. Gibson "has already rendered me great assistance voluntarily," Woodward wrote to James. "He has in various ways acquired no small degree of familiarity with the methods and practices to be inquired into, and has placed his information freely at my disposal. If I may be permitted to express a preference, I think his selection would prove judicious." Woodward left the perhaps misleading impression that the president was amenable to Gibson's addition, telling James that he had spoken to Garfield about the matter, and he "seemed rather acquiescent." (This was almost certainly a misapprehension or a fib on Woodward's part, given how negatively Garfield later reacted to learning of Gibson's hiring.) With James indicating his "earnest approval" of the idea, Woodward was allowed to bring Gibson on to the prosecution team—a move that many people, both inside and outside the investigation, would come to lament.[36]

The budding investigation came under fire almost immediately. "No sooner had this work begun than bitter and malignant attacks appeared in the columns of 'Star Route' organs on the president, the attorney general, the postmaster general, and whoever else was suspected of a disposition to promote clean, honest, and business-like methods," Postmaster General James later noted. "Swarms of contractors, their attorneys, and beneficiaries raised a deafening clamor, and made common cause against the administration." Strident criticism seemed to come from everywhere, which some within the investigation took as a sure sign that they were on the right track.[37]

James and Woodward did their best to ignore the mounting public clamor caused by their work. Armed with information they had gleaned from Gibson, Spencer, and other sources, the two men made their way to the White House to see President Garfield in the early part of April 1881. The postmaster general and the lead investigator laid out for him "the most corruptly manipulated routes" by using "facts and figures laboriously collated" in the preceding month, as James later described it. Garfield expressed great surprise at the information and pressed the men on whether their documentation was reliable. As he began his presidency, Garfield did not want to embark on a wild-goose chase that might end up embarrassing his administration and possibly alienating his allies within the Republican Party. James and Woodward assured him that they were compiling solid evidence that would hold up in court.[38]

Over the next several weeks, Garfield's journal entries reflected his growing concern with Star Route corruption and how his administration should handle it. He noted that James and Woodward had visited the White House "and reported what they had discovered concerning the Star contract service. Great frauds have been discovered and I will clear out the contract office" of the Post Office, which apparently had facilitated the crimes. A few days later, after learning more about the investigation, the president wrote, "The situation will require the removal of several prominent officers." He noted later in his journal: "The corruption and wrongdoing has been of a very gross and extensive kind. I am surprised that it could have so long escaped the notice of President Hayes's administration."[39]

Such was the enormity of these revelations that a second White House meeting addressing Star Route graft was held shortly thereafter. This gathering brought together not only the investigator Woodward, Postmaster General James, and President Garfield but also Attorney General MacVeagh, whose Justice Department would have to lead any efforts to prosecute contractors or Post Office officials. James broached the idea of initiating civil suits, rather than criminal proceedings, to recover the ill-gotten Star Route money. Garfield dismissed this suggestion and affirmed the idea that criminal cases should be instituted if the facts warranted such action.[40]

At this point, MacVeagh spoke up and urged Garfield to think carefully about the chain of events he might be setting into motion. From the evidence that Woodward and James already had compiled, there was no doubt that the Star Route investigation could lead to viable criminal indictments since "the figures were so startling and the uniformity of evidence of mismanagement was so absolute wherever we touched the matter," as MacVeagh later said. But the attorney general wondered if Garfield had taken the time to "consider the full implications of what he was considering" in terms of potentially mounting criminal prosecutions of prominent men within the president's own party. Did he really want to haul his political allies—men like Stephen Dorsey, whose cunning work on the 1880 campaign had been indispensable to his election effort—into court?[41]

That the Star Route frauds had a political dimension was obvious to anyone who had seen Democrats and Republicans squabble over them over the preceding decade. "As practical men," MacVeagh later said, "we all knew these cases would present themselves to anybody's mind—they did to mine certainly—as possibly having certain very grave political complications." He pointed out that Dorsey was no ordinary potential target: he was a former U.S. senator and "had been an active agent of the Republican party in the then-recent canvass which had resulted in the election of the president." His critical role in Garfield's campaign was liable to complicate any investigation of the former senator, especially since it was widely rumored in the press that Dorsey had in his possession correspondence related to the presidential campaign that could somehow embarrass Garfield. If he was backed into a corner and turned desperate, Dorsey might release this material and do harm to the president.[42]

MacVeagh did not say it directly, but everyone in the room understood that Dorsey, who believed his role had been pivotal in the 1880 campaign, was likely to try to attack the president in some fashion if he felt Garfield was betraying him. Without naming anyone specifically, MacVeagh warned Garfield of the potential danger of angering "persons who claim that you are under personal obligations to them for services rendered during the last campaign—and one person in particular who asserts that without his management you could not have been elected." All of those present at the White House meeting knew that he was referring to the former senator from Arkansas.[43]

And then there was the matter of the composition of the Senate as a whole. At the time, the president's party held a one-vote majority in that body. MacVeagh asked Garfield to consider the harrowing possibility of a criminal prosecution leading to the downfall of a Republican senator. (This seems not to have been a reference to Dorsey, who already had left the Senate, but rather to William Pitt Kellogg of Louisiana, whose name often came up in the Star Route investigation.) According to Postmaster General James's recollection, MacVeagh reminded the president that pursuing criminal cases in the Star Route frauds "may result in changing a Republican majority in the United States Senate into a Democratic majority." With the Democrats already holding a healthy majority in the House of Representatives, their takeover of the

Senate would spell disaster for Garfield; the opposition party would control Congress and throttle his administration at every turn.[44]

MacVeagh felt that he had a duty to ask the president to consider these potentially sticky implications before a criminal investigation began in earnest that might oblige him to pursue the president's allies in court. James's proposal—dropping the idea of mounting criminal prosecutions and instead instituting civil suits to reclaim ill-gotten Star Route money—was well worth considering, as it might show a willingness to punish wrongdoing without sparking too much anger within the Republican Party and threatening the balance of power in the Senate. "Look these facts squarely in the face before taking a final stand," the attorney general advised Garfield, "for neither the postmaster general nor myself will know friend or foe in this matter."[45]

To his credit, the new president seemed to disregard the potential political implications of moving forward with the investigation and possibly pursuing criminal charges against members of his own party, including former senator Dorsey. After hearing MacVeagh's words of caution, Garfield paused for a moment and then told James and the attorney general: "No, I have sworn to execute the laws. Go ahead regardless of where or whom you hit. I direct you both not only to probe this ulcer to the bottom, but to cut it out."[46]

During the White House meeting, Woodward was struck by the president's astonishment over the figures that were being presented as proof of chicanery in the awarding of Star Route contracts. "At first," he later said of Garfield, "he could hardly credit their genuineness." But the president overcame his initial shock and resolved to pursue the investigation, whatever the political fallout. "At this interview I first learned that the investigation was likely to lead to criminal prosecutions. The decisive order was given by the commander-in-chief," Woodward later said. Whatever his private doubts, Garfield did not equivocate about the Star Route case when speaking with his subordinates. They were to keep pressing forward.[47]

SETTING A THIEF TO CATCH A THIEF

A Special Prosecutor Is Appointed, Spring 1881

With President Garfield's approval, the new administration adopted a radical and aggressive policy in investigating the Star Route frauds, according to investigator Patrick Henry Woodward. As the government's probe gathered speed in April 1881, Postmaster General James called upon a number of seasoned postal investigators to work with Woodward and figure out if the postal bidding and contracting processes had been corrupted.[1]

Woodward, James, and their colleagues were appalled by what they found. It was evident to them that the value of numerous Star Route contracts had been grossly inflated by fraudulent means. Contractors were able to amend their original bids, and thereby collect more money, by claiming that communities had petitioned them to provide faster and more frequent mail service. "Large and expensive increases were found to be unnecessary, and the methods by which they were worked up [were] fraudulent," James later said. "Many of the affidavits upon which enormous expeditions were based were shown to be rank perjuries." Within a few months, the Post Office's identification of these irregularities allowed it to reduce Star Route expenditures by almost $656,000. (Such cost-cutting measures would be one of the most important practical legacies of the investigation.)[2]

Not everyone welcomed the intense scrutiny now being given to the vagaries of Star Route contracts. Reports of the investigation's progress appeared to send former senator Stephen Dorsey into a frenzy. Once the public became "more fully informed by the startling array of supplemental facts and figures [and] began to realize the enormity of the offenses committed," Postmaster General James later said, "Mr. Dorsey began to actively engage in efforts to shield himself, to bring the investigation to naught, to disturb the relations of the president with his Cabinet, and to convince the country that 'persecution' was the primary motive of the department and the administration." To the dismay of James, who had been given a clear directive by President Garfield to pursue the Star Route investigation, "the most brazen effrontery and reckless prevarication were freely indulged in [by Dorsey], despite the most direct and convincing documentary and oral evidences which abounded on every hand."[3]

At one point early in the spring of 1881, Dorsey became fixated on the notion that his alleged criminal transgressions should be investigated separately, apart from the other men who were thought to have engaged in the Star Route frauds. (He presumably believed that a separate inquiry would leave him relatively unsullied by making it harder to link him to other purported lawbreakers.) The former senator wrote James an open letter demanding his own investigation, and he and his attorney came to the postmaster general's office to plead their case in person.[4]

Later, after Garfield's untimely death, Dorsey would insist that he had made his pitch for a commission directly to the president, who had in fact approved the idea. The proposition included an interesting wrinkle: the commission to investigate the ex-senator would be composed solely of Democrats. (This feature apparently was meant to demonstrate Dorsey's confidence that the charges against him were baseless.) Dorsey would later claim that he had gone to Washington and "laid all the facts before the then president, General Garfield, and requested him to select a commission composed entirely of Democrats to investigate each and every charge that MacVeagh and James caused to be spread abroad. I told him that I would not have counsel appear; that I wanted the naked facts put before that commission, and would abide by any decision arrived at by my most bitter political enemies." According to Dorsey, the president had been receptive to this unorthodox proposal, writing to James and "directing him to select such a commission, with directions to make a most searching and far-reaching investigation, so far as I was concerned." Dorsey would claim that he had taken the president's letter to James, but the postmaster general simply had refused to follow Garfield's directive on how to properly handle the investigation into his conduct.[5]

While Garfield's diary indicated some ambivalence about pursuing Dorsey, it contained no reference to the president having been so openly defied by James in this manner. It seems likely that Dorsey's later story about having received an encouraging response from Garfield was a fabrication—one that of course could not be contradicted by the president, who by then had died.

In the spring of 1881, Robert Green Ingersoll, Dorsey's attorney, spent a good deal of time trying to meet with Garfield and speak with the president about the plight of his beleaguered client. Ingersoll had known Garfield for many years and, therefore, felt that he should have special access to the president. (It was this entitled attitude that apparently led Garfield to deride him as "Royal Bob" when the attorney was out of earshot.) Yet in keeping with the practices of the new administration, he was forced to wait his turn in an anteroom among the throngs of shabby office seekers who also hoped to have an audience with the new president. Much to his dismay, the attorney became a popular figure in the waiting room once it became known that he already was acquainted with Garfield.

"Colonel Ingersoll," one bedraggled man asked him, "can't I have your endorsement? You know me. I want a position as chaplain in the army." His relationship with Garfield notwithstanding, this was an odd request to make of Ingersoll, who at that time was perhaps the most infamous agnostic in the country.

"Yes," Ingersoll said, "I know you. You're a preacher I've met somewhere. You're just the man for my endorsement. You have as little religion as any man I know. You won't hurt anyone." The room erupted in laughter at the joke.

Ingersoll's jocular mood darkened, however, when he repeatedly was forced to wait among the Washington riffraff to speak with Garfield about the Star Route case. An eminent man who had known the president long before he had risen to the nation's highest office, Ingersoll felt that he was being disrespected. "I'm tired of hanging around here, kicking my heels in the anteroom," he announced one day. "I've had too many games of billiards with Jim Garfield to stand this." With that, Ingersoll stormed off.[6]

Dorsey and Ingersoll had better luck in meeting with Attorney General MacVeagh and lobbied him as well. Yet MacVeagh was no more inclined than Postmaster General James to bow to their request for an independent inquiry. The attorney general rightly feared that putting on separate cases would allow some defendants a preview of the evidence that the government planned to use against them. In addition, they would have the convenience of being able to pin the blame on one another. As James later put it, "The attorney general advised me to treat him as everybody else was treated—not to give anyone separate investigation; he said that the ends of justice would not be attained by doing that."[7]

After he failed to undermine, or even influence, James and MacVeagh, Dorsey focused his ire on Tom Brady. The second assistant postmaster general's name long had been connected to numerous Star Route frauds, and he was almost certain to be indicted for bid-rigging, as he appeared to have approved all of the suspicious orders for expedition being examined by the government. Dorsey himself had been linked to Brady's reported criminal activity, and he likely viewed Brady's ouster from the Post Office as a means of discrediting someone who might provide evidence or testimony against him somewhere down the line. To that end, Dorsey met with Woodward and James at the latter's rooms in the Arlington Hotel in Washington. As James later put it, Dorsey "denounced Mr. Brady, the second assistant postmaster general, with great bitterness, and urged that he be immediately removed."[8]

Dorsey's motives in moving against Brady hardly were pure, but Woodward agreed with him that the second assistant postmaster general was manifestly corrupt and should be terminated as quickly as possible, based on the ample evidence of fraud that the investigation was uncovering. When James and Woodward met with Garfield to discuss the matter, the postmaster general asked that Brady be given a chance to at least save face by resigning before he was fired. Garfield initially balked at this idea but then acquiesced. On April 29, 1881, James dispatched a terse letter to Brady that simply read, "SIR: I am directed by the President to request your resignation of the office of second assistant postmaster general, to take effect immediately." (He was replaced by a New Yorker named Richard Elmer.) Brady's forced resignation set the stage for several other departures from the Post Office that were tied to the Star Route fraud investigation, including that of John French, the chief clerk in the Contract Division.[9]

The jettisoning of Brady, which marked the first real punishment meted out to anyone connected to Star Route bid-rigging, touched off a prolonged national media frenzy. "The moment that the resignation of Brady was announced," said one account, "the Star Route topic became an all absorbing one throughout the country. . . . [T]he newspapers almost uniformly began to trade in Star Route exposures." Reporters rehashed the findings of the earlier congressional probes of the frauds and published new information that was being leaked from the current investigation. The result "kept the public mind riveted on the Star Route frauds and on the politics involved in them."[10]

The solidly Republican *Chicago Daily Inter Ocean,* edited by William Penn Nixon, ran a typical story in response to Brady's ouster from the Post Office. It quoted an unnamed Washington insider's views on how the investigation might affect those closest to the president. "As sure as there is a heaven above," the source said, "Tom James has his gun pointed at some of the men who were active in electing Garfield President—the very men who have been supposed to constitute confidential advisers, who were influential in making up his Cabinet, and who have claimed, with more or less reason, to command his attention and favor at all times." The source believed that Garfield wanted a thorough and impartial probe of the Star Route frauds, even if it might pose a threat to his allies in the Republican Party. "I truly believe that President Garfield will not only allow but insist upon having an investigation that will reach to the bottom of the rottenness, if there is any."[11]

Back in Brady's home state of Indiana, many greeted news of his removal from public office with cheers. "Brady is a good man to have out of public life," the *Terre Haute Weekly Gazette* announced. The newspaper's enmity toward the deposed second assistant postmaster general was so great that it not only celebrated his unseating but also mocked his physical appearance, noting, "he is not a particularly handsome man. . . . He might be a bold buccaneer on the Spanish Main from anything to the contrary conveyed by his physiognomy."[12]

As it turned out, Brady's problems were only just beginning. Intensified media coverage put increased public focus on the Star Route affair. Early in 1881, a source approached several newspapers with information about the frauds. The only publication that was eager to fully make use of the material was the *New York Times,* which was fresh off a series of exposés that had contributed to the downfall of William "Boss" Tweed, the corrupt leader of New York City's Tammany Hall political machine. Publisher George Jones saw parallels in the Star Route story and assigned it to Frank D. Root, the *Times's* ambitious and dogged Washington correspondent. Root dove into the material and discovered that it contained detailed information clearly indicating that Brady and the members of Dorsey's ring had engaged in a panoply of illegal activities.[13]

Around the time of Brady's resignation, the *Times* published a bombshell report detailing how some of the Star Route contracts had been manipulated.

Two news articles and an editorial outlined what was described in the newspaper's headlines as "Star Service Corruption" and "The Enormous Profits of the Star Route Ring." The articles explained that Brady had approved expedited service on ninety-three Star Routes, inflating their value from roughly $727,000 to nearly $3 million (the equivalent of almost $77 million in 2021). The newspaper published a table showing how the contracts on all ninety-three routes had been increased, and it named all of the contractors involved, including John Dorsey, John Peck, and John Miner, all of whom had been in the Star Route business with Stephen Dorsey.[14]

As it indignantly exposed what it termed a steal and a swindle, the newspaper stated that it would not be satisfied until "measures are taken to bring Brady to justice and the penitentiary, if possible." But the *Times* was quick to point out that others had been involved in the frauds, most significantly "the Dorsey Gang" and its alleged mastermind. Although the names of Dorsey, Peck, and Miner appeared on the Star Route contracts, they "have acted as blinds for Stephen W. Dorsey, ex-Senator from Arkansas and Secretary of the Republican National Committee." According to the newspaper, Stephen had used his brother John "as a cat's-paw to pull the gold from the public Treasury."[15]

Just months after being feted by Republicans at Delmonico's as their party's savior, Stephen Dorsey was in very deep trouble. He had been publicly named as the leader of a corrupt ring of Star Route contractors. Throughout the spring of 1881, a variety of publications picked up on the revelations in the *Times* and insisted that the former senator should face criminal charges for his role in the Star Route frauds. "It is simply impossible that Dorsey can escape responsibility for what appears to have been a downright fraud on the government," *Frank Leslie's Illustrated Newspaper* stated, "and if there is any law under which he can be punished, it should be enforced against him without mercy or delay."[16]

With the Star Route investigation widening, the government needed additional manpower. Although it was being steered by President Garfield, Attorney General MacVeagh, and Postmaster General James, George Corkhill, as the district attorney for the District of Columbia, was nominally in charge of the inquiry. Corkhill publicly stated that he would need to add attorneys to his staff if he hoped to thoroughly investigate all of the suspicious Star Routes and prepare criminal cases against the men involved. Early in June 1881, the Justice Department gave him the go-ahead to bring on board Albert Gibson, whose revelations in the New York *Sun* had been so pivotal in exposing irregularities in postal contracts, and a Washington attorney named William Cook. Known by many as "Colonel" Cook, in a nod to his military rank in the Civil War, he would be the third federal special prosecutor in the nation's history.[17]

The fate of the first-ever federal special prosecutor, appointed just six years before Cook, showed how ambivalent presidents could be in launching investigations that might ultimately harm themselves or their political allies. In 1875, President Grant had appointed John Henderson, a former Republican senator from Missouri, to investigate the Whiskey Ring scandal. Henderson had taken his charge seriously—perhaps too seriously for Grant's liking. The president had fired and replaced him with James Broadhead when Henderson had targeted his friend and personal secretary, Orville Babcock. Such challenges to the independence of the special counsel would be an unfortunate hallmark of the office from the presidencies of Grant and Garfield to those of Richard Nixon, Bill Clinton, and Donald Trump. Even when they have bowed to public and political pressures and appointed a special prosecutor to investigate a scandal, no president has ever wanted to set into motion an investigation that might harm members of his inner circle or even lead to his own downfall.

From the outset, there was ambiguity surrounding Cook's role, in part because of the title he had been given: special assistant U.S. attorney for the District of Columbia. Cook believed that he had been made a special assistant to Attorney General MacVeagh, but Corkhill thought otherwise. "The district attorney assumed the position," Cook later grumbled, "that I was only an assistant to him."[18]

There later would be intense arguments over the role that the district attorney played—or rather *did not* play—in the Star Route prosecution. Yet it seemed clear to almost everyone from the outset that Corkhill was essentially handing over leadership in the cases to the special prosecutor. When Cook was appointed to his new role, one Washington newspaper reported that Corkhill "has been relieved of the duty of prosecuting the alleged Star Route conspirators." Given that the district attorney's position in Washington formally came under the purview of the Department of Justice, Attorney General MacVeagh almost certainly signed off on this arrangement.[19]

Corkhill himself was explicit in stating his desire to cede day-to-day authority over the Star Route prosecutions, which promised to be both complex and extraordinarily contentious. He wrote to the attorney general, "In view of the fact that these Star Route cases are more of a national than local character, and that from reports they involve a large number of persons, and will array in their defense—should indictments be found—many of the ablest lawyers in the profession, both in this city and elsewhere, and owing to the public interest in them being very great, I do not think that under all these circumstances the whole responsibility of their management should be thrown upon me." He asked MacVeagh to "designate some lawyer a special counsel of government in these cases, who should have the management and control of them." Corkhill made no secret of his eagerness to drop out of the Star Route case entirely and essentially hand it over to Cook: he released his letter to MacVeagh to the press, and it was reprinted in full on the front page of several newspapers.[20]

The appointments of Cook and Gibson delighted the Democratic press, which viewed them as signs that prominent Republicans like Dorsey might not be spared as the Star Route prosecution took shape. Noting the "self-righteous indignation" voiced by many in the Garfield administration over Gibson's appointment, one newspaper observed that his "distinguished service in ferreting out Republican secrets and Republican scandals and Republican thieves have not endeared him to the Republican officials of any grade or shade."[21]

President Garfield, to be sure, was less than enthused that Cook and Gibson would be playing integral roles in the Star Route prosecution. He took a dim view of both men, albeit for slightly different reasons. Upon learning about their appointments, the incensed president wrote in his diary that Cook had "an unsavory reputation," while Gibson "has long been my defamer." Whatever their backgrounds, the pair's appointments should have been cleared with the president in advance. In another diary entry, Garfield noted, "I find there is much feeling among my friends that such men should have been employed without first consulting me."[22]

Gibson was *persona non grata* with the new administration for a variety of reasons. The newspaperman had helped author the Democrats' bitterly partisan *Text Book* in both 1876 and 1880, and he reportedly had been involved in bringing to light some corruption charges against Garfield during his tenure as a congressman from Ohio. (It had been alleged that while he served as chair of the powerful House Appropriations Committee, Garfield took $5,000 from a Washington street-paving contractor.) Garfield also had been implicated in the Crédit Mobilier scandal, which Gibson set in motion through his indefatigable reporting for the New York *Sun*. After being plagued by corruption allegations during his 1880 campaign for president, Garfield was not at all pleased to learn that Gibson, the man behind many of them, was now involved in a prominent prosecution being undertaken by his own administration.[23]

Attorney Robert Green Ingersoll later told Charles Henry, the federal marshal of Washington, DC, that President Garfield had been absolutely livid over Gibson's appointment. "Garfield told me," Ingersoll wrote to Henry, "that it was an outrage." MacVeagh, the new attorney general, apologetically told the president that he had not been aware of Gibson's attacks on Garfield in the *Sun*. According to Ingersoll, the president had said: "But now that MacVeagh does know all about it, why does he not discharge him? I suppose he intends to make me ask it, so that if he fails to convict the defendants in the Star Route case he can put the fault on me."[24]

Many others also were appalled that Gibson was joining the prosecution team. The editor of a Washington newspaper published an open letter to Garfield in which he pointed to the lawyer-journalist's longstanding record of open antagonism toward the president. Noting Gibson's work for the *Sun*, the editor told Garfield that he "denounced you as a bribe-taker, a thief, a perjurer, a liar, and a suborner of perjury and forgery." Moreover, Gibson had launched such unjustified attacks "not once, but repeatedly, and with monotonous iteration and reiteration." The letter expressed shock that Garfield would allow such a vicious and vocal detractor from the opposing political camp to play any role in the Star Route case.[25]

Others expressed their concerns about Gibson privately. On June 20, Garfield received a worried letter from Henry. In addition to being the federal marshal of the District of Columbia, he was a longtime friend and confidant of the president. (The two men had known each other since Henry's days as a student at Hiram College, where Garfield had been president, in the 1850s.) Garfield had asked Henry, a former Post Office inspector, for his opinions about the Star Route investigation. He bluntly told the president:

> The methods and men used in the star route investigations are bad, with the exception of the post office men, who are honest. I am getting some information [about] the way the investigation is being conducted. If anyone says that Gibson is a bad man, the reply comes that the accuser is bought by the ring. From whatever direction I approach it I see the hand of Gibson. I have never known the government before to employ bad men knowingly,

except temporarily as spotters of counterfeiters. I believe Gibson would prefer to ruin innocent men than find out the guilty. . . . If honest men were conducting the investigation, I would feel much better.[26]

While Gibson was probably most noted for his work as a journalist, Cook was a fairly well-known member of the Washington bar. "I had at the time a very large civil as well as considerable criminal practice," he later boasted. The *Evening Star* in Washington described him as being "at the head of the criminal bar of the District," and it argued that his appointment "shows that the Government means business in the prosecution of those cases."[27]

Yet Cook's appointment to such an important position also provoked a negative reaction, as he was not greatly respected by many other attorneys in the nation's capital. One assistant district attorney in Washington, viewing Cook's arrival as an affront to District Attorney Corkhill, eventually resigned his position in protest. The move drew applause from lawyers familiar with Cook's dubious reputation. It was "highly commended by leading members of the bar," according to one news report, because Cook was so poorly regarded in the capital.[28]

These concerns probably were well founded. While serving as corporation attorney in the administration of Washington mayor Sayles Bowen, Cook had been a "legal trickster, feared by many but respected by none," in the words of one critic. Another derided him as a bribe-taker who had facilitated the work of a "set of plundering contractors and leeches" associated with Bowen's regime. It was alleged—often by opposition Democrats—that, among other misdeeds, Cook had committed fraud in connection with a municipal election in 1870.[29]

Ironically, Cook's reputation for rascality was, in the attorney general's view, one of his chief qualifications for the role of special prosecutor in the Star Route case. Henry Van Ness Boynton, the Washington correspondent for the *Cincinnati Commercial Gazette*, discussed Cook's appointment with MacVeagh. When Boynton brought up the attorney's questionable character, MacVeagh brushed off his concerns. "I know all about Mr. Cook," he replied, according to Boynton's later congressional testimony. "I have had him employed in cases before, and he is employed upon the theory of setting a thief to catch a thief."[30]

Cook's appointment to the team investigating the Star Route frauds as a special prosecutor nettled President Garfield. The new special prosecutor earlier had participated in the prosecution of members of the Whiskey Ring, whose diversion of tax revenues had hugely embarrassed the Grant administration in the 1870s. Garfield's assessment of him further diminished after he received a negative report about the lawyer from a member of the Supreme Court. The justice told the president that everyone in Washington knew that Cook was a scoundrel.[31]

After hearing this downbeat assessment, Garfield summoned investigator Patrick Henry Woodward to the White House for a dressing-down. The president, clearly agitated, later noted in his journal, "I sent for Mr. Woodward, Post Office Inspector, to find what was being done in the Star Route investigation, and to know why Gibson and Cook had been employed." He also expressed his concerns about Cook to Boynton, the Cincinnati newspaperman. Unlike MacVeagh, with whom he also spoke about Cook, the president was not happy about the lawyer's appointment. "He said he thought the employment of Mr. Cook was an outrage upon him," Boynton later said.[32]

The president demanded to know why Woodward had gone along with the appointment of the seamy Cook to the prosecution team. Fuming, he explained that a Supreme Court justice "had informed him that Cook was one of the most disreputable members of the Washington bar, and that the selection was a disgrace to the administration," as Woodward later described it. Chastened and scrambling to defend the selection, Woodward echoed MacVeagh's assessment and argued that the attorney's many disreputable associations actually would be an asset to the investigation. He said that, "as the investigation widened, it would be desirable to have in the cases a local lawyer who possessed an intimate and extensive knowledge, not only of the criminal class, but also of the darker elements that go to make up the life of the District." Cook's familiarity with the lowly "social strata" of the area would allow him to ferret out information in a manner that a more respectable attorney could not. "The President seemed partially satisfied" with this justification, according to Woodward.[33]

Cook would make much of his purported close dealings with Garfield in the early stages of the Star Route prosecution, perhaps because he was sensitive to charges that he was not competent or ethical enough to coordinate the government's legal efforts. He later claimed that as the investigation into the postal frauds took shape, Garfield had called him to the White House for several face-to-face meetings. In these conversations, the president instructed

Cook to directly keep him apprised of how the legal cases were progressing. He also acknowledged that, as Cook later paraphrased it, "the case was a delicate one; that it involved many who had been his special friends; [and] that there was no small degree of antagonism in relation to it." Such factors, however, were to have no bearing on how Cook and his colleagues were to go about their work. "He stated that he wished me to make a most thorough, impartial, and fair investigation of all the facts," Cook later said of Garfield's charge, "and wherever they might conduct me to go, irrespective of persons."[34]

According to Cook, Garfield told him that he wanted the special prosecutor to report directly to the president on the progress of the Star Route cases, and thereby essentially bypass his nominal superior, Attorney General Mac-Veagh. Cook later made this assertion in testimony before Congress, creating the impression that the president had placed more trust in Cook than he had in MacVeagh, a member of his own cabinet. Woodward, however, disputed Cook's assertions on this score. In his own later congressional testimony, the investigator said of these claims of being told to report directly to Garfield, "I know with the assurance of certainty that these representations are false." He derided as implausible the idea that Garfield would undercut the authority of a member of his cabinet in order to create a direct channel to Cook, an attorney whose character was questioned throughout Washington (and within the White House itself). "I cannot believe that the executive of this nation arranged a job with a man whom a Supreme Court judge had only a few weeks before denounced to him as disreputable," Woodward later said, "for the purpose of deceiving an honored member of his own official family," Attorney General MacVeagh.[35]

Whatever the exact nature of their relationship, Garfield and Cook met at least once in the presence of Postmaster General James and Woodward to discuss the Star Route case. Cook updated the president on the progress of the investigation and described the work that he and Albert Gibson had done. Garfield did not seem impressed by what he heard. "The president suggested that they were too slow," James later said, "that they should be more earnest in their work, and that they should have the accused parties indicted and tried." The special prosecutor got the message, according to James: "Mr. Cook promised that no time should be lost."[36]

Perhaps in an effort to convince the president of his integrity, Cook also told Garfield that he already had been privately approached by men purporting to represent some potential defendants in the Star Route case, including former second assistant postmaster general Brady. Testifying later before Congress, Cook would say that he had been offered "fees at least double any that the United States would give me" to represent some of the defendants, with one intermediary offering $25,000. Cook proudly reported to the president that he had rebuffed all such propositions, however lucrative, and had chosen to remain in the employ of the government.[37]

Hoping to further "illustrate the total depravity of the Star Routers," as Woodward later described it, Cook told Garfield an elaborate story about how he had resisted an effort that had been made to corrupt him. He claimed that a representative of Brady had arranged a clandestine meeting with him, presumably to propose some kind of bribe or payoff. Cook had insisted on meeting Brady's proxy in his own quarters, but only after "having first prudently concealed a detective under the bed to overhear the conversation," according to Woodward. The hidden detective would be able to vouch for Cook's integrity in handling this approach from Brady's camp.[38]

Woodward was appalled by these strange outpourings from Cook, and he glanced at Garfield to gauge his response. Although the president remained impassive, Woodward, knowing Cook's reputation, was not reassured. "In view of the fact, however, that in a community where he had lived for many years, and where his character was minutely known, the virtue of Mr. Cook had so soon been thus rudely tempted," he later said, "one could not help asking mentally how long it would be able to resist the shock [of the bribery efforts]." The inspector thought it would be only a matter of time before Cook succumbed to temptation and betrayed the government.[39]

Woodward, having recommended that Cook be retained by the government, was already having second thoughts about the apparently second-rate attorney. He later wrote a letter to Benjamin Brewster, MacVeagh's successor as attorney general, describing how Cook had so proudly recounted for Garfield the bribery attempt and his use of a hidden detective. "This extraordinary avowal left a very unpleasant expression on my mind, as only a few days before I had defended the employment of Mr. Cook to the president," an embarrassed Woodward wrote, "which I could not have done had I known that such was his method of conducting business."[40]

Perhaps more disturbing for Woodward was Cook's proposed strategy for dealing with the many criminal offenses of Stephen Dorsey. "Mr. Cook insisted that immunity should be granted to Stephen W. Dorsey," Woodward later said, "on account of his great services to the Republican party." Woodward, who by this time already knew that there was abundant evidence of Dorsey's guilt, opposed Cook's plea for leniency for the former senator. "In answer, I modestly suggested that penal laws and penitentiaries were not devised for the exclusive benefit of Democrats." Garfield agreed with Woodward: whatever his contributions to the party generally and to the president specifically, Dorsey should not be spared. The government had to hold him accountable for his misdeeds.[41]

In his journal, the president noted that he had sent for Cook and criticized him and Gibson for working too slowly on the Star Route case. The impatient Garfield had "suggested that they should be more earnest in their work," as he recorded in the entry, "and that they should have the accused parties indicted and tried."[42]

BUSINESS CONNECTED WITH DORSEY'S TROUBLES

The Investigation Takes Shape, Spring-Summer 1881

With new special prosecutor William Cook getting his charge from the Garfield administration, the work of the investigation of the Star Route frauds moved forward at a brisk pace. Investigator Patrick Henry Woodward and attorney Albert Gibson hunkered down in Rooms 49 and 50 in the Post Office Building and pored over mountains of evidence. It was widely believed that the materials being assembled by Gibson, Woodward, and their colleagues would be damning for those implicated in the Star Route frauds. A St. Louis newspaper observed as the government's investigation took shape, "Men who shared in the ring are anxious and uneasy, and it is predicted that some of them will leave the country." The long-delayed day of reckoning for the Star Route cheats finally seemed to be approaching.[1]

Gibson and Woodward immediately made former second assistant postmaster Tom Brady one of the chief targets of their inquiry. As Woodward later wrote, they were startled by "the orders of Mr. Brady giving extraordinary allowances to certain contractors." And, in their minds, there was no doubt that he had directly ordered that inappropriate changes be made to Star Route contracts. One order—it increased the value of a contract on a route that serviced the silver-mining town of Pioche, Nevada, by almost $30,000—bore the terse command, "Do it—BRADY." There was no mistaking his imprimatur on such questionable directives.[2]

Investigators looked closely at all orders for expedition issued by Brady over a period of one year (the final six months of 1878 and the first six months of 1879). Post Office records showed that in the Western District alone, Brady approved increases worth approximately $2 million. Woodward refused to believe that these increases were legitimate, given both the letter and the spirit of the laws and regulations governing expedition orders. "Did the public necessities so change during the brief period between the appearance of the advertisement and the subsequent inflation of contracts," he later asked, "as to justify even a small fraction of these colossal expenditures?" To the federal investigative team, it seemed unlikely.[3]

Gibson and Woodward determined that, under Brady's supervision of Star Route contracts, "the *bona fide* bidder had no chance whatever," as Woodward later wrote. If one submitted a reasonable proposal for mail service on a particular route, he was sure to be underbid by another contractor. Meanwhile, the "beneficiaries under Mr. Brady's system of administration" were visited by a "prophetic spirit [that] seemed to assure them that the ordinary rules of business might here be safely disregarded." The result was what Woodward termed "a far-reaching scheme for enriching certain combinations [of Star Route contractors] at the expense of the public treasury." Foremost among these combinations was the group of contractors associated with Stephen Dorsey, the well-connected former senator from Arkansas.[4]

In denying that they had engaged in sharp practices, members of the Dorsey combination would point to the fact that the expedition orders approved by Brady had been supported by numerous affidavits and petitions calling for increased postal service along the routes in question. (It was often argued in these materials that increases in postal services were desperately and immediately necessary to foster settlement and boost economic growth in sparsely populated areas in the Great Plains and West.) How could an allegedly secret criminal conspiracy to defraud the federal government, they asked, have been so openly supported by so many people, including prominent politicians? Criminal conspiracies were usually much more clandestine, were they not?

Woodward later explained how cunning contractors essentially manufactured these apparent groundswells of public support. "Having secured the award of certain routes at low figures, favored contractors with a confidence in destiny amply justified by subsequent events dispatched agents to the frontiers to work up petitions among the settlers, asking for more frequent trips, and for the expedition of time. Senators and congressmen were specially solicited to endorse the petitions of their constituents," he wrote. "Anxious to oblige, and ignorant of the scheme, many of them lent the weight of their names quite promiscuously." Woodward grumbled that such ginned-up appeals served as mere pretexts for compliance with regulations by Brady when favored combinations asked to have their contracts fattened through expedition orders.[5]

For Woodward and Gibson, the route connecting Canyon City, Oregon, to Fort McDermitt (located just over Oregon's border with Nevada) typified the Star Route scam. John Peck, part of the Dorsey combination, had been awarded the route in 1878; his contract called for him to be paid $2,888 per year for making one trip per week (which would take 130 hours to cover the 243 miles). Even before mail started to be delivered on the route, Peck began to ask Brady to approve expedited service at a more gainful annual rate. The second assistant postmaster obliged, eventually approving additional trips per week, each at a faster pace. In the end, the route was worth $50,166 annually, more than seventeen times the value of the initial contract awarded to Peck. Subcontractors wound up furnishing the service for roughly $20,000 per year, which meant that the Dorsey combination realized an annual profit of approximately $30,000 solely on Route 44160.[6]

To determine why this route suddenly had become so essential (and remunerative), a Post Office inspector acting under Woodward's authority traveled to Oregon to investigate. He reported that save for the area immediately surrounding Canyon City, there was no settlement along the entire route to Fort McDermitt, and for good reason. "The country is either mountainous or given up to sage brush and practically not cultivable," Woodward later wrote. "It has no mines. For most of the distance, the road was but a trail." This hardly seemed to be an emerging area needing improved—and expensive—postal service.[7]

When Woodward and his colleagues reviewed the records of Route 44160, their suspicions were confirmed. Over the 1880 and 1881 fiscal years, it had generated revenues of $473.69 and $108.58, respectively. With Brady's approval, the Post Office had paid the Dorsey combination and its subcontractors a total of $100,332 to deliver $582.27 worth of mail.[8] And that was just *one* route among many. Woodward and fellow investigators quickly realized that the Dorsey ring, which had successfully bid on 134 contracts, could have bilked the federal government out of millions of dollars.

Not everyone, however, was impressed by the progress of the investigation. Almost daily, Gibson's erstwhile colleagues at the New York *Sun* expressed skepticism over the Garfield administration's commitment to pursuing the wrongdoers, particularly those who were associated with the Republican Party. "It now looks very much as though President Garfield means that the Star Route investigation shall never come to anything," the paper editorialized early in June 1881. "He means to squelch it and save the thieves." A month later, the *Sun* argued: "Brady and Dorsey and all the members of their gang have no occasion for fear. General Garfield will stand by them."[9] The *Sun* suggested that the administration would make a great show of investigating the scandal but then would lose its nerve when it came to fully prosecuting the most obvious targets, Brady and Dorsey, both of whom were prominent Republicans.

Over the spring of 1881, Attorney General MacVeagh had several strained conversations with Dorsey and his attorney, the redoubtable Robert Green Ingersoll. MacVeagh later stated, "we had found certain records in the Department which upon their face were exceedingly unfortunate, it seemed to me, and very persuasive of guilt." If the facts warranted it, there was no point in trying to proceed through anything other than "the ordinary judicial channels"—a formal criminal indictment and then a trial. "I stated to Mr. Dorsey . . . that the matter had gone so far that it would be perfectly useless to attempt to settle it by any other [means] than a judicial investigation."[10]

Dorsey argued with MacVeagh over where Garfield stood on the matter. Hinting that the president actually did not want to drag his political allies into court, the former senator warned MacVeagh not to "disregard the 'orders of the president' or the 'wishes of the president,'" according to MacVeagh's latter account. The attorney general countered that Garfield backed an impartial Star Route investigation, as did the country as a whole. He informed Dorsey that "behind us was the president, and behind him was an aroused public opinion and the press of the country."[11]

Yet it was clear that these approaches had some effect on Garfield, at least privately. The president's journal was peppered with references to his anxiety over the Star Route case. He wrote that he "was kept up until midnight by business connected with Dorsey's troubles." He also admitted to having a great deal of sympathy for Dorsey and harboring some doubts about the wisdom of the investigation that his own administration was conducting. Whatever the evidence, it was not easy for Garfield to abandon a well-connected man who had been such a key operative in his 1880 campaign for the White House.[12]

Members of the cabinet knew that the Star Route cases were weighing on the president. "Of course it would not be telling the whole truth to be silent upon the fact that these prosecutions were a source of very great anxiety, and I might almost say, at a certain stage of them, of distress, to President Garfield," Attorney General MacVeagh later told Congress. "It would have been very strange if it had been otherwise."[13]

MacVeagh himself also seemed burdened by the case. In mid-May, he dropped in on his friend Henry Adams and his wife, Marian. Their discussion of the investigation left her feeling that the attorney general needed the support of the president. "He has a big fight on his hands; if only Garfield has the pluck and decency to support him," she wrote in a letter to her father, "he may yet provide the late Senator Dorsey with board and lodging at the public expense" (that is, he might secure the conviction of Dorsey and send him to prison).[14]

From Dorsey's perspective, the investigation took a dramatic turn for the worse early in June 1881, when his clerk, Monfort Rerdell, made contact with Powell Clayton, the former Arkansas governor and senator. Clayton and Dorsey had been enemies for many years, having found themselves on opposite sides of the bitter Brooks-Baxter dispute in Arkansas in the 1870s. Clayton now was eager to capitalize on the Star Route fraud to embarrass his longtime foe. Perhaps more than anyone, Rerdell knew the inner workings of the Dorsey ring and undoubtedly worried that he might be facing criminal charges in the near future for his role in its operations. As one prosecutor later put it, "either . . . fear or conscience" prompted Rerdell to bare his soul to Clayton. The clerk now "desired to make a clean breast of the matter, and tell the whole story" of the frauds, if Clayton could put him in touch with investigators. This was a potential bonanza for the federal prosecutors, one that could give them an insider's view of how the Star Route frauds had been perpetrated.[15]

Clayton met with George Spencer, the former Alabama senator who had helped catalyze the Star Route inquiry earlier in the year, and the two men talked about the potential implications of investigators turning to Rerdell for information. According to Spencer's later account, Clayton did not have much trust in the clerk: "I think Rerdell is a very bad man," he said. "I do not place any confidence in him." Clayton, however, felt that the testimony and information that he might provide "would make a conviction positive and absolute," as his evidence "referred to all the routes that Dorsey, Vaile, and that combination had—to their general business." Rerdell, in short, knew everything.[16]

Clayton overcame his misgivings and approached Postmaster General James, telling him that Rerdell "desired to make a 'clean breast' of his relations to ex-Senator Dorsey and the Star Route contracts," as James later put it. He suggested that Rerdell take his story to Attorney General MacVeagh, but the clerk insisted that the meeting be with the postmaster general and that Clayton also be present. James agreed and arranged for a meeting involving himself, Rerdell, Clayton, and the investigator Woodward in his rooms in the Arlington Hotel in Washington.[17]

Rerdell initially did not intend to divulge all that he knew to the men leading the Star Route investigation. But the clerk apparently could not hold back once he started explaining the unscrupulous methods by which the Dorsey ring had operated. "In course of the conversation," James later said, "Rerdell evidently went further than it was originally his purpose to go." He eventually laid out how the entire racket had unfolded, and how deeply former senator Dorsey and Brady, the former second assistant postmaster general, had been involved.[18]

Detailing the basics of the dishonest bidding scheme, the clerk described how the men had gathered in Stephen Dorsey's quarters in Washington and prepared Star Route contract bids for John Dorsey, Miner, Peck, and Albert Boone to submit to the Post Office. Rerdell stated that after the bids had been accepted, he had managed the ring's affairs and "attended to getting up influence, petitions, etc., for expedition," which had greatly inflated the contracts' value. Rerdell acknowledged that almost all of these petitions, aimed at providing a rationale for increasing how much the contractors were paid for their routes, were forgeries.[19]

The conspiracy never could have worked if Post Office officials had not been paid off. In the Arlington Hotel meeting, Rerdell explained that the ring had kicked back to Brady sizable percentages of the money it gained through expedition as well as the remission of fines that had been levied for failure to perform service. He eventually produced ledgers indicating that under the pseudonym "William Smith," Brady had received $37,000 for facilitating the bidding scheme. For his part, William Turner, a clerk in the Contract Office, received $600 and some mining stock worth $1,500. (Turner was denoted as "Samuel Jones" in the books.) Rerdell made it clear that everyone involved in the scheme knew that Brady was being paid off. Summarizing the clerk's statement, a prosecutor later said, "it was a perfectly well understood thing that they were dividing their profits with Mr. Brady, and that there was a regular schedule on which the division was made."[20]

When Rerdell showed some of the ring's authentic financial records to James and Woodward, he explained that he had hurriedly prepared a second set of doctored books during the 1880 congressional investigation of Star Route irregularities. (This inquiry had been precipitated by Brady's sheepish request for a massive supplemental appropriation to fund Star Route services through the end of the fiscal year.) Fearing that he would be called before the House committee and asked to produce the firm's records, Rerdell had feigned an illness for over a week and frantically altered records in order to hide the payments that had been made to Brady and Turner. In the falsified records, the kickbacks had been disguised simply as unspecified profits and losses. Woodward later said that in order to show what he had done, "Rerdell also exhibited two balance-sheets purporting to be correct transcripts from the genuine books of Dorsey, and from the amended books prepared during his pretended sickness."[21]

In his conversations with James and Woodward, Rerdell also questioned the integrity of Albert Gibson and William Cook, who had been recently hired to assist District Attorney George Corkhill in the Star Route investigation. "I fully believed those men would betray the government," Rerdell later said. He reported that he had seen Gibson at Stephen Dorsey's house during the 1880 congressional investigation of the Star Route frauds. He also produced documents purporting to show that Gibson had received a payment of $1,500 in mining stock from Dorsey, presumably to shield the former senator from exposure in the pages of the New York *Sun* when Gibson had been employed there.[22]

Rerdell reported that Cook also maintained ongoing ties to Dorsey. "I distrusted Cook," he later said, "because he was holding secret communication with Dorsey after accepting employment from the government." Rerdell disclosed to James and Woodward that he had arranged clandestine meetings between Cook and Dorsey, including one that had taken place the day before Cook's appointment to the prosecution team was announced publicly. When Rerdell mentioned the appointment to Dorsey, the former senator smiled knowingly and said, "That is all right"—the inference being that he knew Cook would protect him.[23]

The postmaster general realized that Rerdell's claims, if true, were a thunderclap, and he advised the clerk to meet with Attorney General MacVeagh. Rerdell did so and essentially repeated what he had earlier told James and Woodward about the Star Route frauds. He also produced a bundle of letters that he and Dorsey had written as part of their crooked contracting scheme. Some of Dorsey's letters showed how he had schemed to drum up fictitious support for the expedition of a postal route in Oregon, instructing the recipient "to get up petitions, to get articles in the newspapers, to get letters written to senators, . . . and giving him a form of affidavit, with instructions not to have any two petitions or letters in the same hand," as a prosecutor later summarized. The letters showed how he had manufactured public opinion that the ring could use as justification for increased services on (and thus additional payments for) its routes.[24]

It was just as Woodward had suspected all along. According to Rerdell's sensational account, the Dorsey combination repeatedly had concocted phony local support to justify the expedition of little-used Star Routes throughout the West. In return for hefty kickbacks, former second assistant postmaster general Brady, working with the clerk William Turner, had approved the unnecessarily lucrative increases in service. Rerdell confirmed everything.

Having long dreaded being found out, Rerdell apparently was relieved to have finally unburdened himself regarding his role in the Star Route legerdemain. He later spoke privately to Woodward and described "the weight taken off his guilty conscience by having made a clean breast of it, having made him a free man, and feeling so much better for the first time in many years," a federal prosecutor later said. He further stated that he hoped some of his coconspirators would similarly admit to having cheated the government, saying, in the prosecutor's words, that "he had been long associated with Mr. [Stephen] Dorsey, and that he was going to endeavor to induce him to make a clean breast of it" with investigators.[25]

Rerdell told MacVeagh that he could provide additional documents to back up his accusations but that he would have to travel from Washington to New York to retrieve them. During his train ride north, he encountered Postmaster General James and explained his mission, stating that he would have to pay a visit to Dorsey's office in the Boreel Building, located on Broadway near Wall Street. James, wanting to make sure that Rerdell would complete this crucial errand without interference from Dorsey, contacted a local postal inspector and instructed him to shadow Rerdell throughout his time in the city. (The inspector later confirmed that Rerdell had visited the Boreel Building.) The following day, taking the train back to Washington, James again encountered Rerdell, who was clutching a package wrapped in newspaper. The clerk said that the package contained the original books of the Dorsey ring, which he would soon turn over to Attorney General MacVeagh.[26]

On the train ride back to Washington, Rerdell told James that he had encountered a troubled Dorsey at the Boreel Building. The meeting had not gone especially well: there had been a stormy scene, as James later put it, with Dorsey charging the clerk with treachery for having spoken with James, Woodward, and MacVeagh about the ring's operations. The postmaster general soon saw for himself that Dorsey was utterly distraught over Rerdell's apparent betrayal and what it might mean in terms of his own exposure to criminal charges. When the train stopped in Trenton, New Jersey, the conductor approached Rerdell with several pleading telegrams that had been dispatched from New York City. "The first one was a request from Dorsey for him to leave the train at Philadelphia and return to New York," James later said. "The next was a piteous appeal, on account of Dorsey's wife and children, to come back— that they must not quarrel." Rerdell assured James that he was steadfast; despite Dorsey's appeals, he would continue to cooperate with the government.[27]

Recognizing the threat posed by Rerdell's disclosures to the government, an increasingly frantic Dorsey scrambled to save himself from prosecution. On June 12, he paid a surprise call upon former senator George Spencer in the latter's room at the Everett House in New York City. Dorsey "was very much excited and worried," Spencer later said, because "he had heard that Rerdell had, as he termed it, 'gone back' on him, had turned informer to the Post Office department, and had tried to give up his books, papers, and memoranda." Postmaster General James was not present at the Everett House meeting, but he later heard from Spencer that Dorsey "was terribly demoralized, smoked incessantly, and drank deeply; that he said his clerk [Rerdell] had 'squealed' and betrayed him," as James later put it.[28]

Eventually, Dorsey and Spencer were joined by Stephen Elkins, a former delegate to Congress from New Mexico Territory who himself had been accused of wrongdoing in connection with the awarding of Star Route contracts. Dorsey "begged them both to help him," according to James, and apologized for having clashed with them previously. He also tried to pump the two men for information, asking if they knew anything about what Rerdell had divulged to the government about the Star Route frauds. Spencer, who had been quietly pushing the Garfield administration's investigation from the start, did not have much to share about the matter. "I told him I did not know anything,"

Spencer later said, "and if I did know anything, I was so situated that I could not tell him."[29]

When Dorsey returned to see Spencer at the hotel on June 16, his mood had changed completely. He "was then in a state of great exhilaration, asserting that everything was all right after all," according to Postmaster General James. He showed Spencer the reason for his newfound sunny disposition: an affidavit in which Rerdell recanted more or less all of the potentially damaging information he had divulged to James, Woodward, and MacVeagh. As James later put it, James Bosler, who worked closely with Dorsey, "had gotten hold of Rerdell, had sat up all night with him, and extorted from him the affidavit in question." Woodward later complained that Rerdell had "yielded to the importunities of his old associates" and had changed his mind about cooperating with the government. The investigators' windfall vanished almost as suddenly as it had appeared.[30]

Rerdell himself later described how he had come to recant so suddenly. After he had met with administration representatives, he and Dorsey exchanged several messages, with the former senator pleading with him to reconsider cooperating with the government's investigation. They eventually met in person in Washington, and Dorsey continued to lobby the clerk. "He made the most eloquent and effective appeals to me," Rerdell later said, "dwelling particularly upon his wife and children," who were sure to be negatively affected if the scandal ruined Dorsey. Rerdell told him that he would attempt to make things right again but that he would not go so far as to perjure himself. "What in hell does an oath amount to when the fate of a friend is at stake?" Dorsey sputtered. "Under such circumstances, I would not hesitate [to lie]."[31]

Bosler, who had formed a business partnership with Dorsey, joined the conversation. The three men then began to collaborate on Rerdell's recantation. The clerk composed portions of it, with Dorsey and Bosler "being present and offering frequent suggestions," according to Rerdell. Dorsey eventually took over the process, writing out the last several pages himself and instructing Rerdell to copy them in his own hand.[32]

This written retraction emboldened Dorsey. Armed with the affidavit, he and his attorney, Robert Green Ingersoll, called upon President Garfield at the White House and demanded the immediate resignations of Attorney General MacVeagh and Postmaster General James. Dorsey insisted that the two men had suborned perjury in their dealings with Rerdell. This pressure left Garfield unmoved; he told Dorsey that Rerdell was a rogue whose retraction could not be believed.[33]

At the time that Rerdell recanted, MacVeagh was traveling in New England. The attorney general received a series of worried telegrams urging him to return to Washington immediately and address the efforts being made by Dorsey to undermine the Star Route case and drive him out of the cabinet (for having allegedly induced Rerdell to make a phony confession). Undaunted, MacVeagh kept to his regular schedule and did not rush back to the capital. "When I came back, I was told . . . that a vigorous effort had been made in my absence to have me turned out," he later said, "and that evidence, or papers purporting to be evidence, had been laid before the president of very gross and very base conduct on the part of Postmaster General James and myself, going to the extent, I think, of suborning witnesses and engaging in a plot to steal papers." MacVeagh met with the president and asked if Garfield had been persuaded by Rerdell's new affidavit. Garfield brushed off the entire matter, telling the attorney general "that if it was left to him the only action he could take upon it would be to have the man who had made [the affidavit] immediately arrested for perjury."[34]

The move by Dorsey to oust James and MacVeagh represented but one front in an expanding war between the federal government and potential defendants in prosecutions stemming from the Star Route investigation. On June 23, before the government had even prepared formal criminal indictments, attorneys representing Stephen Dorsey and other potential defendants in the Star Route matter made a motion in court in Washington "to compel the government to proceed at once and carry the case before the grand jury and have it disposed of. . . . Its apparent object was to force the government before the grand jury prior to its being properly prepared to present any case," as Cook, the special prosecutor, later put it. The potential defendants apparently hoped to catch the government off guard and kill the prosecution.[35]

To support the motion, an impatient Tom Brady filed a letter explaining that the case should move forward immediately so that he could be cleared of scurrilous and unfounded charges as soon as possible and thereby preserve his reputation. The former second assistant postmaster general wrote: "I come here anxious to meet the slanderous charges whenever presented in court of justice, conscious that the inevitable conclusion of an impartial investigation will be to forever annihilate the base fabrications against my official conduct and my good name." He added, "If there are any charges to be presented against me before a legal tribunal for alleged misconduct while in office, I desire that proceedings be instituted in order that I may have the opportunity to appear and vindicate myself therefrom."[36]

Cook was incredulous that potential Star Route defendants like Brady would try to force the government into prematurely heading into court with an incomplete and still-developing case. He told the court that the government took the position that "the United States cannot, must not, [and] will not present any evidence before the grand jury until, after the most cool and tranquil and impartial examination, it appears to be requisite to do so to maintain the purity, the welfare, and the stability of the United States." He further said, "If, after such examination, it becomes necessary to present the most exalted citizens of the United States, or the humblest and the poorest in the walks of life, they should be equally presented." The government probably would be ready to make its case before a grand jury in the fall of 1881, Cook advised.[37]

Echoing Cook's comments, Attorney General MacVeagh later explained why the government had not been ready to seek grand jury indictments against Dorsey and Brady early in the summer of 1881. "It seemed to me that one of the misfortunes of the cases was that the magnitude of them, the extent of territory over which the evidence extended, the period of time it covered, and the character of the testimony," he said, "made it absolutely impossible, in my judgment, for any intelligent presentation of them to be made within the time which some gentlemen seemed to suppose was sufficient." A complicated case—especially one involving such prominent figures—simply required more time to prepare.[38]

The New York *Sun*, with its characteristic skepticism of the government's handling of the Star Route case, mocked prosecutors for having to admit that they were not yet ready to make a presentation to the grand jury in June 1881. The newspaper asserted that the government had spent too much time trying to whip up public opinion against the accused and too little time doing the hard work of adequately preparing a solid case for presentation to a jury. "It is apparent that they made a blunder in beginning a trial by newspaper before being ready for a trial by judge and jury," the *Sun* claimed. "Controversy provoked crimination, and crimination compelled the prosecution to show its hand prematurely."[39]

There was simply no legal authority to back the notion that anxious potential defendants could compel prosecutors to bring criminal charges against them, and the motion went nowhere. If it wished to bring the Star Route cases before the grand jury in Washington in the fall of 1881, the government would have the remainder of the summer to gather evidence and refine the charges it planned to file. It also would have time to shore up political and public support for the prosecutions.

This was the plan, anyway, until disaster struck in July 1881.

The Dalles, Oregon, a town served by a Star Route.
Oregon Historical Society, Portland, Negative 5345.

A Star Route connected Ouray, Colorado, with the outside world. William Henry Jackson,
Ouray, Colorado, William Henry Jackson Collection, History Colorado, Denver, Colorado.

A frontier post office in eastern Montana, circa 1880.
Prints and Photographs Division, Library of Congress, Washington, DC.

A Star Route mail wagon, circa 1892.
Coralville Digital History Library, Coralville Public Library, Coralville, Iowa.

A Star Route stage and mail wagon. John Nopel, *Stage and Mail Wagon*,
John Nopel Photograph Collection, Meriam Library, California State University, Chico.

Second Assistant Postmaster
General Thomas J. Brady.
From *A Biographical History of
Eminent and Self-Made Men of the
State of Indiana*, vol. 1 (Cincinnati:
Western Biographical, 1880).

The Post Office Department building, Washington, DC.
Detroit Publishing Company Photograph Collection, Prints and Photographs Division,
Library of Congress, Washington, DC.

Senator Stephen Dorsey.
Brady-Handy Collection, Prints and Photographs Division,
Library of Congress, Washington, DC.

Throughout the Star Route case, Stephen Dorsey was pilloried by political cartoonists across the nation. Frederick Burr Opper, *Dorsey, the American "Informer"—He Finds One Willing Ear*, from *Puck*, July 25, 1883. Prints and Photographs Division, Library of Congress, Washington, DC.

The opulent mansion of Star Route defendant Harvey Vaile in Independence, Missouri. Historic American Buildings Survey, Library of Congress, Washington, DC.

THOMAS L. JAMES,
THE MAN WHO STAMPED OUT THE STAR ROUTE SWINDLE.

Postmaster General Thomas James. From *Puck*, October 19, 1881.
Prints and Photographs Division, Library of Congress, Washington, DC.

US Attorney General Isaac Wayne MacVeagh.
Brady-Handy Collection, Prints and Photographs Division,
Library of Congress, Washington, DC.

President James Garfield.
Brady-Handy Collection, Prints and Photographs Division,
Library of Congress, Washington, DC.

Charles Guiteau, assassin of President James Garfield.
Photograph by C. M. Bell. Prints and Photographs Division,
Library of Congress, Washington, DC.

President Chester Arthur.
Photograph by C. M. Bell. Prints and Photographs Division,
Library of Congress, Washington, DC.

District Attorney George
Corkhill of Washington, DC.
Brady-Handy Collection,
Prints and Photographs Division,
Library of Congress,
Washington, DC.

Attorney General Benjamin
Brewster. Prints and Photographs
Division, Library of Congress,
Washington, DC.

Star Route prosecutor Richard T. Merrick.
Brady-Handy Collection, Prints and Photographs Division,
Library of Congress, Washington, DC.

Robert Green Ingersoll, defense attorney in both Star Route trials.
Brady-Handy Collection, Prints and Photographs Division,
Library of Congress, Washington, DC.

AN UNCOMPLETED TASK.

McVEAGH. — "Good bye, my brethren; you thoroughly deserve to be bricked up; but I'm afraid I can't wait to finish the job."

Attorney General Wayne MacVeagh resigned before the first
Star Route trial. He is depicted here (*left*) with Stephen Dorsey and Tom Brady.
James Albert Wales, *An Uncompleted Task*, from *Puck*, October 5, 1881.
Prints and Photographs Division, Library of Congress, Washington, DC.

The District of Columbia Courthouse, site of both Star Route trials.
Harris and Ewing Collection, Prints and Photographs Division,
Library of Congress, Washington, DC.

THE HARDER HE PUMPS, THE DIRTIER HIS CASE GETS.

This cartoon depicts attorney Robert Green Ingersoll "pumping" Star Route defendant Montfort Rerdell for information while Stephen Dorsey and Tom Brady look on. Frederick Burr Opper, *The Harder He Pumps, the Dirtier His Case Gets*, from *Puck*, March 7, 1883. Prints and Photographs Division, Library of Congress, Washington, DC.

Attorney Robert Green Ingersoll carries two large bags of money labeled "Counsel Fees" as he leaves the courthouse in Washington after the second Star Route Trial. On the right, wearing tattered clothing, are defendants Tom Brady and Stephen Dorsey. Friedrich Graetz, *The Result of the Star Route Trials*, from *Puck*, June 20, 1883. Prints and Photographs Division, Library of Congress, Washington, DC.

In one memorable illustration relating to the Star Route scandal, Thomas Nast invoked "The Fox and the Lion" from *Aesop's Fables*. Thomas Nast, *A Fable— With a Modern Application*, from *Harper's Weekly*, March 25, 1882.

THE NEWSPAPERS CONFIRMED THE INSPIRATION

The President Falls, Summer–Fall 1881

On the evening of June 29, 1881, investigator Patrick Henry Woodward, Postmaster General Tom James, and special prosecutor William Cook met at the White House with President Garfield to discuss the progress of the Star Route case. Before the meeting ended, the conversation with the nation's chief executive took an ominous turn.[1]

As Woodward later said, Cook offered some "sensational warnings in reference to dangers threatening the president and two of his cabinet." These apparently were not mere political challenges to him or the Republican Party; they were threats to the personal safety of Garfield and his closest advisors. Cook was not explicit about what these alleged dangers might be or who posed them, but he referenced his less-that-sterling professional reputation in claiming that he had become aware that the members of the administration, including Garfield, might be in peril. That was the word on the streets of the capital.

"Mr. President, you know I am a criminal lawyer, and that my associations are not always with angels," Cook admitted, according to Woodward's later statement. "I heard a good deal about what is going on, and I feel that it is my duty to say, from knowledge which has come into my possession, that something dreadful is about to happen. I do not know what it is, but I think I can learn during the coming week."[2]

According to his own later account, Cook told Garfield that "an intense and bitter feeling" was mounting against his fledgling presidential administration. This "feeling of bitterness and vindictiveness" was not merely what might have been expected from Democrats who were angry over the losing the 1880 presidential election; it existed within the Republican Party itself because of ongoing internecine conflicts between the Stalwart and Half-Breed factions. Cook, specifically referencing these intraparty tensions, warned the president that his personal safety might be endangered. As the special counsel later recounted:

> Prior to leaving I said to him that I ought perhaps to suggest that he should be careful of his movements; that, as had been developed by the bitterness of the press favorable to those who were denominated Star Route men, in connection with the excitement growing out of the antagonism between the "Stalwarts" and the "Half-Breeds," that there was an exceedingly bitter feeling prevailing, and that there were connected with these cases men of violent temper and disposition, men of extreme training and character, and that I fear there might be a resort to violence; at least that such was the impression on my mind, and that I made the suggestion accordingly.[3]

Although Garfield initially appeared to react to Cook's admonitions, the president soon brushed off the idea that his safety might be at risk. The warning from the special prosecutor "seemed to touch him but for a moment, as appeared by a nervous or spasmodic change of his position, and he responded and said that he apprehended that there was no danger," Cook later told Congress.[4]

Three days later, on Saturday, July 2, a failed attorney and frustrated political operative named Charles Guiteau approached Garfield at the Baltimore and Potomac Railroad Station in Washington as the president prepared to embark on a vacation trip. In the station's waiting room, Guiteau produced a pistol from his pocket and fired two shots at Garfield from point-blank range. The first shot grazed the president's shoulder, but the second did more serious damage, entering his back and lodging near his pancreas.[5]

Officers quickly apprehended Guiteau and hustled him off to a nearby police station for questioning. When asked why he had shot the president, he exclaimed, "I am a Stalwart of the Stalwarts! I did it, and I want to be arrested! Arthur is President now!"[6]

The second half of the would-be assassin's utterance proved to be premature. Guiteau had gravely wounded Garfield, but the president clung to life and did not immediately lose consciousness. For the time being, at least, Chester Arthur remained vice president.

The first part of Guiteau's statement highlighted the factionalism that had sundered the Republican Party for several years. These divisions often have been later described in terms of a neat cleft between Stalwarts and Half-Breeds. In this framework, the Stalwarts, led by Senator Roscoe Conkling of New York, adamantly defended what was commonly known as the spoils system, an arrangement of political patronage that allowed prominent officeholders to dispense jobs to their allies in return for pledges of political loyalty. (Conkling famously exerted control over the selection of the collector of the Port of New York, perhaps the most coveted patronage position in the country.) The party's other faction, the Half-Breeds, favored reform, believing that the excesses endemic in the spoils system had led to the well-chronicled scandals of the Grant administration. Although Grant had left office, these scandals threatened to haunt Republicans for years to come.[7]

This explanation, however, probably is too simplistic. "Unexamined assumptions and loose terminology," historian Donald Peskin has written, "litter the standard textbook treatments of Republican factionalism during the Gilded Age." Peskin has noted that "this simple picture is clouded by complications" in the composition, methods, and goals of the rival factions. For instance, some accounts do not list Conkling as a Stalwart, while James Blaine, who reputedly led the Half-Breeds, did not refer to the group by that term. (It speaks volumes about Blaine that he referred to this group as "the Blaine faction.") Peskin has cautioned that "historians created the illusion that the Republican party was composed of two symmetrical, well organized, identifiable factions when, in fact, the groupings were much less formal and far more fluid."[8]

The uneasy truce that existed between the party's imprecise blocs broke down when Republicans set about selecting their nominee for president in 1880. The Stalwarts backed former president Grant, while the Half-Breeds advanced Blaine. This split—over the prospect of a third presidential term for Grant—might have been the biggest single matter dividing the coteries within the party. Perhaps not surprisingly, Republican delegates meeting for their party's convention in Chicago were not able to give a majority of their votes to either candidate, and a compromise figure emerged: James Garfield, who actually was present to nominate for president another Ohioan, Treasury

Secretary John Sherman. Garfield—an affable moderate who had not strongly aligned himself with any faction within the increasingly fractious party—won the nomination on the thirty-sixth ballot. The weary delegates then selected Arthur as his running mate.

For many in both major political parties, Arthur was a middling partisan flunky who seemed to personify the spoils system. A New York Stalwart with close ties to Conkling, he had held the prized patronage position of collector of the Port of New York during Grant's presidency. President Hayes, in an effort to rein in patronage in New York, had fired him in 1878. Now, two years later, Arthur found himself politically resurrected and on the Republican ticket, presumably to act as a counterweight to Garfield's mild reform tendencies.

No concrete evidence ever came to light that directly connected Guiteau's violent actions to the Stalwarts. Yet he had in fact called upon Arthur on several occasions during the 1880 presidential campaign. Arthur had given him a meaningless assignment to deliver a campaign speech to a tiny gathering in New York (referencing the Democratic candidate that year, it was entitled "Garfield against Hancock"), which the deluded man mistakenly believed had been crucial to electing Garfield. The assignment had also helped convince Guiteau that he was an intimate and trusted ally of the vice president.[9]

The toxic political environment of 1881, shaped in part by heated debates over the Garfield administration's handling of the Star Route frauds, further led the delusional Guiteau to believe that he needed to take violent action against the new president. When police arrested him, the assailant had in his possession a variety of newspaper clippings. "I will state at the time of my arrest I had some forty or fifty slips [of paper], editorial slips from the leading newspapers of the country, showing the political situation last May and June," he said late in 1881. "These slips show the action and one of the forces which impelled me on to the president, and they are very important as showing the gist of this whole matter." Guiteau asserted that, prior to the shooting, his ideas about the president had been shaped by newspapers that had been, in his words, "denouncing General Garfield at that time."[10]

Among the newspapers harshly criticizing Garfield early in his administration had been the *New York Herald*, edited by Thomas B. Connery. Prompted by Conkling and Vice President Arthur, his Stalwart allies, Connery had in May run a series of articles that blasted Garfield as weak and incompetent. The most notorious of these was entitled "The Wriggler," in which the president had been ridiculed as an "angry boy" and an altogether "small and pitiable" figure. "We have had some men in the executive chair who were not very strong intellectually . . . but it is doubtful if there ever was an occupant of the White House who has been so completely fooled and blinded as the twentieth president of the United States," the paper had claimed.[11]

Guiteau allegedly had a marked clipping of the inflammatory "Wriggler" article in his possession when he shot Garfield. Connery, in an article published sixteen years after the shooting, later admitted that "when Guiteau was arrested there was found on his person a copy of the *New York Herald*, containing a severe arraignment of the president for his double-dealing with Conkling in the matter of New York appointments. The article was marked by Guiteau, and it is supposed that he carried it about with him, reading it frequently and brooding over it, until his brain became inflamed with the murderous impulse."[12]

Guiteau left little doubt that such incendiary articles had swayed him as he made up his mind to shoot Garfield. At his later trial, he would be asked directly if they had influenced him to act on that fateful day at the railroad terminal.

"The newspapers inspired you?" his defense attorney would ask.

"The Deity inspired me," Guiteau would say.

"Did not the newspapers inspire you?"

"The Deity inspired me and the newspapers confirmed the inspiration. Put it into shape."[13]

Guiteau mainly seemed to be obsessed with the feud between Garfield and Conkling and in vindicating the Stalwarts against the Half-Breeds, but criticisms of the president's handling of the Star Route affair were inextricably bound up in how anti-administration newspapers like the *Herald* in New York and the *National Republican* in Washington lambasted the president and whipped up public sentiment against him. The latter publication's interest in Star Route matters undoubtedly reflected the concerns of its owner, Tom Brady, one of the chief targets of the government's investigation. Brady regularly tried use his paper to derail the case before it landed him in criminal court as a defendant.[14]

The *National Republican*'s near-constant attacks on Garfield in the early days of his administration, and their possible influence on Guiteau, would be examined at considerable length at his later trial. At one point, George Gorham, the paper's editor, would be called to the witness stand, presumably in order to offer an opinion on the merits of the speech that Guiteau had delivered to support Garfield's 1880 presidential campaign. Gorham's testimony would take a turn, however, when Guiteau (who would be allowed to question witnesses at his trial) pressed him on the *National Republican*'s provocative coverage of Garfield in the months leading up to the shooting. Gorham would find himself in the awkward position of having to explain how and why his newspaper had so relentlessly attacked the president.

"I want to know if you did not write a good many editorials in your paper last spring denouncing General Garfield for disrupting the Republican Party? . . . Isn't that the fact?" Guiteau would ask. "And didn't you advise or inspire certain articles denouncing Mr. Garfield in the bitterest terms for wrecking the Republican Party?"[15]

A flustered Gorham would dodge such sharp questions about the *National Republican*, saying he would need to look at the specific articles in question before describing their content and tone. Guiteau, however, would not let the matter drop and would offer some additional damning commentary on the editor and his inflammatory publication. Implicit in his discussions would be the suggestion that he had been egged on to shoot the president, at least in part, by having read vituperative attacks on Garfield in Brady's relentlessly antiadministration newspaper.

"Mr. Gorham is the editor of that paper, and I understand that he does the heavy work on it," Guiteau would say in court. "He inspired them by his spirit and his brain, and I can show as a matter of fact that the *Republican* was denouncing General Garfield in the bitterest terms last May and June for wrecking the Republican Party."[16]

There would be some talk in the courtroom about accessing the *National Republican*'s archives so that Gorham could more thoroughly respond to Guiteau's allegations about the newspaper's coverage of Garfield, but it would come to nothing, and the editor would be allowed to end his testimony without having to extensively defend himself or his publication. Still, the impression would be created that the anti-Garfield *National Republican*—owned by the embattled Tom Brady and brimming with coverage criticizing the administration's handling of the Star Route investigation—had shaped the twisted political views that had prompted a madman to shoot the president.

Guiteau would always fume that he was persecuted for simply acting upon the calls to action issued by papers like the *New York Herald* and the *National*

Republican. "I never saw such a diabolical spirit as some newspapers have towards me; especially those that were cursing Garfield last spring," he would write while in prison. "Since he was shot they have deified him and cursed me for doing the very thing they said out to be done—viz., remove him!"[17]

Whatever his actual connections to Vice President Arthur and the Stalwarts, Guiteau's wounding of Garfield had enormous political implications, as it put Arthur, a Stalwart who owed his political career to the spoils system, on the verge of the presidency. Many wondered if a presumably antireform machine politician would permit his administration to vigorously pursue a sticky political-corruption case.

President Garfield spent much of the summer of 1881 convalescing in Long Branch, New Jersey. As he battled for his life, the government's Star Route investigation temporarily ground to a halt. "The nation and the civilized world were shocked by the announcement that James A. Garfield had been [shot]," special prosecutor William Cook later explained. "That suspended all labor for awhile." For a time, the Star Route case was not a high priority for the shaken administration.[18]

The reeling members of Garfield's cabinet received words of encouragement from colleagues and intimates. Henry Adams wrote to MacVeagh to mourn the condition of "the poor President" and boost his friend's flagging spirits. "He has been hit by one of the disregarded chances of life. What then?" Adams wrote a week after the shooting. "Of course your business is to get him well. In that case he will have an eight-year, popular, and irresistible administration." Adams preferred not to dwell on what might happen if Garfield did not pull through. "Well! We will face the alternative when it comes," he told the attorney general. "Luckily we are a democracy and a sound one."[19]

After prosecutors recovered from the shock of the shooting and regained their bearings, the Star Route investigation made some headway. It often was slow going. Investigator Patrick Henry Woodward later said, "our efforts during the spring and summer of 1881 were of a rather desultory character," in part because the shooting of Garfield, and the subsequent efforts to bring Guiteau to justice, had understandably commanded so much of the administration's attention. Still, federal investigators and attorneys did their best to piece together a complex case that could be brought before a grand jury in Washington. In the capital, "a few witnesses were exposing parts of the sores which had eaten deeply into the public morals and the public purse," as Woodward phrased it. He also noted that postal inspectors on the frontier were gathering valuable evidence about irregular Star Route operations.[20]

Piecing together documentary evidence and witness testimony, Woodward "began systematically to prepare the cases for trial," as he later said. "By means of the files and other departmental papers, I was enabled to dig out the special frauds practiced on each route, and largely to demonstrate the methods pursued by the different rings." As Woodward meticulously delved into "the inside affairs of the various combinations" in the summer of 1881, a few things stood out. Among them was "the exceptionally bad service of the Dorseys." It was obvious that the members of the Dorsey ring had manipulated the bidding process and then failed to provide adequate service on the routes they won. They clearly had prioritized bilking the government over actually delivering the mail in a satisfactory manner.[21]

Woodward himself was unsure about how the case was coming together in the summer of 1881. To be sure, some progress was being made in terms of gathering testimony and evidence, but he wondered if it was going to be enough to secure indictments and convictions against Dorsey, Brady, and others who had been involved in the rigging of the contracts. Comparing the government's evidence to armaments, Woodward later said, "As the sultry summer wore away I became more and more painfully conscious that the condition of our magazines was far from justifying this tone of exultation" found in some newspapers. Although the government had uncovered some valuable evidence, "our armories were practically bare."[22]

If the Star Route prosecutions were like a military campaign, the government felt the need to summon seasoned reinforcements to bolster its attack. Although the prosecution was nominally under the control of George Corkhill, the District of Columbia's district attorney, he was preoccupied with the evolving prosecution of Guiteau for his attempt on the life of President Garfield. Moreover, with the approval of Attorney General MacVeagh, he had largely ceded control of the Star Route case to Cook. For his part, Cook already had been relying on the services of the former newspaperman Albert Gibson, but others joined the prosecution effort later in 1881. Coming into the fold were attorneys Benjamin Brewster, William Ker, and George Bliss.

In September, MacVeagh contacted Brewster, who was practicing law in Philadelphia and had earlier served as Pennsylvania's attorney general. Although they were both Republicans, the two men were not cut from the same political cloth: MacVeagh was a Half-Breed reformer, while Brewster was a one-time Democrat who had followed one of MacVeagh's great political foes, the Pennsylvania political boss Simon Cameron, into the Republican ranks, where he became a Stalwart. Political differences had not, however, stopped them from forming an enduring friendship. MacVeagh later described how the two Pennsylvania attorneys had become acquainted: "In an argument before the court I had indulged with the enthusiasm of youth in a quotation from one of the masters of the English tongue . . . and, as soon as the argument was over, Mr. Brewster came to me with a cordiality of greeting I shall never forget, and insisted upon my going to his house, sitting at his table, and spending the evening in his company; and there in his library he read to me from some of the masterpieces of our prose literature with which he was so familiar—from Milton, Burke, Lamb." Their friendship, rooted in a shared love of literature, would continue until Brewster's death in 1888.[23]

Brewster possessed a keen legal mind, boasted an impeccable lineage (he was a descendant of William Brewster, who had come to Plymouth Colony on the *Mayflower*), and sported a memorable appearance. He had been badly burned in a childhood accident, and ghastly scars still marred his face. But this disfigurement had not impeded Brewster's career. "Here was a man of illustrious lineage and sensitive soul whose face was rendered unsightly by burns at the age of five," one observer later wrote. "He made his own way in the world. . . . He never faltered. He met each responsibility with courage and humility."[24]

At the time MacVeagh approached him in the fall of 1881, Brewster was not familiar with many of the details of the Star Route "peculations" (the legal term then commonly used to describe the misappropriation of public funds). He had read about them only in a casual way. "I had a great deal to learn about them," he later explained. "I knew nothing of the cases except as I had read of them in a general way in the newspapers until Mr. MacVeagh appealed to me." Feeling that he had a duty to help the attorney general, Brewster accepted the offer and soon set about studying the details of the postal case.[25]

Brewster was not viewed as being politically active, and his appointment was seen as a sign that the Star Route prosecutors might not be unduly concerned with protecting the Republicans' Stalwart wing. The press generally praised the move as a necessary step to combat the impressive array of legal talent the defendants had been assembling. A midwestern newspaper was heartened by Brewster's appointment, arguing that "the government will need all the wits and brains it can employ to cope with [the] legal ability" of defense counsel.[26]

George Bliss, who joined the Star Route prosecution team at roughly the same time as Brewster, had served for several years as U.S. attorney for the Southern District of New York during the Grant administration. A graduate of Harvard, he had authored a few legal treatises and served on the commission that revised and consolidated criminal laws in New York City. Bliss's legal credentials were probably less important than his personal and political bona fides. Later termed "one of the most politically well-connected lawyers in New York," he was a Stalwart with longstanding ties to Vice President Arthur and Roscoe Conkling's patronage-friendly New York political machine.[27]

The attorney's connection with Arthur dated back to their service together in the Civil War: Bliss had been assistant adjutant general under Arthur's leadership in the New York State Militia. In the summer of 1861, Arthur, in his role as assistant quartermaster general, had overseen Bliss as the two men worked in concert to furnish soldiers with such essential items as uniforms, blankets, and underclothes. Their relationship had continued after the war, with both men getting drawn into the political orbit of Thomas Murphy, Arthur's predecessor as the collector of the Port of New York. They also had worked together to do the bidding of the Conkling machine in state Republican committees.[28]

Bliss and Arthur shared a fealty to Conkling, at least for a time. At one point, Bliss had been, in the words of a later study, one of "the Conkling machine's main lieutenants," and Conkling had arranged for his appointment by President Grant as U.S. attorney for the Southern District of New York in 1872. "The coterie who then surrounded the president and Mr. Conkling . . . were all my friends," Bliss later wrote in an unpublished autobiography. Yet Bliss apparently had broken with Conkling after the boss failed to fulfill a written promise to make sure that he was reappointed to another term as U.S. attorney. To add insult to injury, Conkling apparently never had consulted with him before deciding that another man should fill the role. Bliss later wrote of his profound disappointment over Conkling's lack of "manliness" in handling the matter, and the two never spoke again.[29]

There was some question as to whether Bliss, given his political ties, would zealously pursue those involved in Star Route graft. It was widely assumed that the attorney would squelch anything in the government's prosecution that might embarrass his longtime friend and political ally Arthur. And, because he was a Stalwart with onetime links to the Conkling machine, few people believed that he was a genuine reformer who cared much about rooting out corruption.

Before he agreed to join the team prosecuting the Star Route cases, Bliss had a frank conversation with Postmaster General James. He candidly addressed the possibility that his chief qualification for joining the prosecution team might be his close connection with the man who seemed to be on the brink of becoming president, rather than his acumen as an attorney. "Has the desire to employ me anything to do with Arthur's possible accession to the presidency?" he asked. If the bond with Arthur factored into his appointment, Bliss would decline the position, as it might "stir up the Star Route 'gang' at the outset of his administration" if Garfield passed away. After James reassured Bliss on this score, he signed on.[30]

Not everyone was sure that Bliss was being chosen purely on his merits as a legal practitioner. Demonstrating an enmity that would be an unfortunate hallmark of the relationships between members of the government's legal team, Cook, the special prosecutor, later said that Bliss was "an attorney of ordinary ability" who was chosen after several more talented men were eliminated from consideration. In his view, Bliss's principal qualification was his connection to the man poised to become president if Garfield died. "The chief and controlling consideration which led to the employment of Mr. Bliss was that he was an intimate personal friend of Mr. Arthur," Cook later said.[31]

Once he joined the prosecution team in September 1881, Bliss realized that getting the Star Route case ready for trial would be a tall order, given its enormous scope and complexity. Investigators and prosecutors would have to sort out a vertiginous array of routes, contractors and subcontractors, and payments in order to present a tidy and comprehensible case to the jury. "The magnitude and difficulty of the job you have got me into," he wrote to Attorney General MacVeagh, "grows upon me." Bliss worked tirelessly to master the minutiae of the cases, often laboring sixteen hours per day and staying up until 2 or 3 A.M. "I worked . . . continuously and constantly," he later said.[32]

It was the newcomer Brewster who suggested the appointment to the prosecution team of William Ker, an attorney from Pennsylvania. Ker hailed from "a family of fighters," according to one account: "They were all born so." He and his three brothers all had served with distinction during the Civil

War. Ker had enlisted as a twenty-year-old in 1861 with Company F, Twenty-Seventh Pennsylvania Volunteers, and the record he compiled in combat was an enviable one. Two of Ker's brothers, Edward and George, died of wounds sustained in battle. "The record of the Ker family as soldiers is a most conspicuous one," one of Edward's classmates recalled. "No family in Philadelphia can overmatch it."[33]

After his exemplary service in the war, Ker had become an assistant district attorney in Philadelphia. Brewster knew of his work and thought him to be a "faithful, diligent man," as he later put it. Furthermore, Ker was a Democrat, a fact that was sure to help undercut charges that prosecutors were hoping to protect the administration's Republican allies. He had actively participated in Democratic campaigns for many years, zealously promoting the party's candidates and castigating Republicans as corrupt and inept in every election cycle. (Such were Ker's qualifications as a Democrat that the party would later nominate him to run for a seat in Congress.)[34]

At first, Ker's duties were rather narrow—he was to focus solely on the technical aspects of drawing up indictments and pleadings—but he later took on a greater role and eventually helped present arguments in court. His expertise in drawing up pleadings was sorely needed by the prosecution team. According to Brewster, Bliss—whose background had been primarily in civil matters—professed to be hopeless about how to formulate criminal complaints stating a cause of legal action. "I am in a puzzle about the pleadings in these cases. I cannot draw them," he confessed to Brewster. "I have not the proper facility at it, and I have not the time." Preoccupied by other matters relating to the Star Route case, Bliss was happy to leave this technical and sometimes tedious work to Ker.[35]

In drawing up criminal complaints in the Star Route case, both Ker and Bliss realized that they faced a considerable obstacle: the murky and antiquated laws of the District of Columbia. Ker learned that when the nation's capital had been formally organized by Congress in 1801, it had simply adopted the laws of the state of Maryland as its own. Aside from laws that had been specifically amended or added by Congress in the intervening eight decades, those old, borrowed statutes were still in place, even though many of them had since been repealed or altered in Maryland. "This chaos," according to one later account, "made it almost impossible to tell what the law was or where to look for it."[36]

As he attempted to formulate the government's pleadings, Ker, a relative newcomer to the bar in Washington, often was bewildered. "I found there was a great deal of difficulty and complication attending the correct interpretation of the law," he later said. "They had their own law and their own practice here [in Washington], and I felt at a loss for want of somebody to consult who knew from experience something about the law and the practice of the courts here."[37]

As he struggled to determine which laws were applicable to the Star Route peculations, Ker might naturally have turned to Cook, who had practiced law in the capital for many years. Incredibly, though, Bliss told him that he was to have no contact with his ostensible colleague. "I was under the impression, and in point of fact I was told directly," Ker later said, "that I was to be especially careful not to converse with Mr. Cook or have anything whatever to say to him about the cases; not to tell him what I was engaged upon and not to let him see any of the indictments." Bliss further barred him from consulting with two other members of the prosecution team, Gibson and Corkhill, despite the fact that, as the district attorney for Washington, Corkhill presumably had some expertise on the district's laws and how they might be interpreted.[38]

Corkhill was a former newspaperman—he had once edited the *Washington Chronicle*—who was said to have owed his appointment as district attorney to his connection to U.S. Supreme Court justice Samuel Miller. (Both men had roots in Iowa, and Corkhill had married Miller's eldest daughter, Olive.) His friends loved and admired him. "An Irishman will give you the last penny in his pocket, a Scotsman will walk to the end of the earth to serve you, an Englishman will fight for you if you are in the right," one later wrote. "Corkhill was a happy combination of all three."[39]

Corkhill's new colleagues took a dimmer view of him. Bliss later said that he did not believe that the district attorney, a man with myriad social and political connections to the accused, "was in entire sympathy with the prosecution." In private communications with Brewster, Bliss was adamant that Corkhill should be removed from his position, insisting "that he would leave the cases if Mr. Corkhill was not dismissed from the District attorneyship, because he had no faith in him," as Brewster later put it. "He said Mr. Corkhill was treacherous; . . . that he was a trouble and a hindrance to the prosecutions, and if he were not removed would be the means of absolutely frustrating the work he, Mr. Bliss, proposed to do in the cases."[40]

It was generally understood that neither Postmaster General James nor Attorney General MacVeagh were especially fond of Corkhill either. Before long, word of their displeasure leaked to the press. "James, MacVeagh and other officers engaged in this prosecution have no confidence in District Attorney Corkhill whatever, and they make no secret of this fact," the *St. Louis Globe-Democrat* reported. "They do not charge that Corkhill has been influenced by any money considerations to favor the star-route ring, but they believe that social and personal relations, to say the least, so influence him. All officials concerned in the prosecution maintain that Corkhill has obstructed their progress from the first."[41]

The district attorney's dubious commitment to the Star Route cases was a central topic of discussion in September, when the prosecutors traveled to Elberon, New Jersey, the coastal hamlet where President Garfield was convalescing. It is unclear whether the bedridden Garfield's directly participated in any meetings related to the Star Route case, but most of the prosecution team, along with Postmaster General James and Attorney General MacVeagh, were present and discussed how the postal-fraud case would be presented to the grand jury in Washington. In these meetings, Gibson and Cook made plain their distrust of Corkhill, "stating substantially that he was in the interest of the other side," as Bliss later put it. He knew that MacVeagh "shared in the distrust of Colonel Corkhill."[42]

Although his handling of the Star Route case was suspect, there was one major impediment to removing Corkhill as district attorney: the shooting of Garfield. Guiteau had gunned down the president at the Baltimore and Potomac Railroad Station in Washington, which meant that his trial would take place in the nation's capital and that Corkhill, as district attorney, would prosecute him—potentially for murder, if the president failed to recover. Whatever his failings, many were reluctant to move against Corkhill as he prepared to try such a momentous case. Removing him might mean that Guiteau would walk free, which would be a disaster for the country and an everlasting embarrassment for Republicans.

Chief among those protecting Corkhill at this critical juncture was Vermont senator George Edmunds, the influential chairman of the Senate Judiciary Committee. Edmunds was present at the Elberon talks in September and made it plain that he thought Corkhill should remain in office, at least for the time being, so that the prosecution of Guiteau could proceed smoothly.

According to Bliss, the senator "took the position very decidedly that he would not under any circumstances assent to the confirmation of anybody in place of Colonel Corkhill as long as the Guiteau case was going on" and that the government "ought not to remove Colonel Corkhill at that time." Edmunds's view ultimately prevailed, and Corkhill remained in his post, even though almost no one believed that he was equal to the formidable tasks he now faced.[43]

As the government's attorneys squabbled over Corkhill's fate, they struggled to determine how to frame their case for presentation to the grand jury. Although it was apparent from the evidence that a massive fraud had been committed in rigging bids for Star Route contracts, Ker and Bliss labored to find which federal laws, if any, had been broken.

According to legal scholar Matthew Stephenson, "there wasn't a single turning point" in the battle to control political corruption in the United States. "The fight against corruption in the U.S. was a long slow slog, one that unfolded over generations." In the eighteenth and nineteenth centuries, there were scattered federal laws adopted to control bribery, extortion, theft, embezzlement, and mail fraud. For instance, the Crimes Act of 1790 contained provisions designed to protect the integrity of the judicial process, including a section specifically prohibiting the bribery of federal judges, while the Crimes Act of 1825 banned extortion under color of office. Yet these tepid measures were not zealously enforced and failed to make much of a dent in political corruption at the federal level. The state and local laws then in place were not much better at controlling or punishing wrongdoing by public officials. This permissive legal context had contributed to the rampant corruption of the Grant administration. Although over one hundred men would be convicted for their roles in the Whiskey Ring case, public officials generally seemed untroubled by the prospect of being held legally accountable for peculation.[44]

With federal law being so weak, Ker wondered if any of the prospective defendants, including former senator Dorsey and former second assistant postmaster general Brady, could be charged individually for their obvious misdeeds in manipulating Star Route contracts, such as having concocted (or accepted with a knowing wink) the many forged petitions that had been used to justify increased payments. But he strained to find any federal statute that would be applicable to the fraudsters' individual actions. "I studied that matter out very carefully," Ker later said, "and came to the conclusion that if every one of these people, Dorsey, Brady, and the others who were afterwards indicted, had done any one of these acts separately they would undoubtedly have been able to escape punishment, because there was no United States statute that met the case—nothing even at common law." They would have to be charged together—or not at all.[45]

Ker discussed the matter with Bliss, who said that only one viable alternative presented itself. As Bliss later noted, "In these cases, the United States criminal statutes are in a measure so defective that the conspiracy section was almost the only one which could be applicable." If they were to be brought to justice in court, the Star Route cheats would have to be charged together under Section 5440 of the Revised Statutes of the United States with having engaged in a criminal conspiracy.[46]

Even after they had found a law that might prove applicable to the Star Route frauds, prosecutors still faced some challenges. Section 5440 had been amended by Congress just two years earlier, in 1879, and the alleged offenses they were investigating had occurred both before and after the new measure went into effect, meaning that some defendants might have to be charged under two different versions of the same conspiracy statute.

Then there was the wording of the revised federal conspiracy statute, which stated that a crime is committed "if two or more persons conspire either to commit any offense against the United States, or to defraud the United States in any manner or for any purpose, and one or more of such persons do any act to effect the object of the conspiracy." The government would argue that Brady and the Star Route contractors had conspired to commit fraud—but against which agency of the government had they conspired to cheat? After scouring the pertinent statutes and case law, Ker came to the conclusion that federal law only specifically banned fraud against the Internal Revenue Department and not the Post Office itself. "You can defraud any other department as much as you please," he later testified, "[but] the revenue department is the only one around which any protection is thrown by statute."[47]

Ker and Bliss had to come up with a novel approach to the fraud question, as there had to be a specific criminal offense at the heart of the alleged conspiracy. Ker finally hit upon the notion that, even if the Star Route ring could not be charged with having attempted to defraud the Post Office, "Congress had created a new offense, a 'conspiracy to defraud the United States,' and that under that head would come any fraud which was made such at common law."

This expansive definition of fraud would be at the heart of the government's conspiracy case.[48]

For conspiracy charges to stick, it would not be enough for the government to show that members of the Star Route Ring had merely discussed how they planned to commit fraud in bidding on (and then inflating the value of) postal contracts. Prosecutors also had to demonstrate that the alleged conspirators had performed "any act to effect the object of the conspiracy" to commit fraud. They believed that they had ample evidence of overt acts that had furthered the conspiracy, such as the creation and submission of many forged petitions and affidavits that had been used to justify increased payments for expedition on the Star Routes.

Bliss concluded that it would be difficult for the government to prove that a criminal conspiracy had existed among the Star Route contractors and their confederates if prosecutors focused on irregularities in a contract for a single postal route. He believed that showing patterns of irregularities in multiple routes would offer the government its best chance to prove that a conspiracy had existed. In his view, "as you increase the number of routes . . . the aggregation, it seems to me, carries with it an increased presumption or inference of guilt which makes a case of that kind much stronger than any case based on a single route could be." Evidence of cheating in multiple Star Route contracts would create a kind of mosaic depicting, when viewed as a whole, a broader conspiracy.[49]

Prosecutors planned to reference a variety of Star Routes to show a clear pattern in how contractors had fabricated documents that were used to justify expedited service, which brought with it heftier payments from the Post Office. In their review of postal-contract irregularities, investigators had repeatedly found bogus affidavits stating that more men or horses were needed on particular routes or phony petitions from citizens purporting to call for faster and more frequent service to their towns. "There were all sorts of little frauds in connection with the business," Bliss later said, and, taken together, they provided evidence of a larger criminal enterprise.[50]

There were some risks in adopting this expansive approach. While it offered the advantage of showing patterns of fraud and offering abundant evidence, it inevitably meant charging more men for having been involved in the alleged conspiracy. It would be relatively straightforward to show that, say, three men had conspired to rig bids on a few postal contracts and then had performed overt acts to further the conspiracy. But charging a half-dozen men or more with a conspiracy that had involved myriad contracts would be an exponentially more complex task for prosecutors. Could the government prove that all of the alleged conspirators had known and had directly interacted with each other? And what if some had engaged in overt acts to further the conspiracy but others had not? Such matters would vex prosecutors throughout the Star Route case.

Yet another thorny question for prosecutors centered on who should be charged with having participated in the Star Route conspiracy. Investigators had uncovered evidence of deception in scores of postal routes throughout the Southwest, West, and Pacific Northwest, and they sensed that dozens of men—including the notorious Bradley Barlow, whose name had been almost synonymous with the frauds since the early 1870s—might have engaged in criminal activities. Attempting to charge and try all of them was sure to be a logistical and political nightmare that would be doomed to almost certain failure.

For prosecutor George Bliss, one group stood out: the Dorsey ring. The former senator and his accomplices, including Brady, had engaged in the grossest abuses of the contracting process, and there was plentiful evidence to prove it in court. "I stated that it was a strong case, and I state now, and am prepared to stand by it, that that case was the strongest one we had available to us for months and months," Bliss later declared, "and that I selected it, so far as I had anything to do with the selection, deliberately as the strongest case." For him, there was no question that Dorsey had been involved in the Star Route conspiracy. "I never expressed any doubt of his guilt," he later said.[51]

Special prosecutor William Cook believed that something other than an impartial weighing of evidence drove Bliss to so zealously pursue Stephen Dorsey and his accomplices in court. He later said that there "was unquestionably manifest personal feeling on the part of Mr. Bliss toward Mr. Dorsey." When asked if "Mr. Bliss decided to try that case on account of his personal enmity to Mr. Dorsey," Cook responded, "To a considerable extent."[52]

Whatever Bliss's motives, the prosecution eventually would settle on targeting several core members of the Dorsey combination for conspiracy to defraud the government: former senator Dorsey; his brother, John; and the men with whom they had bid on, and then manipulated, Star Route contracts: Rerdell,

Miner, Peck, and Vaile. Also facing legal jeopardy would be Brady, who had facilitated the scheme and received kickbacks during his tenure as second assistant postmaster general, and Post Office clerk William Turner.

Prosecutors would choose not to focus on a few men in Stephen Dorsey's orbit, at least for the time being. Albert Boone and James Bosler had deep connections to the former senator and his ring. Because they were so enmeshed in Dorsey's business dealings, their names would come up frequently as the federal prosecution developed. Yet they were never seriously targeted by prosecutors, ostensibly because the government hoped to keep its Star Route conspiracy case as narrow as possible.

Bliss was aware that prosecutors could not wait indefinitely to bring charges against the Dorsey combination, as there was a three-year statute of limitations in the federal conspiracy law. There seemed to be a consensus that charges needed to be brought within three years of the overt acts taken to further the conspiracy, which in this case chiefly were the actions benefiting the Star Route contractors taken by the second assistant postmaster general. In short, the clock was ticking.[53]

All seemed to be in order for the prosecution team when it came back from its visit to Elberon on September 15 and prepared to present the case against the Dorsey combination to the grand jury in Washington. There was just one problem: there was no grand jury to hear the Star Route case. Corkhill, the district attorney, had adjourned it until October 3. By then, the statute of limitations would have passed on several of the overt acts that had been taken to further the Dorsey ring's conspiracy. The prosecutors were sickened once they realized that it might be too late for them to take legal action against some of the men who had so brazenly defrauded the government.

MacVEAGH'S WATERLOO
The Prosecution Falters, Fall 1881

S pecial prosecutor William Cook learned of the grand jury's adjournment when he returned to Washington from visiting the ailing president's compound in coastal New Jersey. A colleague approached him at the train depot and gave him the unsettling news that the jurors had taken a formal break.

Cook was blindsided. District Attorney Corkhill had failed to tell him directly of his plan to let the grand jury recess from September 15 until October 3. "Neither from the district attorney nor from the grand jury or any member of it, or anyone else," he later complained, "had I any notice or information, direct or indirect, of the proposed recess, nor could I have anticipated it. It was unusual and extraordinary." Cook was especially bothered because it seemed that the grand jury would not go back into session until after the expiration of the statute of limitations on prosecuting many of the illicit acts of the Dorsey ring.[1]

Corkhill's baffling move to adjourn the grand jury for several weeks (ostensibly made because several jurors had asked to briefly leave Washington for vacation and business) threatened to kill the Star Route prosecution before anyone had even been indicted. Cook later grumbled that "it came near destroying all of the work in this case" just as prosecutors were on the brink of finally being ready to present their findings in court. For him, there was only one reason why Corkhill would do this: the district attorney wanted to scuttle the case. "I have never been able to ascertain any reason for the adjournment, unless it lay in the fact that by that adjournment it was supposed that the statute of limitations would operate against a number of cases that had been made up against star-route contractors," Cook later said. His impression "was that the grand jury was adjourned so as to prevent indictments being filed in the Star Route cases."[2]

News of the grand jury's adjournment was, in words of one newspaper headline, "A Startling Surprise," and it occasioned an avalanche of criticism in the press. Perhaps mindful of his role in the impending prosecution of Guiteau, many newspapers were hesitant to question Corkhill's motives in letting the panel take a break. A Boston newspaper stated that the unexpected recess was "a step which perhaps District Attorney Corkhill can explain, but the explanation is not apparent on the face of things." Another publication noted that while the adjournment "may have been [made] without reference to the Star Route cases," it undoubtedly helped the accused fraudsters and "was not accidental."[3]

The grand jury's problematic adjournment disconcerted the new prosecutor, who never had been much of a fan of Corkhill. "It was a surprise to me," Bliss later said of the adjournment. "I knew nothing about the circumstances under which it occurred, and I know nothing about the disputed facts as to how it came about, but at all events we found ourselves with the grand jury having adjourned." Yet Bliss did not think that Corkhill had acted in bad faith in allowing this pause for several weeks at a critical juncture in the Star Route prosecution. It had been nothing more than a predictable misstep from an incompetent and overmatched attorney.[4]

Corkhill fought back and publicly stated that he was blameless for the debacle. Responding to widespread criticism that he had bungled the Star Route case (perhaps on purpose), the district attorney insisted that it never really had been his to mishandle in the first place. Corkhill stated that after Cook had been brought in as special counsel for the cases in the previous spring, the district attorney "publicly withdrew from the care of them," according to one published report. To formalize this arrangement, Corkhill had written to Attorney General MacVeagh at that time and stated that he was retiring from the Star Route case and leaving it to Cook. (This assertion was easily substantiated: several newspapers had published the letter.) "He said that from that day to this, no one had consulted him regarding the cases, and he knew nothing of them. . . . From the outset of the investigation, he had been in absolute ignorance of every fact concerning the Star Route cases." Not being connected to the cases in any substantive way, he had been completely in the dark about Cook's plans to bring the case before the grand jury in Washington. (In his explanation, Corkhill conveniently omitted the fact that he previously had held that Cook, because of his title, could not present cases to the grand jury himself.)[5]

Cook and others complained that Corkhill's decision to allow a recess meant that the statute of limitations might expire before the Dorsey combination could be charged by the grand jury. In response, the district attorney pointed out that he could have brought the panel back into session at a moment's notice had anyone on the prosecution team explained the urgency of the situation to him. But, according to Corkhill, no one approached him on the matter. His explanations were, of course, self-serving, but it was not too farfetched to think that he had been completely preoccupied with the Guiteau case since early July and simply had trusted that the special prosecutor, Cook, would handle the details of the Star Route prosecution.[6]

Suspicion also fell on Attorney General MacVeagh, albeit for slightly different reasons. Some newspapers, noting his general displeasure with Corkhill, speculated that the attorney general had indeed signed off on the adjournment as a means of delaying the Star Route case until the district attorney could be removed from office. It was reported that MacVeagh had countenanced the recess (the possible statute of limitations issue notwithstanding) because he did "not wish that [Corkhill] should have anything to do with the Star Route cases."[7]

While members of the prosecution team tried to blame one another for the grand jury adjournment fiasco, the nation received devastating news: after battling for more than two months, President Garfield finally succumbed to his gunshot wounds on September 19, 1881. The fate of the Star Route cases now rested in the hands of a new president, Chester Arthur.

The elevation to the presidency of Arthur, a Stalwart and a thoroughgoing machine politician, anguished many who had hoped to see the Republicans finally repudiate the spoils system and embrace genuine reform. There was a widespread impression that he was little more than a machine lackey who would soon be overwhelmed by the responsibilities of office. "My God! Chet Arthur in the White House!" an incredulous friend was said to have exclaimed upon learning of Garfield's death. It was difficult to find anyone who believed that Arthur was equal to the herculean task of running the country.[8]

Arthur's unlikely rise to the presidency apparently gave some hope to those who were possibly facing criminal charges in the Star Route case. The new president was no Half-Breed; his wing of the Republican Party, the Stalwarts, was known for its resistance to reform. And so there was some question as to whether he would pursue the Star Route case as zealously as had Garfield, a man who had shown a greater willingness to confront corruption. One newspaper reported that the accused "lifted up their heads and came forth from their hiding-places in great glee when Garfield died," feeling that the danger of them being charged had passed.[9]

Arthur's well-known links to Stephen Dorsey led to widespread speculation that the former senator might be spared by the new administration. Dorsey's much-noted efforts (in Indiana and elsewhere) as secretary of the Republican National Committee had helped the Republican presidential ticket win a narrow victory in 1880; without his work in defeating the Democrats, Arthur might not have been in a position to ascend to the presidency. His apparent sense of obligation had been underscored at the celebratory dinner held in Dorsey's honor at Delmonico's in New York earlier that year, when the vice president–elect had directly and fulsomely praised his work on behalf of the campaign. The two Stalwarts apparently enjoyed a warm relationship grounded in their unswerving devotion to their party.

To the surprise of many, Arthur did not prove to be an inveterate enemy of reform once he occupied the White House. He took a pragmatic approach that balanced the needs and expectations of his party with the general public's desire to see the spoils system curtailed. Shockingly, Arthur would cut his ties to Conkling, who had been his political patron in New York, and, in 1883, he would sign into law the landmark Pendleton Civil Service Act, which codified the idea that positions in the federal government should be awarded to job applicants on the basis of merit rather than political patronage, the system so treasured by Stalwarts.

William Crook, a longtime White House factotum who served through five presidential administrations, later wrote that insiders realized Arthur had performed admirably in trying circumstances. "An administration that had promised to be torn by dissension, the prey of spoilsmen, defeated by the quarrels of Republicans among themselves, somehow straightened out into order, efficiency," he later wrote. "That is the sort of thing that becomes apparent to an office force. Somehow everything that had to be done was done, without regard to party or personal friendship. Conkling, Star Routers, [the] Navy—all could affirm that." (Arthur fought a long battle to bring the Navy into the modern era.) According to Crook, "Whoever did it, there was more work done, more order created, less of political scandal during Arthur's administration than the White House has often witnessed." This was telling praise from Crook, who had served in the scandal-plagued administration of Ulysses Grant.[10]

An early signal of Arthur's grudging tolerance—if not cautious embrace—of reform came with his handling of the Star Route case. He made it known that the prosecution was to proceed largely as it had under Garfield. As one study put it, the new president "showed from an early date his determination to probe the cases in a fair manner."[11]

Predictably, Bliss, Arthur's friend and political ally from New York, was quick to praise the president's commitment to prosecuting the Star Route case. Countering rumors that some lawbreakers would be shielded from prosecution because of their political connections, he publicly stated: "It is suggested that there is an intention to protect someone. There is no such intention." Bliss touted both his own determination to seek justice in the case as well as the new president's resolve: "If anyone believes that Chester A. Arthur will either directly or indirectly interfere to prevent the ends of justice from being accomplished, he doesn't know him; and if anyone believes I propose to 'let up' on any seemingly guilty man, unless he can be of use in convicting someone bigger or more guilty than himself, I am vain enough to think he doesn't know me." Contrary to popular belief, the Stalwarts would not stymie the Star Route prosecution.[12]

Bliss's comments were echoed by Brewster, who had joined the prosecution team only a week before Garfield died. From the outset of his administration, Arthur made it clear that he still wanted the Star Route prosecution to be a vigorous one. "When I went into office the first thing the president said to me was, he wished me to give [the Star Route cases] special and careful attention," Brewster later said, "and he would do any and all things that I should call upon him to assist me in having the cases thoroughly investigated and tried."[13]

President Arthur demonstrated his resolve to pursue the Star Route case in a variety of ways. When a worried Dorsey attempted to have a private interview with the new president (presumably to push once more for the case against him to be dropped), Arthur told him that he would have to abide by his customary practice of keeping his door open, thereby making secret discussions impossible. Dorsey redoubled his attacks on Postmaster General

James and Attorney General MacVeagh and continued to demand that he be investigated separately. Arthur, however, remained firm and refused to give him preferential treatment. "Arthur did not respond to Dorsey's importuning," in the words of one later account. "Perhaps he believed that the Star Route matter had gone so far that a public trial was necessary to satisfy everyone, and that a special investigation of Dorsey at this point would look like Arthur was trying to protect Dorsey."[14]

Albert Gibson, the newspaperman-turned-prosecutor, came to the conclusion that Dorsey's connections to Arthur, combined with the former senator's shameless and unrelenting lobbying for special treatment, actually made it impossible for the president to spare him. Showing leniency in such circumstances might have crippled the new administration from the outset. "Mr. Dorsey, having been connected prominently with politics, made a great deal of disturbance at that time," Gibson later said, "and owing to the fact that the gentleman who became president by the death of General Garfield had presided at a banquet at Delmonico's and made a speech in which Mr. Dorsey was eulogized, the administration felt incumbent upon itself, I suppose, to proceed against Mr. Dorsey, and I think that was the reason that case was taken and pushed." Ironically, Dorsey's closeness to Arthur was the very thing that made it difficult for the president—a man who was understandably sensitive to charges that he was little more than a stooge for the Republican Party's Stalwart wing—to show him favor.[15]

In addition to not intervening on behalf of Dorsey, Arthur began to remove from their positions several Post Office officials who had been implicated in the Star Route frauds. First Assistant Postmaster General James Noble Tyner, who had close ties to Brady, was among those forced out. Tyner did not seem to be directly implicated in any Star Route frauds. But a few years earlier, he had been dispatched to the West to investigate irregularities in postal contracts and services and had prepared a written report of what he had uncovered. Tyner had never published or otherwise distributed his findings, and there were accusations that he had suppressed the potentially unflattering write-up so that, in 1880, Congress would pass an emergency appropriation to fund the Star Routes for the remainder of the fiscal year. With Arthur's approval, Postmaster General James demanded Tyner's resignation when he learned about this matter.[16]

With Arthur's ascension to the presidency, the balance of power in the prosecution team shifted. Cook later said that Bliss, because of his longstanding relationship to the new president, essentially took over the Star Route case and shut him out of the decision-making process. "The significance was this: that because he was a friend of President Arthur's, the suggestions and views of Mr. Bliss in the conduct of the cases must be carried out, and that suggestions that might come from me would, of course, be of little or no importance if they antagonized those of Mr. Bliss," Cook later said. "Then Mr. Bliss had assumed to act wholly independently of me and ceased to hold any consultation with me." Always quick to point out real or perceived slights to his authority, he complained of being essentially demoted in favor of the better-connected Bliss.[17]

Cook claimed that Attorney General MacVeagh, recognizing Bliss's relationship to Arthur, approved the change in control and coordination. Having approached MacVeagh to protest "some of the spasmodic actions of Mr. Bliss," he was told to stand down. The attorney general informed him "that Mr. Bliss was an intimate friend of President Arthur's, and that as a consequence he would be compelled to place Mr. Bliss in control of the cases and allow them in the mode which he deemed best," Cook later said.[18]

Now working for a new president, the members of the fractious prosecution team tried to figure out if they could move forward with their case without securing indictments from a grand jury. As Gibson later said, the matter was examined in excruciating detail, with all of the attorneys scouring legal texts and canvassing their colleagues for ideas. Eventually, they hit upon the novel idea that they could proceed against the Dorsey combination by filing an "information" in police court. This unconventional route, which apparently had never previously been attempted in the District of Columbia, would allow prosecutors to bypass the grand jury altogether.[19]

The information would in effect replace a grand jury indictment, although the case would now have to be heard in police court rather than the district's criminal court (which was somewhat grandly known then as the Supreme Court of the District of Columbia). The venues were not equal: the police court typically dealt with only minor offenses, such as breaches of the peace, while the criminal court addressed more serious misdemeanors and felonies.

The prosecution team debated whether sidestepping the grand jury and simply filing an information would hold up in court, especially when the move was sure to be attacked by a bevy of very capable defense lawyers. At first, Bliss did not like the relatively unproven nature of the idea, and he opposed it. But seeing few other immediate options, he eventually came to favor it as a means of initiating criminal proceedings against some of the Star Route crooks before the statute of limitations expired.[20]

To research the possibility of filing an information in a conspiracy case, Bliss acquired and studied some rare English treatises on the law of conspiracy. Early on, he saw that the question of filing an information "turned upon the question of whether conspiracy was an infamous crime," as he later put it. He wrote to Cook about his understanding of the purview of the police court and how it might affect how they proceeded with the Star Route case. "Is the syllogism [that] police court has jurisdiction of all crimes not misdemeanors?" Bliss wondered. "If this is not an infamous crime, the police court has jurisdiction. If it is infamous, then an information cannot be granted."[21]

Intent on going through the police court, Bliss prepared a lengthy memorandum discussing whether or not conspiracy was an infamous crime. His research, though extensive, provided few clear answers. The District of Columbia's antiquated statutes were characteristically unclear on the subject, and there were no judicial precedents for the government's team of attorneys to reference from within the jurisdiction. The defendants were sure to challenge the information in court; in response, the prosecution team would have to invoke rulings from other jurisdictions and interpretations from legal treatises, neither of which would necessarily sway a judge.[22]

The deep and enduring fissures that characterized the work of the prosecution team were evident when it came time to formally draw up the counts of the information. Bliss trusted Cook so little that the ostensible colleagues separately drew up the two counts of the information. As Bliss later put it, the idea was, "I should nurse my baby and he should nurse his."[23]

The results were, in Bliss's later estimation, a disaster. Bliss paid little attention to Cook's count of the information until it had been sent to the printer. Upon reviewing the page proof, he realized that Cook had not named any of the parties in his count, choosing instead to simply reference the first count of the information, where Bliss had named all of the parties being charged. The horrified Bliss immediately recognized that any competent attorney would attack Cook's count as defective and have it thrown out of court. "Now, I do not pretend to be a criminal draftsman," he later noted, "but I was a good deal shocked at that carelessness." Prosecutors eventually rectified Cook's mistake, but it would not be the last time that they made a careless error in drafting materials to be submitted in court.[24]

On September 30, the government filed an information in police court against former Second Assistant Postmaster General Brady; John French, the former chief clerk in the Post Office's Contract Division; William Turner, another clerk in the same division; and Star Route contractors Samuel Brown and George McDonough. Prosecutors asserted that the men had conspired to use fraudulent methods in the manipulation of a contract for a route between Santa Fe, New Mexico, and Prescott, Arizona. As one newspaper report put it, they were charged with "conspiracy to defraud the United States by procuring irregular and extravagant additional compensation for carrying mails." The government alleged that the overt act that had furthered conspiracy had transpired on October 1, 1878, which meant that the three-year statute of limitations would have expired the following day.[25]

One name was notably absent from the two counts of the information: that of former senator Stephen Dorsey, who had been widely expected to be charged in some form for his role in the Star Route frauds. Other members of the Dorsey ring, including his brother John and his former clerk Montfort Rerdell, also were not named in the information filed by prosecutors in police court. Their absences puzzled many who had been following the case. Would they all get off so easily, without even having to defend themselves in court?

Bliss assured the press that Dorsey and his cronies had not been forgotten. "His case will be attended to next," he said of the former senator from Arkansas. "The other cases will be brought up in the regular way before the grand jury." The prosecution felt that they would not need to resort to filing an information against some key members of the Dorsey ring because it had been determined that many of their criminal activities could still fall within the statute of limitations. (This was one advantage of putting together a case that covered so much peculation over such an extended period: prosecutors believed that if they kept digging, they were bound to find crimes that fell within the statute of limitations.) There was still time for their cases to be handled in the customary manner by securing a grand jury indictment.[26]

Even with Dorsey's absence from the charges, many viewed the filing of information as a welcome sign that at least some of the Star Route conspirators finally were being brought to justice. "There is no longer any doubt," the *Mil-*

waukee Daily Sentinel observed, "that the Star Route mail cases are to be prosecuted with vigor." Another Wisconsin paper stated: "The Star Route thieves
. . . are trembling in their boots. They are satisfied that President Arthur's
administration will give them no rest—to their souls or their soles."[27]

Seeking to cut off criticism, several members of the prosecution team
spoke with reporters about the filing of an information and the quirky circumstances that had made it necessary.

"Is not this a new form of proceeding?" a reporter asked Bliss.

"Yes, but we were forced to do it by the adjournment of the grand jury until
next month," he replied. "We feared that before we could secure an indictment
before the grand jury, the three years' statute of limitation, within which our
case must be presented, would expire. The method we have selected is equivalent to an indictment and a warrant of arrest."

The reporter then zeroed in on why prosecutors, despite months of preparation and investigation, had not been able to present the Star Route case to
the grand jury in the customary fashion. "Then the adjournment of the grand
jury might have prevented a misfortune?" he asked.

"Yes," Bliss stated. "Whether it was done intentionally or not, I do not know.
Colonel Corkhill says it was not, but it came near destroying all of the work in
this case. But for the action we have taken this might have been accomplished."

Bliss was then asked how he thought the case would turn out. "Well, I gave
up, long ago, predicting the result in criminal cases, but on the testimony on
hand we shall ask twelve men to send the defendants to the penitentiary," he
stated. "In my opinion the evidence is ample and ought to convict."[28]

Prosecutors Gibson and Cook also defended the decision to file an information in police court. It was "regular in every respect," Gibson said matter-
of-factly. "It is not only provided for in the United States statutes, but there
is a long line of decisions from some of the ablest judges in the country to
sanction it." Hoping to make it seem like a routine occurrence, he asserted,
"a procedure by information is universally recognized in United States courts,
and in the courts of many of the states it is commonly practiced." For his part,
Cook claimed, "I can show a dozen opinions of the ablest judges to sustain the
regularity of the proceeding." The way prosecutors talked about it, the filing of
an information sounded like a run-of-the-mill legal maneuver.[29]

These assertions failed to impress the attorneys who represented the initial group of Star Route defendants, and they assailed the prosecution's novel

decision to proceed by an information. One unnamed lawyer told a reporter that, at least for the time being, the defendants would take a wait-and-see approach regarding the prosecution, as the government's move in police court was so unprecedented. He dismissed the government's filing as a ridiculous maneuver that would never hold up in court in Washington, even if it had been used with success in other jurisdictions. "It is hardly possible that they intend to try the cases simply on an information," he stated. "We have nothing to fear from them. We are confident of success, but we shall resist all irregular proceedings by every means in our power."[30]

Attorneys for the defendants quickly went to work, moving on October 4 to quash the information in police court before Walter Cox, a judge on the Supreme Court of the District of Columbia (who would soon preside over a far more grave proceeding—the murder trial of presidential assassin Guiteau). They argued that the court lacked jurisdiction in the matter, as the alleged offense, conspiracy, was an infamous crime that should have been heard in criminal court after the defendants had been indicted by a grand jury. Police court simply was the wrong venue for the case.

The attorneys making these arguments were an impressive group. Their number included veteran Washington lawyer Enoch Totten; Jeremiah Wilson, a former Republican congressman from Indiana; and Robert Green Ingersoll, the widely known orator and freethinker. Although he is perhaps best re-membered today for his iconoclastic lectures and essays (which earned him the moniker the "Great Agnostic"), Ingersoll was an accomplished lawyer who had once served as attorney general of Illinois. His presence in the case signaled that the government would have its hands full in court, however the proceedings played out.

In court, the defense attorneys divided up their task, each attacking the information as defective on different grounds. Wilson, representing Brady, asserted that there was simply no statute on the books in Washington that provided for proceeding through an information rather than securing an in-dictment. If prosecutors wanted to put the defendants on trial, he claimed, they had to first appear before the grand jury and secure a criminal indict-ment. That was the way it was done in the nation's capital.[31]

Ingersoll took a slightly different approach. While Wilson stressed the law, he focused on the facts alleged in the information that the government had filed. As presented by prosecutors, these facts were, in the defense attorney's view, jumbled and implausible. "I shall insist that the facts set forth in each and every count are contradictory, absurd, and impossible," he stated in court. "It is impossible any such acts should be done in any such way." Moreover, even if one could untangle the facts that had been alleged by prosecutors, they did not amount to any crimes as defined by federal law.[32]

As he addressed Judge Cox in court and endeavored to counter these arguments, Bliss spent a good deal of time trying to explain why the government had taken the unusual step of filing an information. "We have no desire to avoid the grand jury," he assured Cox, but the government had been left with little choice if it wanted to bring charges against this group of defendants. "We have no desire, under ordinary circumstances, to proceed outside of the general practice in criminal cases," Bliss said, "but the grand jury was not sitting when the statute of limitation was set to expire." The prosecutor acknowledged that filing an information was not a customary move, but he invoked a variety of legal authorities and judicial precedents to try to justify it.[33]

In his ruling on the defense's motion to dismiss the charges, Judge Cox zeroed in on whether the defendants were being charged with an infamous crime. Filing an information in police court might be appropriate for minor offenses such as misdemeanors. More serious crimes were another matter, however. Cox believed that Congress, in formulating federal law, "drew the line between infamous and non-infamous crimes at the wall of the penitentiary," as one newspaper put it. A crime punishable by a prison term was infamous and therefore required prosecutors to secure a grand jury indictment.[34]

This distinction was crucial in the cases at hand because the Star Route defendants had been charged with conspiracy. If found guilty, they faced sentences of several years in prison. In Cox's view, this meant that the defendants were accused of having committed an infamous crime. As a result, a grand jury indictment, not an information, was the only proper instrument for the government to bring them into court. "It seems to me, therefore, that the effect of the legislation we have been considering is to classify the offense here charged among the infamous crimes, and thereby to secure the defendants from prosecution of it, except on indictment," the judge ruled. "If that be so, of course the information never could have been rightfully filed." Cox threw out the information and told prosecutors that they needed to obtain a grand jury indictment if they wanted to bring conspiracy charges against the defendants. Although Cox's ruling applied only to the defendants in the immediate case, prosecutors knew its broader implications: they almost certainly could not come back to police court with serious charges in *any* Star Route case.[35]

Few people faulted Judge Cox for his ruling against the government. Federal prosecutors, however, were widely panned for having put themselves in the position of needing to attempt such an idiosyncratic legal ploy. If they had simply communicated with one another and thereby kept better track of the grand jury's schedule, they would have been able to take a more conventional route in pursuing the Star Route thieves, and their case would not have been thrown out of court. Their "neglect has caused a humiliating break-down on the part of the government," one newspaper sputtered, "and possibly a total miscarriage of justice." The *Milwaukee Daily Sentinel* joined in the chorus of criticism of the prosecution team, stating in an editorial: "It is not too much to say that the people will feel an intense disgust at the manner of the collapse of the Star Route cases yesterday. That the decision of Judge Cox in throwing the cases out of court is correct, is very probable, but this does not lessen the unpleasant character of the news, which indicates that the legal proceedings have been so shamefully mismanaged on the part of the government as to make it impossible to try the cases upon their merits at all."[36]

Other newspapers singled out the district attorney for having so badly bungled the Star Route prosecution. "But what of the poor, dawdling imbecile Corkhill?" the *Galveston Daily News* asked in a scathing editorial. "He has but two horns to his dilemma—fool and knave. On one or the other he is impaled—it may be both—for his mismanagement of the affair, and his boyish bickering with his associate counsel afford ample suspicion that he is free from neither the one nor the other."[37]

The *Chicago Daily Tribune* placed the blame squarely with the attorney general. The newspaper termed Judge Cox's ruling in the Star Route case "MacVeagh's Waterloo."[38]

The donnybrook was serious enough to make the new president's closest associates reconsider the composition of the apparently faltering prosecution team. A friend of Arthur's reported that Thomas C. Platt, the New York political boss, was urging that New Hampshire politician and attorney William Chandler "must be put in charge of the case at once" in order to salvage the Star Route prosecution and save the administration from further embarrassment.

(It was not the first time Chandler's name had come up: early in Garfield's term, he had been considered as a candidate for the position of solicitor general, but the attorney general had squelched the idea.) As for MacVeagh, he was "whining and begging . . . like an Irish biddy," Arthur's friend reported in a letter to Chandler. "He looks very blue."[39]

THIS LAMENTABLE FIASCO
The Prosecutors' Civil War, Fall–Early Winter 1881

Judge Cox's ruling represented a spectacular public failure for the federal government's team of attorneys in the Star Route case. Chastened and more than a little embarrassed, they attempted to regroup afterward and come up with new strategies to keep the prosecution moving forward. As always, serious questions lingered: Who was really in charge of the government's effort in this prominent corruption case? Were all of the prosecutors genuinely committed to bringing the culprits to justice? And, if so, could they work together effectively?

Despite the gloom and disarray, a beleaguered George Bliss soldiered on, working long hours to prepare the Star Route case for presentation to a new session of the grand jury in Washington. "Matters move slowly," he wrote to Attorney General MacVeagh in December 1881, "and you have no idea of the immensity of detail involved." Still, Bliss felt confident about the progress being made in the prosecution team's pursuit of the Dorsey combination, telling MacVeagh: "The Dorsey case is about ready for the grand jury. Only a few finishing touches are needed." And he was confident that the government would be able to take other tainted postal-route contractors to court as well. Although the Dorsey ring probably had garnered the most attention, the evidence being collected by federal investigators appeared "to indicate equal rascality" on the part of other contractors, and they could be pursued with the same vigor.[1]

MacVeagh, the nominal head of the prosecution effort, had found himself in an awkward position since President Garfield's death in September. A reformer, he had little interest in serving in the administration of the Stalwart Arthur and made it known that he intended to leave the cabinet as soon as was practicable. That he had been roundly criticized for his role in the police court debacle only made it more likely that he would leave the administration before the end of 1881. He publicly indicated that he intended to do so.

In a later conversation with the journalist Robert Underwood Johnson, MacVeagh explained that he had felt no personal hostility toward Arthur. He had found the new president to be a "good fellow" who had handled the grim circumstances of his succession to the nation's highest public office with dignity and tact. But Arthur had only "wanted to be a gentleman when it was not inconvenient," MacVeagh told Johnson. The president had shown no real interest in pursuing any reforms—or prosecuting any cases—that might upset his Stalwart allies or jeopardize his chances of becoming the Republicans' presidential nominee in 1884.[2]

On his way out the door, MacVeagh also exerted nominal control of the prosecution of Guiteau for the assassination of President Garfield. In November 1881, after the resounding failure of the Star Route cases in Judge Cox's court, it became clear that President Arthur was concerned that District Attorney Corkhill might not be up to the task of handling the Guiteau case. Politically, Arthur simply could not afford to let his predecessor's killer go free. Some in Washington worried that there would be a repeat of the notorious case of Congressman Daniel Sickles, who had successfully pleaded insanity after killing attorney Philip Barton Key in 1859. No one in the administration—and probably few people in the entire country—wanted a similarly unsatisfying outcome to be reached in the case of the man who had murdered the president in cold blood.

It was widely reported that Arthur pressed MacVeagh (who had formal control over Corkhill) about the Guiteau case at a tense November cabinet meeting, expressing concern that Corkhill was overmatched and needed assistance to handle the prosecution. MacVeagh tersely said that it was the job of the district attorney, not the attorney general, to ask for additional manpower if he felt it was needed. He also rebuffed Arthur's suggestion that, given the importance of the Guiteau case, MacVeagh himself should appear in court and represent the government. "MacVeagh maintained his position," according to one account of the meeting, "that it was beneath the dignity of the attorney general to appear in a criminal case."[3]

President Arthur reportedly was incredulous that MacVeagh, the nation's chief law-enforcement officer, apparently was reluctant to even lift a finger to help make sure that Guiteau, the nation's most infamous criminal defendant, was prosecuted and convicted. One report of the cabinet meeting stated that the incensed president told his attorney general that he should repair to the nearest law library and review the federal statutes that defined the duties of his office, as he seemed not to understand them.[4]

When descriptions of the strained exchange between the president and the attorney general emerged in the press, MacVeagh protested that they were complete fabrications. He insisted that he and Arthur had a wonderful working relationship. Few in the press believed him, however, and he received another hiding. "The country wants an attorney general in working clothes who is prepared to handle important cases without gloves," the *Chicago Daily Tribune* complained.[5]

Arthur also pressed MacVeagh regarding his involvement, or lack thereof, in the Star Route case. The president wanted the attorney general to play a more central role in the prosecution, but MacVeagh resisted, saying that he did not think it was appropriate. "I explained to him, at the time," MacVeagh later said, "how comparatively slight my relation to it had been; how, as a matter of fact, it had never entered my mind that I was to prosecute them in person; that, as a political officer, as well as the professional representative of the government, I thought it was impossible for the attorney general to undertake to try questions of that character in the criminal courts." He simply had no enthusiasm for the idea.[6]

At around this time, Arthur pressed MacVeagh to either stay in the cabinet or remain in the government's employ as a special prosecutor so that the Star Route case could be prosecuted satisfactorily. The draft of a letter from the president to his attorney general demonstrated Arthur's desire to maintain continuity. "It is apparent that the star route prosecutions are exciting & will continue to excite great public interest & concern," he wrote. "From the outset you have been connected with these cases & indeed in the general estimation identified with them. I greatly fear that your retirement from the control of them now might seriously imperil their success. Let me again express my sincere hope that you will reconsider your determination to resign from your office immediately and that you will continue [to be] its occupant at least until the cases in question have been disposed of."[7]

In his later conversation with Johnson, MacVeagh said the president had urged him to remain involved in the Star Route case at least in part because it was "a legacy of the Garfield administration" and not something that Arthur and his administration had initiated. To MacVeagh, it seemed as though the president wanted to keep the attorney general as a buffer between himself and the prosecution.[8]

MacVeagh doubted Arthur's resolve. The attorney general asked the president to remove from their positions some Justice Department employees who were sympathetic to the Star Route defendants, but Arthur demurred. He sensed that Arthur wanted him to remain in the Star Route case so that the attorney general could "be a screen between him and the people," shielding the president from criticism and responsibility. This was not an option for MacVeagh, a man who prided himself on his integrity. "MacVeagh said that he saw that it was hopeless to convict in the presence of the public sentiment inspired by the new administration. . . . His position was frankly, plainly and repeatedly stated to Arthur by MacVeagh and, as he phrased it, the sinning was deliberate and against the light," as Johnson later wrote. Summing up MacVeagh's feelings about Arthur's approach to the Star Route case, the journalist stated that the new president simply was "not earnest in the matter."[9]

After much speculation, MacVeagh's stormy tenure as attorney general drew to a close. His confidant Henry Adams despaired over what his departure signified for the future of reform, writing to the Massachusetts Republican Henry Cabot Lodge: "Our friend MacVeagh, after an heroic and desperate as well as prolonged struggle to drag President Arthur into the assertion of reform principles, has utterly and hopelessly failed. The new administration will be the centre for every element of corruption, south and north. The outlook is very discouraging." Shortly thereafter, he invited Lodge to Washington but warned, "You certainly will not find many reformers; all that swarm have vanished like smoke, and even I have ceased to lisp the word."[10]

Adams wrote directly to MacVeagh and expressed his sadness over the circumstances of his friend's departure from the cabinet. "I assume as a matter of course that the machine is to rule us henceforth," Adams stated, "and that there can be no place for you in an administration of that nature." He despaired that MacVeagh's resignation meant that he was now without any reform-minded allies in Washington; everyone else, it seemed, was a Stalwart. "I do not like to be left alone in Washington without a single individual to sympathize in my feelings. A single man in a hostile crowd is about equally ridiculous whether he cries out, or holds his tongue. You have rather a gift at crying out."[11]

MacVeagh's successor as attorney general was none other than his friend Benjamin Brewster, who had been part of the prosecution team in the Star Route case since September. Echoing Adams's lament over MacVeagh's departure, the wife of James Blaine, the Half-Breed leader, wrote: "Brewster is made attorney general. All the Stalwarts are going in, and though the mills of Arthur may seem to grind slow, they grind exceedingly fine."[12]

Aware that his predecessor's commitment had been questioned, Brewster made it clear that he intended to continue to pursue the Star Route case with genuine dedication. "These prosecutions must be earnestly pressed; the trials must be earnestly pressed; the trials must be prompt and the cases must be well prepared," he stated. And he would continue to play a hands-on role. "I have resolved that my duty will require me to take active part in the trials in court, and propose to present with you and in person lead the prosecution for the United States," Brewster wrote to Bliss.[13]

Brewster, unlike MacVeagh, felt that he had the full backing of President Arthur in pursuing the Star Route prosecutions. "When I went into office the first thing the president said to me was, he wished me to give them any especial and careful attention, and he would do any and all things that I should call upon him to assist me in having the cases thoroughly investigated and tried," Brewster later said. "And, from the beginning to the end, he has continued to act in that spirit, has always assisted me, confided in me, and strengthened me in everything I have done. I feel that the President's help and confidence have been of very great value to me in pursuing those cases." In Brewster's view, there was no ambivalence in the White House: with the nation watching, Arthur wanted an assiduous prosecution in the Star Route case.[14]

According to Brewster, the president seemed pleased with the progress that had already been made in the Star Route case (the grand jury and police court debacles notwithstanding) and expressed his desire to see it continue. "I want this work to be done as you are doing it, in the spirit in which you are doing it; I want it to be done earnestly and thoroughly," Arthur told Brewster. "I desire that these people will be prosecuted with the utmost vigor of the law. I will give you all the help I can. You can come to me whenever you wish to, and I will do all I can to aid you."[15]

As MacVeagh left office and Brewster took over as attorney general, Arthur himself publicly affirmed his commitment to pursuing the Star Route case. In his first annual message to Congress, submitted late in 1881, Arthur referenced the development of the prosecution, and promised that it would continue until all of the bad actors, whatever their status or political affiliations, were brought to justice in court. "I have enjoined upon the officials who are charged with the conduct of the cases on the part of the government, and upon the eminent counsel who, before my accession to the presidency, were called to their assistance," he noted, "the duty of prosecuting with the utmost vigor of the law all persons who may be found chargeable with frauds upon the postal service."[16]

Arthur's annual message that year also was notable because, as a biographer later put it, "the erstwhile party hack proclaimed his support for civil service reform." This came as a shock to just about everyone. The Stalwart referenced an earlier statement in which he had claimed that "no man should be the incumbent of an office the duties of which he is for any cause to perform; who is lacking in the ability, fidelity, or integrity which a proper administration of such office demands." In calling for reform, the president held out the British civil-service system, with its emphasis on using merit and professional experience in evaluating job candidates, as a model.[17]

Arthur's belated call for change came as a happy surprise to reformers like E. L. Godkin of the *Nation,* who termed it "an encouraging sign of the times." Spurred in part by Arthur's apparent souring on the spoils system, Democratic senator George Hunt Pendleton of Ohio promptly reintroduced a dormant bill aimed at revamping and modernizing the federal civil-service system. For the time being, Pendleton's bill went nowhere, but the fact that it had been introduced at all encouraged reformers, who had despaired over Arthur's ascension to the presidency.[18]

Even with Arthur warming to reform, several lingering problems still threatened to derail the Star Route prosecution as Brewster took over the Justice Department late in 1881. No one, for instance, seemed pleased with District Attorney Corkhill, who was nominally in charge of both the Guiteau murder prosecution and the Star Route case. Brewster himself professed to think that Corkhill ought to take command of the postal-corruption case, but other members of the prosecution team insisted that the apparently overmatched district attorney was actively undermining their work. Prosecutors Ker and Bliss approached the attorney general and informed him that Corkhill "would refuse to sign the indictments when they were presented to him, and would put them in his pocket, and the practical result would be that the statute of limitations would have run," as Brewster later summarized. In their view, if the Star Route case was to have any chance of succeeding, Corkhill had to be ousted from his position.[19]

President Arthur apparently signaled to Brewster that he would remove Corkhill if he found it absolutely necessary, but the attorney general hesitated because of the district attorney's leading role in the prosecution of Guiteau. Brewster believed that, as he later put it, "it would be a very unfair thing and a very impolitic thing to put him out of the district attorneyship when he was in charge of that case, which was one of national importance." Unsure of what he should do, Brewster spoke with George Edmunds, the influential chair of the Senate Judiciary Committee, which would have to give its imprimatur to Corkhill's ouster and the appointment of his successor. Edmunds had been approached earlier in 1881 about the possibility of removing Corkhill, and he remained opposed to the move because it might compromise the prosecution of Garfield's assassin. "We talked the matter over," Brewster later said of his conversation with the senator, "and he agreed with me it would be a very harsh and a very impolitic thing to put Mr. Corkhill out at that time and under the circumstances." Simply put, the timing was awful.[20]

With matters reaching the point of crisis, Brewster eventually confronted Corkhill with his concerns. Mincing no words, the attorney general made it clear that, with the full backing of President Arthur, he could end the district attorney's tenure in office at any time if he doubted Corkhill's integrity or found his performance to be lacking. "It is in my power now," Brewster warned, "to remove you on the spot."[21]

Corkhill realized that his job was on the line and did his best to reassure Brewster that he was still capable of fulfilling his duties as district attorney. He acknowledged that he found himself in an awkward position regarding the Star Route case "because he had personal relations with some of the defendants, and it would have been an unpleasant thing to have had to proceed against them," as Brewster later put it. But "notwithstanding that consideration, he would have proceeded against them" if the prosecution team had not botched the process of bringing cases before the grand jury before its term expired in October. That gaffe had not been his fault, Corkhill said. He had been transparent with everyone—including MacVeagh, Brewster's predecessor as attorney general—about his plans.[22]

In referencing the concerns voiced by Ker and Bliss, Brewster told Corkhill that the prosecution team doubted that the district attorney possessed the will or wherewithal to proceed with the Star Route case if grand jury indictments were secured. Corkhill insisted that he would pursue the case if the chiselers were indicted and said that he would face the consequences if he failed to move forward. "Mr. Attorney General, if you will produce those bills of indictments to me, instead of caviling over them as you have been told I would, I will put my name to them on the spot, in obedience to your command," Corkhill declared, "and if at any time in the course of the proceedings you find me or hear of me doing anything which indicates that I am not faithful to the Government, I am willing to be removed."[23]

Even with Corkhill's role at least momentarily clarified, the prosecution team still faced internecine warfare. Just as some people doubted the district attorney's commitment to the Star Route cases, others continued to wonder if attorneys William Cook and Albert Gibson really were serving the interests of the government. Patrick Henry Woodward was particularly reluctant to question the principles of Gibson, as the Post Office investigator had been largely responsible for bringing the former New York *Sun* reporter into the prosecution fold in the spring of 1881. In short order, however, he came to realize that Cook and Gibson were in fact not fully devoted to the prosecution's cause.[24]

Gibson's peculiar behavior throughout the fall and winter of 1881 was a cause for concern for both Woodward and Bliss. "In August or September, 1881, the attitude of Mr. Albert Gibson towards certain combinations [of contractors] . . . underwent a sudden and remarkable change," Woodward later said. In addition to prosecuting contractors who had engaged in fraudulent bidding, Post Office officials were working to reduce services and bring down the overall costs of existing postal routes. Gibson, who previously "had been the zealous advocate of sweeping reductions of service," now argued that the government "was going too fast and too far" in trying to cut costs. This strange change of heart—Gibson had, after all, made a career of decrying waste and fraud during his days with the *Sun*—raised eyebrows in the government camp, and several insiders, including Brady's successor as second assistant postmaster general, Richard Elmer, "began to suspect him of treachery," according to Woodward.[25]

Woodward pointed to a curious incident involving defense attorney Robert Green Ingersoll, who represented several allegedly crooked postal contractors (and would later play a major role in the Star Route trials). One day, Ingersoll met with Elmer and sought to clarify a matter involving one of his clients.

Elmer, unable to hide his suspicions that Gibson was working for the other side, laughingly told him, "Yes, your associate counsel, Mr. Gibson, took the same view."[26]

Woodward's displeasure with Gibson only intensified after he received potentially damning information from an acquaintance named William Lilley, who was intimately familiar with shady dealings in Washington. In December 1881, Woodward learned from Lilley that at some point Gibson had become the paid agent of the contractors on a route from Phoenix to Prescott, Arizona, that had drawn intense scrutiny from prosecutors as having been fraudulently contracted. Thus alerted, Woodward checked the government's files on the Arizona route and found a document written by Gibson that flatly declared, "There is no proof of fraud in this case." Gibson's analysis found that there were suspicious circumstances surrounding the route, among them the fact that the value of the contract had increased by a factor of seventeen since it had been awarded (from the original bid of $680 to $11,640). Nonetheless, he found that the additional payment was warranted by the improved services that the contractors were providing on the route.[27]

Woodward could not fathom Gibson's internal report on the suspicious Arizona route. Among all of those being reviewed by prosecutors, "this is one of the very worst routes of the lot," the seasoned investigator later said, "not more than two or three being able to compete with it in pre-eminence of bad-ness." He found that the annual pay for the route actually had increased by a factor of forty-eight in a period of nine months, from the original bid of $680 to $32,640. If Gibson could not find fraud in such a brazen manipulation of a postal contract, then "there is no proof of fraud in any case arising under the administration of Tom Brady," Woodward later told Congress. "If there was no proof of fraud in this case, it was the duty of the investigators to confess to their superiors that they had raised a clamor about nothing; to close their rooms, to seek other work, and to save the Government the cost of pursuing a useless inquiry further."[28]

Bliss also was stunned by Gibson's oddly lenient analysis of the irregular Arizona postal route. "The papers [files] indicated that it was one of the very worst cases of all," he later told Congress, with the documents showing that payments had increased exponentially immediately after the contract had been awarded. Yet Gibson inexplicably had found that no fraud had been committed, despite the abundant evidence to the contrary. "Mr. Woodward was as much astonished at finding this report on file as I was," Bliss stated.[29]

Finding Gibson's sunny review of the obviously fraudulent Arizona contract was the breaking point for Bliss. "From the time my eyes struck that report," he admitted, "whatever remaining vestiges of belief I had that Mr. Gibson was honest and sincere in his efforts on behalf of the government, were all dissipated." In his mind, there was no longer any doubt that Gibson's integrity had been compromised.[30]

Although he had been largely responsible for bringing the former reporter into the prosecution team, Woodward reached a similar conclusion. "The presence of Mr. Gibson had become unbearable," he later said. "No one could foresee what might be the next manifestation of his apparently innate and incurable depravity."[31]

Gibson would not survive the calendar year as part of the prosecution team. He was forced to resign his position on December 28, 1881. Gibson chalked up his departure to politics. When he was later asked why he had been forced out, he claimed, "I don't know, further than it was supposed that I was not of the same politics [as] the gentlemen in power." Gibson made no mention of the allegations that he had betrayed the prosecution.[32]

10

FROM THE SEWERS OF CALUMNY

The Press v. the Prosecutors, Winter 1881-1882

William Cook endured withering criticism throughout the Star Route case. His appointment as special prosecutor in the spring of 1881 was widely panned, with many observers expressing astonishment that a lawyer with such a miserable reputation had been placed in such a consequential role by the federal government. Matters did not improve as the case sputtered forward. His fellow prosecutors repeatedly questioned his tactics and motives, as did many newspapers. Cook was repeatedly denounced, for instance, by the *National Republican*, a caustic Washington newspaper that rarely had anything good to say about the government's handling of the Star Route case (or, as assassin Charles Guiteau so often pointed out, President Garfield).

Tom Brady, one of the primary targets in the Star Route prosecution, reportedly had an ownership stake in both the *Evening Critic* in Washington and the *National Republican*. That the former second assistant postmaster general (and onetime Muncie, Indiana, newspaper owner and editor) had close ties to the *National Republican* was an open secret. In his home state, the *Indiana State Sentinel* noted, "General Tom Brady owns a Gatling gun in the shape of a newspaper. The gun is in Washington." In the East, other newspapers routinely ridiculed the *National Republican*'s links to those accused of having manipulated postal contracts. In Washington, the *Evening Star* termed it the "evening organ [of] the Star Route gang"; in New York, the *Sun* called it the vehicle of Dorsey and joked that the newspaper would soon receive a glowing endorsement of its views "signed by all the Star Route ring."[1]

Judging from the *National Republican*'s coverage of the postal fraud scandal, it was not hard to see why rival publications mocked it as a mouthpiece for

Brady and others under investigation. Brady was widely assumed to have been involved in the scheme to manipulate Star Route contracts, but the *newspaper* ignored the mounting evidence indicating his guilt and doggedly defended him against accusations of wrongdoing. "There is not a single particle of proof that General Brady secured a single dime by means of any contracts that were created, extended, expedited, or in any other way affected by his action," the paper argued in one typical editorial. It categorically denied that Brady had done anything wrong.[2]

And the *National Republican* even went a step further. It often suggested that *no one* had committed any crimes in relation to postal contracts and that the government's investigation amounted to little more than a political witch hunt. "It has not yet been ascertained that there are any 'Star Route thieves,'" the newspaper claimed in June 1881, "or that anything has been stolen." At one point, it memorably dismissed the government's entire investigation into the matter as being "the exhalations of mephitic gases from the sewers of calumny."[3]

Brady's newspaper went to great lengths to claim that it did not necessarily object to the idea of the government investigating the possibility that frauds had been committed in connection to Star Route contracts. It contended that it instead took issue with the government's methods of probing what had—or, in the case of Brady, had not—happened. "The *Republican* has not at any time opposed or discouraged the investigation," the paper editorialized. "What it does denounce violently is the gross and open determination of Gibson, Woodward & Co. to befoul men in advance of investigation. It is a crime to assassinate reputation." And throughout 1881, the *National Republican* was especially concerned about protecting the reputation of a man reputed to be one of its owners, the much-maligned Brady.[4]

The *National Republican*'s clearest effort to derail the Star Route case came, perhaps not coincidentally, not long after Brady was forced from his position as second assistant postmaster in the spring of 1881. After Brady's demise, the newspaper made good on a series of threats to release correspondence that might embarrass President Garfield. On May 5, newspapers throughout the country published a letter that Garfield had written in the previous summer to Jay Hubbell, the chairman of his presidential campaign. "Please say to Brady," the Ohioan had written, "that I hope he will give us all the assistance possible. I think he can help effectually." (Given Brady's wealth, it was assumed by readers that this assistance would come in the form of substantial cash donations to the campaign.) He went on to inquire, "Please tell me how the departments generally are doing." Many believed that this mention of "departments" was a reference to the dubious custom of forcing government clerks to contribute to political campaigns, an element of the patronage system that civil-service reformers had long wanted to eliminate.[5]

The dissemination of what would become known as the "Dear Hubbell" letter was almost assuredly the work of an embittered Brady, and his newspaper made the most of the revelation to discredit President Garfield. The *National Republican* pointed to the letter's contents as evidence that Garfield had engaged in "the extortion of 'campaign funds'" from federal employees and Star Route contractors to help him win election the previous fall. It also deplored "General Brady's treatment," as one headline put it, wondering, "Was it honest to demand this money of Brady?" The implication was that Garfield was a rogue, and a hypocritical one at that, for having solicited financial help from Brady and Star Route contractors—the very men he was now persecuting—during his 1880 presidential campaign.[6]

The "Dear Hubbell" letter embarrassed Garfield, but he refused to let Brady and the *National Republican* deter him from pursuing anyone who might be implicated in the Star Route swindles. "I determined when I entered upon the performance of my duties to have a thorough investigation of the alleged Star Route frauds," he said in a public statement after the letter was released. "Having made up my mind to have this, nothing could swerve me from my course." The inquiry into the irregularities in postal-service contracts "will proceed until its results can be made equally [as] public" as the Hubbell letter. And Garfield proved true to his word in his brief time in office: under his watch, the investigation moved forward despite the fact that it threatened to implicate prominent supporters of his presidential bid, including Brady and former senator Dorsey.[7]

Although its campaign against President Garfield proved ineffective, the *National Republican* did not stop trying to shore up Brady's embattled reputation. A large part of this rehabilitation effort involved merciless attacks on Postmaster General James, who helped engineer Brady's removal from office. Whenever the opportunity presented itself, the newspaper lashed out at James and accused him of impropriety. Under the headline "Prosecute Him," the *National Republican* claimed that he had enriched himself with thousands of dollars in fines and forfeitures, "a plundering of the public Treasury for which he should be branded a Star Route thief and handed over to [William] Cook for indictment. . . . Let no guilty man escape." This was all pure fiction, of course; James had a sterling reputation, and few people questioned his integrity.[8]

The newspaper's attitude toward the current postmaster general was perhaps best summed up in a line from an editorial it published in November 1881: "Oh humbug!" the *National Republican* huffed. "Thy name is Thomas L. James."[9]

James was not the only government official singled out for criticism by Brady's newspaper. During his brief but rocky tenure as attorney general, the *National Republican* pilloried Wayne MacVeagh, routinely characterizing him as lazy and woefully ineffective. The headlines of one typically negative story in June 1881 asserted that he was "Neglecting His Duty" and "Not Earning His Salary."[10]

For Henry and Marion Adams, the attacks in the *National Republican* only served to enhance the stature of MacVeagh, their great friend. She wrote in a letter to her father of her sympathy for the attorney general and James, "whom the papers owned by Brady and Dorsey here are blackguarding in a way calculated to raise them in the esteem of all decent folks." She suggested that the attacks—coming as they did from scoundrels—burnished the reputations of both members of the cabinet.[11]

Prosecutors William Cook and Albert Gibson were scarcely better than MacVeagh and James, according to the *National Republican*. The newspaper expressed outrage when Cook was appointed as a special prosecutor in the Star Route case: it referred to his ignominious legal career by calling him "Fifty-dollar Billy" (presumably because he used cash payoffs to secure acquittals for his clients) and insisting that he was notoriously "skilled in manipulating perjurers." When they got to work on the Star Route case, the *National Republican* alleged, Cook and Gibson were predictably underhanded suborners of perjury who proved fond of "committing felonies to procure testimony" against perfectly innocent public servants like Brady.[12]

Almost the entire prosecution team came under fire from the *National Republican* in November 1881, after the government, having failed to secure grand jury indictments, stumbled in its effort to pursue the Star Route case in police court by filing an information against several of those accused of wrongdoing. One headline in the newspaper blared, "The Duplicity of Cook, Gibson, James, and MacVeagh Exposed—The Proceedings a Shameful Fiasco."

Returning to a familiar theme, the *National Republican* openly wondered if the government would be able to mount any kind of case against any of the alleged Star Route thieves, among them the wrongly accused Brady. "It will soon be in order to inquire whether Wayne MacVeagh, Albert Gibson and William Cook are actually in possession of any evidence which would convict anybody of postal frauds, in that *they* may be indicted as accessories after the fact for concealing such evidence," the newspaper thundered. "William A. Cook cannot look solemn enough or wise enough to make anybody believe that he and his associates would not gladly and immediately produce some evidence of unlawful conduct on the part of Thomas J. Brady if they had any."[13]

Curiously, one name was generally absent in the *National Republican's* frequent attacks on the Star Route prosecution team: George Bliss. Although the newspaper often dragged his colleagues through the mud, Bliss usually escaped censure. There was no disparaging wordplay based on his name, no mockery of his lawyering abilities, no dredging up of past indiscretions.

This kid-glove treatment might have been a function of Brady's reported efforts to sell the *National Republican* to a group of investors who were sympathetic to President Arthur and wanted to establish a publication in Washington that was closely allied with his administration. As another newspaper put it, "There is no doubt but that this paper is to be recognized by Mr. Arthur as, to some extent, a mouthpiece of the administration." The ranks of the investors interested in the Brady's newspaper included none other than Bliss, the well-connected Star Route prosecutor.[14]

Although the details of the transaction remain murky, it is clear that Bliss was part of a group of men who negotiated with Brady to purchase the *National Republican* in the fall of 1881 and the early months of 1882. Banker John Walsh, who seemed to know many of the details of this peculiar deal (and many others), later said of Bliss: "I understood that he, with twenty-nine other gentlemen, friends of President Arthur, purchased the paper, each putting in $1,000. . . . Mr. Bliss commenced negotiations with Mr. Brady for the purchase of Brady's interest in the paper about the time the prosecutions began" in the Star Route case.[15]

Walsh claimed that Bliss was joined in this venture by the ever-present William Chandler, the New Hampshire Republican who became Arthur's secretary of the navy early in 1882. Other reputed shareholders in the *National Republican* included First Assistant Postmaster General Frank Hatton (who would be appointed postmaster general by Arthur in 1884). Walsh was indignant that a newspaper that was so vocal about the Star Route cases came under the control of these "friends of the administration," particularly Bliss, a member of the prosecution team. "The spectacle was presented," he sputtered, "of a gentleman engaged as a representative of the government in prosecuting certain defendants, while at the same time the paper of which he was part owner was denouncing the prosecution and abusing the witnesses for the prosecution." Walsh accused Bliss of becoming enmeshed in the *National Republican* deal with Brady while the former second assistant postmaster general was being investigated for his role in the Star Route frauds. As Bliss was framing criminal charges against Brady, Walsh asserted, the two men were involved in a business transaction—one that was designed to help burnish the blotchy reputation of President Arthur.[16]

Bliss vigorously denied these assertions of wrongdoing. "I had no negotiations with Brady," he later said. "I never spoke to Brady in my life in any manner; the only time I ever saw him was when I was prosecuting him. I had no negotiations with him, and nothing to do with him." The *National Republican* itself also denied that Bliss had bought the publication from Brady. "It is not true," the paper later stated flatly, "that the *Republican* has been purchased by Mr. George Bliss."[17]

Prosecutor William Cook later contradicted Bliss and the *National Republican* on this score, insisting that Bliss had divulged his efforts to purchase the newspaper. He also stated that Bliss had wished to keep the negotiations a secret from his fellow prosecutors. "It is true that Mr. Bliss did state, earnest and emphatically to me, that he had purchased the *Republican*," Cook later said in testimony before Congress, "but that I should not let it be known to Mr. Gibson or anyone else." The news had perplexed Cook, who had immediately recognized the enormous conflict of interest of Bliss doing business with such a prominent defendant in the main postal fraud case. As he later said in his testimony, "I did say that I regretted, in view of Mr. Bliss's connection with the Star Route cases, that he had been engaged in any way in the purchase of the *Republican* from Mr. Brady or anyone else; that I would not have, under any consideration, engaged in negotiating with anyone involved in the alleged Star Route crimes."[18]

In his later testimony before Congress, Bliss made contradictory statements when he attempted to explain his role in the acquisition and operation of the *National Republican*. At one point, he stated that he never had influenced the newspaper's coverage of the postal fraud case or of anything else. "I had no control over it," he said of its reporting, "and I had nothing to do with it." But Bliss also claimed that he had been motivated to become involved in the newspaper because he had hoped to make its coverage of the Star Route case more sympathetic to the prosecutors, which seemed to suggest that he could in fact influence the reporting. "I went into it for the purpose of seeing if I could prevent some of the attacks which were being made upon the prosecution," Bliss stated, "and from the time that the paper passed into the possession of the gentleman who purchased it in connection with me, those attacks ceased." He later claimed that he had forced the dismissal from the *National Republican* of a few reporters who had written items for the paper "that had no business to be there."[19]

Many people who followed the *National Republican*'s coverage of the Star Route cases doubted whether Bliss was able to make its coverage any more favorable to the government. The *New York Times* argued that he was mistaken in his claim that the Washington paper's tone changed once he, Hatton, and other Arthur backers took over its control early in 1882. "A reference to its files passim will show that long after [they] became responsible for its conduct," the *Times* stated, "it continued to heap abuse of all kinds upon the persons engaged in the effort to get the Star Route thieves behind the bars."[20]

Chandler's biographer, Leo Richardson, later would do his best to gloss over his subject's role in the *National Republican*, arguing that he had done his best in an unusual situation. Richardson placed most of the blame for the paper's overheated coverage on Hatton. He "seems to have been in command and under him the journal maintained a steady opposition to all types of reform," Richardson noted. (Hatton also reportedly used his position in the Post Office to benefit the paper.) But the biographer was forced to admit that the *National Republican* had a vile reputation even after it was taken over by Bliss, Chandler, Hatton, and the others who were aligned with President Arthur. He noted that the *Nation*, in its criticism of the newspaper, declared that "a more shameless and disreputable sheet of a political kind does not exist."[21]

As Bliss and his fellow Arthur disciples took control over the *National Republican* early in 1882, the Star Route prosecution team reached a milestone. After a series of embarrassing delays and missteps, the government's lawyers began to lay out their case before a grand jury in Washington. Securing an indictment there would allow them, at long last, to make their primary case before a jury in criminal court.

Like almost every legal process connected to the Star Route case, it proved to be agonizingly slow going. The grand jury was drawn on December 7, 1881, but it was not fully organized before the start of the holiday season later in the month. When the calendar turned to January 1882, subpoenas were issued to compel testimony from a number of witnesses, many of whom lived in the West. Not much progress was made by the end of the month, and reporters began to wonder if the government would ever manage to indict anyone associated with the postal-fraud cases. The *New York Times* complained about the "unaccountable delays in the Star Route cases" and noted that "time runs on as inexorably as the statute of limitations." Again, the clock was ticking.[22]

Grand jury proceedings ostensibly are secret, so reporters were forced to pass along to their readers tidbits of gossip and rumors that were leaked by those involved in the proceedings. By early February, newspapers were reporting that several members of the Dorsey ring were being presented for indictment. Reporters were uncertain about the fates of the two biggest names associated with the Star Route frauds, former second assistant postmaster general Brady and former Arkansas senator Stephen Dorsey. Many still doubted that the Arthur administration would indict two prominent Republicans, both of whom had provided crucial help in recent presidential campaigns (Brady in 1876 and Dorsey in 1880).[23]

By mid-February, after hearing from more than fifty witnesses, the grand jury indicted several men associated with the Dorsey combination, including Brady and Dorsey, for their roles in Star Route bid-rigging. Also among those charged were Dorsey's brother, John, and some of the men with whom they had done Star Route work: John Miner, Harvey Vaile, John L. Sanderson, and Montfort Rerdell. Post Office clerk William Turner also was charged. The news apparently came as a shock to the defendants and their attorneys; they had believed that the grand jury would not return any indictments. Instead, it had dealt a heavy blow to the members of the Dorsey ring.[24]

The heart of the indictments claimed that members of the Dorsey ring had "fraudulently, and for . . . benefit, gain, and profit" manipulated "written orders for increase and additional service on and over . . . post-routes, and for the increase of the number of trips each week on and over each of" them. On some routes, as prosecutors later claimed in court, these additional allowances were "utterly unnecessary and unjustifiable, whether judged by the productiveness of the route, the importance of the route, the wishes of the people, or the amount of mail matter." With the connivance of Brady and Turner, the accused contractors had secured these unwarranted increases from the Post Office by concocting phony petitions and letters that "did not represent in any sense the wishes or desires of the people of the locality."[25]

The indictments varied slightly (depending on the individuals named, the postal routes involved, and the alleged frauds committed), but they generally followed the same pattern. In one typical count, the government described the crimes allegedly committed by members of the Dorsey combination in connection to Route 44155, which provided postal service between The Dalles and Baker City in Oregon:

> In further pursuance of, and further to effect the object of their said unlawful, fraudulent, and malicious combination, confederacy, conspiracy, and agreement, [they] did fraudulently make, write, sign, and cause and procure to be made, written, and signed, did fraudulently send, transmit, deliver, and cause and procure to be filed in the said office of the Second Assistant Postmaster-General [Brady], among the papers relating and pertaining to the said post route numbered 44155 a large number of false and fraudulent petitions, applications, and papers purporting to be the petitions and applications of persons residing upon and in the neighborhood of the said post route, to the said Postmaster General for an increased and additional service in carrying and transporting the said mails on and over the said post route, the said petitions, applications, and papers then and there being fraudulently signed with a large number of fictitious names, and the names of persons not residing upon and in the neighborhood of the said post route.[26]

Although members of the Dorsey ring had been involved in operating dozens of postal routes, prosecutors ultimately decided to focus on only a fraction of them (in part because the statute of limitations already had passed on apparently criminal actions connected with some routes). According to the charges, members of the Dorsey combination had conspired to commit fraud to inflate the value of contracts for nineteen Star Routes. Scattered throughout some of the most rugged and remote parts the West, the routes at issue connected myriad small communities, places like Toquerville and Adairville in Utah Territory (Route 41119); Vermillion and Sioux Falls in Dakota Territory (Route 35015); Pueblo and Rosita in Colorado (Route 38134); and Tres Alamos and Clifton in Arizona (Route 40113). These were mostly new and developing communities that relied on Star Route service to keep them connected to the outside world and to each other.[27]

Although there would be protracted wrangling over their content, everyone could agree on one thing: the indictments seemed to be interminable. According to one account, they totaled 106 pages, approximately the length of a short trial transcript. One defense attorney, Enoch Totten, later said that reading them aloud in court would take no less than five hours. Tongue in cheek, he would say in court, "I want to suggest to the court that the Constitution of the United States prohibits cruel and unusual punishments, and to make a man stand up and listen to the reading of that indictment would be clearly within the prohibition contained in that instrument." The judge would go along with the joke, asking rhetorically about the reading of the ponderous charges, "Would that be infliction of punishment before trial?"[28]

Whatever their length, the indictments were cause for celebration at the *New York Times,* which over the preceding few years had relentlessly called for the prosecution of the Star Route crooks. After they were announced, the newspaper lauded the formal charges, calling them "the first important step in the progress of the prosecution that has been set on foot by the government." The *Times* was especially gratified to see that Brady and Stephen Dorsey were among those who had been charged with crimes by the government, as there had "been many predictions that money, legal skill, and political influence would save these two men from ever being brought to trial for their part in the great conspiracy." In the end, such privileges had not shielded the two corrupt former officials, and now they could "suffer the full penalty of their crimes like common swindlers and thieves."[29]

The *Times* excoriated Dorsey at great length for his infamous role in the Star Route frauds. He was no small-time mail contractor or minor Post Office clerk trying to bilk the system for a few extra dollars; he was a former U.S. senator who had abused his power and betrayed the public's trust in order to enrich himself. In the newspaper's estimation, there was little doubt that he had "used his position and influence to secure corrupt contracts in the name of others and made himself a go-between of the Contract Office [of the Post Office] and the manipulators of bids and routes. He doubtless relied on his influence among politicians and officials to prevent exposure of the proceedings in which he was concerned, and the same consideration gave confidence to his co-conspirators." Having committed those offenses, he fully deserved to be hauled into court by the government.[30]

Other publications also expressed satisfaction over the long-overdue indictments. The *New-York Tribune* announced in a headline, "The Ringleaders Coming to Grief." The newspaper enthused over the thoroughness of the case made by the prosecution before the grand jury, quoting one observer who said that if the defendants knew how much evidence against them had been amassed by the government, they would "either commit suicide or leave the country."[31]

For his part, prosecutor George Bliss was ecstatic. He, too, touted the strength of the evidence that the government had presented to the grand jury and said that it had been gathered over the preceding year with diligence and care. "I have had some experience in criminal practice," the attorney claimed, "and I never saw any case in which the evidence was collected with so much energy, intelligence, and ability as in these." The indictments vindicated not only President Arthur, "who has insisted from the first that justice should have full sway in these cases, and that the guilty, if there were any, should be punished," but also the prosecution team, including Bliss himself. "I have said all along that these parties ought to be indicted," he gushed, "and I believed they would be."[32]

William Cook, Bliss's fellow prosecutor, took a dimmer view of the indictments. The Dorsey ring had contracted for a total of 134 Star Routes, and 19 of them were included in the formal charges filed by the federal government. The result was, in Cook's view, a case that was too complicated, too sprawling, and too disconnected. "In this indictment," he later said, "there are two, three, four, five, six, seven—quite a number of different routes, involving different contracts and different parties, in which there was no common interest." He felt that cramming so much into a single case would pose enormous problems when the prosecutors had to make their arguments in court to a jury comprising citizens who were of average intelligence and possessed limited attention spans. "It was, in my opinion, a grave error to embrace so much in one indictment as to render it difficult for either court or jury to form a clear, concise, brief conception of the facts." For the sake of simplicity, Cook would have focused the indictments on a single route in which the Dorsey ring had committed fraud. Doing so, he believed, would have made the case much easier to present to a jury.[33]

11

SELLING YOU OUT TO THE OTHER SIDE
Prosecutors with Suspect Loyalties, Winter 1882

That there were serious flaws in the indictments soon became apparent to everyone involved in the Star Route case.

William Ker had been brought into the prosecution team specifically for his proficiency in drafting indictments, and he toiled at a feverish clip to get them ready. "I worked sometimes all night," he later said. "I generally got back to the hotel about 4 or 5 o'clock in the morning, took an hour or two of sleep and a bath, and went back to the office, because I had to keep my assistants supplied with copy." As he labored on the indictments, Ker was supplied with the names of those to be indicted; these included "M. R. Rerdell" and "J. L. Sanderson." He was concerned by the reliance on initials rather than full first names (commonly called "Christian names" at that time). "I went to George Bliss and told him that I would like to have the Christian names of the people that were given me to be included in the indictment," he later said, "because in some localities the courts were very particular about the Christian names, while in others they were not." Bliss, however, apparently did not supply the appropriate first names to Ker in time, and in the indictment, Rerdell and Sanderson were referred to by their first initials.[1]

And there was another potential problem with the names in the indictments. Ker later said that he had been informed that Vaile's Christian name was "Henry," which is how it appeared in the indictment—erroneously, as it turned out. His actual first name was "Harvey."[2]

The mistakes riled special prosecutor William Cook. Ker had been added to the prosecution team largely because of his purported expertise as a legal draftsman, and he had been expected to handle the indictments with ease. Yet, as Cook later put it, the indictments contained "a most stupid and unjustifi-able use of the initials of two parties," Rerdell and Sanderson, plus the error in Vaile's first name. "No expert would have perpetrated so manifest and plain a blunder as that indictment contained." He later derided Ker as "a supposed expert from Philadelphia."[3]

The miscues were of no small consequence to the prosecution. Rerdell, Sanderson, and Vaile all could plausibly argue in court that the government's charges had not really named them at all, and that, as the indictments pertained to them, they should be thrown out.

Critics jeered that the Star Route prosecutors had blundered yet again. One Missouri newspaper, noting that the government had made a similarly clumsy drafting error in a separate case involving corruption at the New York Custom House, wryly observed, "A singular fatality seems to pursue the United States prosecuting officers in the matter of making mistakes in the names of the parties against whom they secure indictments." The government did not stand much chance of prevailing in court if it could not even spell the defen-dants' names correctly.[4]

When the matter was argued in court, Ker gamely tried to defend the indictments as being valid as they related to the three accused men who had not been identified precisely. Cook was less than impressed. "I heard it ar-gued," he later said. "I was amazed." Judge Andrew Wylie, who was handling the Star Route case in the Supreme Court of the District of Columbia, agreed with Cook, and the indictments were thrown out as they related to Rerdell, Sanderson, and Vaile.[5]

Prosecutors were particularly nervous about the possibility of allowing Rerdell to escape their grasp. The clerk had played a key role in the operations of the Dorsey ring, and his affidavit in the spring of 1881 had laid out in vivid detail how the swindle had worked. He had then retracted the affidavit and ac-cused Attorney General MacVeagh, among others, of having suborned perjury. Prosecutors felt that Rerdell needed to be held to account for his misbehavior on this score. They also wanted to find a way to introduce as evidence the clerk's since-retracted affidavit because it had highlighted in vivid detail the illegal behavior of Stephen Dorsey.

While they tried to sort out the redrafting of the indictment, prosecutors filed an information against Rerdell in police court and charged him with a variety of crimes, including subornation of perjury. Filing an information in police court had proven to be a spectacularly unsuccessful ploy for prosecutors in the fall of 1881, but they now felt that they needed to try something with Rerdell "on account of the invalidity of the old indictment against him," as one Washington newspaper put it.[6]

The proceedings against Rerdell in police court were mainly a back-up plan, however. Chastened by Wylie's ruling, prosecutors redrafted the portion of the criminal indictment relating to Rerdell and Vaile and inserted their full first names. The grand jury then reindicted the two men, and the cases against them were permitted to proceed in criminal court.[7]

Prosecutors felt that the case against Sanderson was relatively weak and incomplete, and they decided to drop him as a defendant, at least for the time being. Ker was "perfectly willing to leave [Sanderson] out of this case" because it was "understood that his turn was to come next," according to the prosecutor's later account.[8]

But the move to at least momentarily spare Sanderson gave rise to rumors that the Star Route contractor had bought his way out of being prosecuted. Ker later responded indignantly to gossip about an alleged payoff. "I have heard it reported," he later said, "that Sanderson paid some money for that. Colonel Bliss has said that he did not receive any, and I now say that I never saw any of Sanderson's money; never got a cent of it, or anything whatever from him. I never met Mr. Sanderson or any of his friends, and if he was induced to pay any money to have his name omitted from that indictment, why it was a great outrage upon him." The accusations were completely baseless, Ker insisted.[9]

As the prosecution team finally readied for trial, its roster changed. Late in March 1882, Attorney General Brewster appointed Richard Merrick as his representative to conduct the Star Route cases in court. A Maryland native who had served in that state's legislature, Merrick was known as a capable attorney. Among his most prominent clients had been John Surratt, who in 1867 had been tried for his alleged involvement in the plot to assassinate Abraham Lincoln. (Although his mother was found guilty and hanged, Surratt's own trial ended in a mistrial.) He also had been part of the team of attorneys who had represented failed presidential candidate Samuel J. Tilden at the Electoral Commission of 1877.

As important as Merrick's legal talents were his political affiliations. He was a Democrat who would later be described by journalist Frank Carpenter as a noted Copperhead (a common term for "peace Democrats," who had called for a negotiated truce with the Confederacy during the Civil War). It was thought that Merrick's appointment by a Republican administration could inoculate the prosecution from charges of partisanship. (This had also been a factor in the hiring of Ker, another Democrat.) A later account noted that Merrick's addition "was considered a shrewd move on the part of the government" as it tried to shore up the prosecution team and shield it from criticism.[10]

Although Merrick enjoyed a generally favorable reputation among members of the bar, his political sympathies and social views were not necessarily popular with everyone in the nation's capital. In 1871, the attorney stood as the Democrats' candidate for the District of Columbia's delegate to Congress. The contest focused on one volatile issue: whether public schools in the capital should be integrated. Frederick Douglass, the great abolitionist and orator, said that Merrick represented the "good old days of slavery" because he vehemently advocated for segregated schools. "I say shame, eternal shame on any colored voter who supports Richard T. Merrick," Douglass declared, "and withered be the black man's arms and blasted be the black man's head who casts a vote against General N. P. Chipman," his opponent. With Douglass's support, Chipman prevailed in the contentious race.[11]

When he later explained to Congress why Merrick had been hired, Attorney General Brewster said that the idea had come from George Edmunds, the powerful chair of the Senate Judiciary Committee. Edmunds's push for Merrick had been driven at least in part by political considerations. "Mr. Merrick was selected for the reason that it was considered a proper thing to dissociate the cases from all political feeling," Brewster later said, "and to select a prominent Democrat to appear in them for the government with the other counsel already employed, so there could not be any charge of anything being done that was not known to all parties, and so that the prosecutions should be manifestly in the interest of the public and not of any party."[12]

Merrick's arrival was necessitated by the departure of Cook, whose tumultuous tenure with the Star Route prosecution team ended once the indictments came into focus and preparations were made for trial. Bliss, convinced that Cook had become a liability to the prosecution team, pushed for his ouster. He believed that Cook had downplayed the potential of some strong Star Route cases and prioritized weaker ones in order to help his friends and associates. "I became dissatisfied with the manner in which Colonel Cook was proceeding with the star-route cases," Bliss said, "and I did not like his associations by any means."[13]

Bliss insisted that, for the sake of moving the case forward, Cook needed to be forced out of the prosecution team, and Brewster ultimately agreed. "You may say that I advised the attorney general to get rid of Colonel Cook," Bliss later admitted.[14]

As he later put it, Cook had felt that he had been the victim of a "gradual freezing out process" from the prosecutors since the death of President Garfield, who had brought him into the Star Route case early in 1881 and had relied on his counsel before his mortal wounding by Guiteau. The marginalization of prosecutor Albert Gibson had led Cook to believe "that it would not be long before I was retired from the cases" as well.[15]

As he exited, Cook made it known that he felt that he had been slighted by the Arthur administration. President Garfield had met with him in the White House to discuss the Star Route case and strategize, but neither Arthur nor any of his lieutenants had taken similar steps to consult with him and solicit his opinions about the conduct of the prosecution. "In fact, I have received no encouragement," Cook complained, "nor have I been sent for or given the confidence of President Arthur or his cabinet." Cut off from support, he felt that he had been forced to retire from the case.[16]

Predictably, Cook's parting lament was mocked by the ever-critical *National Republican*. With no shortage of irony, the newspaper lambasted the Arthur administration for having slighted the attorney during the Star Route prosecutions: "We blush for the Administration. What! Not send for William Affidavit Cook? Will wonders never cease?" ("Affidavit" was a play Cook's middle initial, A.)[17]

In a gentler tone than the *National Republican,* prosecutor William Ker also disputed Cook's account of the reasons behind his departure from the prosecution team. Ker was, as he later said, surprised that Cook had "claimed that he was slowly being frozen out from the prosecution. So far as I could see, he had no reason to believe anything of the kind." Attorney General Brewster had assumed formal control of the Star Route case, and he "was not obliged to call a council of the assistants whom he employed. He had a perfect right to tell Bliss or to tell me what to do without consulting Cook or any of the others. The attorney general had the cases in charge, and no one in connection with the cases could expect to be his equal." It had been presumptuous of Cook, a subordinate, to think that the attorney general—or President Arthur, for that matter—had needed to confer with him before making decisions relating to the case.[18]

Attorney General Brewster was incensed by Cook's suggestion that his departure had been necessitated by President Garfield's death and the change in administrations. He bristled at the idea that progress in the Star Route prosecution was narrowly contingent on the whims or political orientation of whoever resided in the White House. "You were not responsible to any particular administration, as a political responsibility," Brewster wrote in a curt private letter to Cook. "Nor were these cases, or are they, to be confused or associated with any idea of policy supposed to be connected with any ad-ministration. They are instituted for the purposes of justice, and justice only. They will be conducted by counsel upon principles that regulate the orderly administration of justice, and not with reference to the wishes or policies of any President, no matter what his name may be."[19]

The circumstances of Cook's departure were further muddied by accusa-tions that he, like Gibson, had fed information to the Star Route defendants. "I had no question in my mind," Bliss later told Congress, "that Mr. Gibson and Cook had in their possession evidence, and that some time before the trial of the Dorsey case portions of that evidence were given to the defendants." Speculating about how the evidence could have made its way to the Dorsey ring and its bevy of attorneys, a congressman asked him, "Your belief, then, was that Gibson and Cook were selling you out to the other side?" Bliss replied that he felt no hesitation in saying so.[20]

When Brewster took over as attorney general late in 1881, he asked Bliss if he still trusted Cook and Gibson. "Mr. Bliss privately to me took serious objection to Mr. Cook and Mr. Gibson," Brewster later said, "and expressed the opinion it was not safe to have them in the case, and told many things . . . which went to the discredit of those two persons, and make it quite uncom-fortable and improper to have them in the case." Bliss made it clear to him that he thought the two men were actively helping the Star Route defendants by taking sensitive papers from two iron government safes and providing them to the defense. "He stated also that he was of the opinion they were disclosing the information contained in the papers to people upon the other side—to the defendants." Cook and Gibson were so widely suspected of stealing documents, Brewster later said, that investigator Patrick Henry Woodward and Bliss felt compelled to change the combinations of the locks on the safes.[21]

Cook was accused of passing copies of prosecution documents to the defense through Charles Cole, his law partner. The documents in question related to the government's long-simmering investigation of George Brott and Fred Lilley, two men outside the Dorsey ring who also had been implicated in Star Route peculation. In March 1882, shortly after Cook's departure from the prosecution team, William Lilley called on Woodward to complain about a statement given against his son Fred by Brott. Woodward was astounded that the elder Lilley had obtained the document because, as far as he knew, "the original was locked up in one of our safes," as he later put it. When he asked the gentleman how he had gotten his hands on the document, Lilley said he obtained it from Brady, "who had a large stack of our papers."[22]

Appalled that the Star Route defendants had obtained confidential prosecution documents, Woodward asked William Lilley to approach Brady again and ask him how he had acquired the statement in question. Although Brady did not directly tell Lilley how the pile of prosecution materials had come into his possession, "the conversation proceeded on the assumption that he had obtained them from William A. Cook, through his partner, Cole," the investigator said.[23]

Woodward was not the only member of the prosecution team to have doubts about how Cook handled sensitive paperwork connected to the Star Route case. Throughout the early months of 1882, Bliss hounded Cook to return to him documents relating to the Star Route contracts that had been manipulated by the Dorsey combination. (These were abstracts, or summaries, of sixteen routes that had been operated fraudulently.) At first, Cook claimed that he did not have the documents, but he eventually returned them to Bliss at the end of March—a few weeks after he had left the prosecution team. For Bliss, there was only one plausible explanation for his decision to hang onto the documents: "I simply say that, in my opinion, they were retained for the purpose of being copied for the benefit of the other side."[24]As the Star Route case developed in mid-1882, it became clear to prosecutors that the defense was using pilfered documents to shape its approach to the upcoming trial. An indignant Bliss later told Congress, "We simply learned that they had sixteen of our abstracts, and it appears that there were just sixteen returned by Colonel Cook to the Department of Justice." When pressed on this point, Bliss did not waver. The same sixteen documents were involved, and the only possible explanation was that Cook had passed them along to the defense.[25]

For his part, Cook vehemently denied all wrongdoing. "All statements or insinuations that I retained papers or had copies made, or furnished any to the defendants or any other persons," he later said, "are utterly false." In his later testimony before Congress, he went so far as to say he had never possessed, or even seen, the papers in question. Cook also said that he had returned all of the documents he did possess in a timely and appropriate fashion once he had left the prosecution team.[26]

Cook's protests of innocence rang hollow, and accusations of impropriety dogged him for several years. In 1883, Attorney General Brewster told a Philadelphia newspaper that the defendants in the Star Route case had "used the proceeds of their robberies [to] buy up ex-counsel of the government." When he was asked to name names, Brewster said that he had been informed that the defendants had paid "several thousand dollars [to] the law partner of Mr. William Cook and [to] Mr. Albert Gibson. Both Mr. Cook and Mr. Gibson were originally retained by the government in these cases, and I dismissed them because I felt that their services could be dispensed with."[27]

Cook responded to Brewster's accusatory comments with several outraged letters. "The intellectual and moral depravity which tempted and impelled you to malign and misrepresent me as you have done," he sputtered in one missive, "I am unable to comprehend." The claim that he had been bought by the Star Route defendants was "utterly false." (This was one of the attorney's favorite phrases when he spotted an apparent falsehood.) In his anger, Cook also took a swipe at the circumstances of Brewster's elevation to attorney general, suggesting that he had capitalized on President Garfield's assassination and perhaps his own chicanery. "An attorney general of the United States cannot assail my professional or personal character with impunity," Cook wrote, "especially one who attained his distinguished position amid the smoke of an assassin's pistol, and possibly by means which reflect little or no credit on exalted manhood."[28]

A tell-all book published in 1885 offered an especially salacious explanation of how and why Cook allegedly aided the defense in the Star Route cases. An entire chapter was devoted to the escapades of a Washington lawyer who almost certainly was Cook (although he was identified only as "X" in the text). According to this account, Brady and Stephen Dorsey paid an attractive and flirtatious young woman to pose as an heiress from Texas and ask X for legal help. The gullible lawyer was so smitten with the damsel in distress that he offered to represent her without payment and began to neglect his duties in the Star Route case. More importantly for the defendants, "In her bewitching way she extorted from X just the information the conspirators wanted and also furnished them copies of letters, and in two instances original documentary evidence, the possession of which enabled the Star-routers to snap their fingers in the face of justice." If this gossipy account of Cook's foibles is to be believed, "there is no denying the fact that she was the means of saving Brady & Co." (According to the book, Cook apparently only figured out that he had been duped after he traveled to Texas and learned that the woman was a notorious con artist.)[29]

Gibson also struggled to shrug off claims that he sold prosecution documents to the defense after he had left the team. Bliss later told Congress that he quizzed James Bosler, who kept the accounts of the Dorsey combination, about a payment of $2,500 that had been made to Gibson. He wanted to know why the attorney had been paid. "I know you are not one of those men," Bliss told him, "who pay something for nothing." Bosler was evasive at first, but he finally relented after Bliss threatened him with prosecution.

"I paid for information, you know," Bosler finally admitted.

"Albert Gibson had been government counsel, and you paid it to him for information?' Bliss asked him, just to be certain.

"Yes,'" Bosler conceded.[30]

It was sometimes easier to determine which of the government's various attorneys got along than it was to untangle their many feuds, power struggles, and allegations of wrongdoing. Ironically, two of the Democrats of the group representing a Republican administration, William Ker and Dick Merrick, were generally well regarded by their colleagues. (Ker's mistakes in drafting the indictments were attributed to simple carelessness rather than malice or chicanery.)

The New York *Sun*, Gibson's erstwhile employer, decried the utter lack of harmony in the government's legal team. The newspaper scoffed that before leaving office late in 1881, Attorney General MacVeagh had "succeeded in bringing around him a number of men, some of whom were mutually distrustful, some distrusted everyone else in the case, and some of them were more or less jealous of others. A more discordant, mutually distrustful number of special counsel, agents, and detectives probably never worked together on a case."[31]

THE CHARGE HERE IS CONSPIRACY

The First Star Route Trial Begins, Spring–Summer 1882

N one of the defendants in the Star Route case were in any particular hurry to get their criminal trial underway. Although they previously had gone to court in an effort to expedite the case and clear their names as quickly as possible, the accused now adopted the opposite strategy and stalled at every turn. They knew that repeatedly postponing their day of reckoning in court would test the resolve of prosecutors and the political will of the Arthur administration. Brothers Stephen and John Dorsey were especially reluctant to appear in court, and their foot-dragging made it difficult for prosecutors to move forward with the case as a whole, as the alleged conspirators were to be tried together. Delays for a few meant delays for everyone.

At a court hearing early in May 1882, prosecutor George Bliss complained that John Dorsey was not present and had not yet entered a formal plea in the case. Bliss made a cutting remark about Robert Green Ingersoll, suggesting that the defense attorney, in a sneaky effort to further delay the trial, had deliberately misled the court by offering an intentional misstatement about whether Dorsey would show up in person and enter a plea.

"You're a liar!" Ingersoll thundered, jumping to his feet in outrage at the attack on his integrity. He then exclaimed "You're a liar!" again, this time slamming his fist onto a pile of books.

Judge Andrew Wylie had to intervene before the clash between the two attorneys spiraled completely out of control. He chastened both men about their fiery exchange, saying that Bliss's comment was "uncalled for and inexcusable, and Mr. Ingersoll's beyond propriety."[1]

Try as they might, the defendants could not delay the proceedings forever.

After months of postponements, false starts, infighting, and missteps, federal prosecutors finally were ready to take the Star Route case to trial before Wylie in the Supreme Court of the District of Columbia. The case to be heard in his courtroom would be officially known as *The United States v. John W. Dorsey, John R. Miner, John M. Peck, Stephen W. Dorsey, Harvey M. Vaile, Montfort C. Rerdell, Thomas J. Brady, and William H. Turner for Conspiracy.*

The inclusion of Peck's name reflected an ongoing—and profound— misapprehension about the defendants. Although prosecutors believed that he had been involved in the alleged conspiracy, Peck had died of tuberculosis in the fall of 1881, months before the case could be brought to trial, and could not face charges in court posthumously. (It was a testament to the Brobding- nagian nature of the Star Route case that befuddled jurors would return a verdict against him anyway.)

The son of a college president (his father had been the first president of Indiana University and had established that institution's law school), Judge Wylie was known as a fair and principled man who was not afraid to stand up for what he believed to be right. In 1860, the judge had lived in Alexandria, Virginia, and was reputed to have been the only man in the city to have voted for Lincoln for president—this despite the fact that he had been warned be- forehand that he would be shot dead if he did so. The day after the election, he had been enjoying a drink on his front porch when someone had fired a shot at him, shattering the glass he held in his hand. Wylie had then moved across the Potomac River to Washington, but he had refused to be intimidated into abandoning his party.[2]

No one doubted that Wylie took his judicial duties seriously. An attorney who practiced in his courtroom, Nathaniel Wilson, said that after one high-profile trial, Wylie spoke to him "of the awful burden and responsibility that rested upon the man appointed to sit in judgment upon the lives and rights of others, and of the inevitable isolation of the judgment-seat. These, he said, are the hard conditions that belong to the service performed by judges, but if that service were not performed, justice would perish from the earth." With the steady and honorable Wylie in charge, the Star Route trial would be in capable hands.[3]

The proceedings would take place in Washington's newly refurbished courthouse. Delays had plagued construction of the building, which had orig- inally been designed by architect George Hadfield to serve as the capital's City Hall, until its completion in 1849. In the middle of the nineteenth century, the stucco-covered brick structure had fallen on hard times: one later account characterized it as being "unfinished, dilapidated," and "decrepit." (The term "veritable ruin" often was used to describe the building.) Funds finally were appropriated for renovations, and the addition of a new north wing commenced in 1881. Construction of this portion of the building would continue throughout the Star Route trial, and the resulting racket occasioned more than one complaint from attorneys struggling to be heard above the din.[4]

One could argue that the courthouse—long in disrepair but not without the potential to be rehabilitated—was a perfect metaphor for the federal government's imperfect prosecution in the Star Route affair. The government's case was, in modern parlance, a bit of a fixer-upper.

To be sure, in many quarters there was not much optimism about the government's chances of prevailing in Judge Wylie's courtroom. According to one later account, the Star Route trial started "amid general public agreement that Dorsey and Brady were guilty, and that they would never be punished because of their positions within the Republican party," not to mention the infamously lackluster quality of the administration of justice in the nation's capital.[5]

Prosecutors were aware that many people believed that their employer, the administration of President Arthur, might not fully back their efforts to convict individuals who had profited from rigging Star Route contracts. Prosecutor Dick Merrick later told Congress that "it was generally thought that the administration did not desire the conviction of" prominent Republicans like Brady or Stephen Dorsey. According to him, the "idea was abroad in the community . . . that the administration was against the prosecution" because it might damage his political allies within the Republican Party. (Merrick himself, though an inveterate Democrat, did not believe this to be true.)[6]

Merrick, among many other observers, contended that the press played an integral role in creating the perception that the prosecution was doomed to fail. According to one later study, "The control by the Star Routers of most of the Washington newspapers also proved a serious handicap to the government. As a result of this situation, the papers of the District, by pouring out a steady stream of abuse upon members of the prosecution, were able to create an atmosphere favorable to the defendants."[7]

And it was not just the provocative *National Republican* that attacked the prosecution. Merrick was particularly incensed by the relentlessly negative coverage of the case offered by two local newspapers, the *Capital* and the *Eve-*

ning Critic. The latter publication "was most virulent, unpardonably virulent, in its attacks upon the court and upon the counsel and witnesses for the government," the prosecutor later told Congress. The *Critic's* attacks were especially bothersome because it was edited by Mornay D. Helm, who at the time also held a plum position in the federal government's printing office. Helm's criticisms of the prosecution in the *Critic* were so relentless and scathing that Merrick lobbied to have him removed from his federal position. (This eventually would happen, but not until after the first Star Route trial's conclusion.)[8]

Newspapers like the *Critic* did enormous damage to the government's efforts in the Star Route case, Merrick later told Congress. Thanks to their efforts, he believed, "public sentiment in the District of Columbia was very much influenced in some way against the prosecution from the start."[9]

Prosecutors also had to grapple with the simple fact that the Star Route trial was being held in the nation's capital. Washington teemed with men who were directly employed by, or were somehow indirectly connected to, the federal government. Juries drawn from this sea of government employees were notoriously reluctant to return convictions in political-corruption cases. "Few men have ever been punished for fraud in Washington," one cynical newspaper noted, "the juries of that city apparently having an inborn conviction that the government is a proper object of plunder." For many, corruption was just a fact of life in the capital, much like the sticky summertime weather.[10]

Whatever the makeup of the jury selected for the Star Route trial, it would have to make sense of the government's charges and the evidence that prosecutors would present in court to back them up. Some members of the prosecution team worried that they were headed into court with a hopelessly complex case that would be far too tangled for any jury, even an impartial one, to unravel. Merrick was certain that the government would present a solid case in court—he later said, "the evidence in this case satisfied me beyond all possible doubt of the guilt of all the parties"—but he worried that he and his fellow prosecutors might not be able to sufficiently tie all of the defendants together and prove that they had conspired with one another. Investigator Patrick Henry Woodward later said that Merrick, after reviewing the government's case, "told me that bricks were abundant but mortar scarce; that he had the materials for the walls of the edifice, but little cement to bind them together."[11]

What the government needed, Merrick told Woodward, was for an insider to testify about how the far-flung conspirators had plotted out and executed their scheme. Rerdell had provided exactly this kind of cement in his confession back in mid-1881, but, under pressure from Stephen Dorsey, he had since retracted his potentially devastating statement. Prosecutors would either have to find a backdoor way to introduce Rerdell's confession or produce another insider to testify about how the Dorsey combination had operated. This information would provide the cement that Merrick felt was needed to hold the government's case together.[12]

As prosecutors put their case together for presentation to the jury, they still struggled to keep themselves organized. The government's team in the Star Route case remained disjointed even after the departures of problematic attorneys Albert Gibson and William Cook.

William Ker had not expected to take part in the trial of the Dorsey combination. Hired primarily for his expertise in drawing up indictments, he had assumed that his work would be done after the case was presented to the grand jury. But Attorney General Brewster, acknowledging Ker's abilities (and perhaps recognizing that George Bliss was becoming overwhelmed by the expansive case), asked him to stay on. "I want you to see Colonel Bliss and tell him that you will take the witnesses and examine them privately and quietly to ascertain what they can testify to; write out a brief of what you find they will testify to, and hand it to Colonel Bliss, so that at the trial he may know just what the witnesses are going to say, and in that way he will be relieved of a great deal of trouble," Brewster told Ker. "I want you to attend particularly to that branch of the case." Ker did as instructed and relayed the attorney general's instructions to Bliss, who promptly shot down the idea. "He said he would attend to that himself, that he did not want anybody to interfere in that business," Ker later said. "I said no more."[13]

Even though he declined Ker's offer of assistance, Bliss struggled to stay on top of the challenging case. He later called the labors associated with the Star Route trial "the most exhaustive and confining work that I ever had imposed upon me." It was a complex and high-profile case involving multiple defendants, mountains of evidence, and enormous public pressure. Trying it would challenge any attorney, no matter how experienced.[14]

To make matters worse, Bliss and his fellow Star Route prosecutors had to contend with a small army of extremely capable defense attorneys. These ten men ranked among the most skilled legal thinkers and orators in their profession. In addition to Robert Green Ingersoll, they were Lemon Galpin Hine,

Jeremiah Wilson, John McSweeney, Enoch Totten, Jefferson Chandler, Charles Cole, Richard Carpenter, Solomon Henkle, and Arthur Williams. Altogether, fourteen attorneys would appear in the Star Route trial. (The prosecution team now numbered Bliss, Ker, Merrick, and Attorney General Brewster, the last only nominally overseeing the case but who would offer a closing argument at the end of the trial.) One journalist said that this collection of defense and prosecution attorneys constituted "the greatest assemblage of legal talent which had at that time ever been gathered at one trial within the confines of the United States."[15]

The defense team hailed from far and wide. Carpenter, who had made his name practicing law in Kentucky, was once described as "a very peculiar man, wandering about the country and constantly changing his abode." At one point, he had been a judge in South Carolina and had been nominated to run for governor on the Union Reform ticket in 1870. Chandler had graduated from the University of Michigan's law school and practiced law in Missouri. McSweeney was a well-known member of the bar in Wooster, Ohio. Totten, meanwhile, already was a familiar face in the Washington courthouse, as he was a prominent local attorney who had served as corporation counsel for the city and was held in high regard in the capital's legal community for his talent for nurturing young lawyers.[16]

Williams knew the law from both the perspective of an attorney and that of a defendant. In 1876, he had been implicated in a bribery scheme involving Richard Harrington, who was then an assistant U.S. attorney. Williams allegedly had given Harrington a $15,000 bribe to drop murder charges against two of his clients. But the charges against the attorney eventually had been dropped, and Williams had been able to continue with his legal practice.[17]

Among the defense team, Ingersoll probably enjoyed the greatest reputation. A loyal Republican, he had famously nominated James Blaine for president at the party's 1876 convention in Cincinnati by asserting that the senator was like "an armed warrior, a plumed knight" who had "marched down the halls of the American Congress and threw his shining lances full and fair against the brazen foreheads of every defamer of his country and maligner of its honor." Such speeches helped earn Ingersoll a reputation as one of the age's great orators. On the lecture circuit, he was a fearless iconoclast, boasting of his agnosticism and attacking the shortcomings of organized religion and ideological orthodoxy. In the nineteenth century, few Americans had the temerity to travel the country and utter such things in public. Walt Whitman wrote, "He lives, embodies, the individuality I preach. I see in Bob [Ingersoll] the noblest specimen—American-flavored—pure out of the soil, spreading, giving, demanding light." Ingersoll was "always such a vitalizing force," the poet declared, "I look on immortality as in some way implicated with him."[18]

The likes of Elizabeth Cady Stanton, Mark Twain, and Thomas Edison were said to have sat in rapt attention through Ingersoll's speeches, which included a notorious defense of the "Great Infidels." This speech paired praise for the reason of thinkers like Voltaire, Denis Diderot, David Hume, and Thomas Paine with an unrelenting attack on religious superstition. Ingersoll's condemnation of the concept of hell typified his opinions on the specious origins of common religious beliefs. "The idea of hell was born of ignorance, brutality, fear, cowardice, and revenge," he said. "This idea testifies that our remote ancestors were the lowest beasts. Only from dens, lairs, and caves, only from mouths filled with cruel fangs, only from hearts of fear and hatred, only from the conscience of hunger and lust, only from the lowest and most debased could come this most cruel, heartless and bestial of all dogmas."[19]

The globe-trotting journalist Frank Carpenter covered the Star Route trial for the *Cleveland Leader*. He was fascinated by Ingersoll and wrote a memorable description of the attorney: "Ingersoll is a peculiar-looking man. His head is as round as a cannon-ball, and it is as though the Lord forgot his neck when He put him together. His kindly eyes are blue, his forehead is high, and the top of his head is bald. His small nose is slightly turned upward." According to Carpenter, Ingersoll "looks for all the world like an overgrown boy, and it is not unfair to say that he often acts like one. Sometimes he puts his hands into his pockets when he is speaking, and when he makes a joke, he joins the audience in the laughter it provokes." But Carpenter observed that Ingersoll was anything but a comic figure when he plied his craft. Such was the defense attorney's charisma that "when he rises to speak," the journalist wrote, "the courtroom is quieter than when the judge renders a decision."[20]

With Ingersoll and so many other attorneys appearing for both sides, there were bound to be some strange bedfellows in the Star Route case—almost literally. Postmaster General Timothy Howe, who had succeeded Tom James in that post late in 1881, lived in the home of defense attorney Enoch Totten, who was his son-in-law. And then there was the odd matter of Charles Cole, the law partner of former prosecutor William Cook, representing the defense.[21]

It was sometimes difficult to ascertain which attorneys were representing which defendants. Cole had been retained by Stephen Dorsey to represent Rerdell, and Hine represented Miner and Vaile. Miner also was represented by attorney Henkle. Stephen Dorsey himself had his interests defended by McSweeney, Carpenter, Ingersoll, and Chandler, while Brady had hired Totten and Wilson, who also represented Turner. It was never clear who formally represented John Dorsey, but this did not seem to matter. During the trial itself, the attorneys would loosely coordinate their activities and generally defend the accused as a group; there would be very little finger-pointing among the defendants. In court, they would present a more-or-less united front against the government.

Even before the parties began making their respective cases before the jury, these seasoned attorneys jockeyed for any advantage they could find. "There were all sorts of preliminary struggles," prosecutor George Bliss later complained. "The defendants attacked everything; in every way, everywhere, and everybody. Demurrers, motions to quash; every description of motion that criminal pleading permits, and some things which it does not permit, were resorted to." Ruing the defense attorneys' relentless pretrial maneuvering, the *New York Times* complained that "dilatory and obstructive methods . . . characterized their work."[22]

Eventually, the time came to select a jury. With so many defendants involved in the case, the matter of challenges vexed Judge Wylie. After a good deal of contentious back and forth with the attorneys on both sides, he eventually decided that the government would be granted three challenges, while each of the eight defendants would be allowed four, giving them a total of more than thirty. This imbalance put the government at a disadvantage, and prosecutors exhausted all of their challenges before the sixth (of twelve) jurors had been selected.[23]

The parties eventually were able to agree on a dozen men. Jurors included a real estate and claims agent (this was the foreman, William Dickson), a printer, a lawyer, a livery-stable clerk, and a shoemaker. The panel was integrated, as two jurors, a teacher named William Brown and Thomas Martin, a barber, were Black men.

The men eventually selected as jurors for the Star Route trial could have been forgiven if they failed to immediately understand all of the intricacies of the case before them. As the trial began, prosecutors laid out a jumbled account of a complicated case, one that extended over many years and involved numerous individuals and alleged crimes. Jurors needed to keep straight not only the eight defendants themselves but also dozens of subcontractors and Post Office officials who had not been charged. Their crimes would be shown with the aid of mountains of evidence: prosecutor Bliss promised to share the many "false and fraudulent petitions, applications, and papers" that the defendants had used to further their scheme. (It was later said that over 1,00 exhibits were presented to the jury during the course of the trial, but no one seemed quite sure of the exact number.)[24]

And then there were the suspect Star Routes themselves, each denoted by a different five-digit number. In all, nineteen routes were involved in the case: Route 44160 (Canyon City, Oregon, to Fort McDermitt, Nevada), Route 38113 (Rawlins, Colorado, to the White River Ute Agency in Colorado), and Route 38152 (Ouray to Los Pinos, Colorado), among others. The physical landscape of the case was incredibly vast, stretching from Oregon to Arizona to Dakota Territory and touching on numerous small towns that few people in the eastern United States had ever heard of. To further complicate things, different crimes had occurred in relation to different routes and contracts, and not all of the defendants had been involved in all aspects of the frauds.

Nor was the law itself easy to grasp. The defendants were charged with having engaged in a criminal conspiracy, which required the government to show that they had agreed to commit illegal acts *and* that they had engaged in an overt act to put their illegal scheme into motion. While this seemed straightforward enough in theory, it raised a host of practical questions about the relationships between the various men who had been charged by the government. For instance, could individuals who had never met or communicated with one another engage in a conspiracy together? It might be easy enough to show that the Dorsey brothers had entered into a criminal conspiracy together, but what about, say, Brady and Miner?

The prosecution's principal theory—that the far-flung defendants, some of whom were total strangers to one another, had schemed together to commit an elaborate fraud—was mocked by some in the press. In Washington, Mornay Helm's ever-skeptical *Evening Critic* summed up this view by arguing that the government would struggle to prove "a long range conspiracy in which the 'conspirators' are not on speaking terms."[25]

The press recognized that the conspiracy case against the defendants was vertiginous, involving as it did so many individuals and routes. "The exposures of the transactions of Brady, Dorsey, and the rest would have excited much more public indignation had it not been for the difficulty of understanding them," the *New York Times* observed as the Star Route trial began. "The work of the Star Route ring was to ordinary peculation what confidence operators are to sneak-thieving."[26]

As Bliss put it later in the trial, the prosecution's case rested on the notion that the members of the Dorsey combination had conspired to commit fraud in making preposterously low bids on Star Route contracts and then, once the routes were in operation, using phony support materials—the aforementioned "false and fraudulent petitions, applications, and papers"—to claim that the Post Office should increase their value. All this transpired with the connivance of defendants who were in the employ of the Post Office, Contracts Division clerk William Turner and Second Assistant Postmaster General Tom Brady. According to prosecutors, Brady was paid a kickback for approving changes for each suddenly lucrative contract. He also received illegal payments for forgiving fines levied against members of the ring who were not properly executing their contracts.

"The charge here is conspiracy," Bliss said later in the trial. "We charge them with a conspiracy, and we allege that in connection with the conspiracy they made certain false and fraudulent oaths and declarations. That was part of their scheme." Their criminal plot involved "falsely and fraudulently [stating and describing] the number of men and animals required to perform the service of carrying the said mail on and over each of said post-routes." The defendants had knowingly fabricated these details, prosecutors argued, in order to enrich themselves.[27]

Brady, who allegedly had used his authority as second assistant postmaster general to further the scheme, was the cornerstone of the government's case. Bliss outlined his alleged crimes at great length in his opening statement to the jury. This was only appropriate, the prosecutor explained. "In the first place, if guilty, we regard him as the most guilty of all the parties before you, for he was a high public official," he said. "Of course we expect to satisfy you that Mr. Brady is guilty. We believe that we can do it. I think in your minds you will agree with me that if I can prove one-half of the statements I have made to you hitherto, Mr. Brady must be a guilty man."[28]

Although he spent a good deal of time pillorying Brady in his opening statement, Bliss did not slight the other defendants. Stephen Dorsey was "the chief spirit in the conspiracy" who "had no right to be interested in any contracts with the government" while he was serving as a U.S. senator from Arkansas. Meanwhile, the indispensable Rerdell served as "the factotum of all the parties to the conspiracy."[29]

On dozens of Star Routes, various members of the Dorsey ring had submitted low initial bids. Almost immediately, they had provided flimsy or simply fraudulent justifications for fattening the contracts they had been awarded, claiming that increases in the rate and frequency of deliveries now were needed. Relying on specious documents, Brady (with Turner's help) had rubber-stamped the requested increases, enriching both the contractors and himself, as money had flowed back to him, kickbacks from contractors that usually amounted to about one-third of the increase that he had granted. Mail deliveries had then been executed with varying degrees of reliability—or sometimes not all. An incredulous Bliss pointed to several routes where contractors affiliated with the Dorsey ring apparently had failed to deliver even a single piece of mail.[30]

As he finished his opening statement, the prosecutor told the jurors that he was confident that they would reach a guilty verdict. "I will simply say, gentlemen," Bliss concluded, "that unless we greatly misjudge and miscalculate the force and nature of the testimony, and that unless we greatly misjudge you, we shall expect at your hands a verdict of conviction against these defendants."[31]

Bliss's marathon opening statement—it lasted for nearly ten hours over two days—met with mixed reviews in the press. "Bliss made a very strong opening address before the jury in the Star Route conspiracy case, and if the government succeeds in proving half that Bliss promises to prove, the conviction of Dorsey, Brady and the rest is almost certain," the *New York Truth* reported. "Whatever the result of the trial, it is now plain that the government is doing its best to secure a verdict against the Star Routers." With its characteristic scorn for the prosecution, the *Evening Critic* in Washington took a different view, faulting Bliss for being obtuse and longwinded. His meandering argument "could have been clearly and concisely stated in two hours," rather than the ten he had consumed.[32]

After Bliss came the parade of the defendants' many capable attorneys. Jeremiah Wilson, counsel for Brady and Turner, addressed the jury first. A former judge who had represented Indiana in Congress, Wilson had an excellent reputation as an attorney and would later serve as dean of Georgetown

University's law school. His appearance in the crowded courtroom, like that of Ingersoll, signaled that the prosecution was in for a tough and protracted fight.

Wilson began by acknowledging that the Star Route case "had attracted a great deal of public attention" over the previous year thanks to the government's sustained efforts to publicly vilify the defendants and whip up public sentiment against them. "Regularly, from day to day, from week to week, from month to month, through more than a year," he complained, "there has gone out to the country, through the press, the most garbled, the most unfair, the most untruthful accounts in regard to the matters that are now before you, in which these defendants have in the most unstinted way been charged with being thieves and robbers."[33]

The evidence would tell a different story, Wilson promised. Yes, Star Route contracts had been adjusted over time, and his clients, Turner and Brady, had signed off on increased payments to contractors. But this kind of tinkering was to be expected, given that, at least initially, no one really knew much about postal routes in remote areas of the West beyond the number of miles involved. "Will you tell me how the officials, in making up these advertisements, can tell just how much speed can be made on this new route that is marked out by Congress through an untraveled country?" Wilson asked. "Will you tell me how the official could know just how many trips a week ought to be put on this new route? He cannot know." Given that the terms of the initial Star Route contracts had been based on little more than educated guesses, it was hardly surprising that they subsequently had been adjusted. (Wilson never mentioned the curious fact that these adjustments always had been made to increase mail service and boost the value of the contracts. Somehow the initial Star Route agreements never had been changed to diminish their value.)[34]

In making these changes, Brady had simply done his job and exercised appropriate discretion in his role as second assistant postmaster general, the lawyer continued. And he had not exceeded or abused his authority: federal law and Post Office regulations gave him the latitude to amend contracts to reflect necessary increases in the speed and frequency of mail deliveries on particular routes. Brady was not infallible, and he might have made a few minor mistakes in professional judgment in adjusting some Star Route contracts, but these good-faith errors hardly amounted to crimes, argued Wilson.[35]

As he finished his opening statement, Wilson told the jury that the government would not be able to produce even a shred of evidence to show that

Brady or Turner had enriched themselves by engaging in a criminal conspiracy with the other defendants. "Now, gentlemen, I defy this prosecution to prove that my clients ever entered into a conspiracy," he said. "I throw down the gauntlet to them now, and I defy them to prove, by any testimony that is reputable, or has any approximation to reputability, that a single farthing of the Government's money ever went improperly into the pocket of either of my clients." There was no evidence for the simple reason that they never had received any illicit payments from contractors.[36]

During a break in Wilson's opening statement, a reporter overheard some attorneys and judges discussing how artfully he was framing the defense's case for the jury. They were uniformly impressed by his approach. "Jeremiah Wilson is making a magnificent opening speech," one of them told the reporter. "He is dealing in facts—something George Bliss cannot do."[37]

Newspapers that favored the government offered a different appraisal of Wilson's performance. The *New York Times* expressed bafflement that Brady now was apparently changing his justification for his actions in handling postal contracts. "When the shameful and intentional extravagance of the star route management was first exposed," Brady had claimed in the press that he had approved of changes in postal contracts in order to boost economic development and population growth in the West. "Now we are told," the newspaper stated, "that he had no discretion in the matter and was simply doing what the law compelled him to do in accepting the statements made to him" in transparently phony letters and petitions.[38]

After Wilson finished, attorney Lemon Hine spoke on behalf of defendants John Miner and Harvey Vaile. Hine asserted that in bidding on and then securing Star Route contracts, his clients simply had engaged in ordinary business transactions. They "came into it the same as any other honest citizens come into any contract or legal relations one with the other," he explained. "The parties bid as they were invited to bid by the government, and bidding upon those contracts secured them. Why? Because they were the lowest bidders. Hence, of course, being the lowest bidders and the acceptance of their bid being for the interest of the government, they so far certainly did not enter into any conspiracy to injure or defraud the government." None of this had been done with criminal intent, and it hardly amounted to a conspiracy, as the government contended.[39]

In his statement on behalf of Miner and Vaile, Hine highlighted a huge potential weakness in the government's conspiracy case: the apparent lack of connection between some of the defendants. He claimed that Miner had only encountered his codefendant Brady once. That meeting had not concerned Star Route matters, and it had been so unpleasant that Miner, stung by the ill treatment he had suffered, resolved to never deal with Brady again. Miner "has never had any business relations with him since, and has never spoken to him," Hine insisted, "one never recognizing the other from that time to this." Mocking the idea that the two men were intimates who had cooked up a criminal plot together, the lawyer laughingly called them "pretty conspirators!"[40]

One of Stephen Dorsey's attorneys, John McSweeney, spoke next. In the courtroom, McSweeney cut an interesting figure. "His appearance is peculiar," wrote one reporter who was covering the Star Route trial. "He is tall and broad-shouldered. Thin locks of brown hair are plastered closely to his head, and they break into ringlets below his collar. He wears a bushy brown beard, and upon his nose, which is not prominent, are fixed eyeglasses which are far below his eyes, and which close his nostrils in their embrace." Whatever the peculiarities of his appearance, there was no doubt that McSweeney was a skilled orator: "His voice is rich and strong, and he uses it skillfully. He chooses the short Saxon words, and embellishes his arguments with simple and homely comparisons and illustrations."[41]

McSweeney brought all of his talents to bear in his opening address to the jury. The sheer distance between the defendants had made it impossible for them to have engaged in a conspiracy, he stated. Scattered around the country, the defendants had been "separated by thousands of miles," Dorsey's attorney told the jury. "Brother Wilson has said that this conspiracy must have been made at long range. I take another view of it and another figure. Conspiring is being together. Now, it would make those fellows perspire a good deal to conspire and breathe together across the continent."[42]

In his opening statement for the government, Bliss had vilified Dorsey and mocked his excuses for having become entangled in the Star Route contracting scheme. At one point, he had compared the ex-senator to a notorious Shakespearean villain who exploited others and lined his own pockets through cunning and deceit in financial matters. McSweeney, in his review of the substantial financial losses that Dorsey alleged that he had suffered in

Star Route contracting, mocked the idea that his client was any such criminal mastermind. "Senator Dorsey, the Shylock!" he said with a chuckle.[43]

There were more attorneys involved in representing the defendants, among them the illustrious Ingersoll, who would play a sizable role in the trial as it progressed. But only Wilson, Hine, and McSweeney made opening statements to the jury, laying out the basic contours of the defendants' overall case. After McSweeney finished up, the prosecution began its case.

Many of the government's first witnesses were low-level Post Office functionaries who took on the laborious task of explaining how Star Route contracts were handled and by whom. Thomas Kirby, who had been Postmaster General David Key's private secretary, testified about various postal laws and regulations; an assistant journal clerk stated that there was no general order or directive governing the handling of increases in Star Route contracts for expedition. ("Nothing in my books that I can find," the clerk said.) John Falconer, a statistician, reported the number of Star Routes in 1878 (8,811), the number of miles that those routes covered (206,777), and the "aggregate mileage of the carriage" on them during the year (an astounding 61,435,682 miles).[44]

This last number—which is roughly equivalent to the distance separating Earth from Mars—seemed to startle Judge Wylie, and he questioned Falconer about it. Did he mean "the number of miles that the mails are carried backward and forwards through the year?"

"Yes, sir," Falconer told him, "during the whole year."[45]

This kind of testimony hardly was the stuff of high drama, but prosecutors felt that they needed to explain the inner workings of the Post Office before they outlined how Brady, Turner, and the rest of the Dorsey ring had flouted its rules.

The trial proceeded at a sluggish pace, at least in part because there were so many attorneys struggling to be heard in the courtroom. At one point early in proceedings, an already weary Judge Wylie noted, "The first witness examined this morning was examined by three on one side, and, I believe, four on the other." All of the lawyers felt that they had a right to be heard, and they often spoke at the same time. (When their voices overlapped too much, the court reporter sometimes threw up his hands in confusion and simply noted in the trial transcript that "SEVERAL OF THE COUNSEL FOR DEFENDANTS" had spoken.) Their endless objections and arguments—punctuated by occasional questions posed by Judge Wylie and jury foreman William Dickson—broke up the trial's flow, making it difficult for jurors and spectators to follow how the case was developing.[46]

From the outset of the trial, the judge expressed concerns about the potential danger of having so many attorneys presenting evidence, examining witnesses, and arguing over the finer points of law. Reflecting on one moment when the proceedings devolved into a kind of legal free-for-all, Wylie lamented that "the evil became manifest."[47]

To lighten the mood, Judge Wylie and the attorneys sometimes joked about the testimony itself or the atmosphere in the courtroom. Noise and sound from the ongoing renovations to the courthouse seemed to be a consistent source of merriment. McSweeney once noted the racket caused by the hammering of workmen who were erecting the building's north extension.

"To proceed, with that noise, will be very annoying," the defense attorney complained.

"We will have to do the best we can in trying the case with that noise," Judge Wylie stated. "We cannot stop. That noise has continued ever since this case began. Today is not the first time."

Defense attorney Enoch Totten chimed in, "It is the first time they have been pounding on iron bars."[48]

This comment elicited laughter in the courtroom, but it did not seem to have much of an effect on Wylie, who announced that the proceedings would continue. The judge, however, had his own troubles in hearing testimony above the din of construction, although he ascribed the problem to the individuals on the witness stand.

"There must be something the matter with that Post Office building," Wylie said. "None of the witnesses from there speak loud enough to be heard."

Totten, who rarely missed an opportunity to jibe at the prosecution, thought he knew why the Post Office employees spoke so quietly: the unfair scrutiny they had received during the government's investigation of the alleged Star Route frauds. "They have become suspicious, your honor," he said, "under the proceedings of the last year."[49]

Issues of volume notwithstanding, Totten began to lose patience with the initial parade of prosecution witnesses because their testimony seemed to be so irrelevant. None of the low-level Post Office functionaries brought forward by the prosecution appeared to be able to offer any testimony that was directly related to the alleged crimes at issue in the case. "We want to know how the light is coming in," the exasperated lawyer said to Judge Wyle. "When these gentlemen have begun the proof of the unlawful conspiracy, we want to know something about it."[50]

Totten stressed the idea that if the government hoped to prove its charge of conspiracy, it needed to show that the defendants had worked in concert. He noted that the case involved "nineteen contracts, which were awarded to [several] different sets of men" supposedly operating under the umbrella of Stephen Dorsey and getting help from Second Assistant Postmaster General Brady. Merely showing that Brady was a bad actor hardly proved that he had entered into a complex and far-reaching conspiracy with numerous other men. If the government could not show how and why the alleged conspirators were connected, its case would fall apart.[51]

Attorney Jefferson Chandler, who represented Brady, highlighted the problem of focusing a conspiracy trial on the alleged bad acts of a single person (his client). "You cannot affect half a dozen co-defendants by the personal conduct of one codefendant," he argued. "You cannot prove a joint crime, a crime necessarily joint, by circumstances, unless the circumstances themselves be joint. Now, they are not offering here any circumstance, or any fact in which these defendants participated together."[52]

And there was another issue with the conspiracy charge. The government not only had to prove that the defendants had plotted together to commit a crime but also had to demonstrate that they had engaged in some overt act to bring their collective criminal plan to fruition. "The conspiracy is one thing, and something done under the conspiracy, in the language of the statute, is another," Judge Wylie explained. "Unless they prove not only the conspiracy, but some act done in accomplishment or in pursuance of the conspiracy, they fail." For the government, showing that the defendants had planned to commit crimes was only half of the battle.[53]

In the early days of the trial, defense attorney Robert Green Ingersoll mused that the government, with its cavalcade of minor witnesses, was being painfully slow in showing that the defendants had taken any overt act to further their alleged conspiracy. "I suppose this evidence does not go to any overt act, yet," he grumbled from the defense table. "They are tuning the fiddle. They have not struck a tune yet."[54]

Totten used another analogy to criticize the government's case during the testimony of Star Route subcontractor Charles French. On the witness stand,

French explained that he had subcontracted Route 34149 (which ran from Kearney to Kent, Nebraska) from John Peck, who had been acting on behalf of John Dorsey.

Totten interjected that French's testimony did little to prove the alleged crimes at the heart of the Star Route case. "We are beginning at the top of the house," he groused. "We have no proof here at all of the conspiracy."

Amid the din of the courthouse renovations, Judge Wylie warmed to the house-construction metaphor, but he did so in a manner that was sympathetic to the prosecution. "I have seen many houses underpinned, and very effectually, too," the judge responded. "Sometimes that is done." (Underpinning is the process of bolstering the foundation of an existing building.)

"They were underpinned after they had been built, your honor," Totten responded. "You never saw a man begin at the top of a chimney to build a house. That is what my learned friend was doing here."

Wylie told him, "I do not know whether this is the top of the chimney or not, but it seems to me that it is not only competent but important in relation to the issue involved in these proceedings."[55]

Although he allowed French's testimony to continue, Wylie clearly struggled with the prosecution's slow and somewhat disjointed approach to legal house-building—that is, its effort to prove the totality of the defendants' alleged conspiracy, both in its planning and in the overt acts that had set it into motion. His doubts were manifest when the prosecution called former attorney general Wayne MacVeagh to the stand.

The government planned for MacVeagh to recount for jurors a crucial piece of evidence: the June 1881 confession by which defendant Monfort Rerdell had laid out, in considerable detail, the workings of the entire Star Route conspiracy. "I expect to prove by Mr. MacVeagh," prosecutor Dick Merrick stated, "that Rerdell admitted to him that he was in a combination with Dorsey, Brady, and others of these defendants to obtain mail contracts, and by various fraudulent devices to have the pay stipulated for in those contracts enlarged by the improper exercise of official authority on the part of Brady." A credible report of a confession that had been offered by a participant in the alleged conspiracy—this was blockbuster stuff.[56]

Rerdell's confession (which, problematically for the prosecution, he later retracted) provided an essential overview of the alleged conspiracy from the perspective of one of its central figures. Without it, the government would struggle to prove that the Dorsey ring had, with Brady's help, manipulated Star Route contracts and intentionally defrauded the government.

Ingersoll, recognizing the danger that Rerdell's confession posed to his client, objected to MacVeagh's testimony, arguing that the government needed to show that the Star Route conspiracy existed before it could introduce Rerdell's since-repudiated confession about its operations. Judge Wylie agreed, telling Merrick that "you must first prove that there was a conspiracy" before the jury could hear about Rerdell's confession. He ruled out MacVeagh's testimony regarding Rerdell until the government offered sufficient proof that the clerk had been part of a criminal scheme.[57]

Wylie's ruling represented a resounding defeat for the prosecution as well as a public embarrassment. The *New York Times,* which generally favored the prosecution in the Star Route case, noted that "the representatives of the government were overmatched" by Ingersoll and his colleagues for the defense. Moreover, the judge's ruling emboldened an already intransigent defense team. The *Times* soon observed that defense attorneys were "offering trivial objections to every document offered in evidence" by the government. The defense team was "again using the dilatory and obstructive methods which characterized their work before the trial began. Encouraged by their success in barring Mr. MacVeagh and the Rerdell confession, they are now objecting to the introduction of every scrap of paper which the prosecution wishes to place before the jury."[58]

As the trial wore on, the defendants and their attorneys made periodic efforts to amuse and distract themselves, sometimes with the aid of supporters. One Sunday, when court was not in session, the Dorsey brothers, Brady, and a few other defendants joined some lawyers and well-wishers for a cruise on the Potomac River on an excursion steamer, *The Mystic.* The weather was stifling, but "a first-class dinner, with cooling liquids, made amends for the intense heat and the star routers managed to pass a very pleasant day," according to a newspaper account.[59]

For the defense, not every day in the Star Route trial passed so happily. A story was later told about Ingersoll trudging home after an especially long and contentious day in court. In a dark mood after sparring with Judge Wylie, the defense attorney passed an ornery mule, and it snapped at him.

"What court are you judge in?" the harried Ingersoll asked the animal.[60]

NOT SO HOPELESS
The Prosecution Makes Its Case, Summer 1882

At least temporarily unable to make much headway with a potential star witness, former attorney general Wayne MacVeagh, the government resumed questioning a series of minor officials: the cashier of the city post office in Washington; a notary public from Colfax County, New Mexico; George Sears, the postmaster of Greenhorn, Colorado; and a bookkeeper from the Post Office's Finance Division. Their testimony provided mind-numbing details about the paltry revenues of various Star Routes, presumably to show that the defendants should not have received from former second assistant postmaster general Tom Brady hefty increases for expediting services on them.

In one especially stultifying moment in the trial, prosecutor George Bliss reviewed the gross revenues of a particularly poor-performing Star Route that had drawn suspicion. He related that its gross revenues were, "for the fourth quarter of 1878, $3; for the first quarter of 1879, $2.43; for the second quarter of 1879, $1.89; making for the fiscal year commencing July 1, 1878, the gross revenues, $10.32. For the fiscal year commencing July 1, 1879, the gross revenues were $9.90. For the fiscal year commencing July 1, 1880, the gross revenues were $2.43." Throughout the trial, Bliss trumpeted this kind of detailed information about individual Star Routes to bolster the government's claim that members of the Dorsey ring had received special treatment from the Post Office (in this case, increased pay for underperforming routes), but such tedious presentations almost certainly put jurors to sleep.[1]

The defendants' attorneys repeatedly mocked the government for going into such wearisome detail about matters that did not directly show that their clients had entered into a criminal conspiracy. After one of Bliss's lengthy expositions about gross revenues on some western Star Routes, defense lawyer Enoch Totten joked that before any hard evidence of a conspiracy was presented in court, "I might get lost in the sands of Utah."[2]

The trial eventually developed into a pitched battle in which prosecutors repeatedly found themselves on the defensive, struggling to demonstrate that they were building a conspiracy case against the defendants. Prosecutors George Bliss and Dick Merrick realized that the government's case was teetering on the brink of disaster, and they valiantly tried to salvage the situation by reiterating how the evidence being presented in Judge Wylie's courtroom added up to conspiracy. Granted, innumerable small (and perhaps unspectacular) pieces of evidence composed the government's proof against the defendants. When viewed together, however, those small bits of information clearly showed that a conspiracy had existed and that the defendants had furthered it through overt acts. Or at least that was what the government argued to the jury.

As could be expected, defense counsel raised doubts at every turn of the prosecution's case. The phalanx of attorneys representing the Dorsey ring hammered away at the weakness of the conspiracy charge whenever they could. To help them reach their ultimate goal—persuading the jury that the government had not proven its case beyond a reasonable doubt—they tirelessly lobbied Judge Wylie for rulings that would undercut the conspiracy charges. Wylie did not need much convincing. "In my view," he said after several weeks of testimony, "the conspiracy has not yet been made out."[3]

In the early stages of the trial, Wylie seemed to especially struggle with the prosecution's efforts to show how Brady had acted illegally in using his authority in the Post Office to sweeten the Dorsey combination's contracts. Strategically, it made some sense for the government to essentially begin its case with Brady, as his granting of increases for expedition was pivotal to the alleged conspiracy. And, for the most part, Wylie seemed to understand what the prosecution was trying to prove vis-á-vis the former second assistant postmaster general.

But what evidence was the prosecution using to support its case against Brady? Throughout the trial, much was made of the many allegedly fraudulent petitions that had been presented to him as evidence that particular Star Routes merited expedition. A typical one read: "We, the undersigned, citizens of Springfield, Lane County, Oregon, respectfully represent that, in their opinion, the mail facilities on the route from Eugene City to Bridge Creek, Oregon, are not sufficient for the actual necessities of the people. We therefore earnestly recommend that service on said route be changed from one trip a week to that of a daily service route, and that the speed be greatly increased." This plea was accompanied by a reassuring note from P. A. Kennedy, the Springfield postmaster, stating that he was "personally acquainted with a large number of the signers of the . . . petition, and [had] good reason to believe that each name was written by the person as above represented."[4]

The government seemed to suggest that Brady knew, or at least should have known, that such petitions were phony and that his willful ignorance on this matter was evidence that he was furthering the Star Route conspiracy. Judge Wylie, however, struggled to see how the spurious petitions implicated Brady in any crimes. The documents had been prepared and submitted by others, and it was absurd to have expected the second assistant postmaster general—a busy man with a broad purview within the Post Office—to individually validate hundreds of scrawled signatures from places like Oregon and Arizona Territory. During a discussion of one route, the judge interjected: "You are claiming that this was a fraudulent allowance on the part of Tom Brady. So far as I have heard these petitions they do not tend to establish that charge. And why the court and the jury and everybody should be detained listening to evidence that don't even seem to tend to make out the charge, I do not understand."[5]

Wylie's reservations should have represented a red flag for the team of federal prosecutors in the Star Route case. If a judge known for his forbearance and fairness was losing patience with their case, one could only imagine how jurors—ordinary men with no special training or interest in the law—were feeling.

As the trial dragged on into late June 1882, it seemed apparent to many observers that the proceedings were getting bogged down in the prosecution's lackluster presentation of arcane evidence. One newspaper noted in the trial's third week that jurors were "already likely enough to be bewildered with the mass of evidence presented to them." Not long after this observation was published, the jurors themselves expressed some restlessness over the trial's listless pace. With proceedings dragging on, the jury's foreman, William Dickson, said to Wylie: "Allow me to state, your honor, that the jury are exceedingly anxious to get through with this case, and as far as they are concerned they would sit on Saturdays, and even on Sundays, if need be. We are anxious to see this case terminated in some shape."[6]

Wylie, who was himself growing impatient with the prosecution's seemingly interminable examination of allegedly fraudulent Star Route petitions and other documents, despaired that the parties might have to spend their entire summer together in the courtroom. While acknowledging that "this is a very intricate and difficult case to understand and comprehend," he urged the prosecution to streamline its presentation.[7]

"I see now that there is a great deal of time wasted in reading these petitions, and I want to economize a little," the judge told prosecutors. "We have spent almost a month now. . . . If we go on at the rate and in the way that we have been going in the past, I do not see but that it will take three months to try the case."[8]

As the summer wore on, the trial's length made some in the court wax philosophical and poetic. At one point in mid-July 1882, prosecutor William Ker asked Judge Wylie if some extraneous documents could be introduced as evidence as part of a government report.

"Yes, they can all be regarded as in the report," Wylie responded. "It saves time, and that becomes a very important consideration. I do not know how much time we are to have in this world."

"Art is long, and time is fleeting," defense attorney John McSweeney chimed in, quoting an aphorism attributed to the Greek physician Hippocrates and later used by the American poet Henry Wadsworth Longfellow in his poem "A Psalm of Life." (Scarcely a day went by in court without one erudite attorney quoting some piece of literature or scripture.)

"I do not desire to spend all the balance of my days trying this case," Wylie said, "and I don't suppose the jury does, or anybody else."[9]

The avuncular McSweeney often seemed to find himself in the middle of gently needling exchanges between the attorneys. When the Ohioan referenced legal practices in his home state, prosecutor Dick Merrick baited him by interjecting: "Laws introduced by representatives from Ohio have established inquisitorial proceedings against citizens—the most outrageous that were ever passed in the world. We have had enough of Ohio."

"Mr. McSweeney," prosecutor George Bliss asked, "do you defend everything from Ohio that has been brought into this district?"

"Except Hayes," McSweeney said, referring to the former president, a Republican who had represented Ohio in Congress and served two terms as the state's governor. (McSweeney was an unapologetic Democrat.)[10]

Later in the trial, McSweeney objected to some testimony that Merrick was attempting to enter into the record. Merrick shot back that he had already established grounds to introduce the evidence in question.

"I think I have got it about every way," Merrick said. "I fixed it around on all sides of the compass, and your honor said my foundation was completely laid."

"No such foundation was by any man built," McSweeney protested. "He says he has got it all around. I object to it."

"It is not quicksand that my foundation is upon. It is a good foundation."

"It is slow sand," McSweeney cracked, referring to the ponderous pace of the prosecution's case.[11]

Not all of the exchanges in the courtroom featured good humor or clever wordplay. As often happens in long and contentious legal cases, attorneys' tempers periodically flared. The sharp-elbowed Merrick in particular seemed to delight in offering caustic asides about the defense team. During one session, a minor dispute arose as to how attorney Solomon Henkle had registered an objection to a particular piece of testimony. A quick check with the court reporter revealed that Henkle had not actually stated his objection.

"I made a mental objection, your honor," Henkle said sheepishly.

"That is the first one of the kind the gentleman has made," Merrick cut in to say.[12]

A short time later, Merrick and Henkle sparred over how candid the defense attorneys were being in the presentation of their case. Merrick implied that they were withholding information in a manner that benefited their clients.

"You admit what suits you," Merrick said, "and deny what suits you."

"My admissions are a great deal more reliable than the testimony of your witness," Henkle shot back.

"I think the proper way is to wait until your time comes," Merrick said, "and not cast doubt upon the matter by admitting some and denying some."

Here, an indignant Jeremiah Wilson cut in. "We always admit the truth," the defense attorney stated.

"I think that is the thing they do not admit," Merrick retorted.[13]

Throughout the trial, all of the attorneys in the cramped courtroom, as well as Judge Wylie, invoked legal treatises of various kinds to support their arguments. This often led to detailed exchanges about where potentially relevant interpretations of the law—principally American but sometimes British—could be found in particular editions of books.

"From what page of Roscoe do you read?" Judge Wylie said at one point to Merrick. He was referring to *Roscoe's Digest of the Law of Evidence in Criminal Cases,* an English work first published in 1827 and widely used by American attorneys and judges during the nineteenth century. Merrick was referencing the book's discussion of the law of conspiracy (which included the statement, "If a conspiracy be formed, and a person join it, afterwards, he is equally guilty with the original conspirators").[14]

"I read from side page 416," Merrick replied. "My edition is the 7th American, from the 8th London."

"I have the same edition," noted Wylie.

"Then your honor will be able to follow me."[15]

The lawyers' libraries contained more than the even-popular "Roscoe," as it was called. During the Star Route trial, they referenced numerous other treatises devoted to evidence, including "Starkie on evidence" (*A Practical Treatise of the Law of Evidence,* by Thomas Starkie), "Burrill on circumstantial evidence" (*A Treatise on the Nature, Principles and Rules of Circumstantial Evidence, Especially That of the Presumptive Kind, in Criminal Cases,* by Alexander Burrill), "Greenleaf on evidence" (*A Treatise on the Law of Evidence,* by Simon Greeleaf), and "Ram on facts" (*A Treatise on Facts as Subjects of Inquiry by a Jury,* by James Ram). Another oft-mentioned book was "Bishop's criminal procedure" (*Commentaries on the Law of Criminal Procedure, or Pleading, Evidence, and Practice in Criminal Cases,* by Joel Prentiss Bishop). Nearly every day of the trial, Wylie or an attorney appearing before him cited such works to back up their interpretations of the law.

As the Star Route trial progressed, it turned out that the prosecutors were not quarrelling only with belligerent defense attorneys, bored jurors, and an increasingly impatient judge. Internecine squabbles continued to plague the prosecution team. At almost every turn, they seemed to be battling among themselves.

William Ker later told Congress that internal discord and suspicion impeded the government team throughout the trial. As the prosecutor told it, a large part of the problem had been that one of their number was ambivalent about prosecuting perhaps the main target in the Star Route case, former senator Dorsey.

According to Ker's later congressional testimony, Dick Merrick told him that their colleague George Bliss hoped to shift the government's strategy in the Star Route case. While the trial was underway, Merrick said to Ker of Bliss, "Well, he wants me to let Dorsey go."

Merrick's claim startled Ker. He could not believe that Bliss actually wanted to let Dorsey escape justice while still attempting to secure convictions of minor players who had been involved in his combination. It seemed absurd to prosecute, say, Rerdell but let Dorsey—who had so clearly directed the former's actions—go free. The ex-senator was a linchpin of the whole case.

"What does he mean by that?" Ker asked, seeking clarity about Bliss's comment regarding Dorsey.

"Why," Merrick stated emphatically, "he wants to let Dorsey escape. He says we can convict the rest, but he wants to let Dorsey go."

Ker still could not take these alleged remarks at face value. Perhaps Bliss had just been speculating about the possibility of eliminating defendants somewhere down the road if the trial took an unexpected turn. (The prosecution team had engaged in innumerable conversations of this type as the Star Route case had taken shape over the preceding year.)

"No," Merrick said firmly. "He means it."

Ker continued to defend Bliss, insisting that Merrick had either misunderstood their colleague's comments or that Bliss had uttered them in an offhand manner in a moment of passion or frustration. Merrick, however, held his ground. Ker, as he later told Congress, was sure that "Colonel Bliss did not mean any harm, or did not mean anything wrong by the suggestions; but Mr. Merrick was very firm in his conviction that Colonel Bliss did mean something wrong."

And there was one more thing. According to Merrick, Bliss also wanted to kick Ker off the prosecution team. "I will tell you what he wanted me to do," he told his colleague. "He wanted me to go to the attorney general and tell him that there were too many in the case, and that the attorney general had better dismiss you and let him and myself [meaning Bliss and Merrick] run the case."

It was to Ker's credit that he persisted in defending Bliss's motives even after hearing this surprising allegation. Perhaps he had a legitimate concern about cutting expenses by reducing the number of attorneys representing the government?

Merrick recognized that Ker was an invaluable part of the prosecution team and said that he had refused to help orchestrate his colleague's ouster. If

Bliss forced Ker out, Merrick would leave also. In the meantime, he insisted that Ker stay on board, at least in part to help him maintain the integrity of the Star Route case. Merrick wanted him to help monitor Bliss and keep their fellow prosecutor in check. Ker said that this would be an unpleasant task.

"Well," Merrick told him, "we are going right ahead, and you must keep watch and see that everything goes on all right."[16]

Merrick and Ker later had slightly different recollections of the exact wording of this conversation. But Merrick never shook off the idea that Bliss was hesitant to prosecute Dorsey because he "bore very intimate and close political, and I thought personal, relations to Dorsey," as he later put it.[17]

Although they seemed to disagree about Bliss's dedication to seeing justice served, both attorneys would stick with the case. Bliss's apparent ambivalence about prosecuting Dorsey persisted throughout the trial (perhaps most notably in his closing argument to the jury, about which more later), and his disagreement with Merrick on this score played out in public when both men gave separate interviews about the case to the *New York Herald*. Speaking to a reporter from the newspaper, Bliss responded to claims from attorney Robert Green Ingersoll, who was defending Dorsey, that the jury would find the government's case against the alleged Star Route thieves to be defective. "Mr. Ingersoll will find out before the trials are over," Bliss stated, "that the cases contained a good deal of meat for the government."

But even as Bliss expressed his overall confidence in how the prosecution was progressing, he confessed that a case against one of the defendants might be lacking, at least in comparison to the others.

"The one against Mr. Dorsey, defended by the brilliant colonel, is admitted to be the weakest of the lot," Bliss said, referring to Ingersoll by the military title he had earned during the Civil War, "but in all the others a verdict for the prosecution is confidently looked for, and even that may be decided in the same way." In a later letter to the *Herald*, he claimed to have been misquoted, but this attempted correction really only served to reinforce his claim about the relative weakness of the case against Dorsey. "I have never by word or thought questioned ex-Senator Dorsey's prominence in the Star Route conspiracy," Bliss wrote. "I have only said that, owing to the exclusion of testimony by the court, the case proved was not as strong against Dorsey as against others."[18]

The *Herald* later published a story in which Merrick expressed a markedly different opinion about the comparative strengths of the cases against the individual defendants. Merrick had grown tired of Bliss's equivocating over the case against the former senator from Arkansas, which he told the paper was not weak at all. "Mr. Merrick evidently does not share the views expressed by his colleague, Mr. Bliss . . . that the case against ex-Senator Dorsey is 'the weakest of the lot,'" the newspaper reported. In contrast, Merrick "finds in both the law and the evidence abundant materials for making" for making a strong case against Dorsey. "He declares," the *Herald* noted, "that while Brady was the central figure, ex-Senator Dorsey was the life of the conspiracy."

In speaking to the newspaper, Merrick used vivid language to assert that the government had amassed more than sufficient proof to show that Dorsey had engaged in illegal conduct and merited conviction under the federal conspiracy statute. It was the former senator "who led them all, who stood in the van like Satan among his fallen hosts," he said. The government's evidence showed "enough ill-gotten gains in Dorsey's pockets to weigh him down before any honest jury in any honest country."[19]

Defense attorneys delighted in the apparent public disagreement between the two prosecutors over the strength of the government's case against Dorsey. Jeremiah Wilson said in court that the *Herald* stories indicated that there was a "very wide difference that existed between Mr. Merrick and Mr. Bliss upon this subject." Alluding to the possibility that the dispute might have to be resolved by their boss, the defense attorney said that it remained to be seen if the attorney general "was going to side with Bliss in saying that this was not much of a sprinkle so far as Dorsey was concerned, or whether he was going to side with Merrick and say that it was a flood so far as Dorsey was concerned."[20]

Throughout its sometimes helter-skelter case against the Star Route defendants, the government made much of the allegation that the Dorsey ring had cynically misrepresented public sentiment about support for expedition on particular routes. Although the term would not come into widespread use until a few years later, the government argued that Stephen Dorsey in particular essentially had conducted a misleading public-relations campaign to give the Post Office justification for expediting various routes (and thereby swelling the ring's coffers). The petitions, letters, and newspaper articles that poured into Brady's Washington office all had been part of a disingenuous effort to defraud the government.

To make this part of its case, the government presented a series of witnesses who allegedly had been part of the combination's public-relations push.

Bliss explained that one man had been put on the witness stand because the government expected "to show that Mr. Dorsey transmitted to this witness and wrote to this witness a letter, directing him to go to work and get up petitions and generally to manufacture public opinion; that he not only wrote one letter, but he wrote several; that he sent dispatches upon the subject; [and] that thereafter this witness did do those things." According to Bliss, "these letters and petitions which this witness dealt with were the petitions and letters which Mr. Dorsey transmitted to the Post Office Department, or to the second assistant postmaster general [Brady], as the basis of this order of expedition." There never had been any legitimate groundswell of public support to enhance services of any of the nineteen suspect Star Routes; it had all been manufactured by the ring. Had the case been heard in the twenty-first century, prosecutors might have asserted that these purportedly grassroots efforts had been "astroturfed" by Dorsey and his associates.[21]

At one point or another during the trial, all of the defense attorneys asserted that this line of argument was paradoxical, given the central charges in the case. The government alleged that the defendants had engaged in a conspiracy to manipulate the value of their routes, and conspiracies were understood to be, in common if not legal parlance, secretive. But if the members of the Dorsey combination had been intent on plotting in secret, why had they drawn public attention to their purported scheme by circulating petitions, eliciting letters, and planting favorable stories in newspapers? Was mounting a public relations campaign not the *last* thing a shadowy cabal of conspirators would do?

Defense attorney John McSweeney made this point with particular vehemence. If Dorsey and his compatriots really had been engaged in a conspiracy to defraud the government, "why freight souls with employing agents to call the attention of the world to the matter in public print that could catch [them] at a trick? Conspiracies are not done in public newspapers."[22]

Judge Wyle also balked at the notion that there was anything particularly sinister about the defendants having attempted to "manufacture public opinion," as Bliss derisively had put it. He was puzzled by the suggestion that the Dorsey ring had engaged in wrongdoing (and thereby furthered its criminal conspiracy) by planting factually accurate stories in western newspapers. "For the purpose of procuring expedition upon a route, it is perfectly legitimate to have articles published in the papers, it seems to me, certainly if they are true in fact, and an article published in a newspaper that is true in regard to a postal route, that states the facts, is not an objectionable method of proceeding in my view," the judge said. Focusing on such articles was, in the end, a waste of the court's time. "I do not see how it would tend, in the slightest degree, to make out the charge of conspiracy if it was allowed to come in; and, as time is valuable, the court does not think it right to spend the public time and its own time and tax counsel in an investigation which can lead to no result."[23]

Wylie also lost patience with of the government's unrelenting focus on the "false petitions" that it alleged the Dorsey combination had drummed up to justify expedition on particular Star Routes. Prosecutors put a seemingly endless string of witnesses on the stand to testify about the suspicious circumstances in which the petitions had been gathered, but there were some obvious flaws in this strategy. The government was not alleging that these witnesses had been involved in the Star Route conspiracy, and it did not seem that submitting a fraudulent petition to the Post Office to support expedition on a Star Route was any kind of federal crime. (And even if it was, the defendants had not been charged with it.) Wylie wondered what purpose was served by the testimony about the origins of the petitions, and he eventually urged prosecutors to turn to evidence more pertinent to the heart of their case.

After subjecting the jury to weeks of prosaic testimony about the minutiae of Star Route contracting, the government eventually made some headway in its case against the Dorsey ring. It did so by calling to the stand three crucial witnesses: John Walsh, former attorney general Wayne MacVeagh, and former postmaster general Tom James. Their testimony probably would do more to prove the government's conspiracy case than anything else heard or seen at the entire trial.

Walsh, a banker and sometime postal-route contractor, had known Brady since he had gotten caught up in the Whiskey Ring affair in New Orleans several years earlier, and his name had popped up throughout the Star Route scandal. He was widely known to have been involved in a dubious financial transaction between James Price and Senator William Pitt Kellogg (for which Kellogg later would be tried) and had offered startling testimony about irregularities in Star Route contracting before a House of Representatives investigative subcommittee in 1880. Although he seemed to have been involved in many of the same questionable activities that had landed members of the Dorsey combination in court, Walsh himself artfully dodged the authorities for many years.

In the Star Route trial, Walsh testified that he had loaned Brady "various sums of money" over the years. Although the precise amount was in dispute, he claimed that the former second assistant postmaster general wound up owing him upward of $40,000. Walsh, after suffering through a series of financial reversals, had approached Brady late in December 1880 to see if a settlement between the two men could be reached. He had made it clear that he wanted to collect Brady's debt.[24]

According to Walsh's testimony, the two men had bickered over the aggregate size of the loans, with Brady reminding him that a contract for a Star Route he had subcontracted from the Dorsey ring—the much-disputed Route 40101, which provided service from Santa Fe, New Mexico, to Prescott, Arizona—had been enhanced by the Post Office, thereby greatly increasing its value. Brady had explained that his expedition of Route 40101 had reduced his previous financial obligation to Walsh. Having enriched Walsh through the improved Star Route contract, Brady now owed him less.

Walsh's trial testimony was potentially explosive because he claimed that Brady, in recalibrating his massive debt (it was the equivalent of approximately $1 million in 2021), had explained to him in considerable detail how the Dorsey ring operated and how Brady raked in a small fortune from kickbacks from the combination. When the two men had discussed the expedition of Star Routes, he had stated that Walsh "must not suppose for a moment that it afforded him any special amusement to indulge" in enhancing their value. Rather, Brady had said, he boosted the contracts because a portion of the increase was kicked back to him. "I asked him to please indicate . . . what the terms were," Walsh said in court. "He told me that as a rule it was 20 per cent per annum [of] the amount of expedition."[25]

In other words, Brady had allegedly admitted to Walsh that his cut of every Star Route expedition was one-fifth of its yearly value. (Other estimates put this figure at one-third.) This was graft, plain and simple.

Prosecutor George Bliss stressed that the corrupt arrangement described by Brady to Walsh—he would grant expedition on postal routes in return for a kickback—had been his standard operating procedure in handling Star

Route contracts, and that it had been more or less an open secret. In outlining the bribery scheme, Brady had informed Walsh that "such was his invariable practice as second assistant postmaster general in every case where he made an order for expedition and allowance of pay," as Bliss put it in court, "and that the witness and everybody engaged on the mail routes knew and understood that this was his practice." In short, if you wanted the Post Office to beef up your Star Route contracts, Brady would have to get a cut for making it happen. This was his standard practice, and everyone involved in Star Route contracting knew it.[26]

After outlining for Walsh how the Star Route kickback scheme worked, Brady had tried to recalibrate his outstanding debt. He had reminded Walsh that his approval of the expedition on Route 40101 had increased its annual value from $74,000 to $135,000, a yearly difference of approximately $60,000. Twenty percent of the annual increase in the contract's value over the course of its three-year term amounted to about $36,000. This is what Walsh owed him for the expedition of the route, Brady had explained.[27]

But Walsh owed him even more, Brady had said in their December 1880 meeting. As Walsh stated in court, "He then reminded me of the fact that I had been requested to pay $8,000 to what was known as the congressional corruption fund, a fund which he insisted had been necessary in order to secure the appropriation for the Star Route deficiency." This had been the notorious slush fund used to pay off congressmen earlier in that year to secure their votes for ongoing funding for the Star Routes. Walsh did not feel that he should be obliged to pay into the fund; he already had done his part by holding his tongue about Star Route corruption in his testimony before the House appropriations subcommittee.[28]

This, too, was startling testimony. Walsh was not just claiming that Brady had orchestrated a kickback scheme; he also was asserting that the second assistant postmaster general had managed a "congressional corruption fund" financed at least in part by shady Star Route contractors. Much of the previous testimony offered by prosecution witnesses—about such pedestrian matters as fraudulent petitions and suspicious newspaper articles—paled in comparison.

On cross-examination, several defense attorneys took a crack at Walsh, all hoping to discredit him as a confidence man who had an ax to grind. "I want to show the animus of this man towards Tom Brady," Jeremiah Wilson said. Much was made of the fact that Walsh had filed a lawsuit against Brady to recoup the money that allegedly was owed to him and that there had been some minor inconsistencies in Walsh's accounting of who owed how much to whom.[29]

McSweeney went in a different direction in assailing the idea that there was any truth to Walsh's testimony. The defense attorney mocked the idea that anyone would make a detailed and damning confession in the manner Brady allegedly had done to Walsh. "Was there ever, since God made man, and man made Star Routes, such a confession in such humor made by one fellow to another as between brother Walsh and Mr. Brady?" he said while Walsh was on the witness stand. "Brady, with his $40,000 note in his hand, says, 'I want you to understand that I am the biggest rascal unhung, and I am running it here on ten thousand star routers. Just go now, and tell it.'"

"That is an elegant story," McSweeney said, dismissing Walsh's account with a chuckle. "That is a splendid thing."[30]

The press feasted on Walsh's testimony for several days. Several newspapers exulted that the Star Route trial, after almost two months, finally had hit its stride. With Walsh's testimony, "the first direct evidence of corruption was given," the Boston Daily Advertiser noted, and "the real interest in the case now begins." In Cleveland, the Daily Herald trumpeted the astonishing new revelations that bolstered the prosecution's flagging case.[31]

Among the news media, the general consensus seemed to be that Walsh's testimony about Brady had finally provided the moribund trial with a long-overdue jolt of energy and intrigue. Day after day throughout June and July, the prosecution had seemed intent on lulling the jury into a stupor with testimony about petitions and the minutiae of postal contracts. Some observers even had wondered if the trial would soon grind to a conclusion, given that the government had seemed to be running out of evidence to present. Now, with Walsh's spectacular testimony about Brady, something genuinely dramatic had transpired in the courtroom: a witness had directly implicated one of the principal defendants in serious wrongdoing. As a result, people were once more talking about the case. "The Star Route trial has taken a new hold upon public interest by the introduction of Walsh's testimony," a Chicago newspaper reported. "It introduces a new element into the trial, and what the result will be cannot be foreseen."[32]

Understandably, Brady was apoplectic. Not only had Walsh testified against him, but the banker also had elaborated on his testimony in several lengthy newspaper interviews. Reached by a sympathetic reporter from the *National Republican*, Brady expressed his dismay that Walsh had "made extended statements to newspaper men, with a view of influencing public opinion, and possibly the court and jury, in regard to this case." For his part, the defendant would not make any extensive statements about the Star Route case outside of the courtroom. "I cannot be persuaded," he said of Walsh, "to follow his bad example."[33]

Earlier in the trial, the government had attempted to introduce Wayne MacVeagh's testimony about Montfort Rerdell's confession, but Judge Wylie had ruled then that it was premature. The government, the judge had found at that time, had not yet laid a sufficient foundation to show that this defendant had entered into a conspiracy with the other men on trial. But after Walsh's testimony, Wylie was willing to give the former attorney general a chance to recount his dealings with Rerdell. Like Walsh's account of his interactions with Brady, this was potentially damaging testimony that might show a broad plan involving multiple members of the Dorsey ring.

Throughout the trial, both sides of the case had struggled with how a complicated conspiracy—one involving (if you included the deceased Peck) eight far-flung men and nineteen Star Routes in some of the most remote parts of the United States—might be proven to the jury. Judge Wylie had not always provided the clearest guidance on this matter; it sometimes seemed that he expected prosecutors to have proven the Dorsey ring's alleged conspiracy before he would allow them to present evidence of (or testimony about) it to the jury. MacVeagh's testimony about Rerdell led to a characteristically muddled discussion in which defense attorneys attempted to figure out exactly what the government intended to prove by calling the former attorney general to the witness stand.

"Your honor holds," defense attorney Solomon Henkle tentatively stated about MacVeagh's proposed testimony regarding Rerdell, "that it is competent for the purpose of proving the conspiracy."

"For the purpose of proving his connection and the character of his own acts with that combination," Wylie responded. He seemed to be suggesting that whatever MacVeagh reported about Rerdell should only be viewed as pertaining to Rerdell himself and not the Dorsey combination as a whole.

"Then it is not admitted for the purpose of proving the conspiracy," Henkle said. After all, the defendants were on trial for allegedly having jointly entered into a criminal conspiracy, not for allegedly having committed crimes as individuals.

"I do not intend to express my opinions in your language," Wylie said in a noncommittal way. "That is all."[34]

On the witness stand, MacVeagh related what Rerdell had admitted about the Dorsey ring to federal investigators in June 1881. He testified that Rerdell had explained his jack-of-all-trades role in preparing and submitting Star Route bids on behalf of the combination as a whole. It had been understood, Rerdell had said, that the Dorsey group would low-ball their bids and then have the value of the contracts inflated by Brady after they had been awarded. He had divulged that "the plan was to take them at much lower bids than they were worth," as MacVeagh put it in his testimony, "and then have them expedited and the service multiplied by Tom Brady."[35]

Of course, Second Assistant Postmaster General Brady had been rewarded for playing such an integral part of the Star Route fraud, Rerdell had told MacVeagh. "He said that Tom Brady was a party to this plan," the former attorney general said from the witness stand. "When the expedition for the increase of service had been allowed he stated some percentage that Brady was to have, but I am not clear about the amount. It was in the neighborhood of thirty or forty percent." (This was slightly more than the 20 percent that Walsh had reported as being Brady's standard kickback for facilitating Star Route expeditions.)[36]

According to MacVeagh, Rerdell also had mentioned that Stephen Dorsey had made a one-time payment of $7,000 to Brady. The former attorney general could not recall the details of this payment, but it seemed consistent with Walsh's earlier testimony about having been asked to contribute $8,000 for the so-called congressional corruption fund. (Dorsey had left the Senate by the time Congress addressed the Star Route funding deficiency in 1880.)[37]

Rerdell's confession had not reflected well on Dorsey. The former senator essentially had been portrayed by his former clerk and Arkansas friend as the mastermind of the entire criminal enterprise, MacVeagh stated in his testimony. To make matters even worse, Rerdell had said that Dorsey's role in orchestrating the scheming of the Star Route combination had started, as MacVeagh put it in his trial testimony, "while Senator Dorsey was in the Senate."[38]

MacVeagh's account was buttressed by the testimony of former postmaster general Tom James, who also had been present when Rerdell had outlined the machinations of the Dorsey ring. At that time, Rerdell had explained how he had prepared bids and "then attended to getting up of influence, petitions, etc., for expedition, and after the contracts were expedited . . . he managed the business of the combination," according to James. The former postmaster general also recalled that Rerdell had mentioned Brady's standard demand for a kickback after he permitted expedition on a Star Route: an amount equivalent to a third of the increase. And he had mentioned that Brady had expected a payoff for remitting contractors' fines and penalties (half of the forgiven amount).[39]

The government had hoped to call George Spencer, the former senator from Alabama, to the witness stand as well. Although he had been in Nevada since Garfield's assassination a year earlier, Spencer had been instrumental in helping launch the government's investigation of the Star Route frauds early in 1881, and prosecutors seemed eager to have jurors hear what he knew about the Post Office swindles. Spencer himself, aware of how the government had turned on some of its own witnesses, was less enthusiastic about testifying, but he responded to a subpoena and traveled to Washington.[40]

Among other matters, prosecutors hoped that Spencer would testify about his interactions with Stephen Dorsey. In the course of the Star Route investigation, the former Alabama senator had told Postmaster General James that he had witnessed Dorsey placing as many as six $1,000 bills into an envelope and then handing it over to Second Assistant Postmaster General Brady—a bribe for Brady's help in fattening the ring's Star Route contracts. As James paraphrased it, Dorsey had told Spencer that he had intended to demonstrate "how he did business" by passing along the cash-filled envelope to Brady. In a listless trial, this would be a spectacular revelation: one former senator providing firsthand testimony about another former senator offering a bribe to one of the central targets in the case.[41]

When he arrived in the capital, Spencer booked a room in the Arlington Hotel that adjoined the quarters of prosecutor George Bliss. Over the next week, he made repeated attempts to meet with Bliss and determine what, exactly, prosecutors were seeking from his testimony; he did not want to open himself up to prosecution by revealing too much of what he knew. Bliss repeatedly avoided the Alabaman even after a mutual friend (the omnipresent Secretary of the Navy William Chandler) tried to intervene and broker a meeting. Wary of the prosecution and fed up with Bliss, Spencer left Washington and traveled to New York, where he discussed the matter with Roscoe

Conkling, the Stalwart boss who was no fan of the prosecution after having fallen out with both Garfield and Arthur. Conkling, an attorney by training, inspected the subpoena that had been served on Spencer and announced that it was invalid.[42]

Spencer then vanished. The government received reports that he had returned to his home in Nevada and also had been seen in Hastings, Minnesota, but it could not find him and serve him with another subpoena. The former senator's disappearance was all the more galling because he was still a government employee, serving as government director of the Union Pacific Railroad. It was said that the matter was brought to the attention of President Arthur, but this did not seem to help the government's search efforts. Wherever Spencer was, he never took the stand at the Star Route trial.[43]

There was much speculation regarding Spencer's reluctance to testify. Some wondered if he was concerned about possibly incriminating himself. Another theory was that he had been caught telling a tall tale to the postmaster general about having witnessed Dorsey bribing Brady and did not want to admit on the witness stand that the story was a fabrication or exaggeration. Spencer later told Congress that he did not know how prosecutors had gotten the idea that he claimed to have seen an illicit transaction between the two men. "I have no recollection of ever making such a statement," he declared.[44]

The government questioned a few minor witnesses in subsequent days, but its case against the Dorsey ring effectively ended after jurors heard from Walsh, MacVeagh, and James. Their testimony late in the trial provided potentially devastating revelations about Brady, Dorsey, and Rerdell, strongly suggesting that they had orchestrated a conspiracy to defraud the federal government by grossly inflating the value of Star Route contracts and arranging for Brady to receive hefty kickbacks. Even with Spencer failing to testify, these dramatic disclosures provided some encouragement to those who hoped that all of the defendants would be convicted.

Buoyed by the prosecution's late-trial surge, the New York Times noted that "the conviction of the Star Route gang is not so hopeless as it recently appeared." The prosecution now seemed to have a fighting chance.[45]

14

WAS NOT THAT A FRAUD?
The Defense Stumbles, Summer 1882

The defense opened its case on July 31, 1882, almost two months after the Star Route trial had begun. By that point, it was unclear how effective the prosecution had been in proving its case to the jury, but the defense had to assume that the testimony of Walsh, former attorney general MacVeagh, and former postmaster general James had done some damage to the men who were on trial. If their statements in court about the Dorsey ring were not counterbalanced by persuasive testimony from defense witnesses, it was possible that the jury would buy the prosecution's theory of the case and convict the defendants of conspiracy.

The defense sought to undercut the government's case by attacking some of its central premises. In making their case to the jury, prosecutors had stressed the idea that the lucrative orders for expedition made by Brady on the disputed Star Routes had been unnecessary and that the push for these needless orders had been generated solely by the money-grubbing members of the Dorsey combination looking to commit fraud. When its turn to present evidence arrived, the defense countered these claims head-on with evidence purporting to show that many of the orders for expedition made by Brady had been perfectly legitimate and that he had been urged to make them by numerous people, not just members of the Dorsey combination.

"They charge that Tom Brady in making these increases and expeditions," defense attorney Jeremiah Wilson said of the prosecution's theory, "made them knowing that this service was not needed, and all that." The witnesses called by the defense, he promised, would show otherwise.[1]

For the most part, the government's witnesses had been a motley assortment of government clerks, western postmasters, and Star Route contractors, many of them hardscrabble men who probably had never stepped foot in the nation's capital before being summoned to testify at the trial. The defense countered with a succession of prominent individuals, including several senators and congressmen, all of whom freely admitted that, as part of their official duties, they had called upon Brady and practically begged him to expedite service on various Star Routes. Many said that they had done so because they strongly believed in the importance of Star Route mail service in catalyzing economic and population growth in sparsely populated regions of the West. This was noble public service, not corruption, and the defense witnesses spoke of it proudly.

John Mitchell, a former senator from Oregon, testified about his efforts to expedite service on Route 44140 which ran from Eugene City (now simply known as Eugene) to the town of Mitchell. Having received several petitions calling for increased service on the route, the then-senator had met with Brady to add his voice to the lobbying effort. "I stated, in a general way, unquestionably that I thought it was an important route for the interest of the people," Mitchell testified, "and for that reason I recommended that he comply with the wishes of the petitioners, because I had a great many petitions sent me asking for the increase of this service and expedition."[2]

The former senator might have felt a special affection for the town of Mitchell—it apparently had been named in his honor—but he testified that his efforts to expedite mail service had been grounded in a genuine commitment to serving the best interests of his constituents in Oregon, women and men who desperately wanted and needed improved mail service. When asked why had called upon Brady and advocated for improved service on several Star Routes, including Route 44140, Mitchell explained that "the interests of the people on and along the routes . . . demanded it. That was the only reason I had or could have had." Making money had nothing to do with it.[3]

Other lawmakers gave similar accounts of their interactions with Brady regarding the expedition of Star Routes. Edward K. Valentine explained that when he had taken office in 1879 as Nebraska's lone congressman, he had been besieged by constituents calling for upgraded mail service and facilities in his state. Valentine had not needed much convincing on this score.

"I was personally acquainted with a good portion of the state, and knew personally that it did not have such facilities as I thought it ought to have in that direction," he testified. He had been specifically concerned about the relatively poor quality of mail service in the northwest region of Nebraska, which seemed to be impeding settlement there.[4]

On the witness stand, Valentine stated that he had "repeatedly called upon Tom Brady, who was then the second assistant postmaster general, and urged increased mail [service and] facilities for my state." Defense attorney Robert Green Ingersoll asked the congressman how often he went to see Brady about bolstering Star Route service in Nebraska.

"Almost every day," Valentine said.

"For about how long?" Ingersoll asked.

"At least for the first three or four months after I came in, I called almost continually," Valentine said.[5]

The star defense witness was not a former politician but rather a former military leader, William Tecumseh Sherman. Although he is probably best remembered for his exploits as a merciless Union general during the Civil War, Sherman also later served as commanding general of the U.S. Army in the 1870s. In that role, he focused on making western and Great Plains states and territories safe for white settlement by eradicating the Native American tribes living in them. Several major campaigns against indigenous peoples were undertaken during Sherman's tenure, including the Modoc War, the Great Sioux War of 1876, and the Nez Perce War.[6]

Sherman, like the members of Congress who had preceded him on the witness stand, had lobbied the Post Office Department for expedited services on various Star Routes. He had written to the postmaster general, for instance, about Route 38113, which ran between Rawlins, Colorado, and the White River Ute Agency (now Meeker) in Colorado. Conditions in the area had been volatile; a revolt by Native Americans in 1879 had resulted in eleven deaths. "There were very serious troubles at that very time," Sherman said on the witness stand, and he had believed that improved mail service on the route would make it easier to subdue the restive Native American populations in the area. In a letter to the postmaster general, he asked that service "be increased from three times per week to seven times per week, and, if practicable, that the running time on said route be reduced from the present schedule to 36 hours, thereby accommodating the important business interests" of the region.[7]

The government disputed the relevance of Sherman's testimony, but Ingersoll insisted that it showed that the expedition of Star Routes served legitimate public-policy interests. "Here is a great general fact," the defense attorney said. "That great general fact is that the general of the Army had made up his mind that the increase of mail facilities became a great factor [in] the settlement of the Indian question." This undercut the government's argument that the expedition of Star Routes only resulted from the greedy scheming of members of the Dorsey ring.[8]

In their effort to prove that the Star Route expeditions had not been profligate, defense attorneys relied on the testimony of other Post Office employees who were familiar with how changes in the contracts had been handled. They did this at some risk, as so many men in the department had been accused of wrongdoing and removed from office after being charged with manipulating Star Route contracts.

One such potentially tainted witness was John French, the former chief clerk in the Post Office's Contract Division. French had worked under Brady, and in the second assistant postmaster general's absence, he had often temporarily assumed his superior's authority. In that "acting" role, French had approved several of the expedition orders at issue in the Star Route trials. For instance, for Route 46247, which ran between the northern California towns of Redding to Alturas, French had signed off on an order providing for three weekly trips (at an additional overall cost of roughly $28,000 per year).

Ingersoll argued that French, acting in Brady's absence, had made these orders honestly. He hoped to show that French "belonged to no combination, never received a dollar from any contractors, and that General Brady never suggested to him the doing of a dishonest or of a dishonorable action." The testimony of the clerk, who had not been named as a defendant in the case, would tend "to show that there was no conspiracy about the expedition of these routes." It had been ordinary Post Office business.[9]

French's testimony did present a potential problem for prosecutors. If the clerk had in fact been involved in fraudulently expediting Star Route contracts as Brady's underling, why had he not been charged as a conspirator? Fortunately for the government, impeaching French proved to be a relatively straightforward matter. On cross-examination, he was asked why Postmaster General James, shortly after taking office, had removed him from his position in the spring of 1881. French was forced to admit that he had been terminated because, it was alleged, he "had sat by Tom Brady and . . . had known of wasteful extravagance and had failed to report it to the postmaster general or to the president of the United States." In ordering the dismissal, James had not claimed that French had violated any laws, but rather had said that the clerk had been negligent in failing to properly report Brady's repeated transgressions in granting expeditions on Star Routes.[10]

The defense gambled again when Harvey Vaile took the witness stand early in August. With the Fifth Amendment protecting their right against self-incrimination, the defendants were not required to testify at the Star Route trial, and none of them had been heard from directly in the first two months of the proceedings in Judge Wylie's courtroom. Testifying represented a double-edged sword: it would allow them to make their case directly to the jury, but it also would expose them to potentially damaging cross-examination by the prosecution team. Among the defendants in the Star Route trial, only Vaile—apparently believing that it would be relatively easy to prove that he had not been part of the alleged conspiracy—decided to take that risk. It proved to be a colossal miscalculation on the Missourian's part.

Vaile's attorney was the capable Lemon Galpin Hine, a prominent and extremely active member of the Washington bar. Vaile's strategy in taking the witness stand seemed straightforward enough. Questioned by Hine, he told jurors that he barely had any acquaintance with his fellow defendants until he acquired an interest in some mail contracts late in the summer of 1878. A few months later, "there was an agreement and a division . . . of the Miner, Peck, and Dorsey mail routes," as he put it on the witness stand. Vaile had obtained 40 percent of the more than one hundred routes held by the group; Miner had taken 30 percent; and John Dorsey and Peck (through their representative, Stephen Dorsey) had taken 30 percent.[11]

Vaile had acquired six Star Routes as a subcontractor from Peck and John Dorsey: Vermillion to Sioux Falls, Dakota Territory; Kearney to Kent, Nebraska; Bismarck to Tongue River, Dakota Territory; The Dalles to Baker City, Oregon; Canyon City, Oregon, to Fort McDermitt, Nevada; and Colton to Julian, California. Although a subcontractor and not the original bidder for the routes, he had exercised full authority in their operation. "I and my men had absolute control of them. I may say I had as absolute control over them as anyone could have," he testified. "They were in my charge the same as if I had bid for them." Vaile stated that he had no interest in, or knowledge of, any of the remaining routes taken up by the Dorsey combination.[12]

After the routes had been divided in the spring of 1879, Vaile testified, he had virtually no contact with the other members of the combination.

"I never met Mr. Peck in my life," Vaile stated. "I never saw John W. Dorsey from that time and before until this trial. I never met Stephen W. Dorsey but once since that time, and that, I think, was in June last—this last June."

"Have you had any correspondence with any of them?" Hine asked.

"None whatever," Vaile said.

"Did you ever have any with Rerdell?"

"I think not."

"Since that time?"

"No, sir."

"Have you ever spoken to him since April, 1879?"

"I have not."

"Or conspired with him?"

"No, sir, I have not," Vaile stated.

Vaile and his attorney made a point of distancing him from Stephen Dorsey, perhaps the government's biggest target in the Star Route trial. They pointed out that the two men, far from being chummy coconspirators, had actually not gotten along very well.

Asked by Hine about his relations with the former senator, Vaile said, "Well, we were very unfriendly."

"That commenced from the time you met him in your first business transaction with him?" Hine asked.

"Yes, sir," Vaile said.

"You quarreled the first time you met?"

"Yes, sir."

"You have never made up since?"

"We have been more friendly since this trial. We have spoken," Vaile acknowledged. "But I think as soon as this trial is ended we shall be as far apart as ever."[13]

Up to this point, Vaile's testimony generally seemed to support the idea that he, at least, was innocent of the conspiracy charges leveled by the government. He did a capable job of explaining how he had acquired his subcontracts on several Star Routes, describing the manner in which they had been operated under his watch, and delineating how he had essentially steered clear of most of his alleged coconspirators after the combination's routes had been divided up.

But Vaile's testimony veered horribly off course when he was cross-examined by prosecutor Dick Merrick. Vaile—unwisely, in retrospect—had in his direct testimony described when and how he had taken over various Star Routes from the Dorsey combination as a subcontractor. This allowed Merrick to delve into the suspicious circumstances of that transaction. It turned out that the subcontracts entered into by Vaile had been backdated so that they would supersede any other subcontracts that the combination might have entered into. Such tinkering seemed to belie the notion that he had been an ethical subcontractor who had always played by the rules.

"You, being afraid that some of your investments might be jeopardized by the existence of previously executed contracts," Merrick asked, "caused your contracts to be antedated in order to cut out any such previously executed contract. That is so, is it?"

"That is so," a sheepish Vaile admitted.

Judge Wylie commented, "That is a square, honest, answer."

"That is a square, honest, answer," Merrick countered, "but the transaction was not."

Relentless in his effort to portray Vaile as crooked, the prosecutor honed in on the backdating of the documents.

"You said just now that you had the subcontracts antedated?" Merrick asked later.

"Yes, sir," Vaile stated.

"In order to cut out any prior contracts which these parties may have been executing?"

"Yes, sir."[14]

As Merrick quizzed him about the backdating of the subcontracts, Vaile explained that he had not been sure that any prior contracts existed.

"I did not go to the [Post Office] department before I took these subcontracts to know whether there were any other contracts on file or not," Vaile testified. "But there was a distrust or a fear, I might say, perhaps, in my mind, that some of my investments would be jeopardized, so that these contracts were antedated to get in, in advance—"

"Of any others?" Merrick asked, cutting in.

"Of any others," Vaile replied. "That is true."

Merrick then asked the obvious question about the backdating of the sub-contracts.

"Was not that a fraud on the others on its face?"

"That is a question for you to settle," Vaile said.

"That is a question of law," Merrick said.

"That is a question of law," Judge Wylie interjected, "which he is not competent to settle."[15]

Both Merrick and Wylie seemed genuinely surprised that Vaile had opened himself to such a damning line of questioning from the prosecution. Himself a lawyer by training, the witness should have known that his testimony about the subcontracts on direct examination might leave him open to questioning on cross-examination about the dubious character of the contracts themselves. It was an almost inexplicable self-inflicted wound.

"Are you a lawyer by education?" Merrick asked.

"I am," Vaile said.

"And you have been in court for the last eight weeks?"

"Indeed I have."

"And you have been closely attending to the rulings of the court in the progress of the examination of witnesses?"

"I have."

"Those kind of people," Wyle interjected, referencing the damage that Vaile had inflicted on himself, "do not make the best witnesses."[16]

From there, things only got worse for Vaile. Further questioning from Merrick revealed that Vaile, prior to completing arrangements to subcontract routes from the Dorsey combination, had spoken with Second Assistant Postmaster General Brady about the status of the routes. It seemed that some of those being acquired by Vaile as a subcontractor never had been put into operation by the Dorsey combination, a breach that normally would lead the Post Office to impose fines for nonperformance. Vaile had told Brady that he was preparing to subcontract routes and said he hoped that the official would extend the deadline for getting them up and running.

"I said to him as I left, 'If you will extend the time, I will go home and consult my friends, and I may possibly join them,'" Vaile said on the stand, referring to his associates in the Dorsey combination.

"Did he extend the time?"

Vaile initially responded "No." Then he backtracked, offering a convoluted explanation detailing how Brady might have handled the proposed extension. Merrick smelled blood and pressed the witness.

"Did he extend the time?"

"Yes, sir, he must have extended it."

"Do you not know that he extended it?"

"Oh, yes."

"Why did you not say so?" Merrick asked, clearly peeved that Vaile had given the opposite answer to the same question just moments earlier.

"Yes, sir, he extended the time," Vaile acknowledged.[17]

Further questioning from Merrick revealed that one of the routes subcontracted by Vaile (Canyon City and Fort McDermitt) had skyrocketed in value late in 1878 because of an expedition order approved by Brady. (This was the desolate route in the Pacific Northwest that had attracted so much scrutiny from investigator Patrick Henry Woodward back in early 1881.) In light of Vaile's testimony regarding the need to have extensions granted for some of the Dorsey combination's routes, the expedition order seemed curious to prosecutors. How could the Post Office possibly have known that the route needed to be expedited when it had not yet been put into operation?

Merrick asked Vaile what he knew about the timing of the expedition order on the Canyon City route, which had dramatically increased its value. The massive boost "was under an order made before the service was put on the whole route, was it not?"

"That I could not say. It may be so and it may not be. I do not know."

"What is your best recollection?"

"Well, my best recollection is that it was."[18]

At another point in his withering cross-examination, Merrick asked Vaile about the expedition of a route by Brady that increased its value by $19,318.

"Do you recollect that?" Merrick asked.

"No, sir," Vaile said.

"You don't know anything about it?"

"No, sir."

"You got the money, did you not?"

"At the expiration of the quarter I—"

Here, Merrick cut in to attempt to ferret out who, exactly, had asked for the expedition that had so handsomely benefited Vaile. The contractor feigned ignorance of the matter, saying he did not know, or could not recall, who had made the request.

Foiled in his efforts to determine who might have requested expedition on the route, Merrick turned to the documentation that must have been submitted to support the change in the contract. Throughout the trial, much had been made of the bogus petitions and affidavits that had been used to justify Brady's orders for expedition.

"You don't know who made the affidavit?"

"No."

"You don't know whether any affidavit was ever made?"

"I do not."

"You don't know who filed it?"

"I do not."

"You never had any talk with the contractor about it?"

"Never."

Merrick was incredulous over Vaile's explanations, or lack thereof. He seemed to be suggesting that the expedition order had just mysteriously appeared, like a holiday gift left by Father Christmas.

"Then the government was a Kris Kringle, acting voluntarily—"

"I don't know anything about that."

"—carrying around sugar plums?"

"They did not give them to me."

"You got the money?"

"Yes, sir."

"Yeeeeeessss, well . . . ?" Merrick said.

"It was not very sweet, though," Vaile conceded.[19]

Realizing that Vaile had shot himself in the foot with his testimony, defense attorneys scrambled to distance their clients from him. When John McSweeney jumped in to question Vaile, he attempted to underscore the fact that the witness professed to having had minimal contact with his client, Stephen Dorsey.

"When did you meet Senator Dorsey after the spring of 1879?"

"I think it was in June of last year," Vaile said, referencing their meeting in 1881.

"Did you see, communicate, conspire, or breathe with him since?"

"Never, nor before."

"That is conspiracy at a long range," McSweeney said.

Merrick interjected, "We will bring it close enough for you."[20]

Vaile's testimony was a thoroughgoing debacle not only for himself but also for the defense as a whole. Up until that point in the trial, the government had mainly relied on secondhand admissions of wrongdoing (provided by Walsh, MacVeagh, and James) and piles of confusing documents. Now, however, a member of the alleged conspiracy was speaking from the witness stand about how Star Route contracts apparently had been manipulated, and he could not offer plausible or straightforward explanations to account for how and why so many lucrative expedition orders had been granted by the Post Office. Vaile's admissions were a bonanza for the prosecution. It was, the *Washington Evening Star* marveled, "really remarkable testimony."[21]

There were a few more witnesses after Vaile, including some rebuttal witnesses put on the stand by the prosecution. The government recalled Albert Boone, who had been deeply involved in the Dorsey ring in its early operations, to testify about how records had—or, rather, had not—been kept. (Prosecutors privately remarked that Stephen Dorsey's abrasiveness made it easier for them to persuade witnesses like Boone to offer damaging testimony against him.)[22]

"You told us, I think, that you kept no letter-book?" Merrick asked. (A letter-book was a binder containing copies of business correspondence.)

"Certainly not," Boone said, scoffing at the idea. "The company did business on grave-yard principles."

This homespun comment drew some chuckles in the courtroom.

"What principles?"

"Grave-yard principles; [we] kept no books," Boone clarified.[23]

Boone's inference was clear. The Dorsey ring had kept no records because, in this thoroughly corrupt enterprise, it had been important for everyone to remain as silent as the grave.

A NATIONAL HUMILIATION
The Controversial Verdict, Late Summer 1882

L ate in August 1881, as President Garfield lay dying in New Jersey, a woman named Julia Isabella Sand dispatched a remarkably candid—and completely unsolicited—letter to Vice President Arthur, a man she had never met. Sand herself was a great admirer of Arthur, but others were, she wrote, somewhat less confident of his abilities. "The hours of Garfield's life are numbered—before this meets your eye, you may be President," it began. "The people are bowed in grief; but—do you realize it?—not so much because he is dying, as because *you* are his successor."

So began a remarkable correspondence between Sand and Arthur, who would in fact soon become president. Sand, who lived in New York City, was not especially prominent or well connected. She was a self-described invalid (she suffered from a variety of ailments, including chronic troubles with her spine) who would be institutionalized for mental illness in 1886. Sand was, however, a keen observer of political life. In the twenty-three letters that she sent to Arthur between 1881 and 1883, she offered shrewd reflections on the major political issues of the day, such as the Rivers and Harbors Act (he should veto it) and the Chinese Exclusion Act (also worthy of a veto). She likened herself to a "little dwarf" in a royal court who could tell a king the unpleasant truths that everyone else was afraid to articulate.[1]

As the Star Route trial drew to a close, Sand felt that Arthur needed the counsel of someone outside his inner circle in Washington. Her advice about the postal-corruption case was straightforward: he should remain steadfast, even if it meant hurting or alienating his political allies within the Republican Party. On August 15, 1882, she wrote:

And may I say one thing more? Do not, at the last moment, do anything weak in the Star Route cases. I know it is one of the most painful things in life to turn away from a friend, [and] let the cold, hard hand of Justice fall with full force, where it was expected to mitigate the blow. I am almost certain that this thought is troubling you now. But do not waver. Remember that your duty to the country stands above all else. If you must suffer, by all means suffer for the sake of truth [and] justice. What we suffer for wrong, degrades us—what we suffer for right, gives us strength.[2]

Arthur apparently did not respond in writing to Sand's remarkable letters, but they clearly struck a chord. On August 20—just five days after she urged him to stay the course in the Star Route case—the president made an unplanned visit to Sand's home on East 74th Street in New York. Their impromptu discussion left Sand dissatisfied; the presence of members of her family made it impossible for her and Arthur to have a frank discussion of political matters. (She later complained that it probably had been "a very stiff visit" for the president.) Arthur did, however, tell her that she should not believe everything that she read in the newspapers, which was perhaps an allusion to reports that he was wavering in his commitment to prosecuting the Star Route case.[3]

As Arthur was being counseled by Sand to maintain his resolve in the Star Route case, closing arguments in the trial got underway. They would consume the better part of a month. For several weeks, jurors would hear attorneys from both sides try to sum up the evidence that had been presented in court in a manner that pointed toward either conviction or acquittal. Their longwinded efforts—marked by hyperbole, humor, and an impressive range of literary and religious allusions—would stretch from the first week of August until the beginning of September. Attorneys from the opposing sides would more or less take turns making their final pitches to the jury over that period.

Prosecutor William Ker addressed the jury first. He began by underscoring the importance of the Star Route case, which he called one of the most significant legal proceedings in the nation's history. "Now, this is not an ordinary case," he stated. "There is not a man who is within the sound of my voice who will ever live to see the equal of this case again, and none of you twelve gentlemen will ever again sit in the jury-box on a case that is as important as this, and one that will go down into history among the legal records as one of the celebrated cases of the country."[4]

Such was the magnitude of the case, the Philadelphia attorney continued, that people throughout the country were anticipating the jurors' verdict. "There is not a hamlet, a city, a town, a county, a state, from one end of this great Union to the other, that does not know of this case, and where the people are not anxiously and eagerly waiting to know what you are going to do and what your verdict is," Ker stated. "Their verdict is already made up and they are waiting for yours. It is a matter of the greatest importance to them."[5]

Ker did manage to clarify—at least somewhat—the prosecution's stance toward one of the named defendants in the case, the deceased John Peck. He did not mention Peck's demise a year earlier but admitted that the government had put forth almost no evidence or testimony relating to him during the entire trial. "I wish to God that John M. Peck's name were out of that indictment," Ker conceded. "For I believe if there ever was a man injured, if there ever was a man who has gone to a higher tribunal and whose good name and fame and credit and reputation have been traduced and brought into infamy and disgrace, it is John M. Peck. There is not an act in the whole of this transaction that puts John M. Peck before you as a criminal. Not an act." Ker effectively told jurors that they were not to consider the question of Peck's guilt (which they could not have done posthumously anyway).[6]

As he finally finished up his closing address, Ker reminded jurors of their obligation to evaluate without bias or prejudice the evidence presented at the trial. "Now, gentlemen, when it comes to that point in the case do not forget that you have a great duty to perform," he said. "Do not let the ties of friendship interfere with you. Do not let the animosities of hate step in. Take the evidence as it is, and act as one man should act toward another." If they did so, Ker argued, they could only reach one decision: verdicts of guilty for all of the defendants.[7]

After Ker's closing argument, a procession of defense attorneys began making last-ditch pleas to the jury for their clients. Richard Carpenter, one of the stable of attorneys who represented Stephen Dorsey, gave an argument that spread over four days and attacked the prosecution on multiple fronts.

Characteristically forsaking legal nuance, Carpenter offered blunt criticism of how the federal government had botched the Star Route case. He began by noting that District Attorney George Corkhill had forsaken his position and turned over the government's case to a team of special prosecutors operating under the broad authority of the attorney general. "This, so far as I know, is without a precedent in the annals of the country," Carpenter intoned. "I have known of no other district attorney abdicating his position in favor of any man." It was perplexing to the defense attorney that the government had taken this unusual step in order to bring so much power to bear in the Star Route case. "Has not the Government power enough under ordinary circumstances and with ordinary means? Why this excessive exercise of power?" he asked. "Why establish this precedent for the first time in more than a hundred years of the national existence?"[8]

After suggesting that the Star Route defendants were the victims of prosecutorial overkill, Carpenter attempted to turn the jurors' attention to a delicate subject that had not been directly referenced in the trial up until that point: Stephen Dorsey's ties to the late President Garfield and his successor, Chester Arthur. In another apparent attempt to cast doubt on the legitimacy of prosecution as a whole, Carpenter questioned why President Arthur would countenance the prosecution of Dorsey, "his friend, his familiar, his acquaintance, one with whom, upon terms of intimacy and kindness and hospitality he had lived for years; one with whom he was associated in political life for years." To foreground the connections between the two men, Carpenter reminded jurors that grateful Republicans—Arthur among them—had feted Dorsey in New York City not long after the 1880 presidential election. "On the 11th day of February, 1881," the attorney said, "there was the most remarkable convocation of gentlemen that, perhaps, has ever occurred in the United States, in the city of New York, at Delmonico's."[9]

On that occasion, of course, Arthur and former president Grant had heaped praise upon Dorsey for his efforts in securing the Republican ticket's victory. Arthur himself had gone so far as to make sly but unmistakable references to the former senator's critical (and almost certainly underhanded) work in defeating the Democrats in Indiana. As he launched into his account of this celebratory event, Carpenter seemed to be building an argument that Arthur, now president, might not have actually favored the prosecution of Dorsey, purportedly his great ally.[10]

None of this, of course, had anything to do with determining whether or not Dorsey and any of his fellow Star Route defendants had conspired to defraud the federal government. Judge Wylie sustained prosecutors' vehement objections to Carpenter's detour, instructing the attorney that he would have to confine his closing remarks to the evidence that had been introduced at the trial. (This clear admonition would not dissuade other defense attorneys from attempting to reference the Delmonico's dinner in their own closing arguments.)[11]

Reined in by Wylie, Carpenter assailed the heart of the government's case. In what he derided as "an interminable indictment," prosecutors alleged that the defendants had engaged in a conspiracy, but the evidence presented during the trial had shown this charge to be, in Carpenter's estimation, utterly untrue. The attorney reminded jurors that, in order to prove the conspiracy charge, the government needed to demonstrate that the defendants had taken an overt act to further their scheme. But what had members of the Dorsey combination done? Legitimate businessmen seeking a profit, they merely had bid on and then secured postal contracts, after which they had sought increased payment of expediting services along their routes—all perfectly legal deeds and not the stuff of a sinister and wide-ranging criminal conspiracy.[12]

"You cannot make a crime out of innocent acts or any number of innocent acts," Carpenter insisted in court, "and there is not an act proved against any one of the defendants in this case, I undertake to say, that is sufficiently charged in this indictment on trial alone or sufficiently proved by this evidence that would authorize you for a moment to convict a single defendant in this case, not one." The government had absolutely "no right to pick up a little suspicion here and accumulate a little suspicion there and gather a little distrust elsewhere and put the three together and apply them in this case. That is not the way crime is proved."[13]

Carpenter's most notable contribution might have been his effort to minimize the overall importance of the Star Route case. Hardly a matter of historical import, the dispute over the postal routes was an ordinary controversy that had been blown completely out of proportion by the federal government. "It is magnified by the fact that the government is involved in it," Carpenter stated. "The government comes here with all its pomp and circumstance and show of power and inflates its case to an importance which it really does not have." The fate of the republic did not rest on the conviction of some well-meaning postal contractors and a couple of minor post office officials.[14]

During a colloquy after Carpenter had completed his remarks to the jury, defense attorney John McSweeney echoed his colleague's effort to downplay the significance of the Star Route case. "The whole thing," he observed, "is a scrubby affair."[15]

After Carpenter finished up, the alternating closing arguments continued with George Bliss. The prosecutor began apologetically, telling the jury that it was his "duty to inflict upon you gentlemen some remarks in connection with this case." Bliss warned that he would have to review a staggering amount of material in order to properly summarize the government's case against the Star Route defendants. "Now in this case, gentlemen of the jury . . . if I seem to weary you in going a little into detail," he said, "you must bear in mind the extraordinary mass of minute evidence that there is in this case." Bliss mentioned that upward of 1,000 exhibits had been entered into evidence, "a larger number than ever have been known to be proved in a case, certainly within our time." It would take time, he warned, to offer even a rough outline of this material, not to mention the fifty days of testimony the court had heard.[16]

Bliss insisted that conscientiously working through all of that evidence could lead the jurors to only one possible outcome: returning guilty verdicts against all of the Star Route defendants. "I claim that with the evidence this record bears there can be no doubt in the minds of one honest juror, and I am not going to think I have been addressing any but honest jurors," he stated. "I leave the case with you, gentlemen, as men who have taken an oath, as men who desire to stand well before the community, as men who desire to stand well before your maker, to find a verdict that the government has made out its case, and that the defendants have been guilty of a gross and outrageous conspiracy to defraud the government of the United States."[17]

For those who suspected that Bliss, the loyal Stalwart, was going easy on some of the defendants because of their service to President Arthur, his closing argument featured some notable holes. Although he touted the overall strength of the government's case against the Star Route defendants, he did not seem overly concerned with highlighting the guilt of former senator Stephen Dorsey, who had been so instrumental in the Republicans' 1880 presidential campaign. This omission was so glaring that Attorney General Brewster later would feel compelled to address the jury himself and rectify the error.

In their closing arguments to the jury, attorneys on both sides of the Star Route case mostly limited themselves to the facts and the legal issues at hand. But in an effort to make a lasting impression on bored jurors, almost all of them adorned their arguments with rhetorical flourishes of various types. The Bible and the works of William Shakespeare were referenced most frequently. (*Hamlet* seemed to be a particular favorite.) Attorneys also mentioned *Aesop's Fables* and the work of poets John Greenleaf Whittier and Lord Byron. One attorney invoked "From Greenland's Icy Mountains," a missionary hymn written in 1819 by Reginald Heber, an English bishop. If they were still paying attention to the proceedings, jurors received what might later be thought of as a kind of minicourse in the arts and humanities.

Defense attorney Enoch Totten's approach was typical. Addressing the jury after Bliss, he quoted lines from William Makepeace Thackeray's poem "The White Squall" (1844):

> And when, its force expended,
> The harmless storm was ended,
> And as the sunrise splendid
> Came blushing o'er the sea;
> I thought, as day was breaking,
> My little girls were waking,
> And smiling, and making
> A prayer at home for me.[18]

The quotation reinforced a running theme in all of the closing arguments offered by the defense attorneys: although the federal government had likened the Star Route frauds to a deluge of corruption, the case amounted to little more than a passing and altogether harmless rain shower.[19]

Defense attorney John McSweeney next addressed the jury in his typically homespun fashion. As Carpenter had done before him, McSweeney referenced the Delmonico's dinner from February 1881. Not long after Dorsey had been feted by former president Grant, Vice President–elect Chester Arthur, and other Republican dignitaries for his pivotal efforts on behalf of the party in the 1880 election, his purported allies betrayed him by allowing the completely baseless Star Route prosecution to proceed. "He has been stabbed in the house of his friends," the attorney said. "Scarce had the shoes grown old that stamped their loud approval of Senator Dorsey—two months—nay, not two months—until the roar of accusations burst out against him."[20]

McSweeney then created a stir in the courtroom by brandishing the bill of fare (or program) for the Delmonico's event. He did so not so much to highlight Arthur's purported fondness for Dorsey but rather to embarrass prosecutor George Bliss, who, like the president, once had been a cog in Roscoe Conkling's redoubtable New York political machine. Although he later claimed not to have been in attendance at the dinner honoring Dorsey, Bliss's name had appeared in the program for the event.

"Here is a little book that you may look upon, inscribed George Bliss," McSweeney said as he held the program aloft. "It is not in evidence."[21]

As the defense attorney well knew, this was completely irregular; the jury could not consider materials that had not been entered into evidence and were irrelevant to determining the defendants' innocence or guilt. Judge Wylie sustained prosecutors' objections to McSweeney's reference to the bill of fare, but the point had been made: Bliss, one of the prosecutors, was among those in President Arthur's orbit who had complicated ties to Dorsey. The clear inference was that the administration might not want to see the former senator convicted.

In his later congressional testimony about the Star Route trial, prosecutor William Ker recounted how McSweeney had "pulled out of his pocket a little book" that had been given to him by Bliss. To Ker, there was no doubt as to the defense attorney's intentions in attempting to show to the jury the program for the Dorsey dinner at Delmonico's. "This bill of fare was exhibited by Mr. McSweeney to show that the President and prominent men had favored Dorsey in the days of his influence," he testified. "The effect that Mr. Mc Sweeney wanted to produce, or the idea that he wanted to convey to the minds of the jury, was—and being a red-hot Democrat he could do it in that case a good deal better than a Republican could—the idea he wanted to convey was that the higher powers did not want Dorsey convicted." (Ker could not resist adding that the Delmonico's dinner might not have been such a great honor for Dorsey after all: he cited rumors that the former senator, in an effort to puff up his reputation as Garfield prepared to take office, actually had paid for the elaborate event himself.)[22]

Coming after McSweeney's theatrics, prosecutor Dick Merrick's closing presentation to the jury seemed subdued and workmanlike. Merrick knew something about high-profile cases: he had been involved in the spectacular trial of John Surratt, who had been tried in 1867 for plotting to kidnap and assassinate President Lincoln In his view, the Star Route trial ranked among the most important in American history, and as such, it commanded the attention of the entire nation. "Gentlemen of the jury, you are trying these defendants, but the whole people of the country are trying you and me," he declared. "This is no ordinary case. This is no common litigation."[23]

For Merrick, the Star Route case was significant in part because it had the potential to inaugurate a new, and salutary, period in American history, one in which corruption in public life became a relic of the past. "This jury, by its verdict, will mark one of two eras," he stated. "It will mark the commencement of an era of official purity, under honest and virtuous principles, and with a just appreciation of legal and moral duty, or it will mark an era of official peculation and conspiracy against the Treasury of the United States under the sure protection of perverted law." Jurors could help the nation embark on this new era, he argued, by returning guilty verdicts for the defendants.[24]

Well, for *most* of the defendants, anyway. Merrick said in his closing argument, "in the name of the Government of the United States I demand from this jury a verdict of guilty against John W. Dorsey, John R. Miner, Stephen W. Dorsey, Harvey M. Vaile, Montfort C. Rerdell, and Thomas J. Brady." Two names were notably absent from that list: those of the deceased John Peck and William Turner, who was still very much alive. The former Post Office clerk was no saint, but the government no longer believed that he had been a party to the conspiracy. "In reference to Turner," Merrick said, "evidence does not leave my mind free from doubt; and whilst I do not believe him unstained by criminal conduct in receiving money . . . I do not believe that these men introduced him into their confidence and made him familiar with the secrets of this conspiracy as a member of the conspiracy."[25]

The government was abandoning its case against Turner, and he would face no punishment. Merrick hoped that the clerk would learn something from his narrow escape. "For him, therefore, repentance and reflection," the prosecutor said. "And since he has heard the grating of the penitentiary doors so close to him, let that sound go with him through life and serve to quicken the better sentiments of his nature, elevate and improve his character, and make him hereafter a better and more useful man."[26]

As for the remaining defendants in the case, the jury should show no mercy. "I would have you [be], like justice, cold as icicles and firm as steel," Merrick continued. "If there is a plea to be interposed at all by me it is a plea for my country. It is a plea for the United States and the preservation of her institutions."[27]

Defense attorney Robert Green Ingersoll was one of the great speakers of his era, a man who regularly packed auditoriums for his fiery lectures on freethought, politics, history, and myriad other topics. Now, Ingersoll brought his remarkable oratorical skills to bear in his closing statement in the Star Route trial, delivering an address that captivated spectators in the gallery and jurors alike. (Such was the quality of his argument that it would later be included in published collections of his greatest works.) "Ingersoll's speech before the jury was one of the great efforts of his life—full of pathos—tender, logical, and though it consumed five hours time, yet it was to the point, and listened to by a great crowd," according to one account of the trial. "Many ladies were present and held their handkerchiefs to their eyes, while everyone in the room, even the hardened bailiffs, was touched with his wonderful powers of persuasive eloquence."[28]

Ingersoll lauded the defendants as decent and honest men who had done nothing sinister in bidding on, and then executing, Star Route contracts. His client, Stephen Dorsey, was particularly noble: according to his defense attorney, the former senator was "a man with an intellectual horizon and a mental sky, a man of genius, generous, and honest." Dorsey's accusers, however, were cut from an altogether different cloth, Ingersoll stated. They were so misguided that they had asked the jury "to violate the law of nature. They have maligned mercy. They have laughed at mercy. . . . Think of it."[29]

Ingersoll insisted that, despite the enormous length of the Star Route trial, prosecutors simply had not proven their case. None of the evidence presented in court demonstrated that the defendants had engaged in a conspiracy to defraud the government. "I have shown you that the indictment is one thing and the evidence another," Ingersoll said. "I have shown you that not one single charge has been substantiated against John W. Dorsey. I have demonstrated to you that not one solitary charge has been established against Stephen W. Dorsey—not one. I believe that I have shown to you that there is no foundation for a verdict of guilty against any defendant in this case."[30]

Many observers of the trial contrasted Ingersoll's full-throated defense of Stephen Dorsey with the prosecution's seemingly half-hearted efforts to secure the former senator's conviction. As one historian later put it, there was widespread "public suspicion that the administration was not sincere in its efforts to secure his conviction." There was a feeling that the government wanted to go through the motions of prosecuting some Star Route fraudsters without actually putting any prominent Republicans in any real legal jeopardy. Among those criticizing the government's approach was the *Washington Post*, which labeled the trial a roaring farce. The *Post* had particularly harsh words for Bliss, who seemed intent on "working up a hypothetical case against Brady and Dorsey, while avoiding the plain case he might have made against them." That prosecutor's closing argument, which only fleetingly mentioned Dorsey, did nothing to quell rumors that the Arthur administration's heart really was not in the Star Route case.[31]

There was some controversy over who would follow Bliss's lackluster performance and wrap up the prosecution's case. Although the federal government's team had operated under his authority, Attorney General Benjamin Brewster had not been on hand for most of the trial. (This was understandable, given his broad and time-consuming duties in leading the Department of Justice and serving in Arthur's cabinet.) Defense attorneys resisted the idea that Brewster, having largely sat out the proceedings up to that point, could now choose to appear at the trial. They argued that it would be inappropriate and unfair for the government to be able to bring another attorney—especially one of such stature—into the case in the final hour. But Judge Wylie saw no reason why the government should be barred from having its foremost attorney appear, especially since Brewster had been a special prosecutor on the case before his appointment as attorney general.

According to Brewster, the prosecution team asked him to deliver a closing argument to the jury. The government's attorneys were eager to have him address provisional (or interlocutory) rulings issued by Judge Wylie during the course of the proceedings. Brewster later said that it would have been "a very improper and unexplainable thing if I did not appear and speak" at the Star Route trial, given the enormous importance of the case. With the nation watching, the attorney general simply had to appear in court and tie together the government's case.[32]

When he was preparing his closing remarks, Brewster summoned prosecutor William Ker, and the two men brainstormed about how the attorney general might address the jury. As the pair reviewed the trial record, they determined that Stephen Dorsey's name had appeared nearly one hundred times in various transactions related to the nineteen Star Routes named in the government's indictments. The evidence clearly showed that he had been "the head and front of the whole affair," as Ker later put it, but during the trial, prosecutors had done a relatively poor job of highlighting Dorsey's leading role in the scam. His prominence had gotten lost in the morass of details presented to the jury. Ker and Brewster determined that the attorney general should rectify this strategic error in his closing argument. As the trial drew to a close, he would make a point of emphasizing the guilt of the former senator from Arkansas.[33]

After consulting with Ker, Brewster decided to narrow the focus of his closing remarks to Wylie's interlocutory rulings from the bench and the culpability of Stephen Dorsey. As he prepared to wrap up the seemingly interminable Star Route trial, the attorney general saw no point in attempting to review all of the evidence that had been mustered by the government.[34]

The colorful attire worn by Brewster in court occasioned much comment. It was so memorable that a later history of the courthouse, published in 1919, included a description of what the attorney general had sported for his closing address to the jury in the Star Route trial: "He wore a ruffled shirt of the finest cambric, with brass buckles and other features of the regalia of the Lord High Chancellor of England," that country's high-ranking judge. Other comments were less charitable, insisting that the attorney general looked like a dandy or a fop.[35]

Clearly stung by defense attorneys' objections to his presence, Brewster made a point of defending his right to be in court as the Star Route trial concluded. Although rash things had been said by defense counsel—they had suggested that he "did not understand the case"—there was nothing irregular about the attorney general stepping in to wrap up arguments in a significant federal prosecution. If anything, it would have been odd if had *not* appeared in court.[36]

At the core of this important case was Stephen Dorsey. According to Brewster, the former senator had been the central actor in the Star Route sham. Dorsey's figurative fingerprints were all over the nineteen routes that had been named in the indictment: the evidence showed that his name appeared approximately one hundred times in documents relating to them. Dorsey was mentioned so frequently because he essentially had been the connective tissue holding the various other conspirators together. His brother John, his brother-in-law Peck, his Arkansas acquaintance and clerk Rerdell, former second assistant postmaster general Brady—all of them had been bound into the conspiracy by Stephen Dorsey, according to the attorney general.

Brewster mocked the idea that Dorsey and his accomplices were honorable men who had innocently joined together in an ordinary and aboveboard business arrangement. From the start, their intent had been sinister. "They come from the different quarters of the compass to enter into this arrangement, they tell you honestly and by a kind of divine impulse!" the attorney general stated. "I say it was a diabolical impulse. Their object was conceived in corruption and executed in the same wicked spirit. Their object was plunder, *plunder!*"[37]

As Brewster was assailing Stephen Dorsey in court, the former senator was attempting to use the press to fight back against the prosecution. During closing arguments, Dorsey renewed his efforts to discredit the government's pursuit of him and his codefendants. He did this clumsily, first releasing letters he had written to President-elect Garfield early in 1881 in which he had leveled harsh criticisms at James (who would be postmaster general), MacVeagh (attorney general), and Bliss (special prosecutor). In one letter—written on February 7, 1881, around the time of his triumphant dinner at Delmonico's—Dorsey had mentioned that he recently had met with Bliss and Henry Knox, a college classmate of Garfield's, and discussed who might represent New York in the president-elect's cabinet. "It cannot be possible that you would call upon George Bliss, much less Mr. Knox, to give advice respecting so important a question to you and to the people of this state," Dorsey had written in the letter to Garfield. The two men might be decent fellows, he had said, but they "do not represent the people of New York, no more than I represent the King of Siam. All such advice is idiocy, and if you are occupying your time listening to men like these, I wish to express in the most emphatic way that your administration will prove to be a lamentable failure." He had also declared, "I am tired of this blathering talk about MacVeagh to the cabinet from Pennsylvania, and James, from New York."[38]

In the letter to Garfield, Dorsey had paired his blistering criticisms of Bliss, MacVeagh, and James with praise for the New York Stalwarts who had been so critical to the Republicans' triumph in 1880. "If you want advice in New York," Dorsey had written to the president-elect, "why don't you send for Conkling or Arthur, the two men who elected you, with the aid of Grant?" He had suggested at the dawn of the Garfield administration that these important machine politicians, not the likes of James and MacVeagh, should be consulted in important matters.[39]

In releasing this letter and a few others as the Star Route trial drew to a close, Dorsey seemed to think he could tie together his connection to the fallen president with his earlier warnings about some of the principals involved in the prosecution, all while currying favor with the current president. This ill-conceived effort backfired in breathtaking fashion. The *New-York Tribune* said that the letter "expresses exactly the spirit which has made the Stalwart faction odious to four-fifths of the people of these United States." Worse than this newspaper criticism was the apparent displeasure of the nation's chief executive, who was unhappy with having his name dragged into the Star Route fracas by Dorsey. "There is some talk tonight that Dorsey has overreached himself," the *Boston Globe* reported in a dispatch from Washington, "and that President Arthur is annoyed beyond measure at the publication of the letter."[40]

Dorsey's legal fate would be decided, of course, not in the newspapers or the White House but in Judge Wylie's noisy courtroom. Before he handed the case over to the jury, Wylie heard from attorneys on both sides about possible instructions that he might give to the panel to guide its deliberations. With so many attorneys involved, there was no shortage of proposed instructions: one defense attorney provided forty-eight of them, while another furnished twenty-three. Most of the proposed instructions dealt with, in one way or another, how the jury should determine if, when, and how the defendants had entered into a conspiracy to defraud the government. No other issue was more crucial to the government's case.

It was up to Judge Wylie to reconcile the various proposed instructions in a concise manner and then send the exhausted jurors off to deliberate. Providing a proper charge to the jury after a long, complicated, and contentious trial—a fraught proceeding that had captured the nation's attention for several months—was a critical task. Wylie acknowledged its importance by quoting a Latin proverb: *Judex damuatur curn nocens absolvitur* (roughly, "the judge is at fault when the wicked escape"). He knew that if he did not wrap up the case properly, the jury might falter.[41]

"You have a duty to perform," Wylie told the jurors. "If you believe these defendants innocent, if you believe the charge against them not made out beyond a reasonable doubt . . . then you should acquit them without regard to any amount of clamor, without regard to the opinions of the world." Likewise, the men were duty-bound to return guilty verdicts if they felt that the government had sufficiently proven its case.[42]

Wylie chose not to prepare a written charge to the jury. It would take too long, he said, and might only serve to further bog down what were already sure to be tense deliberations. Instead, the judge spoke at great length about the legal issues in the case, verbally summarizing the main points the panel would have to resolve in determining its verdict.

Wylie zeroed in on how the federal conspiracy statute should be applied to the Star Route case. It would not be enough for the jury to simply find that the defendants had reached an agreement to commit an illegal act. "Our statute requires that there shall be a conspiracy followed by an overt act by one or more of the conspirators, and that overt act is binding upon them all, although committed by but one," the judge explained. "So if you acquit one of the conspirators and there is no other overt act than his in the case, you must acquit them all."[43]

In making this point about the evidence of overt acts, Wylie specifically referenced the former second assistant postmaster general, who was generally regarded (along with Stephen Dorsey) as having been one of the key players in the alleged Star Route conspiracy. "For example, if you were to acquit Mr. Brady in this case, who has been called the master key in this conspiracy, and no other overt act than his can be found proved, of course the indictment must fall and the prosecution must fail," he explained. "So in case you acquit any of these defendants, and are deliberating about the guilt or innocence of the others, you must see whether the overt act was committed by someone still remaining among the conspirators."[44]

After receiving Wylie's charge and warning, the jury retired at 2:53 P.M. on Friday, September 8, 1882. Eight-one days after Bliss had made his opening statement for the government, the jurors began their deliberations in the Star Route case.

Judge Wylie instructed the jurors to return at 6 P.M. that day. When he asked them if they had reached a verdict, William Dickson, their foreman, reported that they had not done so "except as to one of the defendants." Wylie was unwilling to accept such a partial verdict and instructed the panel to return to the jury room for additional deliberation and then retire for the evening. After the marshal, Charles Henry, said that he would provide overnight accommodations for the men, the judge, mindful of the possibility that the jurors might be tampered with, warned them, "Take care that you do not let any of the jury-fixers approach you at the hotel or anywhere else."[45]

The jury reported back at 10 A.M. the following day (again, with no verdict) and then once more at 6 P.M. "We simply desire to report to the court," Dickson stated, "that the jury have come to an agreement as to some of the defendants named in the indictment and not as to others." Wylie again stated that he was unable to accept what he termed an "imperfect verdict—a verdict as to some of the defendants and no verdict as to others." Prosecutor Dick Merrick agreed, telling the court: "There can be but one verdict, your honor, in any case. It cannot be divided." The judge ordered that the government would have to lodge the jurors together, after which they would resume their deliberations.[46]

Little progress was made on the following day; nothing much had changed with the jurors. Wylie called them back into the courtroom twice, only to be told by Dickson that the panel had made no further progress. On the morning of Monday, September 11, the foreman told Wylie: "I will report that the jury stand the same as they did on Saturday last when my report was made. They have decided as to four of the defendants, and do not agree as to the others." The judge gave the jurors one final chance to reach an acceptable verdict before calling them back at 2 P.M. that day. After Dickson once again related that they had made no further progress, Wylie gave up; he would have to accept whatever verdict they had reached.[47]

Dickson said that the jury, heeding the prosecution's decision to abandon its cases against both men, had found John Peck and William Turner not guilty. John Miner and Montfort C. Rerdell had been found guilty as indicted. As for defendants John Dorsey, Stephen Dorsey, Harvey Vaile, and Tom Brady, "the jury are unable to agree," the foreman reported.

It was later revealed that the jurors had decided to acquit Turner by their fourth ballot. Their next ballot had resulted in the acquittal of Peck and convictions of Miner and Rerdell. (The delay in rendering not-guilty verdicts against Turner and Peck was inexplicable, given that the government had specifically abandoned its cases against both men.) Jurors also had come within one vote of convicting John Dorsey on five successive ballots.[48]

Attorneys for the two convicted men, Rerdell and Miner, immediately filed motions requesting a new trial. The motion on behalf of Rerdell cited as its grounds misbehavior on the part of the government, wrongdoing by members of the jury, and prosecutorial misconduct (in the presence of the jury, the government's lawyers had referenced the defendant's constitutionally protected decision not to testify on his own behalf). Rerdell's motion also argued that the verdict was contrary to the evidence and unreasonable. Miner's motion made essentially the same points.[49]

In arguing for a new trial for Miner, defense attorney Solomon Henkle underscored the obvious flaw in the jury's verdict: if jurors had not returned a guilty verdict against Tom Brady, perhaps the central figure in the entire alleged conspiracy, how could they have found lesser alleged conspirators (Miner and Rerdell) guilty? "Now, it seems to me, if the court please, that it is necessary and essential to this indictment that Brady must be in it; and if you knock him out, it is all gone," Henkle argued. "If that be so, then there can be no conspiracy under this indictment that does not include him."[50]

Almost everyone who had closely followed the Star Route trial agreed with Henkle's reasoning. It seemed illogical—and profoundly suspicious, given the ongoing accusations of jury tampering that had surrounded the trial—that the two central figures in the conspiracy (Brady and Stephen Dorsey) would not be found guilty while two comparatively smaller players (Miner and Rerdell) were convicted.

Even prosecutors were baffled by the jury's conclusions. "The government of the United States itself is not entirely satisfied, by any means, with this verdict," prosecutor Dick Merrick said in court after the motions from Miner and Rerdell were heard. "It is a verdict which subjects the masters to a retrial, and convicts the servants and the minions." The two convicted men did not have clean hands, he stated, but they merely had been acting on the orders of Stephen Dorsey and Brady. "It is apparent to all men, that, deeply guilty in point of morals and law as Rerdell and Miner are, the guilt they did, the criminality that they perpetrated, were the scheme and device of others." Inexplicably, though, the jury had not convicted those other individuals, even though they were even more culpable for the Star Route conspiracy.[51]

In an extraordinary step that highlighted the infirmity of the jury's partially hung verdict, Merrick announced that the government would not object to the motions for new trials made by Miner and Rerdell. The government hoped to "bring to trial again both masters and servants, in order that full justice may be done," he stated. "The government of the United States, may it please your honor, seeks no victim. It seeks simply justice. When a verdict apparently trifles with justice, it cannot meet the approval of the government of the United States."[52]

The disappointed Merrick concluded, "The verdict is thoroughly inconsistent with any rational theory as to the guilt of those found guilty, the rich are let go and the poor punished, the masters free and the servants in jail."[53]

On September 15, 1882, Judge Wylie granted the motions made by Rerdell and Miner and set aside the jury's partially hung verdict. He cited not only the very real possibility of jury tampering but also the general unreasonableness of the outcome. The judge was puzzled that the jury could have only found guilty "these two men [who] seemed to be at the two ends of the line" of the conspiracy. "It did not seem to my mind that they could have gone into a conspiracy without having some of the others along." An unbiased jury also might have come to this unlikely conclusion, but Wylie felt that there was a strong possibility that this panel had been bribed or coerced into reaching such an inconsistent verdict.[54]

With Wylie's ruling, the Star Route prosecution was almost back to square one. If the government desired to convict the Dorsey group, there would have to be a retrial.

For the most part, Judge Wylie received favorable reviews for ably presiding over a long and difficult trial. Although the government had lost, Attorney General Brewster placed no blame on him for the jury's problematic verdict. "I think Judge Wylie deserves praise for the way in which he presided in these cases," Brewster later testified before Congress. "He had a very serious, laborious, and difficult duty to perform, and he performed it with signal ability."[55]

It was difficult, however, to find many people who were pleased with the verdict reached by the jury in Wylie's courtroom. The prosecution team was befuddled and angered that the panel had convicted Miner and Rerdell but had somehow failed to return similar verdicts against Tom Brady and Stephen Dorsey, the two men who had led the alleged conspiracy. "It was not possible," prosecutor George Bliss later complained, "for those two gentlemen to have been guilty, acting under orders from Brady and Dorsey, and not to have found Brady and Dorsey guilty, the parties who gave the orders." The prosecutor later fumed to Congress that "it was actually and legally impossible that the little fellows could have been guilty, unless the big fellows were also. The verdict was a solecism and an absurdity."[56]

Prosecutor Dick Merrick was no more pleased than Bliss about the verdict in the Star Route trial. Explaining why he had not contested defense motions for a new trial, he later told Congress, "I regarded [the verdict] as disgraceful to the records of the court and of the government, and felt it to be my duty not to allow it to stand." The issue of the verdict's illogic aside, Merrick was troubled by reports that the jurors might have been tampered with and had referenced prohibited (and possibly prejudicial) materials during their deliberations.[57]

There was an overwhelming consensus that the government had so badly bungled the prosecution that jurors (issues of possible tampering aside) had been justified in their confusion in evaluating the evidence and applicable law. Charles Cole, Rerdell's attorney, later said that the jury had reached an entirely erroneous and inconsistent verdict because of the convoluted manner in which the case had been presented by prosecutors. "Take that mass of testimony put in before that jury, and the confusing arguments of counsel and the charge of the court, and it is a wonder to me that a set of men could make anything at all out of it," he later told Congress.[58]

Even former members of the prosecution team faulted the government for the verdict. "As the case was presented, my verdict would have been that the men were not proven guilty," William Cook, the much-maligned special prosecutor, later said. "Under our law, I would be compelled to have brought in a verdict of not guilty." Cook believed that the prosecution had erred in including too many defendants and postal routes in its indictment. A streamlined case, including a handful of routes and mainly targeting Stephen Dorsey and Brady, undoubtedly would have proven less confounding to the jury, he argued.[59]

The press spent weeks lamenting the verdict, which was, after years of buildup, a colossal anticlimax. A midwestern newspaper offered a typically perplexed assessment of the Star Route jury's unwillingness to convict either Stephen Dorsey or Brady, asserting in an editorial, "It is very difficult to imagine how two spokes of a wheel turn around without the hub and the tire turning also, and if two of the conspirators were guilty of defrauding the government, it is difficult to see how the officials through whom this fraud was perpetrated can be innocent."[60]

Papers throughout the country echoed this sentiment and bemoaned the verdict. In New York, it was called illogical and indefensible (the *Sun*) as well as a ridiculous disappointment (the *Graphic*). In Philadelphia, newspapers criticized the verdict as "a national humiliation" (the *Record*), a blow against justice, and a profound miscarriage of justice (the *Times*). In Atlanta, the *Constitution* complained that "the evidence in the case is spurned and justice [is] laughed at."[61]

Many newspapers looked for a silver lining in the trial's conclusion. Although the outcome had been legally ambiguous, there was a general feeling that all of the defendants had been proven guilty in the court of public opinion. "They are disgraced," the New York *Sun* argued, while in Massachusetts, the *Springfield Republican* said that the defendants had been left "stripped in character." The *Philadelphia Record* noted that, whatever the verdict, the defendants were "not vindicated. For the rest of their lives they must run the gauntlet of deserved obloquy. There is hardly a man, woman, or child in the Union that has not some notion of their infamy." In Baltimore, the *American* claimed that the trial fixed "an ineffaceable brand upon each of the conspirators" by showing the public how they had conspired to hoodwink the government.[62]

★16

INCONSISTENT AND PECULIAR
Charges of Jury Tampering and a Purge, Fall–Winter 1882

In his final remarks to the jurors in the Star Route trial, Judge Wylie felt compelled to address the proverbial elephant in the room: the prospect that the jury had been tainted.

Throughout the proceedings, there had been numerous newspaper reports about alleged efforts by both sides of the case to improperly influence the jury. (These stories had appeared in the press almost daily.) More seriously for Wylie, the foreman, William Dickson, solemnly reported to the judge that he had been approached by someone purporting to represent the government and hoping to influence the verdict. At least for the moment, Wylie did not believe that Dickson or any other juror had been compromised, but he nonetheless issued a stern warning to them all.

If Dickson's report was true, then "there are men engaged in the business, as it is technically called in New York, of fixing the jury," Wylie stated. "It would be very natural that any of you who have been approached in that way should feel indignant. You would be very likely to experience such a revulsion of feeling from this scandalous, degrading offer and insult as to be repelled to the other side. You ought to be careful about that, and not even let that interfere with a calm, dispassionate exercise of judgment." The judge called on the jurors to resist the temptations of bribes and remain true to their oaths. "If any of you have been approached with a bribe, be so brave, be so true to *yourselves* that not even that insult shall disturb the equanimity of your consciences and judgments."[1]

Wylie might not have been fully aware of it at the time, but efforts to fix the jury had started even before the men had begun to hear the case—or at least the prosecution believed so.[2]

The final two jurors selected for the Star Route trial in the spring of 1882 were Hugh T. Murray, a clerk in the House of Representatives folding room, and a broker named Zachariah Tobriner. During *voire dire*, prosecutors did not attempt to strike the two men from the panel, but they publicly speculated that Marshal Charles Henry, who had organized the pool of prospective jurors, had intentionally selected them from a group of men who were known to be sympathetic to the defense. Attorney General Benjamin Brewster was so suspicious of Henry's handling of the matter that he called the marshal in for an interview and had a stenographer on hand to record what was said.

Brewster took a keen interest in Murray, whose integrity had been questioned by prosecutor George Bliss. Marshal Henry was adamant that he had impartially selected Murray from the pool and had no knowledge about his sympathies to the defendants.

"If this miscarries, the censure shall fall upon you," Brewster warned. "You will never escape it as long as you live."

"I am not one who will try to escape responsibility," Henry replied.

The marshal was incensed that his integrity was being questioned by the attorney general, and he told him so.

"I only sent for you to learn what you had done," Brewster explained.

Henry responded, "I challenge the closest investigation into [my] conduct."

"If there is a just acquittal by twelve responsible men, I will rejoice," Brewster said. "If one man holds out against eleven the people will say, 'How came that jury to be put in that condition?' This thing of jury fixing I will not tolerate."[3]

The government's campaign against Henry continued after his confrontation with the attorney general. Bliss suggested that Stephen Dorsey had gone to Henry's office during jury selection and extracted a promise that the marshal would do his best to aid the defense. Henry explained that the former senator had in fact briefly visited, but only for a perfectly innocent reason. "The only time that Dorsey was ever in my office was one day when he called for a match to light his cigar," he said. Henry was adamant when asked if there was any veracity to the charges that he was beholden to the defendants: "Not even the substance of a shadow."[4]

Stung by Bliss's accusations of wrongdoing, Henry responded angrily. In an intemperate and altogether ill-advised newspaper interview, the marshal said of the prosecutor, "He don't amount to much, anyway. He is too full of genuine, downright meanness to ever amount to much as a man." Bliss—who everyone knew to be a crony of Chester Arthur—was "continually trying to hedge and throw distrust around the administration of President Garfield, and those who know Bliss best pay but little attention to the pompous fellow."[5]

Henry's friends believed that the government, possessing neither the will nor the evidence to convict the Star Route defendants, already was looking to pin responsibility on someone if the prosecution ended in failure. Don Albert Pardee, a federal judge in New Orleans, wrote to Henry, "I am a little concerned about the attempt to blame you in connection with the Star Route jury, for I have been of the opinion for some time that the administration did not desire a conviction, even if there is a case, which is doubtful, but would want a scapegoat." The government had "no case against the Star Route crowd," Pardee declared. "I have no doubt of the conspiracy as charged, but where is the evidence coming from? And when there is a failure, then there will be a racket. Then there must be a scapegoat." He suspected that this fall guy might be his friend Henry.[6]

The marshal later said that Brewster Cameron, a special agent of the Department of Justice (and the attorney general's nephew), had approached him during jury selection for the Star Route trial and stated that he hoped the panel would be stacked with jurors sympathetic to the prosecution. To that end, Cameron had attempted to give Henry a list containing the names of four or five men who would make, in his view, good jurors because of their sympathy toward the government. Henry later said that he had refused to even look at Cameron's list. "I became very excited, a little indignant, and refused flatly to have anything to do with it," he later testified in an 1885 court proceeding. "It would depend, I told him, upon the evidence, and I would summon good men, good and reputable citizens." (Henry admitted, however, that he had never reported Cameron's alleged approach to Judge Wylie, and the attorney general later called the entire story a preposterous lie.)[7]

In April 1882, as the selection of the Star Route jury was underway, one prospective juror, Frederick Shaw, received a note from Howard French, who was then an employee of the Census Bureau. The two men subsequently met for a drink, and French introduced him to William Rice, a well-connected politician in the capital. Rice subsequently passed along small sums of money to Shaw in return for information about his fellow prospective jurors; he told Shaw's wife that the two men "had a developing business relationship which would be for their mutual benefit." In these conversations, Shaw learned that Dorsey, the former senator from Arkansas, had given Rice $12,000 "to fix the jury" in the Star Route trial.[8]

Rice's entreaties to Shaw and another prospective juror, William Holman, ultimately did not yield results for the defense, as neither man ultimately was picked for the jury. Nonetheless, Rice and Shaw continued to work together on Dorsey's behalf to influence the men who were selected for the jury, among them a shoemaker named Edwin Doniphon. Dorsey gave Rice $1,000 to buy Doniphon's vote for acquittal, but the juror apparently needed additional convincing. Shaw received another $250 from Dorsey and passed it along to the juror as a gesture of good faith. Doniphon later confirmed that Shaw had offered him money to vote for Dorsey's acquittal.[9]

Prosecutors later told Congress that they had monitored the jury throughout the trial because they feared that the defense would make such surreptitious efforts to influence the panel. According to George Bliss, after "people brought us various stories of this juryman and that juryman, that he was doing queer things and meeting with queer people," the government had hired detectives to watch jurors who seemed to be engaged in suspicious behavior. "I am perfectly willing to say this, that during the first trial we caused the jury or many of the jurymen to be watched—where they went, their talks, and everything of that kind. We got reports." All of this had been done to guarantee the integrity of the panel, Bliss said, and not to influence its verdict. The detectives had been given strict instructions not to communicate with any jurors they monitored.[10]

The members of Congress who later reviewed the activities of the government's detectives were not impressed by their work. During a hearing on how the Star Route prosecution had been conducted, one of them cracked that "the principal occupation of these detectives seems to have been to take drinks and ride on street cars."[11]

There were plenty of accusations that the prosecution had gone further than simply monitoring the jury, although most of these were later determined to be spurious and concocted to deflect attention from the improper efforts of the defendants to sway the panel. The most spectacular claim on this score came from the foreman, Dickson, who stated in an affidavit to Judge Wylie that Henry Bowen, claiming to represent the Department of Justice, had approached him in an effort to influence the outcome of the Star Route trial.

According to the affidavit, Bowen had approached Dickson one evening at Driver's restaurant in Washington and asked to speak with him about the trial. Dickson, adamant about maintaining the integrity of the jury, had rebuffed his initial overture. "I replied that I had studiously refrained from conversation in reference to that matter," he later claimed, "and preferred that no allusion be made to it; that my position as a juryman in the case debarred me from indulging in any conversation on the subject, and I chose, while holding that position, to remain silent."[12]

Bowen had persisted, however, and eventually the two men began discussing the Star Route case. Bowen had said that Attorney General Brewster "was deeply interested in the final result of the Star Route cases," especially after newspapers controlled by Tom Brady had "commenced their tirade of abuse and vilification of the administration and its officers." Furthermore, Brewster had come to believe that his personal and professional reputations were at stake in securing convictions. With so much at risk, Bowen allegedly told Dickson, the attorney general felt that Brady and Dorsey must be convicted by any means necessary, even underhanded ones.[13]

Bowen had then said, "Dickson, you are a politician, and you know that 'politics is politics.' You are a man of superior intelligence, and the brains of the jury. The attorney general has a high appreciation of you, and knows all about you. If you are so disposed, you can accomplish what [Brewster] desires, and I will fully guarantee that there is 25 in it for you."

Dickson had then asked, "Twenty-five, what do you mean by that?"

"Why, $25,000," Bowen had replied. "The money will be placed in escrow."

Dickson later said that when he had expressed surprise at this startling overture, Bowen told him: "You are a man of the world and know when you are in a fight you must use every means in your power to win. This is now the attorney general's fight, and he must succeed—'tis life or death to him. . . . He desires this trial to be his greatest triumph."[14]

According to the foreman's account, Bowen had assured him that he need not worry about the ultimate fates of the defendants if he accepted the attorney general's bribe and helped secure a conviction. He had said that Arthur would pardon everyone convicted, perhaps within a month of the trial's conclusion, after the dust settled. And when Dickson had expressed some skepticism about his bona fides, Bowen showed him some documents (unrelated to the Star Route case or the postal bribery scheme itself) that appeared to bear the seal and signature of the attorney general.

"I am fully authorized to act by the attorney general, and will satisfy you if you assent to the proposition," Bowen had said of the bribe offer, "but if you do not, and the conversation should leak out, I'll deny every [damned] word of it."[15]

After the Star Route trial ended, Dickson's spectacular bribery charges, along with the other claims that had been circulating throughout the proceedings, prompted the government to launch an investigation of the jury's conduct. Prosecutors William Ker and Dick Merrick headed up this inquiry, with help from a special investigator for the Department of Justice, Henry Horatio Wells, a former U.S. attorney for Virginia and the District of Columbia. Wells would pen the government's report on the matter.

Shortly before Wells's findings were presented to Attorney General Brewster on October 21, defense attorneys doubled down on accusations that the government had tried to improperly influence the jury during the Star Route trial. They produced several affidavits from individuals claiming to know of bribery attempts that had been made by men purporting to represent the Department of Justice. Several of these accusations related to a detective named Frank H. Fall, who had been employed by Cameron, the Justice Department special agent, as a government investigator during the trial.

"The sordid, confusing story of the jury bribery," as one historian later called it, "was difficult to untangle, particularly as it related to the double-dealing of Fall. Employed to monitor the defendants' efforts to influence the jury, Fall had gone a step further by apparently approaching a juror named William Brown with the offer of a bribe. He had explained in a letter to Cameron that he could ensure that the jury would return guilty verdicts—so long as the government provided him with something in return. "I am certain that I can control two (2) men on the Petit Jury," he informed Cameron, "if I can have placed at my disposal 3 or 4 (three or four) 'clerkships' under the patronage of some *Senator that you can be safe to deal with* and will not get back on *me*."[16]

Cameron had not employed Fall to engage in jury tampering, and he worriedly passed along the letter to his uncle, the attorney general. Brewster was empathic in his response: the government no longer wanted to have anything to do with the unscrupulous Fall. "Best dispense with his services," he had written, "as the gov't cannot retain in its employ anyone who even suggests that an attempt be made to control a jury-man." Fall was duly fired.[17]

Brewster later told Congress that Fall had been involved in an effort to entrap Cameron and thereby discredit the prosecution generally and the attorney general specifically. In his report to the attorney general on efforts to tamper with the Star Route jury, Henry Horatio Wells essentially agreed. He found that Fall had acted on his own without instructions from the government, then further suggested that the rogue detective's intrigues had been part of a setup engineered by the defense. "It is apparent, from the whole history of the alleged attempt upon Brown's virtue," Wells reported, "that it was not done with the knowledge, in behalf of, or in the interest of the prosecution; that its guilty authors were neither the agents nor acted with the knowledge or approval of any officer of the Department of Justice. It was a deliberate and carefully prepared conspiracy against the administration of justice." He pointed out that "every one of the vile creatures who touched this infamous transaction" completely and immediately admitted, in affidavits provided to the defense, their roles in the jury fixing plot—a telltale sign that they had been trying to set up the prosecution all along. Actual scoundrels never would have confessed in that manner.[18]

After Wells submitted his report on the jury to the attorney general, arrest warrants were issued for Fall, Frederick Shaw, and two other men who had been involved in efforts to manipulate the Star Route jurors. Then jury foreman William Dickson's story about Bowen's attempt to bribe him—which the New York Times termed exceedingly improbable and suspicious—fell apart.[19]

Not only had representatives of the government *not* attempted to offer a massive bribe to Dickson during a meeting at Driver's restaurant (a meeting he had claimed to describe in some detail in the affidavit he had submitted to Judge Wylie), but it also was alleged that he had in fact taken money from the defense. Dickson, too, soon faced arrest. On its front page, the Times decried "Dickson's false charges" and stated that "the foreman [was] deliberately working for acquittal" in the Star Route trial. It was later revealed that Dickson himself had approached a representative of the Department of Justice, special agent Cameron, with an offer to "sell out for $25,000," as the newspaper put it.[20]

Jurors William Dickson and William Brown later were charged with crimes for having violated their oaths and working with the defense to secure an acquittal in the Star Route trial. Brown, whose votes during deliberations the *Times* described as being "inconsistent and peculiar," apparently received eight dollars from representatives for his trouble. (According to later legal filings by the government, he received this payment in the form of a five-dollar bill, two one-dollar bills, and a silver dollar).[21]

The government's efforts to prosecute Dickson for his misconduct as jury foreman would stretch from December 1882 until April 1885. In one police-court proceeding, Bowen was asked about Dickson's account of their alleged meeting at Driver's.

"Did you on that occasion offer Dickson $25,000 for the right to influence his vote in the Star Route trial, or tell him that you would place $25,000 in escrow?"

"No, sir. Emphatically, no," Bowen stated.

Had he ever made any efforts, at any time, to bribe members of the Star Route jury?

"None whatever."[22]

After several false starts, the government secured a criminal indictment against Dickson for having "corruptly endeavored to influence jurymen," and he went on trial in April 1885. It was a muddled affair that featured a morass of charges and countercharges against Dickson, Bowen, Cameron, and Brewster. In the end, jurors (understandably) could not figure out who was telling the truth, and Dickson was acquitted.[23] Even Dickson's acquittal could not conclude the seemingly endless Star Route jury-tampering saga. Dickson soon announced that he was filing a libel lawsuit against former attorney general Brewster for having told a *Philadelphia Press* reporter, "Dickson sold that trial. Bowen was a bad man, too—nearly as bad as Dickson, and that is saying a great deal."[24]

As the federal government tried to determine how and why the jury in the first Star Route trial had gone off the rails, it prepared for a second effort to convict the Dorsey ring in court. Given the prominence of the case, and how much criticism the first verdict had drawn, there was never any question that prosecutors would try again—and quickly. The government could not afford to lose face by simply giving up on the case.

Bliss received his marching orders from Attorney General Brewster, who wanted the Star Route case brought to trial again before the end of 1882. It would be up to him to organize the prosecutors and get them working to meet that deadline. "You know whom to direct. *I do not.* So do not let the case suffer for want of our preparation," Brewster advised in a letter. "I would not on any account have us miss a trial in December. It will give great public dissatisfaction."[25]

Part of prosecutors' efforts in getting ready for the retrial involved reviewing the mistakes they had made in the first go-around. William Ker was appalled to discover that, for the first trial, his colleague Bliss had done a lackluster job of preparing witnesses for their testimony. "In some instances I was surprised to find that they had not told one-half of what they knew, or not more than one-half," he later said. Determined to glean more information from witnesses during the retrial, Ker questioned them at length before they appeared in court.[26]

This type of more rigorous preparation left Ker feeling cautiously optimistic about the government's chances of prevailing in the retrial of the Dorsey combination. Prosecutors were compiling additional evidence that bolstered the case against a few of the defendants in particular. "It was principally implicating the Dorseys. The strongest part of the evidence was against the Dorseys, showing that they were in the case—Senator Dorsey, especially—as deeply as anybody." Ker insisted that "the case was made a great deal stronger against Stephen Dorsey [for] the second trial. It was made so strong that there could not be a shadow of doubt about it in the mind of any intelligent person."[27]

To signal its seriousness in continuing to pursue the charges, the government made several moves to punish those believed to have improperly aided the defense in the first Star Route trial. Among those dispatched from their official positions were Metropolitan Police Force detective George Miller, who had furnished daily intelligence reports to defense attorneys and had helped concoct bogus affidavits purporting to show that the government had attempted to bribe the jury.

Also seeing the door was Mornay Helm, who had held a plum job in the Government Printing Office. During the first trial, when he was not working for the government, Helm had regularly assailed the prosecution in the pages of the *Washington Evening Critic*, of which he was editor. Prosecutor Dick Merrick had been apoplectic over the newspaper's coverage and later said that the *Evening Critic* "was most virulent, unpardonably virulent, in its attacks upon the court and upon the counsel and witnesses for the government." During the trial, he had urged Bliss to approach President Arthur and suggest that Helm be removed from his lucrative government post immediately. "I told him that he, as a friend of the president," Merrick later testified, "ought to go to the president and have the man put out." Helm held on for a time but eventually was forced out.[28]

Charles Henry, marshal of the District Columbia, was ousted from his position as well. In his role as marshal, Henry—an Ohioan with close ties to former President Garfield—allegedly had failed to exert much, if any, control over the Star Route jury, allowing at least two of its members to be essentially bought by the defense. Moreover, he had given an indiscreet newspaper interview in which he had assailed Bliss. A still-smarting Bliss later said that Henry was dismissed "for a flagrant violation of his duty in aiding the defendants."[29]

Henry's dismissal raised some eyebrows, as many respected him for his integrity. "No end of justice can be forwarded by injustice," the *Cincinnati Gazette* editorialized. "The honest prosecution of the Star Route accused can not be advanced by accusing the innocent." The *New-York Tribune* noted that while Henry probably had gone too far in his criticisms of prosecutors, "no one who knows him doubts for a moment the entire honesty of the man."[30]

Henry himself felt that he had been made a scapegoat for the government's failure to secure convictions in the Star Route trial. Rumors circulated that, in retaliation, he would attempt to stymie the Senate's confirmation of his successor as marshal.

"No, sir, that is a public matter, and my private interests ought not to interfere with the official act of the Senate," Henry told a reporter who asked if he would oppose the confirmation of his successor. "I will fight to defend my character against this infamous attack, and against the charge that I have in any way sought to obstruct justice."

"What are the charges against you?" the reporter asked.

"Nothing, so far as I know, except those [made by] Bliss and the attorney general. The latter says the marshal of the District is responsible for much of the opposing sentiment, etc. There is not the shadow of foundation for that charge."[31]

Former senator George Spencer was another casualty of the government's posttrial purge. Although he had helped set the Star Route prosecution in motion in the early days of the Garfield administration, Spencer had ignored a subpoena and failed to testify during the first trial, thereby damaging the government's case. He later claimed that Bliss had given him the go-ahead to leave Washington during the proceedings, an assertion that the prosecutor himself vehemently denied. (Bliss would explain that he and others were so eager to find Spencer that government agents had searched for him as far away as San Diego.) The Arthur administration did not believe Spencer's weak explanation for his absence, and he was dismissed from his position as government director of the Union Pacific Railroad.[32]

Bliss strongly favored the housecleaning, viewing it as a necessary move to set the stage for the Star Route retrial. He wrote to President Arthur, "It seems to me important [that] the atmosphere which surrounds the case should be in some measure purified, that everyone may know so thoroughly—that the prosecution is in dead earnest, from the president down." The public needed a sign that the government was still serious about the case.[33]

The defense team, for its part, reacted altogether differently to the moves made by the government before the retrial. Reached by the *New York Times*, attorney Robert Green Ingersoll—who had indignantly refused to cooperate with Wells's jury-tampering investigation—complained that the government had not taken the time to hear from the officeholders before dismissing them from their positions. The defense lawyer announced that "he considered the dismissals by President Arthur as the most outrageous official acts he ever knew an administration to be guilty of on ex parte testimony," the paper reported. Ingersoll thought "the action of the president was taken for the purpose of terrorizing the jury in the coming trial into conviction."[34]

Stephen Dorsey also claimed that Henry's removal was part of the prosecution's effort to influence the jury in the upcoming retrial. He said that the marshal had been fired "in order that the selection of the next jury might be absolutely under the control of the prosecution—that is to say, 'packed.'"[35]

Always with an eye on his bottom line, Ingersoll wondered if his lucrative career on the lecture circuit would suffer because of his work on behalf of the Star Route defendants. He was thus delighted to discover that audiences still flocked to see him. "I am having a great success," he wrote from the lecture trail after the first trial. "The Star Route [affair] has helped, instead of hurt me." Sensing that his audiences were sympathetic to the defendants, he proclaimed their innocence and criticized the prosecutors for dragging guiltless men into court and peremptorily firing the likes of Henry. Ingersoll's efforts drew criticism from the *Nation,* which accused him of trying to influence public opinion—and with it, the minds of potential jurors—in advance of the retrial.[36]

For the Star Route retrial, Ingersoll still anchored the defense team, but its composition changed somewhat. John McSweeney, Enoch Totten, and Lemon Galpin Hine had left the fray, as had Charles Cole. Replacing Cole as Montfort Rerdell's attorney was William Wallace Wilshire, a Democrat who had served in Congress and as chief justice of the Arkansas Supreme Court. Walter Dorsey Davidge, who had been involved in the successful prosecution of Garfield assassin Charles Guiteau earlier in the year, also came on board. Attorneys Jefferson Chandler, Solomon Henkle, and Richard Carpenter reprised their roles from the first trial.[37]

The Star Route retrial began with the defense characteristically making a variety of moves to obstruct its progress. Affidavits from Dorsey's doctors were presented to Judge Wylie, all of them explaining in somber tones that the former senator could not appear in court because an eye infection had essentially rendered him blind. According to Ingersoll, the materials demonstrated "that Mr. Dorsey has lost about eleven-twelfths of his vision; that he is threatened with what is known as atrophy of the optic nerve; that he is in an extremely dangerous condition, [and] that he is liable to lose his sight." Other defendants offered petitions and affidavits of their own arguing the trial should be postponed because inflammatory newspaper coverage made it impossible to find an impartial jury.[38]

In court, the accused pointed to a "libelous report" issued by Attorney General Brewster and published widely in the newspapers. In a letter to President Arthur, Brewster had described how many officeholders in Washington had facilitated the egregious frauds perpetrated by the Dorsey combination. "Some portions of this community who surround these defendants and who have enjoyed or do still enjoy minor official positions know no allegiance to anyone but this band of robbers, and render no service to anyone but these evil employers," he asserted. "From motives of gain or other corrupt considerations they are saturated with affinities for these bad men, and they have contributed by every means in their power at the bidding of their masters to obstruct public justice and to defame its officers with the hope of securing the acquittal and escape of the worst band of organized scoundrels that ever existed since the commencement of the Government." With the attorney general fanning public sentiment in this manner, the defendants argued, it would be impossible for them to get a fair trial.[39]

Ironically, these complaints about potentially damaging press coverage were followed by Dorsey making a variety of confrontational and inflammatory declarations in the pages of the *New York World*. In a long and caustic statement, the former senator recounted his version of how the Star Route investigation had unfolded, starting in the early days of the Garfield administration. He suggested that Garfield himself had favored Dorsey's own suggestion for handling the matter (appointing a commission of Democratic congressmen to investigate the former senator's business affairs). He also claimed that he was being singled out for unfair treatment while other combinations of Star Route contractors were being dealt with by the government with greater leniency.

Dorsey seemed to be outraged by the conduct of Attorney General Brewster, especially after his published letter had stoked such fury among the defense team. "Mr. Brewster has dragged the robes of his great office into the filth and slime of debauchery so many times," Dorsey proclaimed, "that it is to be expected that a person guilty of such atrocious acts of immorality would be guilty of equally infamous acts in the administration of the office he holds and dishonors." He expressed his disgust that, in his letter to President Arthur, Brewster would attack the defendants "in language that would disgrace the merest police-court shyster." For good measure, Dorsey gave a separate interview with the *World* in which he described Brewster's predecessor as attorney general, Wayne MacVeagh, as a "physical, mental, and moral dyspeptic."[40]

Dorsey's public fusillade against the prosecution did little to aid his defense, at least as it played out in Judge Wylie's courtroom. Prosecutors argued that if he possessed the physical capacity to write articles and give interviews attacking their efforts, he should have the wherewithal to appear in court. Wylie agreed and allowed the trial to commence, lamenting as he did so the newspaper coverage of the Star Route case. (Effectively, the ailing Dorsey would be tried in absentia until he testified in March 1883.)

The press evidently had not been chastened by the criticism leveled at it by both the prosecution and the defense during the first Star Route trial. Breathless headlines and articles marked the start of the retrial, with newspapers heralding in headlines the arrival of "The Star Route Cyclone" and demanding that the "STAR THIEVES MUST GO." (But before they went, they should pay up:

"Every Farthing Stolen Must Be Recovered.") In its macabre preview of the trial, one paper announced, "The great fight is to rage all winter, and bloodthirsty people announce that this winter's drama will be a gory one all around."[41]

Bliss found himself wondering what he had gotten himself into by agreeing to become a special prosecutor in the Star Route case. Writing to William Lawrence, the government's first comptroller, about his pay—a persistent sore spot—as the retrial neared, he grumbled that his involvement in the matter had cost him dearly. "I may be permitted to add that had I supposed the engagement would take my time so exclusively as it has, I should never have accepted it . . . at almost any rate," Bliss complained. "It has practically taken my entire time for over a year, which has taken me from my home and my office. It has broken up almost entirely a business which I have spent twenty-five years in building up, and has been a thankless and unsatisfactory business." After reluctantly agreeing to join the prosecution team a year earlier, Bliss had attempted on several occasions to quit, only to be talked out of it by Attorney General Brewster. "I came in unwillingly," he wrote to Lawrence, "and I remain unwillingly, at a personal and pecuniary loss."[42]

Bliss complained to Merrick, his fellow prosecutor, that Brewster's insensitivity to the pay issue might force him to quit. "I have had a very pleasant *taffy* letter from Brewster as to my going out of the cases and wishing me to stay in," Bliss wrote (using "taffy" to mean insincere flattery). "Still I doubt. Lawrence, first comptroller, has hung up my bill, and Brewster don't seem to assert his rights as to it. If he don't do so, out I go."[43]

Other members of the prosecution team likewise complained about the sacrifices required, both financially and professionally, due to their involvement in the Star Route case. In a plaintive letter to Attorney General Brewster, Ker described how his private legal practice in Philadelphia had suffered because of his decision to work for the government. "Whilst I was so employed in the government service," he wrote, "I had to let my private cases go into the hands of other attorneys; the student I left in charge of my office was absent visiting theaters, going to picnics and base-ball matches, and, as I learned from people who had called, my office was closed nearly two months." Ker only wanted the attorney general "to fix some certain and adequate rate of compensation" that properly reflected not only his indefatigable work for the government but also his abandonment of his private practice. If that could not be arranged, Ker would have to return to Philadelphia.[44]

In this turbulent atmosphere, the Star Route retrial got underway early in December 1882. Despite their sensational failure in the first trial, prosecutors did not substantially change their approach to the case, deciding to focus on the Dorsey combination and its alleged conspiracy to defraud the government by manipulating contracts on nineteen Star Routes and kicking back money to Second Assistant Postmaster General Brady. The government believed that it still had an airtight case, although it was narrower in that Post Office clerk William Turner and contractor John Peck—whose prosecutions the government had abandoned during the first trial—were no longer defendants.

That the government had decided not to alter its approach was evident from the outset. Bliss, seemingly unable to stop himself from again plunging headlong into the minutiae of the case, delivered a detail-heavy opening statement that stretched out over three and a half days. By the end of it, he was forced to admit to the jury that he had spoken at "probably unnecessary length" about how the Dorsey combination had operated. He finished by expressing the hope that they would "vindicate the cause of honesty and the cause of the honest administration of justice in the District of Columbia" by returning guilty verdicts against all of the defendants.[45]

For the most part, the members of the defense team were more economical in their presentations to the jury. But if they were more concise, the attorneys for the defense were no less dramatic. Attorney Jefferson Chandler, for example, told the jury: "You are called to the consideration of this case under the most extraordinary circumstances that ever surrounded an American jury. There has been organized and executed up to this hour a tyranny of opinion that was never before felt in the administration of justice under the American flag."[46]

And so it went. The prosecution once again bombarded the jury with facts and figures, while the defense repeatedly offered objections and attempted to dismiss the entire prosecution as nothing more than a tempest in a teapot.

If there was intrigue surrounding the second Star Route trial, it involved the prosecution's persistent effort to track down potential witnesses and compel them to testify. Bliss would not give up on the idea of finding Spencer, the elusive former senator from Alabama, and serving him with a subpoena. Spencer and the government played an international cat-and-mouse game that at one point involved the dispatch of three detectives from the Pinkerton

Agency to Canada. The Pinkertons came up empty, however, as Spencer soon decamped for Europe.[47]

As the second Star Route trial played out in Judge Wylie's courtroom in Washington, another significant drama was unfolding just down the street at the Capitol. There, members of Congress engaged in a long-overdue debate about the merits of civil-service reform. The proceedings against the Dorsey ring provided an essential backdrop for this watershed effort to rein in patronage and graft in the federal government.

The November 1882 off-year elections did not go well for Republicans. The campaign focused on the party's apparent reluctance to curtail the excesses of the spoils system and limit political patronage. On the campaign trail, Democrats throughout the country repeatedly invoked the Arthur administration's apparent bungling of the Star Route prosecution, which had ended in breathtaking failure just weeks before the election. With Republicans losing thirty-four seats and the Democrats gaining sixty-eight, control of the House of Representatives swung to the Democrats. The *New York Times*, in a front-page analysis of the election, pointed to the failure of the half-hearted Star Route prosecution as a key factor in turning voters against the Arthur administration. "The country had become convinced of the guilt of the Star Route defendants," the *Times* observed, "and many persons were watching for indications which might show the feeling of the administration upon the subject." What they saw was a clumsy and disjointed prosecution that seemed to lack much will to pursue prominent Republicans. The inability of prosecutors to get the slippery Spencer to testify "was only a straw, and perhaps it ought not to have had much weight, but it did have weight in the minds of many," showing that the Republicans were not serious about reform.[48]

For many, the electorate—appalled by the failure of the first Star Route trial and exhausted by the scandals that had plagued a succession of Republican presidencies—sent a clear message about the need to separate the operations of government from partisan political activity. The *Civil Service Record* observed: "The complete overturn which has resulted from the November elections, and which amounts to a revolution, must be regarded as a grand popular declaration of the course of the dominant wing of the Republican Party—the 'Spoils' wing, the 'boss' wing, and the 'voluntary contribution' wing.

The recent election sets the seal of the people's verdict upon patronage in politics." That verdict handed Congress to the Democrats.[49]

The circumstances of President Garfield's assassination gave added urgency to the cause of civil-service reform. Late in 1881, Dorman Eaton, a reformer from New York, published an impassioned article entitled "Assassination and the Spoils System." He argued that Guiteau's unhinged and murderous actions had their origins in a thoroughly debauched system that represented an affront to democracy. "In the case of Guiteau, it needs neither logic nor the lessons of history to connect the bloody deed with the cause. It was not left to reformers or pessimists to discover it," Eaton wrote. "The assassin himself has declared it. A whole people has recognized it. Every civilized nation has taken notice of it." The system needed to be quickly and thoroughly overhauled, Eaton argued, before it produced any more Guiteaus.[50]

Calls for civil-service reform were in the air when Congress returned for its postelection "lame duck" session on December 4, 1881. (The newly elected 48th Congress would not convene until the following spring.) President Arthur, acknowledging the election results and the threat they posed to his party, used his annual message to Congress to call for the passage of a civil-service bill. "I trust that before the close of the present session," Arthur stated that month, "some decisive action may be taken for the correction of evils inherent in the present methods of appointment, and I assure you of my hearty cooperation in any measures which are likely to conduce to that end." The president also offered praise for the prosecutors in the Star Route retrial, claiming that "if any guilty person shall finally escape punishment for their offenses, it will not be for lack of diligent and earnest efforts on the part of the prosecution." The government was doing its level best, he claimed.[51]

Arthur did not mention Stephen Dorsey by name in his message to Congress, but he included an implicit attack on the methods that the former senator (and many others) repeatedly had used to raise money for the Republican Party. The president argued that federal law should prohibit federal employees from being forced to make political contributions—a practice that Republican leaders like Dorsey always had relied upon to fill their party's coffers (and thereby help office seekers like Arthur himself in 1880). "I have always maintained and still maintain," Arthur declared, "that a public officer should be as absolutely free as any other citizen to give or withhold a contribution for the aid of the political party of his choice."[52]

The *Chicago Tribune*, startled by the president's sudden embrace of civil-service reform, wryly noted, "In his message to Congress, President Arthur gives the order 'right about face' to the Stalwart army." Many observers felt that the results of the recent election had given him little choice; Republicans surely would be doomed if they did not move to blunt Democratic attacks on the spoils system. "One hears it said on the streets and in the hotels," a journalist noted, "that the President has heard the verdict of the people and been guided by it." Everyone, including Arthur himself, knew what would happen if he did not call for reform after the 1882 election: the Democrats would continue to bludgeon the Republicans over the issue of patronage and take back the White House in 1884.[53]

It was a Democrat, Senator George Pendleton of Ohio, who took up Arthur's challenge. Highlighting what he called "the necessity of a change in the civil administration of this government," Pendleton reintroduced a bill aimed at curbing some of the worst abuses of the spoils system in the federal government. The need for reform in this area "was submitted to the people of the United States in the fall elections," Pendleton argued, and they had delivered a resounding verdict: the party in power had not done nearly enough to clean up the civil-service system. The Ohio senator was frank about how support for reform had gained momentum, claiming that in his state, "dissatisfaction with the methods of administration adopted by the Republican party in the past few years was the most important single factor in reaching the conclusion that was attained" in the election—a rout by the Democrats.[54]

Among other reform provisions, Pendleton's measure—which had been drafted by Eaton, the New York reformer—called for the creation of a federal Civil Service Commission. The new body would have the power to formulate rules, conduct investigations, and administer competitive examinations for thousands of federal positions. It also would ensure that promotions were based on merit rather than political connections. Furthermore, mandatory political contributions (euphemistically known as "assessments") would be banned.[55]

There followed a spirited debate on the floor of the Senate, with members of both parties speaking in favor of or against Pendleton's bill. Some Democrats objected because the measure did not seem to go far enough in eliminating Republicans who were already entrenched in federal offices. Others complained that it went too far and would leave the Democrats without the ability to reward loyalists if the party won the presidency in 1884. On this score, Pendleton reassured his fellow party members, stressing that the measure was limited in scope and would affect only a fraction of all government employees (roughly 11 percent, according to one estimate). Its application was restricted to officials in Washington and—in a nod to recent scandals—employees in major customhouses and post offices.[56]

Just after Christmas, Pendleton's bill passed the Senate with minimal opposition, and then the House of Representatives approved it by an almost two-to-one margin. President Arthur signed the measure into law in January 1883 and appointed Eaton as chair of the newly minted Civil Service Commission.[57]

"It was the beginning of the end of the spoils system," according to one popular history textbook published at the end of the nineteenth century, and it had an unmistakable link to the uproar caused by the Star Route scandal.[58]

★ 17

SUCKLED IN FALSEHOOD

The Star Route Retrial, Winter 1882–Spring 1883

Meanwhile, the Star Route retrial lurched forward. As the Pendleton Act was becoming the law of the land, prosecutors continued to put on their case against the Dorsey ring. It was slow and tedious going, even compared to the snail's pace of the first trial. Judge Wylie had hoped—naively, in retrospect—that the retrial would last only a week; instead, it would stretch out over the first half of 1883.

The government again elicited testimony from an assortment of undistinguished Post Office clerks and Star Route subcontractors, and it once more entered mountains of documents into evidence—contracts, petitions, correspondence, and anything else that might show that the combination's contracts had been handled in an irregular manner. The prosecutors seemed determined to bury the defendants and their attorneys under an avalanche of paper.

It was all too much for John Crane, the jury foreman. After Judge Wylie told him that the jury would not be allowed to take any of the evidence into its possession for review, he complained that he lacked the brainpower to recall so much soporific material from memory. "I do not think I have the capacity," Crane said, "to take eight or ten thousand printed pages of evidence and bring it up ready for use at any time when it is wanted." He could have been speaking for anyone who was closely following the retrial.[1]

Over the course of the two trials, prosecutors and defense attorneys spent a great deal of time battling in court, and it was evident to everyone that they were tiring of each other. At one point, prosecutors put Albert Boone, who had been entangled in Star Route contracting with Stephen Dorsey, on the witness stand. (Boone's presence loomed large in both Star Route trials, but he was not a defendant in either one.) Defense attorney Robert Green Ingersoll wondered where Boone's testimony was headed, as it did not seem to prove that his client, Dorsey, had engaged in any kind of criminal conspiracy to defraud the federal government.

"Where is all this going to end?" he demanded.

His patience wearing thin, prosecutor George Bliss responded, "In the penitentiary."

The snide comment enraged Ingersoll. "You'll be there as soon as my client!" the defense attorney sputtered. "I represent a gentleman! My client is a gentleman!"[2]

If Ingersoll was on edge regarding Dorsey, he had good reason. In the first trial, prosecutors had done a notoriously poor job of proving that the former senator had played a key role in the alleged Star Route frauds. Now, they were determined not to repeat their mistake. To that end, they managed to introduce into evidence some damaging correspondence that had been excluded from the first trial, including letters Dorsey had written asking Arkansas postmasters to certify bondsmen on bidding forms.

Although Ingersoll was quick to defend his client's honor, he was not doing charity work. Like all of the defense attorneys, he expected to be compensated for his long hours on the case, and handsomely at that. With the retrial dragging on in the early months of 1883, the defendants' ability to pay for Ingersoll and his many co-counsel became a pressing issue. There were reports that Dorsey and Tom Brady had paid approximately $75,000 each to the lawyers who had represented them in the first Star Route trial, and no one thought that their respective bills for the second trial would be significantly less.

With their legal bills continuing to mount, the two defendants had to raise money to pay for their attorneys. Brady was forced to sell his palatial house in Washington's Farragut Square for $125,000. The buyer was his old friend and business associate Theodore Vail, who would soon become the first president of Bell Telephone. Vail, who called the criminal charges against his friend "one of the most dastardly political acts ever perpetrated," also bought from Brady a Canadian lumber camp. Dorsey, meanwhile, had to sell off significant pieces of his pride and joy, his massive New Mexico ranch.[3]

The turning point in the Star Route retrial came on Thursday, February 15, when defendant Montfort Rerdell asked to address the court. Thanks in part to the incriminating affidavit he had provided to investigators in 1881, Rerdell had been one of two defendants found guilty in the first trial. Judge Wylie had set aside that verdict, but Rerdell appeared to feel that the second Star Route trial was going so poorly for him that his best hope lay in trying to cut a deal with prosecutors. That the government's attorneys had always harbored doubts about his reliability did not stop them from agreeing to put the mercurial clerk on the witness stand.[4]

"If the court please, I desire to make a statement personally and in my own behalf," Rerdell told Wylie. "After mature reflection and full consideration of the whole subject, I have determined to abandon any further defense of myself in these cases and put myself at the mercy of the court and the government." As he gave up on his own defense, Rerdell said he would testify for the government "to all my knowledge of any facts." He would, in short, tell jurors everything he knew about the operations of the Dorsey ring.[5]

Rerdell's about-face panicked his fellow defendants and their counsel, as they now would have to grapple with potentially devastating testimony from someone inside the ring. Prosecutors feared that Dorsey and Brady were so desperate to avoid conviction that they might arrange to have Rerdell harmed before he could testify. To protect him from attack, he received an armed escort when appearing in court to testify.

A small man sporting a mustache and pointed beard, Rerdell was not an imposing figure. ("He is rather of a rural type, and would pass for a village lawyer or small storekeeper," one reporter wrote.) He appeared to be calm as he took the witness stand to relate what he knew about the ring's operations. According to the clerk's testimony, Stephen Dorsey had been in complete control of the Star Route combination, determining which routes would be bid on, and for how much. Dorsey also had directed him to create fraudulent paperwork to justify increased payments for the bids that the ring had won. Working under Dorsey's direction, he had forged affidavits, doctored petitions, and concocted other false documents that were submitted to Brady at the Post Office. According to Rerdell, Dorsey had masterminded the entire scheme.[6]

Rerdell's direct testimony was especially damaging because he confirmed that Dorsey had kicked money back to Brady. On the witness stand, he detailed various payments that had been made to Brady, stating that at one point Dorsey had shown him a memorandum regarding an $18,000 disbursement to the Post Office official. Rerdell also detailed a June 1879 trip he and Dorsey had made to a Washington bank. According to him, Dorsey had withdrawn a large sum of money and then had immediately gone with it to Brady's office. He had later told Rerdell to note in his account books that he had made a payment to Brady, a kickback for the second assistant postmaster general's favorable tweaking of Star Route contracts.[7]

Prosecutors milked Rerdell's testimony (which paralleled the much-debated affidavit he had made—then retracted—before the first Star Route trial) for all it was worth. Dick Merrick, seeking to impugn Dorsey as thoroughly as possible, stated that the former senator had brought Rerdell "from the wilds of Arkansas to the city of Washington, taught him in the ways of iniquity, and, having debauched him, used the moral wreck he had made for his own personal benefit and emolument." As portrayed by Merrick, Rerdell was like some poor, exploited wretch who had stepped from the pages of a Charles Dickens novel.[8]

Unfortunately for the prosecutor, the defense was amply prepared for Rerdell's testimony. During his cross-examination, Ingersoll gleefully produced an affidavit in which Rerdell had retracted his first sworn statement to prosecutors in 1881. This second affidavit exonerated Dorsey of all wrongdoing and emphatically contradicted almost all of the direct testimony that Rerdell had just given in the retrial. Rerdell scrambled to explain this second affidavit, claiming that he had sworn to it under duress; Dorsey, he said, had threatened to have him prosecuted for perjury for his initial statement to investigators. But he was forced to again admit that he had never actually seen Dorsey give any money to Brady; Dorsey had only told him that he had handed over the kickbacks.

Brady struggled to contain his emotions as he watched Rerdell's provocative testimony. A reporter noted that the former second assistant postmaster general "eyed the witness intently, and with a contemptuous sneer on his face. Once [Brady] smiled. Immediately his associates were nearly suffocated with suppressed mirth, which was only stopped by a stern look from the court."[9]

The dramatic developments of the second Star Route trial were not limited to theatrics in the courtroom. Defendant Harvey Vaile was called home to Independence, Missouri, to attend to his ailing wife. The two trials, and the publicity surrounding them, apparently had taken a heavy toll on Mrs. Vaile: according to the *New York Times,* she "felt the disgrace keenly, and ever since the first trial has been greatly distressed in spirit." (Her husband's humiliation had been compounded by his disastrous testimony in the first proceeding.)

She was reported to have made several ominous comments to acquaintances before ingesting a large dose of morphine. Vaile got word of the overdose and rushed back to Missouri, but his wife died before he arrived. The headline to the *Times* story about her suicide noted that she was "Despondent Over Her Husband's Trial."[10]

Defense attorney Arthur Williams faced legal rather personal troubles. After a citizen's committee in Washington mounted an investigation of the city's detective bureau, a grand jury returned indictments against several individuals for larceny and receipt of stolen property. Those accused included Williams, who was indicted for having received a stolen gold watch and chain. The work of the citizens' committee also resulted in the indictment of George Miller, who had close ties to the defense.[11]

Williams's client, Stephen Dorsey, also found himself in additional trouble. Newspapers reported that during Rerdell's testimony, the former senator called upon William Lilley, the seventy-year-old father of Fred Lilley, the former deputy auditor in the Post Office. Both of the Lilleys had been implicated in Star Route frauds in various ways and were familiar with many of the principals on both sides of the trial, including Rerdell. Dorsey, convinced that the elder Lilley had persuaded Rerdell to become a witness for the government, allegedly struck him in the face and then, as the septuagenarian lay on the floor, kicked him in the abdomen, all the while calling Rerdell a liar. (This assault seemed to belie the notion that Dorsey was too frail and blind to attend the trial.) "Dorsey Growing Violent," a headline in the *New York Times* proclaimed. "He Assaults an Old Gentleman and Abuses Rerdell." Dorsey's defenders admitted that the assault had taken place but asserted that the elder Lilley had provoked him with false accusations.[12]

Another physical altercation involved James Bosler, who had been active in the operations of the Dorsey ring but had not been charged with conspiracy by the government. Prosecutors were keen to have Bosler testify at the second Star Route trial and produce some account books that would back up Rerdell's testimony. But when a deputy U.S. marshal attempted to serve a subpoena on Bosler, he attacked the federal agent with a cordwood stick. Bosler was arrested, but the case was dropped after he issued an apology. More significantly, the subpoena was not properly served, and Bosler (and his potentially consequential account books) never materialized at the Star Route retrial.[13]

These developments reflected the growing tension surrounding the case.

Although the defense was able to blunt the damage of Rerdell's testimony, there was a sense that the prosecution was putting on a much stronger case than it had in the first trial. As a result, some of the accused felt compelled to testify in their own defense. They reasoned that the risk inherent in this strategy—they could be grilled in cross-examination, as Vaile had been during the first trial—was outweighed by the potential benefit of being able to explain themselves directly to the jury.

Stephen Dorsey's appearance on the witness stand made for high drama. The former senator's eye ailment kept him away from the courtroom until March 26, 1883, when Ingersoll took him by the arm and gingerly led him inside. His appearance was nothing if not striking. "He wore dark-blue goggles over his eyes, and with the full brown beard, as he faced the counsel," one newspaper noted, "might easily have sat for a picture of Lieutenant Danen-hower, of the ill-fated *Jeannette* expedition." (In 1881, John D. Danenhower had famously survived the ship *Jeannette*'s doomed journey to the Arctic.)[14]

Before Dorsey could testify, he had to swear an oath, as was customary for all witnesses. Merrick interrupted the process and asked the court "whether the oath is administered in a form which is binding on the conscience of the witness." He then pointedly asked Dorsey himself, "Do you consider an oath binding on your conscience with a view to the future state of rewards and punishments?"[15]

The prosecutor was motivated by more than a desire to learn the defendant's views on how he might be judged by his maker in the afterlife. Dorsey reportedly had told Rerdell in 1881 that committing perjury to protect a friend was acceptable, and prosecutors hoped to discuss the earlier comment in front of the jury at the Star Route retrial as a means of undercutting the former senator's credibility as he took the witness stand and promised to tell the truth.

Merrick's maneuver precipitated a prolonged debate with Ingersoll, who was widely known for his adamant agnosticism. He said in response to the prosecutor's inquiries about Dorsey's willingness to swear an oath:

I object to the projection of the barbarism and ignorance of the infamous past into this court-room in the light of the last part of the nineteenth century. Whether a man believes in the future state of rewards or punishments has nothing to do with his testimony, nothing. If at this time we are to rebuild the fires of hell, if we are to bring into this court-room a literal devil, with a three-pronged fork to stir up the conscience of the average Christian so that he will tell the truth, it seems to me that we bad better go back for three or four hundred years and throw away all of the literature of the present age, all of its splendid discoveries, and all there is of civilization.[16]

Merrick held firm, telling the court that he simply wanted to know if Dorsey "feels that his conscience is involved, and that there is an obligation on his conscience as an immortal creature standing in the presence of high Heaven to tell the truth, as well as an obligation upon him as a man, with the penitentiary in front, if he tells what is not true."[17]

Judge Wylie eventually resolved the oath-swearing dispute by divorcing it from matters of religious belief. Dorsey would be sworn in "not with reference to his belief or disbelief in a future state of rewards and punishments, but the law provides temporal punishments that may be imposed in case of false swearing." The witness, in short, should concern himself not with defending himself at the heavenly gates, but rather with having to answer to the court if he violated his oath and committed perjury.[18]

After the matter of Dorsey's oath was settled, Ingersoll led him through his direct testimony. Not surprisingly, he contradicted Rerdell on almost every major point, insisting that the clerk had not kept books for him and never could have noticed him paying kickbacks to Tom Brady because he never had made such illicit payments to the second assistant postmaster general or to anyone else.

"Now, Mr. Dorsey," Ingersoll asked, "did you ever enter into an agreement with Thomas J. Brady, John W. Dorsey, H. M. Vaile, John R. Miner, and John M. Peck, or with any or either of them, to defraud the Government in carrying the mails, in mail contracts or bids?"

"I never entered into any agreement with anybody, anywhere, at any time, to defraud the government," Dorsey replied.

"Did you ever enter into a conspiracy with any or either of these defendants for any purpose?" Ingersoll asked.

"Never."

"Did you ever pay, or promise to pay, or cause to be paid, any money to Thomas J. Brady for the purpose of influencing his official action in regard to any mail routes mentioned in this indictment?"

"I never had a transaction with Brady, directly or indirectly, to the extent of one cent in my life, and I never paid him a cent in my life."

"Did you ever promise to pay him anything?"

"And I never promised to pay him anything."

"Did you ever authorize anybody else to pay him?"

"I just said 'directly or indirectly.' I never authorized anybody else to."

"For the purpose of influencing his official action?" Ingersoll asked.

"For any possible purpose," Dorsey stated. "I never had a transaction with him of any kind."[19]

At the end of his direct examination, Ingersoll returned to Dorsey's alleged dealings with Brady. The government charged that Brady had demanded kickbacks for fines he imposed on Star Route contractors. Dorsey again was unwavering: he never had furnished such under-the-table payments to the second assistant postmaster general. There never had been any passing of cash-stuffed envelopes, as banker John Walsh had testified in the first Star Route trial.

"Did you ever have any agreement or arrangement with him by which he was to have a portion of the fines that were remitted?" Ingersoll asked.

"I never had," Dorsey responded, "and during the time that I had charge of this business I doubt whether he remitted any fines."

"Did you have any such arrangement?"

"I never had."[20]

Although Dorsey sounded forthright in answering these questions from Ingersoll, he was more circumspect in describing some other matters, including his postal-contracting activities during the time he served in the Senate. As one later study put it, "Dorsey was able to offer plausible explanations for all of his actions after April, 1879," when the combination had divided up its routes, "but he had great difficulty justifying his behavior before that date." He seemed wary of being forced to admit that he had mixed business with public service during his time in elective office.[21]

Brady also testified. Taking the witness stand, the former second assistant postmaster general appeared to be a hearty and confident bulldog of a man. "General Brady is a heavy man, slow of movement and apparently a 'good liver,'" the *New York Times* reported. "He has a full face and a bright complexion, but his neck is so short that his head seems to rest upon his shoulders." Apparently unruffled over five days of testimony, he denied all wrongdoing and insisted that he had served the public interest in his handling of Star Route contracts. "We thought," he said of the work he did with his Post Office colleagues, "that we were doing a good thing for the country, and I think so now."[22]

Brady admitted that he had spoken with Dorsey, but he insisted that the talk never had been related to Star Route contracts. On the witness stand, he explained that he had gotten together with Dorsey in New York City in August 1880, not long before the presidential election that year. The discussion had focused almost exclusively on the Republicans' desperate efforts to prevail in Indiana, Brady's home state, in the presidential election. "We had a long talk about political matters and the way to carry Indiana," he testified. "I had been chairman of the committee out there once, you know, and was presumed to know something about how to carry Indiana." The two men had spoken and strategized at considerable length, but they had said "nothing about Star Routes or mail service. I do not think that question was mentioned the whole evening or afternoon." The outcome of the election had been vastly more significant to them than the details of some piddling postal contracts.[23]

Brady said that he scarcely knew the other defendants. He testified that had never seen John Peck but might have met John Miner at some point, although he could not precisely recall where or when. Whatever his personal dealings with the defendants, Brady had treated their contracts in a routine manner, he affirmed from the witness stand. When some of the Dorsey combination's contracts were in danger of failing, he had said to his subordinates, "Here, give these men some little time now to put this service on, and if they don't do it by a certain time, bust them." This was not special or inappropriate treatment. It was, Brady testified, "my usual expression in these cases."[24]

Brady reluctantly admitted that he had had some dealings with John Walsh, the banker who had testified that a discussion of Brady's debts had led to the former assistant postmaster general describing how he manipulated Star Route contracts for personal gain. But Brady contended that the banker's account of these interactions was entirely false. "Walsh's statement is one that he made out of whole cloth," Brady stated, "with scarcely a word of truth in it from beginning to end."[25]

For some, Brady's direct testimony strained credulity. Here was the former second assistant postmaster general painting himself as a noble public servant who had merely served the greater good—this after stories of his transgressions and abuses of power had filled newspapers for several years. "If Brady speaks the truth," a skeptical Minnesota newspaper editorialized, "the entire gang of Star Route conspirators must be the most self-sacrificing and philanthropic citizens of this great republic. All they did, it seems, was for the benefit of the public at large. They had no selfish or mercenary motives whatever."[26]

During cross-examination, prosecutors tried to poke holes in Brady's story. But as was the case throughout both Star Route trials, the government attorneys allowed themselves to get bogged down in the subtleties of how the contracts of particular routes had been handled. Prosecutor George Bliss inexplicably zeroed in on Brady's handling of a Star Route in a remote part of New Mexico, quizzing him on how and why particular changes had been made. At one point, the two men argued over why the town of Raton had not been connected by a Star Route to the nearby town of Pulaski, which had a railroad station. "I remember very little about this matter," an almost bored Brady said as the discussion dragged on. This was not the stuff of high drama.[27]

Attempting to provide a frame of reference for Brady's numerous orders for expedition on Dorsey combination Star Routes, Bliss referenced the fact that Brady had approved exponentially more such orders than the men who had previously occupied the position of second assistant postmaster general. To Bliss, this suggested that he had engaged in unusual—and therefore suspicious—conduct.

"Do you not know," Bliss asked, "that you made more than ten times as many orders as . . . your predecessors, during a corresponding period in office?" Brady, brimming with confidence, laughed away the comparison, replying: "I may have done so. I thought myself ten times a better second assistant postmaster than they were." Ripples of laughter filled the courtroom after this wisecrack, which typified his insouciant testimony. On the witness stand, he acted as though the trial was a minor annoyance and not a grave proceeding that could result in his imprisonment.[28]

Brady testified over five days. Some wondered if the trial would ever conclude if witnesses continued to speak at such length. "Men who have not passed beyond middle life, and are in fair health," a Delaware newspaper joked, "may hope to see the end of the Star Route trial."[29]

When the retrial finally drew to a close, attorneys for both sides offered their closing arguments. Speaking for the prosecution, Merrick bluntly said that the facts of the case required jurors to return guilty verdicts. His voice suffused with emotion, Merrick said:

I demand this verdict on behalf of the people of the United States, whose public Treasury these defendants have robbed. I demand it on behalf of integrity in the execution of official trust, which they have disregarded. I demand it on behalf of the supremacy of the law of the land, which they have defied with arrogance and spurned with contempt. I demand it on behalf of the truth, honor, and virtue of the American people, which these men by their criminal and nefarious conduct have stained and blackened and exposed to the scorn, the derision, and the contempt of the world.[30]

Adopting a softer tone, defense attorney Robert Green Ingersoll was at his eloquent best in his closing argument. He somehow still managed to hit rhetorical high notes after enduring many grueling months in Wylie's courtroom. "I want a verdict in accordance with the evidence. I want a verdict in accordance with the law," he told jurors. "I want a verdict that will relieve my clients from the agony of two years. . . . I want a verdict that will fill the coming days and nights with joy. I want a verdict that, like a splendid flower, will fill the future of their lives with a sense of thankfulness and gratitude to you, gentlemen, one and all." The only verdict that could accomplish all of that, he said, was one of not guilty for all of the defendants.[31]

Outside the courtroom, Ingersoll articulated a more nuanced view of the case. "There isn't much doubt there was some crookedness," he admitted to reporters, "but they can't prove a conspiracy."[32]

Although the conspiracy originally had included eight men, the jury would now weigh the evidence against only five defendants. John Peck had died, the government had long since dropped its charges against William Turner, and Montfort Rerdell essentially had pleaded guilty.

For a time, it seemed that the composition of the jury itself might also change. On the second day of deliberations, a juror named John Vernon collapsed in dramatic fashion. The trial transcript, usually a fairly dry record of testimony and legal sparring, noted the unusual event as follows: "At 10:37 a.m. the jury came into the courtroom, when, before they had taken their places, Juror John H. Vernon fell on the floor with an exclamation as if in great pain, and was apparently unconscious."

As the fallen Vernon was rushed to another room in the courthouse for treatment, Judge Wylie said that he had seen the juror's collapse coming for several days. "This man has been drinking a good deal; he is a hard drinker," the judge stated. "During the progress of the trial, on one occasion, I took him aside and gave him a pretty sharp admonition, and he promised to abstain; but I have observed from his appearance for several days past that he has resumed his hard drinking." Wylie surmised that Vernon had suffered from a bout of delirium tremens, a rapid onset of confusion usually caused by withdrawal from alcohol, because he had been "confined to the jury-room, and cut off from his supplies" of liquor.[33]

Backers of the Star Route defendants delighted in Vernon's breakdown (which included an injured ankle that he badly twisted in falling to the ground). In the capital's barrooms and saloons, friends and associates of Brady and Stephen Dorsey expressed hope that Vernon's apparent alcoholic prostration would lead to a mistrial or hung jury. Mint juleps, brandy smashes, and other cocktails were raised in his honor, with celebrants offering an ironic toast: "To Vernon's future health and prosperity."[34]

But Judge Wylie was not about to let the alcohol-soaked Vernon's prostration derail the jury's deliberations. A doctor administered some brandy to the stricken man, and the judge allowed Vernon to continue to drink in moderation as a means of preventing another debilitating bout of withdrawal. "I suppose whatever a doctor prescribes for the juror," he said from the bench, "can be taken by him." It was determined that a deputy marshal would permit Vernon to enjoy two drinks per day, but he was under strict orders "to prevent the circulation of a whiskey bottle among the jurors," the *Philadelphia North American* noted. (There was some dispute about the exact number of drinks Vernon would be allowed: some newspapers reported that he would have three rather than two.)[35]

The nation's newspapers regaled their readers with the story of Vernon's plight. In St. Louis, the *Globe-Democrat* ran a lengthy article headlined "A Drunken Juror" that recounted Vernon's boozy exploits during the trial. It was reported that the diminutive Irishman, who owned a restaurant in Washington, had been intoxicated throughout the proceedings, "sometimes stupidly drunk and in no condition to listen to, much less understand, evidence or argument in the Star Route case." His breakdown in the courtroom was "simply outrageous," declared the newspaper.[36]

The tale of the inebriated juror might have gotten so much traction because the nation seemed to have finally tired of the mundane details of the Star Route case. As the retrial drew to a close, the *New York Times* noted that the proceedings were attracting less public interest, in part because Brady and Dorsey, the two chief villains in the drama, already had been diminished by the government's efforts over the preceding few years. "There is an apparent change in the attitude of the public mind toward this trial," the paper noted. "There has been much less interest in it than there was in the former trial, and there is almost an entire absence of feeling in regard to it. Dorsey and Brady are no longer regarded as public characters, with power and influence." Years of accusations—leveled by prosecutors, the press, and rival politicians— already had irreparably damaged the reputations of both men. Whether a jury ever found them guilty, they were now regarded, in the court of public opinion, as crooks.[37]

The jury—including the debilitated Vernon—returned its verdict on June 14, 1883. It was an even worse defeat for the prosecution than the first trial had been: not guilty on all counts for every defendant. The jurors voted 10 to 2 in favor of acquitting Brady and Stephen Dorsey, and 9 to 3 in favor of Miner. (At no time did more than three of the jurors vote that a conspiracy had existed.)

To many, the jury's acquittal of Rerdell seemed to be completely inexpli- cable. The clerk had been found guilty in the first Star Route trial (on the strength of secondhand accounts of a self-inculpatory affidavit), then had of- fered a detailed confession from the witness stand in the second proceeding while effectively, if not formally, pleading guilty. How could the jury have possibly failed to convict him in such circumstances?

Jurors afterward explained that Rerdell's testimony lacked any credibility. Crane, the foreman, later said that "not one of the jury believed a word" of it. Moreover, given Judge Wylie's instructions about conspiracy, they were wary of returning only a single guilty verdict, whatever the strength of the evidence that had been presented. One juror was said to have remarked during deliber- ations: "Rerdell has pleaded guilty of conspiracy. He can't be punished except someone be convicted with him."[38]

The courtroom erupted when Crane read the verdicts aloud. "Hats and handkerchiefs were waved aloft; every rule of decorum was forgotten or swept away, and a wild yell of delight drowned the voices and nullified the attempts of the court officials to restore order," the New-York Tribune reported. Judge Wylie admonished spectators to respect the dignity of his courtroom, but it was a futile effort; the celebrations continued.[39]

Ingersoll, having beaten the government in court for a second time, was mobbed by well-wishers. Grinning broadly, the defense attorney embraced the defendants and shook hands with others who had surged forward to offer congratulations. His colleague Jeremiah Wilson also accepted kudos, his face all the while wearing what the *Tribune* described as "a shrewd 'I-told-you-so' expression."[40]

The defendants themselves were, for the most part, overjoyed when they heard the not-guilty verdicts. While his friends shook one of his hands, Harvey Vaile took out a handkerchief with the other and dabbed his eyes, weeping with relief. Stephen Dorsey pushed through the crowd to find his wife, who had greeted the verdict by shouting "Glory to God!" and clasping her hands above her head. They embraced and cried. Medora Peck, the widow of the deceased defendant John Peck, was so overcome that she fainted. Caught up in the revelry, one defense attorney burned his mustache after confusedly inserting the lighted end of a cigar into his mouth.[41]

Only Tom Brady remained impassive. As "cool and imperturbable as ever," according to one newspaper report, he "received without apparent emotion the verdict and the congratulations which were showered upon him from all sides." True to form, he stayed haughty and above the fray.[42]

The celebrations continued outside the courthouse well into the night. The keeper of a restaurant located nearby was instructed to keep an open house to accommodate all of the revelers. Many of them eventually found their way to Ingersoll's residence. A crowd estimated at 200–300 people gathered there to celebrate the verdicts. They sang songs and listened to brief speeches from some of the defense attorneys, among them Richard Carpenter, who angrily proclaimed that the prosecution had been "conceived in conspiracy, brought forth in perjury, and suckled in falsehood."[43]

Buoyed by the victory, Carpenter still managed to keep his sense of humor. At one point, a reveler shouted to him, "Give the attorney general hell!" The lawyer laughed and responded, "Excuse me, I decline to anticipate providence."[44]

The atmosphere inside Ingersoll's residence was festive as well. The defendants' closest friends and family members toasted the trial victors and sang; women waved their handkerchiefs. The mood was reminiscent of a merry holiday-season affair. Eventually, a member of the jury appeared and was offered a warm welcome. Dorsey's grateful wife led the man around and introduced him to the other well-wishers. Among those greeting the juror was Peck's widow.[45]

Amid the celebration, the evening's host struck a magnanimous tone. "Victory is the only revenge I want," Ingersoll said as he basked in the glow of triumph. "I think it is the most popular verdict that has been given in this country in many years."[46]

The homes of both Ingersoll and Dorsey were visited by members of the Towpath Republican Club, who brought with them a brass band. Between raucous tunes, Dorsey addressed members of this "colored organization," as the group was described in a newspaper report, and praised them for their support. "I thank you for the courage you have shown in the presence of all the dishonor that the government has tried to put upon me," he said. "You are brave enough, you are strong enough to raise up your voice and your right hand against the attempted injustice." Although his reputation was in tatters, his legal ordeal appeared to be over.[47]

While the defendants and their backers celebrated, prosecutors licked their wounds once more. Dick Merrick found it hard to contain his frustration and blasted the verdict as a farce. Defeated in court for a second time, Attorney General Brewster was more diplomatic, telling reporters: "That settles it. When twelve men agree, that settles it." For his part, George Bliss said that he was "very much astonished" by the outcome.[48]

The nation's newspapers were, on the whole, less forgiving. "The whole thing has been a national humiliation," the *Baltimore American* opined after the Star Route retrial ended. The *Boston Herald* termed the verdict "a farce and a burlesque," and the *New York Evening Post* called it "most unfortunate." For the *New York World*, it was nothing less than "a public calamity." In Buffalo, the *Express* said that the outcome was likely "to sicken thoughtful people of our boasted system of trial by jury."[49]

The second Star Route jury, like its predecessor in the first trial, came in for harsh criticism. "Whether or not the failure of justice in these Star Route trials has been due to the ignorance, mental imbecility or rum soaked condition of jurymen, or to bribery, or to what not," the *New York Mail and Express* noted, "the verdict will be received by the American people with indignation, disappointment and disgust." In Columbus, Ohio, the *Daily Times* asserted that the jurors had reached an "astounding verdict . . . that is flagrantly opposed to all the testimony that has twice massed together" in the separate trials.[50]

The *Chicago Tribune* seemed to sum up the prevailing mood in the country when it editorialized: "The verdict which has been found will satisfy the Star Route gang, but it will satisfy no one else. There is not one person of intelligence in the country who has not believed them to be guilty from the beginning, and there is not a person of intelligence who does not believe them guilty now notwithstanding the declaration of the miserable jury to the contrary."[51]

There were a few exceptions to this trend. General William Tecumseh Sherman, who had testified on behalf of the defense in both Star Route trials, said he hoped that the matter had at least been put to rest. "The jury having brought in a verdict of not guilty, that ought to end the matter as far as Brady and Dorsey are concerned," he declared. "Both of them seemed to me to be honorable men."[52]

The public's reaction to the verdict was shaped in part by a general consensus that, as had been the case in the first trial, at least some jurors had been paid off by the defense (if they had not been simply too intoxicated to think clearly). These suspicions were well founded. As one later study pointed out, "there is little doubt that the defense had tampered with" the jury in the second trial.[53]

The furor over jury tampering in the first trial apparently did nothing to temper the defense's efforts to improperly influence the panel in the retrial. Defense attorney Arthur Williams hired a man named James Nelson, a friend of the disgraced Frank Fall, to keep tabs on the jury and make inroads with it however he could. It was thought by the defense that Nelson, a Black man, would be a natural to monitor and approach Black members of the jury. Nelson later said that he had been paid ten dollars daily to "look out and watch the government counsel, government spotters [detectives], and the members of the jury."[54]

Nelson later reported in an affidavit that he had spoken to one juror, Clarence Shields, who had complained that Dorsey had not followed through on a pledge to compensate him for voting for acquittal. Shields, a Black man, had told him that he was doubly upset because Dorsey had fulfilled his promises to pay off white jurors. Nelson also said that he had observed suspicious activity on the part of Crane, the jury foreman. It was clear to Nelson that Crane, through an intermediary, had frequently been in communication with Williams. Such were the defense attorney's connections with him that the two men had worked out a system of signals so that the foreman was able to apprise him about the voting in the jury room. (Crane motioned to an intermediary, who then reported to Williams.)[55]

The failures and shenanigans of two different juries in the Star Route trials were so glaring that they occasioned a great deal of public handwringing about the efficacy of the jury system. Following the rout of the government in the retrial, articles appeared bearing such worried headlines as "Is the Jury System a Failure?" (*American Law Register*) and even "Shall the Jury System Be Abolished? (*North American Review*). The latter article, written by former South Carolina governor and senator Robert Y. Hayne, concluded that juries simply could no longer be relied on to resolve cases in a manner that served the interests of justice. Grousing that the jury system "entails frequent miscarriages of justice, permitting thousands of notorious criminals to escape," Hayne pointed to the Star Route case as an example.[56]

After the Star Route retrial had ended, the satirical magazine *Puck* ran a story recounting an imaginary encounter between a juror and a well-dressed stranger. The two men spoke on a Washington sidewalk.

"Are you a member of the Star Route jury?" the stranger asked.

"I had that honor," the juror responded. There was pride in his voice.

"I am so glad to meet you," the stranger responded. "I have long wished to form your acquaintance. I can't tell you how happy you make me. This is indeed one of the proudest moments of my life. . . . If I talked for a week, I couldn't begin to convey to you my intense satisfaction at having the privilege of making your acquaintance."

The juror wanted to know the stranger's identity. Was he a friend of Stephen Dorsey? Brady? Or maybe he was acquainted with Ingersoll, the vaunted speaker and attorney?

The stranger apologetically said that he was in a rush and simply gave the juror his business card as he hurried away. It read, "Judas Iscariot, Temple Street, Jerusalem."[57]

YES, THE STAR ROUTE BUSINESS KILLED GARFIELD!
Reckoning with the Scandal, 1883-1884

Early in December 1883, not long after the inauspicious conclusion of the Star Route retrial, Congress initiated an investigation of what had gone wrong. It provided a remarkable glimpse of the inner workings of the prosecution team, laying bare how and why the government's attorneys had failed in two attempts to convict anyone associated with the Dorsey ring.

Under the leadership of Congressman William Springer, a Democrat from Illinois, the House of Representatives Committee on Appropriations held hearings that effectively were a postmortem on the government's failed efforts to successfully prosecute the Star Route case. Congressmen heard from, among others, all of the attorneys who had represented the government in the cases (George Bliss, William Cook, Arthur Gibson, William Ker, and Dick Merrick), investigator Patrick Henry Woodward, former attorney general Wayne MacVeagh, and his successor, Benjamin Brewster. Other parties who had been entangled in the case offered testimony as well, including the banker John Walsh.

The Springer committee hearings, as they were known, were a prolonged and complicated exercise in parceling out blame. The prosecutors were asked to explain why they had chosen to pursue the Dorsey combination in the first place and how they had put their failed case together in court. Not surprisingly, they blamed one another for the fiascoes in Judge Wylie's courtroom and insisted that things would have gone more smoothly if only the others had followed *their* advice. There was also much discussion if they had been underpaid or overpaid for their work for the government. (Examining the prosecution's sizable expenditures was the ostensible purpose of the hearings.) Other testimony detailed how the juries in the two trials had been monitored and most likely bribed.

Some of the most intriguing revelations to come from the hearings involved the assassination of President Garfield. Cook, the Star Route special prosecutor, told the committee that, shortly before the 1881 shooting, he had warned the president that he feared "there might be a resort to violence" by those involved in the case. He also stated that, after the shooting, he had learned that the assailant, Charles Guiteau, allegedly had been seen "in one or more establishments seeking a pistol, and that he had been accompanied by two or three persons." Cook testified that he had passed along this potentially crucial information to District Attorney George Corkhill, who apparently had failed to follow up on it.

Cook's testimony regarding Garfield's murder, implying that he had anticipated the assassination and that Guiteau might have had abettors connected to the Star Route case, led to sharp questioning by members of the committee. At one point, Springer asked if Cook had spoken to Corkhill about his suspicions that Guiteau had accomplices. The chairman, following his lead, hinted that these abettors might have had some connection to the Star Route frauds. The attorney said that he had in fact spoken to the district attorney about the matter.

"Did you suggest to him that an investigation would develop the fact that the Star Route defendants were the instigators of this crime?" Springer asked.

"I may not have spoken of the 'Star Routers,' as we called them," Cook said, "but I suggested to him strongly that an investigation might lead to the discovery of the fact that others were associated with Guiteau in the perpetration of the crime."

"But you say that line of inquiry has never been pursued?"

"I do not think it has ever been pursued earnestly," Cook said.

Later in his testimony, Cook stopped short of saying that he had any concrete evidence directly linking any specific Star Route figures to Garfield's assassination. Still, he maintained that he had been concerned that some of the accused men might resort to violence as a means of thwarting the administration's investigation into their flagrant corruption. "Shortly after I entered into the employment of the government, I unquestionably formed the idea that there was a bitter and reckless feeling on the part of those involved in the Star Route investigations," he said. "It was so bitter in words, and so bitter in print, so bitter socially, that I was impressed with the idea that it might be carried into corresponding practice."[1]

At the Springer committee hearings, former postmaster general Tom James also alluded to the possible connections between the Star Route scandal, Guiteau, and the assassination of Garfield. In a prepared statement, he praised Garfield's commitment to the government's investigation of the postal-corruption case. "If he had taken a lower view of his obligations as chief magistrate and as an honest man," James said, "it is my firm belief that he would not have fallen victim to an assassin's bullet."

A congressman pounced on this comment. Was James suggesting that Guiteau's murderous actions had been prompted by any members of the Star Route ring?

James would not go quite that far. In answering, he suggested that the mentally imbalanced assassin had at least been influenced by the intense anti-Garfield sentiment that had pervaded Washington in the early days of the president's administration, much of it whipped up by local newspapers that were critical of his handling of the Star Route case. (Guiteau himself had said as much at his murder trial.) "Taking the warning given by Colonel Cook, and the clamor raised by these people [in] this investigation," James said, "taken together with the fact of the newspaper clippings that were found in the pockets of the assassin, I think that [Guiteau's] head was turned by these assaults upon the president."[2]

There was discussion in the hearing room that some of the articles in Guiteau's possession at the time of the shooting had been torn from the pages of the Washington *National Republican,* which was of course owned at that point by one of the targets of the Star Route inquiry, Tom Brady. At his trial, Guiteau had grilled George Gorham, the newspaper's editor, about its relentless attacks on Garfield prior to the assassination, suggesting that he had been provoked by the publication's intemperate coverage of the president and his administration. It was well known that Guiteau had in his possession inflammatory articles from the *New York Herald* at the time of the shooting, but no one in the hearing could confirm that he had been carrying clippings from Brady's *newspaper.*

James's testimony about the possible connection between the Star Route case and Guiteau resonated with some who tried to make sense of the assassination. Among them was the killer's sister, Frances Marie Norton, whose husband, George Scoville, represented Guiteau at his trial. In 1888, Norton (who herself once had been ruled insane) published a novel that bore the telling title *The Stalwarts; or, Who Were to Blame?* In its preface, Norton wrote that James's congressional testimony opened her eyes to the real forces behind her brother's actions, helping her perceive "the connection between the assassination of Garfield and the final outcome of the 'Star Route' affair—the virtual acquittal of everyone. *Yes, the 'Star Route' business killed Garfield!*"[3]

The novel itself is a roman à clef in which a presidential assassin, Jules Grieveau, acts as a tool for the Star Route conspirators. At one point, the editor of "a leading Stalwart Washington paper, the one of which a prominent 'Star Router' was part owner," is hauled into court to explain his possible connection to the murder. The narrator observes that the editor should have been held to account because his newspaper, prior to the assassination, had "been most rabid in affirming that the country would be better off if some sickness or an accident should remove him." To the frustration of the narrator, however, the editor escapes responsibility for having egged on Grieveau. Any knowledgeable reader at the time of the publication of *The Stalwarts* would have recognized Norton's allusions to Tom Brady, editor George Gorham, and the provocations issued prior to Garfield's murder by the *National Republican*.[4]

As was demonstrated by the detours by Cook and James into the Garfield assassination, the Star Route congressional hearings were a broad-ranging affair. In the end, the proceedings were so contentious and confusing that the Springer committee ultimately threw up its hands and reached only the most general conclusions about what had gone wrong with the government's prosecution. The "committee are of the opinion," the panel's final report stated, "that there were many causes which operated to prevent the successful prosecution of Star Route offenders."[5]

The committee's report noted that "while the evidence against Star Route contractors and public officials was strong and conclusive as to their guilt, and that the government was defrauded of large sums of money, and that large sums of money were also expended to secure indictments and convictions, yet no person was convicted or punished." This was not for want of trying. Federal prosecutors throughout the country periodically took aim at individuals outside the Dorsey ring who had been implicated in crimes related to Star Route contracts. According to one later study, "scores of cases [were] brought into the various courts of the country."[6]

Few, if any, of these efforts bore much fruit. For instance, in February 1882, the federal government tried two Star Route contractors in Nebraska, E. E. Corbin and Charles Iddings, for conspiracy to commit fraud. After an alleged coconspirator refused to testify against them, the defendants were acquitted in the court of federal judge Elmer Scipio Dundy because, in the words of one news report, "the prosecution had utterly failed to show any wrong-doing by the accused."[7]

Although the precise numbers are hard to track, in the end, it appeared that the federal government only scored two criminal convictions in cases related to Star Route frauds. In September 1882, Christian Price and Thomas McDevitt were convicted in federal district court in Philadelphia for having conspired to commit fraud by scheming to use worthless straw bonds to secure Star Route contracts. (The jury acquitted a third defendant who also had been implicated in the scheme.) Both men were fined and sentenced to brief prison terms.[8]

Even such minor victories were not without complications, however. McDevitt's legal odyssey had begun a year earlier, in the fall of 1881, when he had shared information about straw-bond practices with federal investigator Patrick Henry Woodward. Grateful for the information and eager to pursue bigger prizes, Woodward had assured McDevitt that he would not be prosecuted on the basis of what he divulged. When federal prosecutors in Philadelphia had prepared to take McDevitt to trial anyway, Woodward had told him not to worry. "Believing that the implied faith of the government could not and would not be broken," the investigator later said, "I wrote him to employ no lawyer, to go to no expense, and to rest in peace." Yet despite Woodward's efforts to have the charges against McDevitt dropped, they were only postponed. The case eventually went forward, and McDevitt was convicted.[9]

Woodward was troubled by this outcome and tried to make amends. He convinced his prosecutorial colleagues George Bliss, Dick Merrick, and William Ker to write letters recommending that McDevitt be pardoned and prevailed upon former postmaster general James to explain the circumstances of the man's ill-fated decision to cooperate with prosecutors. Woodward himself wrote directly to President Arthur and asked him to commute the sentence, noting that McDevitt had been tried and convicted after he basically had been promised immunity from prosecution. "In the trial and conviction of McDevitt," he told the president, "the solemn pledges of the government have been broken."[10]

In a separate letter to Attorney General Brewster, Woodward alluded to the similarity of McDevitt's fate to that of George Brott, a crooked contractor who also had been prosecuted after cooperating with federal authorities and providing them with valuable information. Although he believed that he had attempted to keep his word with McDevitt and Brott, it rankled Woodward that he had unwittingly contributed to the prosecution of both men. "The innocent part borne by me in this and in one or two other transactions, which somewhat similarly have gone amiss, have caused me intolerable pain and humiliation, and have seriously embarrassed me in the performance of my official labors," he wrote to Brewster in his effort to have McDevitt spared.[11]

It was to no avail. McDevitt served his full term in prison. "In the treatment accorded to him a grave mistake, in my judgment, was made," Woodward later said.[12]

Largely frustrated in criminal court, the government tried other means of seeking justice and recouping at least some of the money that had been lost through the rascality of Star Route contractors. At one point, an effort was made to reach a settlement with prominent contractors (among them Stephen Dorsey) through arbitration. Bliss, for one, favored this move. He "said inasmuch as the criminal cases could not be well made out, if the parties were willing to pay whatever might be found against them, it would be a great advantage to the Government to get them to consent to arbitrate with the delay incident to protracted proceedings in court," stated Attorney General Brewster. The effort broke down, however, when Bliss and Robert Green Ingersoll—the respective leaders of the prosecution and defense teams—emerged as potential arbitrators. To Brewster, this appeared contradictory to the central premise of arbitration, in which an impartial third party resolves a dispute outside the formal structure of the courts. As he later put it, "It seemed to me the proper way would have been to have had some persons selected who had nothing to do with the conduct of the cases as counsel." After the postmaster general agreed with the attorney general that Ingersoll and Bliss should not be involved, the arbitration effort fizzled.[13]

The government also filed at least two dozen civil suits against Star Route contractors for alleged fraud. From the perspective of prosecutors, civil actions had one distinct advantage over criminal proceedings: there was no statute of limitations. Yet the government seemed to have exhausted itself in the two Star Route trials; there was not much enthusiasm for pursuing civil cases. Most of these proceedings dragged on in the courts for many years and ultimately went nowhere. (The last of these was dismissed in 1902, several decades after the two main Star Route criminal trials.)[14]

Federal authorities made a valiant but ultimately doomed effort to recover money from Stephen Dorsey through a civil action. Just after the verdict in the Star Route retrial was handed down, Postmaster General Walter Q. Gresham informed the Justice Department that he had "taken the preliminary steps toward suits for the recovery, on account of fraud, of all moneys paid for expedition on all the routes, save one, that were included in [the Dorsey case]." Attorney General Brewster endorsed Gresham's actions, writing to Bliss that the postmaster general "thinks it his duty not to delay the matter, and I rather coincide with him." A hopeful *New York Times* announced in a headline, "THE GOVERNMENT PREPARING TO SUE FOR LARGE SUMS."[15]

Bliss believed that the government should only pursue civil actions against men with deep pockets, among them Dorsey and Harvey Vaile. The likes of John Miner were "all understood to be impecunious," he wrote in a letter to Brewster, and thus not worth pursuing, as the government was unlikely to ever recover much, if any, money from them. Vaile and Dorsey, however, were different, with Bliss estimating that $200,000 could be recovered from Dorsey alone.[16]

To proceed in court, the federal government needed to access financial records that were in the possession of James Bosler, the Dorsey business partner who had nimbly avoided criminal prosecution for his connection to the Star Route frauds. (He had done this in part by retaining the legal services of former prosecutor Albert Gibson.) Unfortunately for the government, Bosler died in December 1883 before the government could seize the records in question. The documents remained in limbo while Bosler's will was probated. Authorities then made an attempt to serve attachment papers on Dorsey himself, but he proved too elusive, and the civil case against him simply petered out.

Attempts to recover money from other contractors met with similarly dispiriting results. With some in the Justice Department insisting that, in the words of one official, "not an inch can be yielded to these vampires," the government instituted civil suits aimed at recovering money from Dorsey combination contractors Miner and Vaile, both of whom had survived the criminal trials in 1882 and 1883. The suit against Miner apparently never was settled, while the effort against Vaile ultimately was dismissed in 1895 (by which time Vaile was dead.)[17]

Although he was involved with the Dorsey combination, Star Route contractor Albert Boone never faced serious legal jeopardy in either criminal or civil courts. In January 1882, as the government prepared its case against the rest of the combination, Boone was indicted by a Washington grand jury for his involvement in straw-bond bidding, charged with having knowingly relied on fictitious or worthless bondsmen to secure Star Route contracts. After his indictment, Boone complained that he was only being targeted because it served the interests of his former associates in the Dorsey ring, who had broken with him after he had helped secure their lucrative contracts. "The fact is that I am in the way of a clique desiring to control the mail service of the United States," he told the press.[18]

An embittered Boone claimed that he had been jettisoned after doing the heavy lifting for the Dorsey combination. "Within six months after the contracts were secured, the Dorsey party, having no further use for me, threw me overboard," he grumbled. Now, he was being made a scapegoat in order to divert attention from those same men as they found themselves in legal jeopardy. "It is fair to presume that these same parties are the instigators of the prosecution, probably by some of ex-Postmaster General James' friends, who had arranged to secure a big slice of the contracts."[19]

But the straw-bond case against Boone ultimately came to nothing as well. Prosecutor William Cook told Congress that the case was *nolle prossed* (that is, abandoned) after the debacle of the Star Route retrial. By then, it seemed pointless to pursue him any further.[20]

Other civil cases involving Star Route contracts were taken up in 1884 by George L. Douglass, a special assistant attorney general. Nothing if not persistent in his efforts to reclaim ill-gotten Star Route money, Douglass pursued lawsuits in a variety of jurisdictions, including Kansas, where a case was brought against a contractor named Cornelius Cosgrove. The federal government sought to recover from Cosgrove $140,000 that, it alleged, he had fraudulently obtained through expeditions on a Star Route contract. This effort ultimately failed, as did another case seeking to recover $14,342.52 from a contractor in Nebraska named Luke Vorhees. The Nebraska case began with some promise for the government—a newspaper headline reporting Voorhees's detention in 1885 announced that he had been "finally arrested for his official crookedness"—but the U.S. Supreme Court ultimately ruled in Vorhees's favor in 1890.[21]

The knotty story of William Pitt Kellogg—a Republican who represented Louisiana in both the Senate and the House of Representatives and also served a much-disputed term as the state's governor—demonstrated just how difficult it was for the government to make charges stick in Star Route cases, especially when they involved powerful figures in Washington. The prosecution of Kellogg ran roughly parallel to the main Star Route case, and it reached a similarly muddled conclusion. Prosecutors believed that they had clear evidence showing that Kellogg, while serving in the Senate, had accepted a portion of a bribe from a postal contractor in return for his efforts to sweeten a Star Route contract, but the case sputtered along for several years before ending when a jury acquitted him in 1884. (The federal case, plagued by bickering and indecision among the attorneys handling it, ultimately foundered on a faulty indictment: Kellogg was charged with having received "lawful money," but the government could only show that he had received notes and drafts.)[22]

The middleman in the alleged scheme to bribe Kellogg was John Walsh, the unscrupulous banker who testified at the first Star Route trial about his shadowy dealings with Second Assistant Postmaster General Brady. Although Walsh was not a model citizen, he attempted to prod the Arthur administration into being more resolute in its efforts to prosecute those who were involved in the Star Route frauds, including Kellogg. At one point, he penned a passionate letter to the president in which he assailed not only Star Route criminals but also the bungling prosecutors who were failing to bring them to justice. In his missive, he quoted a famous aphorism from the great British statesman and philosopher Edmund Burke:

"When bad men combine, the good must associate; else they will fall, one by one, an unpitied sacrifice, in a contemptible struggle." That the bad men have combined is apparent in the immunity which has, for eighteen months, favored them—an immunity as surprising as it is disgraceful. An immunity explicable only on the grounds that the servants of this great Government are not in earnest in prosecuting these men. . . . It is the first time, I believe, in the history of the Republic that men unblushingly, and in the full glare of day, organized as plunderers, openly defy the power of the State. The laws of the land have been most wantonly and shamefully violated by these men, witnesses for the Government have been terrorized by them and their agents, juries corrupted, officers of the Government made to violate their oaths, and justice itself made a mockery of in the capital of the Republic. Such has been the weak and vacillating character of the prosecution, as a whole, that men knew not on which side the Government was arrayed.[23]

The Star Route trials brought together a disparate cast of characters—politicians, attorneys, entrepreneurs, and civil servants of varying degrees of ability and virtue. After the various postal-corruption cases ran their course in the early 1880s, these men went their separate ways and largely receded from public view.

Chester Arthur battled poor health—he suffered from nephritis, an ailment that causes swelling in the kidneys—and ongoing Republican factionalism throughout his brief but tumultuous term as president. He toyed with the idea of running for president in 1884, but the idea never gained much traction; Arthur was simply too unpopular and never shook the perception that he was nothing more than an accidental (and not especially competent) president. Bowing to the inevitable, he made way for James Blaine, the Half-Breed leader, to be the party's nominee. (Blaine would lose in the general election to Democrat Grover Cleveland.) Arthur's health deteriorated after he left the White House, and he died in November 1886 at the age of fifty-seven.[24]

Stephen Dorsey, once the dust of the Star Route trials had settled, focused on his massive ranch in New Mexico. In 1877, he acquired 160 acres of land near a landmark on the Santa Fe Trail called Point of Rocks. He eventually expanded his holdings to 24,000 acres on which grazed thousands of cattle bearing his Triple Dot brand. The centerpiece of his holdings was a thirty-six-room log-and-stone mansion. The structure's most distinctive feature was an octagonal tower that featured not only carved likenesses of Dorsey, his wife, and his brother John but also two gargoyles that had been sculpted to resemble James Blaine of Maine, the Half-Breed Republican who Dorsey, ever the loyal Stalwart, always detested.[25]

Dorsey tried to dabble in politics in New Mexico, but he met with little success. His business fortunes also plummeted in the 1880s thanks to a dramatic drop in cattle prices, the mismanagement of his Palo Blanco Cattle Company, and the enormous costs of the Star Route trials. He was so strapped for cash that one of his attorneys, Jefferson Chandler, had to sue him to recover $2,500 in unpaid legal fees. When he could not come up with sufficient cash to pay Robert Green Ingersoll, Dorsey was forced to compensate his attorney in land. "Bob took a big slice of the Senator's ranch as part of his fee," an acquaintance later said. To make matters even worse, Dorsey also was accused of having obtained much of his New Mexico property through fraudulent land titles.[26]

At loose ends both politically and financially, Dorsey eventually was forced to auction off all of his New Mexico property. These setbacks in business did not seem to faze the former senator, and he remained in good spirits. "I knew Senator Dorsey quite well and rather liked him," a friend from New Mexico named Miguel Antonio Oterero later wrote. "He was a jovial fellow—kind, congenial, and full of fun." Oterero had a great deal of sympathy for Dorsey, feeling that he had been made the scapegoat in the Star Route affair. "He was no worse than many of the others," he wrote, "but he was caught with the goods."[27]

Others took a less salutary view of Dorsey. "The days of his political glory are past, because, as I am convinced, the leaders and masses of all parties regard him as hopelessly pilloried before the nation as a Star Route thief," the surveyor general of New Mexico, George W. Julian, wrote in 1888. "He smells of the penitentiary, and no fumigation is possible. To every honest man in the republic, his name suggests the striped costume of the crew whose fellowship he escaped through the miscarriage of public justice."[28]

The former senator continued to be involved in a variety of moneymaking schemes—some of them of dubious character—throughout the remainder of his life. According to one account, he spent much of his time "eluding creditors, at which he became particularly adept, and pursuing an endless variety of speculative schemes." He died in Los Angeles in 1916.[29]

Dorsey's reputation in his adoptive state never recovered from the Star Route scandal. Dorsey County, located in the south-central part of Arkansas, had been named in his honor in 1873 after his election to the Senate, but it was renamed a dozen years later after he "rendered himself unpopular with the people of Arkansas," in the words of one history of the state. (It was indicative of the shifting political landscape in Arkansas that it was rechristened Cleveland County after the newly elected president, a Democrat.)[30]

Dorsey's brother and Star Route codefendant died in 1901 in Bridport, Vermont. Unlike his somewhat profligate sibling, John Dorsey seemed to have lived a quiet and industrious life. "The old-fashioned virtues of honor to men and reverence to God early took firm hold of him and could not be shaken off," according to an obituary notice, "even at the expense of being called narrow and Puritanical."[31]

Tom Brady, after battling a kidney ailment and pneumonia, died on April 22, 1904, in Jersey City, New Jersey. Obituaries glossed over his role in the Star Route case and instead stressed his record of military service during the Civil War and his work for the Republican Party. As it marked his passing, the *New York Times* said that Brady had been "a prominent politician of Indiana." In recognition of his military service, he was buried in Arlington National Cemetery.[32]

Harvey Vaile returned to Missouri and tried to piece together a life that had been shattered by the suicide of his wife, Sophie, during the Star Route retrial (which had come, heartbreakingly, on Valentine's Day). He clearly never recovered from this loss. According to one legend, Vaile buried his beloved in his front lawn in a coffin that sported a glass lid—the better for him to look down and see her whenever he wished. Sophie Vaile might have had some trouble letting go as well: it was said that her spirit haunted the mansion for many years. Emotionally broken and alone, Harvey Vaile died of a stroke in 1894.[33]

When prosecutor George Bliss died in 1897, his *New York Times* obituary recounted his lengthy legal career, highlighted his devotion to the Roman Catholic Church, and noted that he was "identified with the Star Route cases." It also referenced the passions caused by those proceedings, noting that there had been an unsuccessful attempt to have Bliss disbarred after the retrial because of his vehemence in criticizing local attorneys and judges.[34]

It would have galled Bliss to learn what became of Montfort Rerdell, who he had so zealously pursued in court during the two Star Route trials. Rerdell eventually made his way to the Panama Canal Zone in the early 1900s and parlayed his legal training into a position as a judge. (It was said that he presided over the first American legal proceedings held in the canal zone.) He also found time to pursue his hobbies. "Rerdell has all of the typical Southerner's love for honest sport and he is an ardent huntsman," one observer stated. "He takes great pride in his fine pack of hounds, and rarely a week goes by that he does not bring down a deer, a tapir, or a tiger cat."[35]

Prosecutor Dick Merrick never stopped being a partisan Democrat. When Republicans were slow to concede the 1884 presidential election to Cleveland, Merrick delivered a fiery speech in Washington that warned of violence if they tried to seat their candidate, Blaine. "I give this warning to the Republican

National Committee. Terror will follow any such proceeding as the seating of Blaine," he thundered. "Cleveland has been elected president, and he is to be inaugurated, peaceably if possible, forcibly if must be. If this government cannot preserve the rights of the people, it had better be torn to pieces." Merrick died a year later, leaving behind a daughter, Mary Virginia Merrick, who would become a pioneer in Roman Catholic social reform.[36]

Benjamin Brewster died in 1888. When he passed away, his friend and predecessor as attorney general, Wayne MacVeagh, said that Brewster "was not only a great lawyer, but was, what is better, a ripe and gracious scholar, and what is better still, a patriotic citizen, who served not only the law, but also the state, who was brave as becomes a gentleman in every circumstance of his life, and who left in the hearts of those who were privileged to know him best such sorrow as will not soon pass away."[37]

During the 1880s, MacVeagh chaired the Pennsylvania Civil Service Reform Commission, but the Republican Party's opposition to such reform so angered him that he switched sides. Becoming a Democrat, he served as the U.S. ambassador to Italy from 1893 to 1895 during Cleveland's second presidential administration. MacVeagh remained active in public life until his death in 1917. As World War I worsened, he penned several articles urging Americans to fully support the Allied cause.

Robert Green Ingersoll died of congestive heart failure in 1899. A century after his death, the attorney's reputation as an orator and pioneering freethinker was revived with the publication of an excellent biography by Susan Jacoby (*The Great Agnostic*) and the republication of some of his greatest speeches and writings (bearing the appropriate tongue-in-cheek title, *What's God Got to Do with It?*).[38]

In the summer of 1886, just three years after the Star Route retrial, George Corkhill, Washington's much-maligned district attorney, died of a stomach hemorrhage. He was only forty-eight years old. For several years, Corkhill had been dogged by the story that Charles Guiteau, James Garfield's assassin, had cursed him and the rest of his legal team after being successfully prosecuted for the president's murder. This rumor was so well known that one obituary of Corkhill recounted in detail how the assassin had "in his semi-lunatic way cursed him and others connected with the prosecution." A friend eulogized him as "one of nature's noblemen."[39]

Albert Gibson, the reporter-turned-prosecutor, never let go of his distaste for Republican corruption. In 1885, he published a screed entitled *A Political Crime: The History of the Great Fraud,* in which he maintained that the 1876 election had been stolen from the Democrats by the likes of Brady, who had been dispatched to Florida to help the Hayes campaign manipulate the vote count. The voters, he insisted, "were deprived of their choice by illegal methods, bolstered by frauds, perjuries, and forgeries." Gibson eventually turned his attention away from the grubby world of American politics—and the United States altogether—by moving to London and practicing patent law. He died in Berlin in 1899.[40]

Special prosecutor William Cook died in 1901. A few months after his death, he was remembered at an Emancipation Day celebration in Washington by Perrin Wellington Frisby, a pioneering Black attorney. "He took an active part in the liberation of the slave," Frisby said of Cook, "and manifested a great interest in all the affairs of the Republican Party." Although some thought that Cook always overstated his connections to President Garfield, Frisby said that "his strong friendship with the martyred president was marked and brought confidential advisory relations with him."[41]

After being forced out of his position as marshal of Washington because of his alleged tinkering with the jury in the first Star Route trial, Charles Henry returned to his farm in Ohio. He later engaged in a variety of business and investigative matters, at one point even traveling to Brazil to track down an embezzler. Henry died in 1906.

While Henry seemed to move on from his entanglement in the postal scandal, his son never forgot his father's "unmerited humiliation," as he termed it, in the early 1880s. In a biography published in 1942, Frederick Henry defended his father's honor and offered a fitting coda for the case. "The whole Star Route prosecution was a shuffling and sordid affair," the younger Henry wrote. "No one connected with the case derived any particular credit from it."[42]

★19★

THE STANDARD OF PUBLIC MORALS HAS BEEN ELEVATED

After the Star Route Scandal, 1884–Present

It is tempting to view the Star Route imbroglio as being nothing more than a flagrant example of the excesses of Gilded Age politics. The sleazy affair seems to reinforce what the historian Charles W. Calhoun has described as "the hoary stereotype" of the period, with its hallmarks "of political corruption and meaningless contention for spoils between the two major parties." This tangled and multifaceted story is a bit easier to follow when it is viewed through such a lens. Cashing in on a classic bid-rigging scheme, Stephen Dorsey, Tom Brady, and others repeatedly and shamelessly used underhanded methods to line their pockets, and they managed to escape relatively unscathed thanks to a bungling prosecution, two corrupted juries, and the general indifference of three successive presidential administrations. In an ignominious political era, the Star Route scandal stood out for its duration and naked rascality.[1]

Yet treating the Star Route scandal merely as a notorious emblem of a debauched political era is perhaps too facile. For one thing, the Gilded Age was notable for more than simply the rapacity of on-the-make politicians and greedy plutocrats. In this pivotal moment in American history, with the nation struggling to emerge from the turmoil of the Civil War and Reconstruction, politicians in both parties worked in good faith to address a broad and complex set of policymaking challenges. To that end, Republicans warmed to the idea that government could and should strategically use its power to affect change (especially in the realm of economic development) and safeguard the public interest. Although graft remained a stubborn problem, politicians gave careful consideration to weighty matters of policy as the nation matured and entered into its second century.

As they grappled with substantive foreign policy and domestic issues, politicians and parties in the Gilded Age meaningfully engaged with the American public in an effort to chart the nation's course and determine the parameters of state power. Along the way, they "glimpsed . . . the broader possibilities for energetic government," according to Calhoun. "In important ways they helped lay the groundwork for the twentieth-century American polity." Before the myriad reforms of the Progressive Era could be undertaken, or the welfare state established, the nation simply had to find its footing and explore the idea that the judicious use of state power could bolster economic and social well-being.[2]

The exposure and prosecution of the Star Route swindlers was an integral—if far from perfect—part of this process. An embarrassing episode of misconduct that lasted for the better part of a decade, the scandal forced Republicans of all ranks and factions to reckon with the cynicism, venality, and corruption that had diminished the party's standing and limited its appeal at the polls. To be sure, they did so reluctantly and haltingly; few members of the party relished the idea of potentially damaging their standing by bringing out into the open the brash corruption of men who had played key roles in Republicans' narrow electoral successes in 1876 and 1880. Yet James Garfield set the Star Route case into motion almost as soon as he took office in 1881, and—to the surprise of many—his successor as president, Chester Arthur, allowed it to proceed through not one, but two high-profile trials in 1882 and 1883. Both presidents and the attorneys general working under them (Wayne MacVeagh and Benjamin Brewster) followed this course of action even though it was not the most politically advantageous one. Although none of them received much credit for it, each man did his duty.

That the Star Route trials ultimately were not formal successes for the federal government (at least in the conventional sense of securing criminal convictions) should not diminish the significance of the fact that they happened in the first place. The postal frauds could have remained swept under the rug. Instead, for the better part of two years, federal officials investigated and prosecuted the Dorsey ring and others who had been involved in the exploitation of lucrative postal contracts. This process, though flawed at best, focused public attention on the necessity of exposing and finally stamping out corrupt practices in government contracting. By the time the case reached its muddled denouement in 1883, it was a settled question that an expanding, more robust federal government would need to replace the spoils system with a more principled framework that foregrounded honesty and efficiency.

The Star Route prosecution also was significant in that it helped further establish and legitimize the nascent role of the special prosecutor (subsequently known as an independent counsel and, finally, a special counsel) in investigating serious allegations of corruption and malfeasance in the federal government. Building on the experiences of the special prosecutors who probed the Whiskey Ring and Star Route scandals, later presidential administrators appointed special prosecutors and special and independent counsels to investigate fraud charges in the Post Office (1903) and the Teapot Dome scandal (1924). The practice continued with the Watergate scandal, the Iran-Contra affair, the sprawling Clinton-era Whitewater scandal, and allegations that Russia interfered with the 2016 presidential election. Whatever its effectiveness in any of those instances, the appointment of such an independent figure became recognized as a legitimate and impartial means of avoiding potential conflicts of interest while investigating and prosecuting wrongdoing in government.[3]

In retrospect, it is easy to second guess the work of special prosecutor William Cook and the other attorneys who represented the government in the Star Route case. There were credible accusations that some of the attorneys (Cook among them) were not fully committed to the cause and might have in fact aided the defendants. But in judging the work of these men almost 150 years later, we must also bear in mind the enormous challenges faced even today by well-trained and highly specialized attorneys who attempt to prosecute complex fraud and conspiracy cases. The Star Route prosecutors faced the added burden of having to argue their cases before juries in the nation's capital that were compromised by tampering—and the jurors' own myriad vices. Taken on the whole, their work was imperfect and uneven but still admirable. Attorneys General MacVeagh and Brewster (in particular) gave a good account of themselves, as did the two Democrats involved in prosecuting the case, Dick Merrick and William Ker.

It is also important to note that the federal government's Star Route prosecution was birthed during a particularly fraught moment in the nation's presidential history. When Garfield took office in 1881, his party was at war with itself, as competing Republican factions battled for supremacy. Garfield barely had time to mend these rifts—or even to govern the nation as a whole—before Charles Guiteau, a madman inflamed by the era's toxic political atmosphere, gunned him down. Upon Garfield's death, a man almost universally considered to be unprepared to become president, Arthur, took office. It was against this uniquely tumultuous and uncertain backdrop that the Star Route prosecution proceeded between 1881 and 1883.

The extent to which the Star Route case influenced Guiteau probably never will be known. Garfield's assassin was not of sound mind when he shot the president in 1881, and it is probably pointless to try to ascribe clear motives to him (as one might with, for instance, John Wilkes Booth, the assassin of President Lincoln in 1865). Yet after the killing, when he attempted to explain why he had become so agitated against the president, Guiteau himself alluded to the anti-Garfield media frenzy that had been whipped up in newspapers like the Washington *National Republican*, the organ of one of the main targets in the Star Route case, Tom Brady. Furthermore, several other observers—including Guiteau's sister, special prosecutor William Cook, and Postmaster General Tom James—suggested that the scandal and some of those connected to it might have influenced the assassin. This is one of the most momentous and tantalizing questions related to the entire Star Route affair, but it might never be fully answered.

If few individuals covered themselves in glory in the Star Route scandal, public institutions—in particular the Post Office—fared somewhat better. Investigator Patrick Henry Woodward (who later pursued a career in banking and died in 1917) said, "Some of the salutary results accomplished by the Star Route prosecutions can hardly be appreciated by persons unfamiliar with the revolution it has helped to effect in the methods of the Post Office Department." Once Star Route corruption was addressed, fraud and waste in the postal service were greatly reduced, with reform-minded officials applying "the pruning knife . . . fearlessly and vigorously to existing abuses." Furthermore, efficiencies increased, and the Contract Division was "transformed into a model of purity and efficiency." The Post Office that emerged from the prolonged embarrassment of the scandal was in many ways more modern, competent, and accountable.[4]

There were broader effects as well, according to Woodward. "We might go still farther and claim that the standard of public morals has been elevated," he said in testimony before Congress. "On the one hand, the people have grown more intolerant of wrong-doing; and on the other, men in positions of trust have grown more timorous about yielding to dishonest inclinations."[5]

In his 1938 book *The Politicos, 1865–1896*, the political journalist Matthew Josephson, reflecting on the ramifications of the Star Route scandal, reached a similar conclusion. Although it did not result in guilty verdicts, "the open stealing from the till of the government was sharply reduced after the famous Star Route trials," he wrote. "The officialdom of the [Republican] Party separated itself from large-scale revenue frauds." Some Republicans made this break more quickly than others—Secretary of the Navy William Chandler was accused of favoritism in awarding shipping contracts in 1883—but members of the party gradually comported themselves more ethically in their official duties.[6]

It would be naive, of course, to suggest that the Star Route scandal so outraged the American public that corruption, bid-rigging, and fraud were swiftly eliminated from the nation's political landscape in the late nineteenth century. This was simply not the case. Politicians found fresh sources of graft in the burgeoning industrial economy, particularly the railroads and public utility companies. And, even today, graft continues to be a problem, even in United States Postal Service (USPS) contracting.

Over the years, the Star Routes have evolved into Highway Contract Routes (HCRs). The days of horses carrying the mail over rugged, dusty trails are long gone, of course. The USPS now employs a small army of private contractors to haul mail over long distances between designated postal facilities in massive semi-tractor-trailer trucks. As was the case in the nineteenth century, this is a sprawling and lucrative enterprise: in 2016, the USPS reported that it paid 8,300 contractors roughly $3 billion to carry the mail. HCR agreements now represent the largest group of contracts managed by the USPS.

After fielding numerous reports of fraud and waste, the USPS Office of the Inspector General, the agency's internal fraud watchdog, scrutinized the management of the HCRs and found it to be lacking in myriad ways. In 2016, it issued a report decrying the limited management and oversight of the private contractors employed by the USPS. Of particular concern to the inspectors was the lack of any "centralized method to manage performance irregularities" in HCRs. With lax regulatory and administrative practices, fraud and waste could easily go undetected.[7]

A series of recent legal proceedings involving HCR contractors has borne out this point. In one case, the government alleged that a Colorado company had committed fraud by having "failed to pay its drivers prevailing wages, ordered falsification of [Department of Transportation] regulated hours of service logs, falsified contract documents, and lied to Federal auditors and investigators during a compliance review." In a similar case, Alexei Rivero, the vice president of Florida Carrier & Brokerage Service, pleaded guilty in June 2019 to two counts of wire fraud for having cheated on some HCR contracts.

Rivero's case, like the Colorado prosecution, demonstrated that the methods allegedly used by crooked postal contractors to defraud the government have changed a bit since the days of the Dorsey ring in the 1870s and 1880s. In his guilty plea, Rivero acknowledged that his firm had not paid payroll taxes for its drivers nor provided them with fringe benefits as its contracts with the USPS had stipulated. The misappropriated funds, which Rivero allegedly pocketed for his personal use and benefit, amount to roughly $2.7 million.[8]

A century and a half after the government fought an unprecedented and epic legal battle to end fraud in postal contracting, a federal official who was involved in securing the guilty plea from Rivero said that the USPS would "continue to aggressively investigate those who would engage in fraudulent activities designed to defraud the Postal Service." Although the times (and alleged crimes) have changed, the spirit of the Star Route prosecutions—grounded in a belief that the government has a fundamental duty to root out corruption and provide honest services to the public—lives on.[9]

NOTES

ABBREVIATIONS

2DT   *Proceedings of the Second Trial of the Case of The United States v. John W. Dorsey, John R. Miner, John M. Peck, Stephen W. Dorsey, Harvey M. Vaile, Montfort C. Rerdell and Thomas J. Brady, in the Supreme Court of the District of Columbia, Andrew Wylie, Justice* (Washington, DC: Government Printing Office, 1883)

DTT   *Proceedings in the Trial of the Case of The United States v. John W. Dorsey, John R. Miner, John M. Peck, Stephen W. Dorsey, Harvey M. Vaile, Montfort C. Rerdell, Thomas J. Brady, and William H. Turner for Conspiracy, in the Supreme Court of the District of Columbia, Andrew Wylie, Justice* (Washington, DC: Government Printing Office, 1882)

GRDOJ   General Records of the Department of Justice, 1849–1989, Record Group 60, National Archives and Records Administration, College Park, MD

HSRE   *Miscellaneous Documents of the House of Representatives for First Session of the 48th Congress, 1883–1885. Testimony Relating to Expenditures in the Department of Justice, Star Route Cases* (Washington, DC: Government Printing Office, 1884)

PREFACE

1. Eugene Coleman Savidge, *Life of Benjamin Harris Brewster, with Discourses and Addresses* (Philadelphia: J. B. Lippincott, 1891), 9–11.

2. Savidge, *Life of Benjamin Harris Brewster,* 9–11.

3. Henry Adams, *The Letters of Henry Adams,* vol. 2, *1868–1885* (Boston: Belknap, 1982), 493.

4. H. Wayne Morgan, *From Hayes to McKinley: National Party Politics, 1877–1896* (Syracuse, NY: Syracuse University Press, 1969), 157.

5. *St. Louis Globe-Democrat,* May 1, 11, 1881; *Chicago Daily Inter Ocean,* May 11, 1881.

6. *New York Times,* October 19, 1898.

7. Mark Wahlgren Summers, *The Era of Good Stealings* (New York: Oxford University Press, 1993).

8. Frances Marie Norton, *The Stalwarts; or, Who Were to Blame?* (Chicago: Frances Marie Norton, 1888), iii–iv (emphasis in original).

1. CELERITY, CERTAINTY, AND SECURITY

1. Daniel Carpenter, "American Democracy Is in the Mail," Boston Review, September 10, 2020, bostonreview.net/articles/daniel-carpenter-american-democracy-mail/.

2. Devin Leonard, *Neither Snow nor Rain: A History of the United States Postal Service* (New York: Grove, 2017), 18–19.

3. "Status and Performance of the United States Postal Service," *Hearings before the Subcommittee on Postal Service of the Committee on Post Office and Civil Service, House of Representatives, Ninety-Second Congress, 2nd Session* (Washington, DC: Government Printing Office, 1972), 647.

4. Office of the Inspector General, United States Postal Service, "Rural and Urban Origins," Report RISC-WP-19-007, August 26, 2019, 5.

5. Cameron Blevins, *Paper Trails: The U.S. Post and the Making of the American West* (New York: Oxford University Press, 2021), 168n18.

6. Blevins, *Paper Trails,* 77–78.

7. Frederic Logan Paxson, *Recent History of the United States* (Boston: Houghton Mifflin, 1922), 62.

8. Winifred Gallagher, *How the Post Office Created America: A History* (New York: Penguin, 2016), 87.

9. Blevins, *Paper Trails,* 78–80.

10. Carl Anderson, *As I Remember It: Reminiscences* (Spencer, IN: Farm Bureau Printing, 1943), 19.

11. Marshall Cushing, *The Story of Our Post Office: The Greatest Government Department in All Its Phases* (Boston: A. M. Thayer, 1892), 40.

12. "The Life and Legend of Mary Fields," Women's History Matters, April 8, 2014, montanawomenshistory.org/the-life-and-legend-of-mary-fields/; Gary Cooper (as told to Marc Crawford), "Stagecoach Mary: A Gun-Toting Black Woman Delivered the U.S. Mail in Montana," *Ebony,* October 1, 1959, 97–100.

13. Uel W. Lamkin, *History of Henry County, Missouri* (Philadelphia: Historical Publishing, 1919), 154.

14. Mark Wahlgren Summers, *Rum, Romanism, & Rebellion: The Making of a President, 1884* (Chapel Hill: University of North Carolina Press, 2000), 71–72; Sharon K. Lowry, "Portrait of an Age: The Political Career of Stephen W. Dorsey, 1868–1889" (Ph.D. diss., North Texas State University, 1980), 248–53.

15. Earl Leland, "The Post Office and Politics, 1876–1884: The Star Route Frauds" (Ph.D. diss., University of Chicago, 1964), 3.

16. Cushing, *Story of Our Post Office,* 24.

17. Cushing, *Story of Our Post Office,* 23–24.

18. Lowry, "Portrait of an Age," 248–53.

19. Lowry, "Portrait of an Age," 248–53.

20. Lowry, "Portrait of an Age," 248–53.

21. Leland, "Post Office and Politics," 14–15; Jacob G. Ullery, *Men of Vermont: An Illustrated Biographical History of Vermonters and Sons of Vermont* (Brattleboro, VT: Transcript, 1894), 158; Frederick W. Baldwin, *Biography of the Bar of Orleans County, Vermont* (Montpelier: Vermont Watchman and State Journal, 1884), 131.

22. Leland, "Post Office and Politics," 14.

23. *Sun* (New York City), April 23, May 15, 1875.

24. *Annual Report of the Postmaster General of the United States for the Fiscal Year Ended June 30, 1881* (Washington, DC: Government Printing Office, 1881), 501. The portion of this report dealing with Star Route contracts was written by Albert Gibson.

25. Blevins, *Paper Trails*, 85–86.

26. Blevins, *Paper Trails*, 76–77.

27. Thomas B. Helm, *History of Delaware County, Indiana* (Chicago: Kingman Brothers, 1881), 203–8.

28. Helm, *History of Delaware County*, 203–8; *War of the Rebellion: A Compilation of the Official Records of the Union and Confederate Armies*, ser. 1, vol. 31, pt. 1 (Washington, DC: Government Printing Office, 1890), 605–6.

29. Charlie Basham, "A Muddy Confederate Flag and the Foiled Plot," *Mountain Democrat* (Placerville, CA), April 14, 2015, www.mtdemocrat.com/prospecting/a-muddy-confederate-flag -and-the-foiled-plot/.

30. *A Biographical History of Eminent and Self-Made Men of the State of Indiana*, vol. 1 (Cincinnati: Western Biographical, 1880), 92–95.

31. John Y. Simon, ed., *The Papers of Ulysses S. Grant*, vol. 22, *June 1, 1871–January 31, 1872* (Carbondale: Southern Illinois University Press, 1998), 400–401.

32. *National Republican* (Washington), February 7, 1871.

33. Thomas Brady to *Rensselaer (IN) Union*, September 3, 1874, quoted in *Galveston (TX) Daily News*, August 20, 1876.

34. *Indiana State Sentinel* (Indianapolis), October 6, 1874; *Indianapolis Sentinel*, October 4, 1874.

35. Joseph E. Holliday, "Daniel D. Pratt: Senator and Commissioner," *Indiana Magazine of History* 58, no. 1 (1962): 17–51.

36. *Biographical History of Eminent and Self-Made Men*, 92–95.

37. Rollin H. Kirk, *Many Secrets Revealed; or, Ten Years behind the Scenes in Washington City* (Washington, DC, 1885), 105. The book was published anonymously but later attributed to Kirk.

38. *Cincinnati Enquirer*, June 11, 1876. Blaine was not yet a senator from Maine at the time of the Cincinnati convection in June 1876; he would be sworn into office a month later.

39. George Ticknor Curtis, *Constitutional History of the United States: From Their Declaration of Independence to the Close of Their Civil War*, vol. 2 (New York: Harper and Brothers, 1896), 414.

40. U.S. House of Representatives, *Presidential Election Investigation, Testimony Taken by the Select Committee on Alleged Frauds in the Presidential Election of 1876*, vol. 2, *Testimony Relating to Florida*, 45th Cong., 3rd sess., H. Misc. Doc. 31, pt. 2 (Washington: Government Printing Office, 1879), 55, 59.

41. U.S. House, *Presidential Election Investigation*, 88.

42. U.S. House, *Presidential Election Investigation*, 51, 60.

43. *Galveston (TX) Daily News*, August 20, 1876.

44. *Biographical History of Eminent and Self-Made Men*, 92–95.

45. *Cincinnati Daily Gazette*, September 2, 1878.

46. *Annual Report of the Postmaster General*, 486; *Ann Arbor (MI) Argus*, November 14, 1879.

47. *Silver World* (Lake City, CO), December 13, 1879; *New Haven (CT) Register*, June 1, 1880.

48. Albert Bigelow Paine, *In One Man's Life, being Chapters from the Personal & Business Career of Theodore N. Vail* (New York: Harper and Brothers, 1921), 140–44.

49. *Terre Haute (IN) Weekly Gazette*, July 6, 1882.

50. Kirk, *Many Secrets Revealed*, 107–8.

2. CHAPTER FIRST IN THE HISTORY OF PLUNDER

1. *Washington Daily Patriot*, January 8, 1872; J. Martin Klotsche, "The Star Route Cases," *Mississippi Valley Historical Review* 22, no. 3 (1935): 407–18; "Testimony Taken before the Committee on the Post-Office and Post-Roads, in Relation to Mail Contracts," in *Reports of Committees of the House of Representatives for the First Session of the Forty-Fourth Congress, 1875–1876* (Washington, DC: Government Printing Office, 1876), 400–409.

2. *Washington Daily Patriot*, January 2, 1872; Klotsche, "Star Route Cases," 407–18; "Testimony Taken before the Committee on the Post-Office and Post-Roads," 400–409.

3. *Washington Daily Patriot*, January 2, 1872.

4. *Washington Daily Patriot*, January 2, 1872; Klotsche, "Star Route Cases," 407–18; "Testimony Taken before the Committee on the Post-Office and Post-Roads," 400–409.

5. *Washington Daily Patriot*, January 2, 1872; Klotsche, "Star Route Cases," 407–18; "Testimony Taken before the Committee on the Post-Office and Post-Roads," 400–409.

6. HSRE, 63.

7. HSRE, 63.

8. HSRE, 64.

9. HSRE, 67.

10. *Washington Evening Star*, January 25, 1872; "Testimony Taken before the Committee on the Post-Office and Post-Roads," 410–27.

11. "Testimony Taken before the Committee on the Post-Office and Post-Roads," 410.

12. *Alexandria (VA) Gazette*, February 5, 1872; *Sun* (New York City), March 21, 1876.

13. *National Republican* (Washington), May 2, 1874.

14. *Sun* (New York City), March 21, 1876.

15. HSRE, 199.

16. "Management of the Post-Office Department," in *Reports of Committees of the House of Representatives for the First Session of the Forty-Fourth Congress, 1875–1876* (Washington, DC: Government Printing Office, 1876), vii–xii.

17. "Management of the Post-Office Department," vii–xii.

18. *Sun* (New York City), March 20, 1876.

19. Leland, "Post Office and Politics," 38; *Sun* (New York City), March 8, 1878.

20. *Sun* (New York City), March 8, 1878.

21. *Sun* (New York City), March 8, 1878.

22. *Concord (NH) Independent Statesman*, May 22, 1873; Nat Brandt, *The Town That Started the Civil War* (Syracuse, NY: Syracuse University Press, 1990), 258.

23. *Little Rock Morning Republican*, Jan 20, 1873; *Biographical Directory of the American Congress, 1774–1961* (Washington, DC: Government Printing Office, 1961), 823–24.

24. *Little Rock (AR) Morning Republican*, Jan 20, 1873.

25. *Little Rock (AR) Morning Republican*, Jan 20, 1873; *Concord (NH) Independent Statesman*, May 22, 1873; *Lowell (MA) Daily Citizen*, July 14, 1874.

26. *Helena (AR) World*, quoted in *Arkansas Gazette* (Little Rock), February 9, 1873; Dallas T. Herndon, ed., *Centennial History of Arkansas*, vol. 1 (Chicago: S. J. Clarke, 1922), 306–7.

27. Carl H. Moneyhon, "Brooks-Baxter War," Encyclopedia of Arkansas, last updated January 10, 2019, encyclopediaofarkansas.net/entries/brooks-baxter-war-2276/.

28. Lowry, "Portrait of an Age," 80–83; *St. Louis Post-Dispatch*, reprinted in *Arkansas Gazette* (Little Rock), February 26, 1875.

29. Mary Clemmer Ames, "A Woman's Letter from Washington," *Independent*, July 2, 1874, 13.

30. Lowry, "Portrait of an Age," 104–5; Theodore Clarke Smith, *The Life and Letters of James Abram Garfield*, 2 vols. (New Haven, CT: Yale University Press, 1925), 1:599; Thomas C. Reeves, *Gentleman Boss: The Life of Chester Alan Arthur* (New York: Knopf, 1975), 217.

31. Allan Peskin, *Garfield* (Kent, OH: Kent State University Press, 1978), 486.

32. *Washington Evening Star*, March 19, 1878.

33. *Washington Evening Star*, March 18, 19, 1878; *New York Times*, March 18, 1878.

34. DTT, 227–28.

35. DTT, 227–28.

36. Warren G. Harding, *The Railways and Prosperity: Address by Warren G. Harding, at the Annual Dinner of the Railway Business Association* (New York: Railway Business Association, 1914), 3–4; Lowry, "Portrait of an Age," 259–68.

37. Lowry, "Portrait of an Age," 259–68.

38. Lowry, "Portrait of an Age," 259–68.

39. HSRE, 602–12.

40. HSRE, 602–12.

41. *Little Rock (AR) Morning Republican*, May 12, 1874.

42. *Arkansas Gazette* (Little Rock), July 22, 1874.

43. HSRE, 602–612.

44. Lowry, "Portrait of an Age," 259–68.

45. Lowry, "Portrait of an Age," 259–68.

46. *Washington Evening Star*, March 24, 1878.

47. Lowry, "Portrait of an Age," 257–68.

48. DTT, 231–32.

49. *Lowell (MA) Daily Citizen*, July 14, 1874; *Washington Evening Star*, April 3, 1878.

50. *Washington Evening Star*, April 3, 1878.

51. Johannes Martin Klotsche, "The Star Route Frauds" (Ph.D. diss., University of Wisconsin–Madison, 1931), 33; Lowry, "Portrait of an Age," 259.

52. Rutherford Birchard Hayes, *Diary and Letters of Rutherford Birchard Hayes, Nineteenth President of the United States,* vol. 4 (Columbus: Ohio State Archeological and Historical Society, 1925), 10–13.

53. Hayes, *Diary and Letters,* 10–13.

54. Albert M. Gibson, *A Political Crime: The History of the Great Fraud* (New York: W. S. Gottsberger, 1885), 53, 65, 110.

3. THE CYNICISM OF THIS

1. Lowry, "Portrait of an Age," 259–68.

2. W. Caleb McDaniel, "In 1870, Henrietta Wood Sued for Reparations—and Won," *Smithsonian Magazine,* September 2019, www.smithsonianmag.com/history/henrietta-wood-sued-reparations-won-180972845/; Carl H. Moneyhon, "Convict Lease System," Encyclopedia of Arkansas, last updated January 10, 2019, encyclopediaofarkansas.net/entries/brooks-baxter-war-2276/.

3. DTT, 212–15.

4. DTT, 212–15.

5. DTT, 212–15.

6. DTT, 212–15.

7. Lowry, "Portrait of an Age," 259–68.

8. Lowry, "Portrait of an Age," 259–68.

9. "Looking Back: Reminiscing about the 'House of Gold!,'" Esoteric Curiosa, June 22, 2010, theesotericcuriosa.blogspot.com/2010/06/looking-back-reminiscing-about-house-of.html.

10. "Looking Back."

11. *Kansas City Times,* quoted in "Looking Back."

12. Lowry, "Portrait of an Age," 259–68.

13. Lowry, "Portrait of an Age," 259–68.

14. Lowry, "Portrait of an Age," 259–68.

15. Lowry, "Portrait of an Age," 259–68.

16. Lowry, "Portrait of an Age," 259–68.

17. Lowry, "Portrait of an Age," 259–68.

18. Lowry, "Portrait of an Age," 259–68.

19. Lowry, "Portrait of an Age," 259–68.

20. Lowry, "Portrait of an Age," 259–68; Leland, "Post Office and Politics," 74.

21. Leland, "Post Office and Politics," 74–75; *New York Times,* December 11, 1879.

22. *Sun* (New York City), December 16, 1879.

23. *Miscellaneous Documents of the House of Representatives for Second Session of the 46th Congress, 1879–1880,* vol. 3 (Washington, DC: Government Printing Office, 1880), 2.

24. Lowry, "Portrait of an Age," 259–68.

25. Leland, "Post Office and Politics," 76–77.

26. *Miscellaneous Documents of the House of Representatives for Second Session,* 159.

27. *Miscellaneous Documents of the House of Representatives for Second Session*, 258.

28. *Miscellaneous Documents of the House of Representatives for Second Session*, 279–80.

29. *Miscellaneous Documents of the House of Representatives for Second Session*, 290.

30. *Miscellaneous Documents of the House of Representatives for Second Session*, 279–80.

31. *Miscellaneous Documents of the House of Representatives for Second Session*, 279–80.

32. Lowry, "Portrait of an Age," 259–68.

33. *New York Times*, April 3, 1880; *Sun* (New York City), January 25, 1880.

34. Lowry, "Portrait of an Age," 259–68.

35. *Sun* (New York City), March 5, 1880.

36. Kirk, *Many Secrets Revealed*, 108–9.

37. Robert D. Marcus, *Grand Old Party: Political Structure in the Gilded Age, 1880–1896* (New York: Oxford University Press, 1971), 42.

38. Lowry, "Portrait of an Age," 259–68.

39. Paul Tincher Smith, "Indiana's Last October Campaign," *Indiana Magazine of History* 19, no. 4 (1923): 332–45.

40. Benjamin T. Arrington, *The Last Lincoln Republican: The Presidential Election of 1880* (Lawrence: University Press of Kansas, 2020), 134.

41. Kenneth Ackerman, *Dark Horse: The Surprise Election and Political Murder of President James A. Garfield* (New York: Carroll and Graf, 2003), 200.

42. Arrington, *Last Lincoln Republican*, 144–46.

43. Mari Grana, *On the Fringes of Power: The Life and Turbulent Career of Stephen Wallace Dorsey* (Lanham, MD: Rowman and Littlefield, 2015), 30; Lowry, "Portrait of an Age," 226; *St. Louis Globe-Democrat*, November 2, 1880; Robert Russell LaFollette, "History of Campaign Funds from 1876 to 1892" (M.A. thesis, University of Wisconsin–Madison, 1917), 26.

44. "The Week," *Nation*, May 19, 1881, 341–43; Leland, "*Post Office and Politics*," 226.

45. David Ross Locke, *The Nasby Letters* (Toledo, OH: Toledo Blade, 1893), 416.

46. Lowry, "Portrait of an Age," 232.

47. Lowry, "Portrait of an Age," 232–33.

48. Smith, *Life and Letters of James Abram Garfield*, 2:1053–54.

49. Smith, *Life and Letters of James Abram Garfield*, 2:1059.

50. *New York Times*, February 12, 1881.

51. *New York Times*, February 12, 1881.

52. *New York Times*, February 12, 1881.

53. *New York Times*, February 12, 1881; David M. Jordan, *Roscoe Conkling of New York: Voice in the Senate* (Ithaca, NY: Cornell University Press, 1971), 375.

54. Grana, *On the Fringes of Power*, 30–31.

55. James R. Doolittle to Thomas A. Hendricks, June 19, 1884, reproduced in Duane Mowry, "Political Letters of the Post-Bellum Days: From the Doolittle Correspondence with Thomas A. Hendricks," *Indiana Quarterly Magazine of History* 5, no. 4 (1909): 171–80. Arthur had become president by the time the letter was written.

56. Matthew Josephson, *The Politicos: 1865–1896* (New York: Harcourt, Brace, 1938), 132; Smith, *Life and Letters of James Abram Garfield*, 2:1085–86.

57. George Frederick Howe, *Chester A. Arthur: A Quarter-Century of Machine Politics* (New York: Dodd, Mead, 1934), 179; Lowry, "Portrait of an Age," 246; Leon Burr Richardson, *William E. Chandler, Republican* (New York: Dodd, Mead, 1940), 266–67.

58. Gibson, *Political Crime*, 53, 65, 110.

59. Marcus, *Grand Old Party*, 43.

4. PROBE THIS ULCER TO THE BOTTOM

1. Justus Doenecke, *The Presidencies of James A. Garfield and Chester A. Arthur* (Lawrence: University Press of Kansas, 1981), 34, 39.

2. Julius Chambers, *The Book of New York: Forty Years' Recollections of the American Metropolis* (New York: Book of New York, 1912), 24.

3. Dorothy Ganfied Fowler, *The Cabinet Politician: The Postmasters General, 1829–1909.* (New York: Columbia University Press, 1943), 168.

4. Fowler, *Cabinet Politician*, 176.

5. T. B. Connery, "Secret History of the Garfield-Conkling Tragedy," *Cosmopolitan*, June 1897, 145–62.

6. Connery, "Secret History," 145–62.

7. Stephen Fiske, *Off-hand Portraits of Prominent New Yorkers* (New York: G. R. Lockwood and Son, 1884), 191–92.

8. HSRE, 1.

9. E. Benjamin Andrews, "A History of the Last Quarter-Century," *Scribner's Magazine*, September 1895, 288.

10. HSRE, 1.

11. Smith, *Life and Letters of James Abram Garfield*, 2:1075; Reeves, *Gentleman Boss*, 219.

12. Jordan, *Roscoe Conkling*, 374–75.

13. Stanley Edgar Hyman, "Comment," *New Yorker*, December 24, 1943, 13; "Isaac Wayne MacVeagh, 1881," Chester A. Arthur—Administration, U.S. Presidents, Miller Center, University of Virginia, millercenter.org/president/arthur/essays/macveagh-1881-attorney-general.

14. Warner Berthoff and David Bonnell Green, "Henry Adams and Wayne MacVeagh," *Pennsylvania Magazine of History and Biography* 80, no. 4 (1956): 493–512.

15. Isaac Wayne MacVeagh, *Law and Democracy: An Address Delivered before the Graduating Classes at the Sixty-Second Anniversary of the Yale Law School, on June 29th, 1886* (New Haven, CT: Law Department of Yale College, 1886), 33.

16. Smith, *Life and Letters of James Abram Garfield*, 2:1086.

17. Lowry, "Portrait of An Age," 271–72.

18. *New York Herald*, August 15, 1882.

19. *Milwaukee Daily Sentinel*, December 2, 1882.

20. Savidge, *Life of Benjamin Harris Brewster*, 119–20.

21. HSRE, 2.

22. HSRE, 2.

23. John N. Makris, *The Silent Investigators: The Great Untold Story of the United States Postal Inspection Service* (New York: E. P. Dutton, 1959), 96.

24. HSRE, 2.

25. Patrick Henry Woodward, *The Secret Service of the Post Office Department* (Hartford, CT: Winter, 1886).

26. HSRE, 334.

27. Savidge, *Life of Benjamin Harris Brewster*, 133.

28. HSRE, 335.

29. HSRE, 54, 334.

30. HSRE, 334.

31. HSRE, 54.

32. Elbert L. Watson, "George Spencer," Encyclopedia of Alabama, November 18, 2010, encyclopediaofalabama.org/article/h-2975.

33. HSRE, 55, 66.

34. Democratic National Committee, *The Campaign Text Book: Why the People Want Change* (New York: National Democratic Committee, 1880), 442, 453–54.

35. Roy Morris Jr., *Fraud of the Century: Rutherford B. Hayes, Samuel Tilden, and the Stolen Election of 1876* (New York: Simon and Schuster, 2003), 122.

36. Patrick Henry Woodward to Thomas James, April 26, 1881, reproduced in HSRE, 915; ibid., 335.

37. HSRE, 3–4.

38. HSRE, 3–4.

39. Smith, *Life and Letters of James Abram Garfield*, 2:1157.

40. HSRE, 4.

41. HSRE, 26.

42. HSRE, 26.

43. HSRE 4, 26.

44. HSRE, 4.

45. HSRE, 4, 26.

46. HSRE, 4.

47. HSRE, 335.

5. SETTING A THIEF TO CATCH A THIEF

1. HSRE, 5, 335.

2. HSRE, 5.

3. HSRE, 5–6.

4. HSRE, 16.

5. *Milwaukee Daily Sentinel*, December 2, 1882.

6. William H. Crook, *Through Five Administrations* (New York: Harper and Brothers, 1910), 257–58.

7. HSRE, 16.

8. HSRE, 4.

9. Thomas James to Thomas Brady, April 29, 1881, reproduced in HSRE, 4–5; Myrtle Trowbridge, "The Garfield Administration and the Star Route Prosecutions" (M.A. thesis, University of Wisconsin–Madison, 1918), 34.

10. Trowbridge, "Garfield Administration," 34–35.

11. *Chicago Daily Inter Ocean,* April 26, 1881.

12. *Terre Haute (IN) Weekly Gazette,* July 6, 1882.

13. Meyer Berger, *The Story of the New York Times: The First 100 Years, 1851–1951* (New York: Arno, 1970), 54–55.

14. *New York Times,* April 25, 1881.

15. *New York Times,* April 25, 1881.

16. *Frank Leslie's Illustrated Newspaper,* May 28, 1881, 215.

17. Lowry, "Portrait of an Age," 278.

18. HSRE, 101.

19. *National Republican* (Washington), June 3, 1881.

20. George Corkhill to Wayne MacVeagh, June 1, 1881, reproduced in HSRE, 915; *National Republican,* June 3, 1881.

21. *St. Louis Globe-Democrat,* June 6, 1881.

22. James A. Garfield, *The Diary of James A. Garfield,* vol. 4, *1878–1881* (East Lansing: Michigan State University Press, 1981), 604; Smith, *Life and Letters of James Abram Garfield,* 2:1161.

23. Lowry, "Portrait of an Age," 278.

24. Frederick A. Henry, *Captain Henry of Geauga, a Family Chronicle* (Cleveland: Gates, 1942), 328.

25. The *Capital* editor's open letter was reproduced in the *National Republican* (Washington), June 6, 1881.

26. Henry, *Captain Henry of Geauga,* 327–28.

27. *Washington Evening Star,* quoted in HSRE, 94.

28. *Boston Daily Advertiser,* September 12, 1881.

29. John H. Crane, *The Washington Ring* (Washington, DC, 1872), 2–23; Democratic National Committee, *The Campaign Text Book: Why the People Want Change* (New York: Democratic National Committee, 1876), 164–65; John H. Crane, *More about the Washington Tammany* (Washington, DC, 1873), 8–11.

30. HSRE, 809.

31. *Sun* (New York City), June 7, 1881.

32. Smith, *Life and Letters of James Abram Garfield,* 2:1161; HSRE, 808.

33. HSRE, 336.

34. HSRE, 95.

35. HSRE, 338.

36. HSRE, 7.

37. HSRE, 93–94.

38. HSRE, 338.

39. HSRE, 338–39.

40. Patrick Henry Woodward to Benjamin Brewster, July 7, 1883, reproduced in HSRE, 915.

41. HSRE, 338.

42. Smith, *Life and Letters of James Abram Garfield,* 2:1162.

6. BUSINESS CONNECTED WITH DORSEY'S TROUBLES

1. *Chicago Daily Inter Ocean,* June 4, 1881; *St. Louis Globe-Democrat,* June 4, 1881.

2. Woodward, *Secret Service of the Post Office Department,* 569; *Testimony of Attorney-General Brewster, together with the Letters and Documents Furnished to the Committee of the House of Representatives Appointed to Inquire into the Expenditures of Department of Justice* (Washington, DC: Government Printing Office, 1884), 31–32.

3. Woodward, *Secret Service of the Post Office Department,* 569.

4. Woodward, *Secret Service of the Post Office Department,* 569–70.

5. Woodward, *Secret Service of the Post Office Department,* 571–72.

6. Woodward, *Secret Service of the Post Office Department,* 577.

7. Woodward, *Secret Service of the Post Office Department,* 577.

8. Woodward, *Secret Service of the Post Office Department,* 577–78.

9. *Sun* (New York City), July 1, 4, 1881.

10. HSRE, 27.

11. HSRE, 27, 28.

12. Klotsche, "Star Route Cases," 407–18.

13. HSRE, 28.

14. Ward Thoron, ed., *The Letters of Mrs. Henry Adams, 1865–1883* (Boston: Little, Brown, 1936), 288.

15. DTT, 115–17.

16. HSRE, 55.

17. DTT, 115–17; HSRE, 6.

18. HSRE, 6.

19. HSRE, 6.

20. HSRE, 6, 337; DTT, 115–17.

21. HSRE, 337.

22. HSRE, 602–12.

23. HSRE, 602–12.

24. DTT, 115–17; HSRE, 337.

25. DTT, 115–17.

26. HSRE, 6–7.

27. HSRE, 6–7; Lowry, "Portrait of an Age," 278–81.

28. HSRE, 7, 58–59.

29. HSRE, 7, 58–59.

30. HSRE, 7, 338.

31. HSRE, 602–12.

32. HSRE, 602–12.

33. Lowry, "Portrait of an Age," 281.

34. HSRE, 29.

35. HSRE, 95–96.

36. *Chicago Daily Inter Ocean,* June 24, 1881.

37. HSRE, 95.

38. HSRE, 27.

39. *Sun* (New York City), June 24, 1881.

7. THE NEWSPAPERS CONFIRMED THE INSPIRATION

1. HSRE, 15.

2. HSRE, 7, 338.

3. HSRE, 97.

4. HSRE, 97.

5. James C. Clark, "The Murder of President James A. Garfield," *Prologue* 24 (Summer 1992): 129–39.

6. Clark, "Murder of James A. Garfield," 129–39. Guiteau's exact words at this moment have been recorded in a variety of ways, but the differences do not seem to be substantive.

7. Allan Peskin, "Who Were the Stalwarts? Who Were Their Rivals? Republican Factions in the Gilded Age," *Political Science Quarterly* 99, no. 4 (1984): 703–16.

8. Peskin, "Who Were the Stalwarts? Who Were Their Rivals?," 703–16.

9. Candice Millard, *Destiny of the Republic: A Tale of Madness, Medicine, and the Murder of a President* (New York: Doubleday, 2011), 94–95.

10. Richard Menke, *Literature, Print Culture, and Media Technologies, 1880–1900: Many Inventions* (Cambridge: Cambridge University Press, 2019), 30; *Report of the Proceedings in the Case of The United States v. Charles J. Guiteau,* in the Supreme Court of the District of Columbia, Walter Cox, Justice (Washington, DC: Government Printing Office, 1882), pt. 1, 326.

11. Jared Cohen, *Accidental Presidents: Eight Men Who Changed America,* New York: Simon and Schuster, 2019, 152; Stewart Mitchell, "The Man Who Murdered Garfield," *Proceedings of the Massachusetts Historical Society* 67 (1941): 452–89; *New York Herald,* May 11, 12, 13, 14, 1881. The infamous "Wriggler" article appeared in the May 11 issue of the *Herald.*

12. Connery, "Secret History," 145–62.

13. *Report of the Proceedings in the Case of The United States v. Charles J. Guiteau,* pt. 1, 696.

14. Clark, "Murder of President James A. Garfield," 129–39.

15. *Report of the Proceedings in the Case of The United States v. Charles J. Guiteau,* pt. 1, 789.

16. *Report of the Proceedings in the Case of The United States v. Charles J. Guiteau,* pt. 1, 789.

17. Charles J. Guiteau, *The Truth and the Removal* (Washington, DC: Charles J. Guiteau, 1882), 155.

18. HSRE, 113–14.

19. Harold Dean Cater, ed., *Henry Adams and His Friends: A Collection of His Unpublished Letters* (Boston: Houghton Mifflin, 1947), 108–9.

20. HSRE, 340.

21. HSRE, 340.

22. HSRE, 340.

23. Savidge, *Life of Benjamin Harris Brewster,* 237.

24. Lewis Cassidy, "The Elder Brewster of Pennsylvania." *Dickinson Law Review* 41, no. 2 (1936): 103–14; Brooks M. Kelley, "Simon Cameron and the Senatorial Nomination of 1867," *Pennsylvania Magazine of History and Biography* 87, no. 4 (1963): 375–92.

25. HSRE, 844.

26. *Chicago Daily Inter Ocean,* September 14, 1881.

27. Jeffrey Broxmeyer, *Electoral Capitalism: The Party System in New York's Gilded Age* (Philadelphia: University of Pennsylvania Press, 2020), 108; Jeffrey Broxmeyer, "Politics as a Sphere of Wealth Accumulation: Cases of Gilded Age New York, 1855–1888" (Ph.D. diss., City University of New York–Graduate Center, 2014), 158–61.

28. George Bliss, "Autobiography of George Bliss," vol. 1, George B. V. Bliss Papers, 1847–1897, Manuscript Collections, Patricia D. Klingenstein Library, New-York Historical Society, 148. I am enormously grateful to Jeffrey Broxmeyer of the University of Toledo for sharing this material as well as his overall insights.

29. Bliss, "Autobiography," 1:247; Broxmeyer, *Electoral Capitalism,* 62.

30. HSRE, 156.

31. HSRE, 124, 126–27.

32. HSRE, 164.

33. "The Ker Fighters," *Seen & Heard by Megargee,* December 25, 1901, 27–30; *Philadelphia Times,* September 12, 1892.

34. *Philadelphia Times,* September 19, 1876, September 11, 1892.

35. HSRE, 848; Klotsche, "Star Route Frauds," 120; *Testimony of Attorney-General Brewster,* 7.

36. Klotsche, "Star Route Frauds," 124.

37. HSRE, 533–34.

38. HSRE, 533.

39. *Boston Globe,* July 11, 1886. This tribute was written upon Corkhill's death by the anonymous columnist known simply as "Howard."

40. *Testimony of Attorney-General Brewster,* 5–6; HSRE, 218.

41. *St. Louis Globe-Democrat,* September 30, 1881.

42. HSRE, 217; *Chicago Daily Inter Ocean,* September 8, 1881.

43. HSRE, 218.

44. Matthew Stephenson of Harvard Law School quoted in "A History of Corruption in the United States," Harvard Law Today, September 23, 2020, today.law.harvard.edu/a-history-of -corruption-in-the-united-states/.

45. HSRE, 534–35.

46. HSRE, 159.

47. HSRE, 535.

48. HSRE, 535.

49. HSRE, 159.

50. HSRE, 226.

51. HSRE, 159, 255.

52. HSRE, 107–8.

53. HSRE, 161.

8. MACVEAGH'S WATERLOO

1. HSRE, 104.

2. *Milwaukee Daily Sentinel,* October 1, 1881; HSRE, 103, 105.

3. *St. Louis Globe-Democrat,* September 16, 1881; *Chicago Daily Inter Ocean,* September 15, 1881; *Boston Daily Advertiser,* September 16, 1881.

4. HSRE, 161, 218.

5. *Chicago Daily Inter Ocean,* November 8, 1881.

6. *Chicago Daily Inter Ocean,* November 8, 1881.

7. *St. Louis Globe-Democrat,* September 16, 1881.

8. Richard Hofstadter, *The American Political Tradition and the Men Who Made It* (New York: Vintage Books, 1959), 173.

9. *St. Louis Globe-Democrat,* October 1, 1881.

10. Hofstadter, *American Political Tradition,* 173; Crook, *Through Five Administrations,* 278–79.

11. Klotsche, "Star Route Frauds," 105–6.

12. *Sun* (New York City), October 4, 1881.

13. *Testimony of Attorney-General Brewster,* 39.

14. Lowry, "Portrait of an Age," 284–85.

15. HSRE, 89.

16. Klotsche, "Star Route Frauds," 105–6.

17. HSRE, 108.

18. HSRE, 108.

19. HSRE, 69.

20. HSRE, 160.

21. HSRE, 161–62.

22. HSRE, 161–62.

23. HSRE, 166.

24. HSRE, 166–67.

25. Klotsche, "Star Route Frauds," 107; *Milwaukee Daily Sentinel,* October 1, 1881.

26. *Milwaukee Daily Sentinel,* October 1, 1881.

27. *Wisconsin State Register* (Portage), October 8, 1881; *Milwaukee Daily Sentinel,* October 1, 1881.

28. *Milwaukee Daily Sentinel,* October 1, 1881.

29. *Chicago Daily Inter Ocean,* October 3, 1881.

30. *Chicago Daily Inter Ocean,* October 3, 1881.

31. *Chicago Daily Inter Ocean,* November 4, 1881.

32. *Chicago Daily Inter Ocean,* November 4, 1881.

33. *Boston Daily Advertiser*, November 5, 1881.

34. *Boston Daily Advertiser*, November 11, 1881.

35. *Chicago Daily Inter Ocean*, November 11, 1881.

36. *Milwaukee Daily Sentinel*, November 11, 1881; *Boston Daily Advertiser*, November 11, 1881.

37. *Galveston (TX) Daily News*, November 12, 1881.

38. *Chicago Daily Tribune*, November 11, 1881.

39. Howe, *Chester A. Arthur*, 182.

9. THIS LAMENTABLE FIASCO

1. George Bliss to Wayne MacVeagh, December 23, 1881, reproduced in HSRE, 164.

2. Robert Underwood Johnson, *Remembered Yesterdays* (Boston: Little, Brown, 1923), 369.

3. *Chicago Daily Tribune*, November 6, 1881.

4. *Washington Evening Star*, November 5, 1881.

5. *Chicago Daily Tribune*, November 7, 12, 1881.

6. HSRE, 24.

7. Dorothy S. Eaton, "Manuscripts," *Quarterly Journal of Current Acquisitions* 16, no. 3 (1959): 133–51; Chester A. Arthur to Wayne MacVeagh, November 7, 1881, Chester Alan Arthur Papers, Library of Congress, Washington, DC. I have very lightly edited this draft for clarity.

8. Johnson, *Remembered Yesterdays*, 368.

9. Johnson, *Remembered Yesterdays*, 368–69.

10. Henry Adams to Henry Cabot Lodge, November 15, 1881, in Worthington Chauncy Ford, ed., *Letters of Henry Adams (1858–1891)* (Boston: Houghton Mifflin, 1930), 331–32.

11. Cater, *Henry Adams and His Friends*, 113.

12. Howe, *Chester A. Arthur*, 161.

13. Benjamin Harris Brewster to George Bliss, December 26, 1881, reproduced in *New York World*, December 30, 1881.

14. *Testimony of Attorney-General Brewster*, 39.

15. *Testimony of Attorney-General Brewster*, 6.

16. *Chicago Times*, December 7, 1881; Chester A. Arthur, "First Annual Message," December 6, 1881, American Presidency Project, www.presidency.ucsb.edu/node/203844.

17. Scott Greenberger, *The Unexpected President: The Life and Times of Chester A. Arthur* (Boston: Da Capo, 2019), 186–87.

18. "The Week," *Nation*, December 8, 1881, 441.

19. *Testimony of Attorney-General Brewster*, 6.

20. *Testimony of Attorney-General Brewster*, 6.

21. *Testimony of Attorney-General Brewster*, 7.

22. *Testimony of Attorney-General Brewster*, 7–8.

23. *Testimony of Attorney-General Brewster*, 7–8.

24. HSRE, 342.

25. HSRE, 341–42.

26. HSRE, 341–42.

27. HSRE, 343.

28. HSRE, 343–44.

29. HSRE, 193–94.

30. HSRE, 166, 193–94.

31. HSRE, 344.

32. HSRE, 86.

10. FROM THE SEWERS OF CALUMNY

1. *Sun* (New York City), January 7, 1882; *Washington Evening Star,* March 1, 1882; *Indiana State Sentinel* (Indianapolis), May 4, 1881.

2. *National Republican* (Washington), June 27, 1881.

3. *National Republican* (Washington), April 26, June 20, 1881; Grana, *On the Fringes of Power,* 34.

4. *National Republican* (Washington), June 14, 1881.

5. Klotsche, "Star Route Cases," 413.

6. *National Republican* (Washington), May 9, 1881.

7. *Cincinnati Commercial Gazette,* May 5, 1881; Klotsche, "Star Route Cases," 413–14.

8. *National Republican* (Washington), October 19, 1881.

9. *National Republican* (Washington), November 2, 1881.

10. *National Republican* (Washington), June 24, 1881.

11. Thoron, *Letters of Mrs. Henry Adams,* 305.

12. *National Republican* (Washington), June 9, 24, October 7, 1881.

13. *National Republican* (Washington), November 12, 14, 1881.

14. *Bangor (ME) Daily Whig and Courier,* February 16, 1882.

15. HSRE, 468–69.

16. HSRE, 468–69.

17. *National Republican* (Washington), March 18, 1882; HSRE, 697.

18. *Washington Evening Star,* March 18, 1882.

19. HSRE, 696.

20. *New York Times,* May 28, 1884.

21. Richardson, *William E. Chandler,* 343; "The Week," *Nation,* January 11, 1883, 23.

22. *New York Times,* January 26, 1882.

23. *New York Times,* February 10, 1882.

24. *New York Times,* February 21 1882.

25. DTT, 716.

26. DTT, 712.

27. DTT, 6, 11.

28. *Washington Evening Star,* March 16, May 20, 1882; *National Republican* (Washington), March 17, 1882.

29. *New York Times,* February 21, 1882.

30. *New York Times,* February 21, 1882.

31. *New-York Tribune,* February 21, 1882; *Frank Leslie's Illustrated Newspaper,* March 4, 1882, 18.

32. *New York Times,* February 21, 1882.

33. HSRE, 122–23, 225.

11. SELLING YOU OUT TO THE OTHER SIDE

1. HSRE, 535–37.

2. HSRE, 535–36.

3. HSRE, 122, 127.

4. *St. Louis Globe-Democrat,* April 24, 1882.

5. HSRE, 128.

6. *Washington Evening Star,* April 26, 1882.

7. HSRE, 128; *Washington Evening Star,* May 20, 1882.

8. HSRE, 543.

9. HSRE, 543.

10. Frank G. Carpenter, *Carp's Washington* (New York: McGraw-Hill, 1960), 34; Klotsche, "Star Route Frauds," 119–20.

11. James H. Whyte, *The Uncivil War: Washington during the Reconstruction, 1865–1878* (New York: Twayne, 1958), 109.

12. *Testimony of Attorney-General Brewster,* 6–7.

13. HSRE, 112–13.

14. HSRE, 112–13.

15. HSRE, 119; *Washington Evening Star,* March 17, 1882.

16. *Washington Evening Star,* March 17, 1882.

17. *National Republican* (Washington), March 18, 1882.

18. *Washington Evening Star,* March 20, 1882.

19. Benjamin Brewster to William A. Cook, March 17, 1882, reproduced in HSRE, 111.

20. HSRE, 195.

21. *Testimony of Attorney-General Brewster,* 4–5.

22. HSRE, 344.

23. HSRE, 344.

24. HSRE, 216.

25. HSRE, 213.

26. HSRE, 115–16, 344.

27. *Philadelphia Press,* May 24, 1883, quoted in William A. Cook to Benjamin Brewster, June 7, 1883, reproduced in HSRE, 129.

28. HSRE, 130.

29. Kirk, *Many Secrets Revealed,* 30–32.

30. HSRE, 196–97.

31. *Sun* (New York City), November 27, 1881.

12. THE CHARGE HERE IS CONSPIRACY

1. *Washington Evening Critic,* May 4, 1882.

2. "In Memoriam: Justice Andrew Wylie," *Washington Law Reporter* (January 6, 1905): 803–6.

3. "In Memoriam: Justice Andrew Wylie," 803–6.

4. Regis Noel and Margaret Brent Downing, *The Court-House of the District of Columbia* (Washington, DC: Judd and Detweiler, 1919), 25–32. Benefiting from several further renovations, the building, located on what is now Judiciary Square, is still in use and currently houses the District of Columbia Court of Appeals.

5. Lowry, "Portrait of an Age," 292.

6. HSRE, 645.

7. Klotsche, "Star Route Frauds," 123–24.

8. HSRE, 643–44.

9. HSRE, 643–44.

10. *Washington Evening Star,* June 16, 1883.

11. HSRE, 346–47, 597.

12. DTT, 107.

13. HSRE, 541.

14. HSRE, 186.

15. Noel and Downing, *Court-House of the District of Columbia,* 67.

16. John S. Reynolds, *Reconstruction in South Carolina, 1865–1877* (Columbia, SC: State Company, 1905), 113; William H. Dennis, "In Memoriam—Hugh Thomas Taggart, Esq.," *Records of the Columbia Historical Society* 18 (1915): 252–62; William O. Bradley, *Stories and Speeches of William O. Bradley* (Lexington, KY: Transylvania Printing, 1916), 101–2; Kentucky Historical Society, "Richard B. Carpenter, Jr.," Civil War Governors of Kentucky Digital Documentary Edition, discovery.civilwargovernors.org/document/N00005226.

17. *Chicago Daily Tribune,* June 18, 1876; Affidavit of Brewster Cameron, June 23, 1884, GRDOJ.

18. Robert Green Ingersoll, *Political Speeches of Robert G. Ingersoll* (New York: C. P. Farrell, 1914), 55–60; Horace Traubel, *With Walt Whitman in Camden,* vol. 8 (Oregon House, CA: W. L. Bentley, 1996), 102.

19. Robert Green Ingersoll, *The Works of Robert G. Ingersoll,* vol. 6 (New York: Dresden, 1901), 101.

20. Carpenter, *Carp's Washington,* 171.

21. Leland, "Post Office and Politics," 166.

22. *New York Times,* June 13, 1882; HSRE, 186.

23. Klotsche, "Star Route Frauds," 128.

24. DTT, 683.

25. *Washington Evening Critic,* June 7, 1882.

26. *New York Times,* June 3, 1882.

27. DTT, 732.

28. DTT, 106.

29. DTT, 107–8.

30. DTT, 136–37.

31. DTT, 147.

32. *Washington Evening Critic,* June 6, 1882; *New York Truth,* June 6, 1882.

33. DTT, 147.

34. DTT, 152.

35. DTT, 160.

36. DTT, 209.

37. *Washington Evening Critic,* June 6, 1882.

38. *New York Times,* June 7, 1882.

39. DTT, 210.

40. DTT, 212–15.

41. *New York Times,* June 8, 1882.

42. DTT, 238, 241.

43. DTT, 225.

44. DTT, 257–52.

45. DTT, 261.

46. DTT, 351.

47. DTT, 351.

48. DTT, 224.

49. DTT, 301.

50. DTT, 334.

51. DTT, 334.

52. DTT, 357.

53. DTT, 368.

54. DTT, 380.

55. DTT, 404.

56. DTT, 280.

57. *New York Times,* June 10, 1882.

58. *New York Times,* June 13, 1882.

59. Leland, "Post Office and Politics," 180.

60. Paine, *In One Man's Life,* 152.

13. NOT SO HOPELESS

1. DTT, 587.

2. DTT, 622.

3. DTT, 741.

4. DTT, 1520.

5. DTT, 819.

6. DTT, 1274; *New York Times,* June 29, 1882.

7. DTT, 1029–30.

8. DTT, 1023.

9. DTT, 1404.

10. *Washington Evening Star,* July 22, 1882.

11. DTT, 2281.

12. DTT, 1453.

13. DTT, 1472.

14. Horace Smith, *Roscoe's Digest of the Law of Evidence in Criminal Cases* (Philadelphia: T. and J. Johnson, 1874), 409–16.

15. DTT, 1678.

16. HSRE, 544–45.

17. HSRE, 650–51.

18. *New York Herald,* August 12, 26, 1882; HSRE, 651.

19. *New York Herald,* August 26, 1882; HSRE, 546.

20. DTT, 2884; HSRE, 655.

21. DTT, 1552.

22. DTT, 1553.

23. DTT, 1578–79.

24. DTT, 1700.

25. DTT, 1700–1701.

26. DTT, 1607.

27. DTT, 1700–1701.

28. DTT, 1700–1701.

29. DTT, 1761.

30. DTT, 1642.

31. *Boston Daily Advertiser,* July 22, 1882; *Cleveland Daily Herald,* July 22, 1882.

32. *Chicago Daily Inter Ocean,* July 22, 1882.

33. *National Republican* (Washington), quoted in *Washington Evening Critic,* July 22, 1882.

34. DTT, 1807.

35. DTT, 1808–9.

36. DTT, 1808–9.

37. DTT, 1812.

38. DTT, 1821.

39. DTT, 1882.

40. Leland, "Post Office and Politics," 185–87.

41. HSRE, 13–14.

42. Leland, "Post Office and Politics," 185–87.

43. *Washington Evening Critic,* August 8, 1882.

44. HSRE, 59; Deposition of George Bliss, November 22, 1883, GRDOJ; *Washington Evening Star,* August 8, 1882.

45. *New York Times,* July 26, 1882.

14. WAS NOT THAT A FRAUD?

1. DTT, 2014.

2. DTT, 2008.

3. DTT, 2005.

4. DTT, 2019.

5. DTT, 2019.

6. The story of Sherman's career has been told in a variety of biographies, including Brian Holden Reid, *The Scourge of War: The Life of William Tecumseh Sherman* (New York: Oxford University Press, 2020).

7. DTT, 2074–75.

8. DTT, 2074–75, 2081.

9. DTT, 2093, 2095.

10. DTT, 2112.

11. Ryan P. Semmes, "From Pea Ridge to the Potomac: Lemon G. Hine and the 44th Illinois Regiment, 1861–1862," *Journal of the Illinois State Historical Society* 104, no. 1/2 (2011): 115–39; *Washington Law Reporter*, January 23, 1914, 49; DTT, 2200–2201.

12. DTT, 2203.

13. DTT, 2204.

14. DTT, 2205–7.

15. DTT, 2205.

16. DTT, 2208.

17. DTT, 2208–9.

18. DTT, 2211.

19. DTT, 2217–20.

20. DTT, 2249–50.

21. *Washington Evening Star,* August 5, 1882.

22. George Bliss to Benjamin Brewster, November 6, 1882, GRDOJ.

23. DTT, 2271.

15. A NATIONAL HUMILIATION

1. Thomas C. Reeves, "The President's Dwarf: The Letters of Julia Sand to Chester A. Arthur," *New York History* 52, no. 1 (1971): 72–83.

2. Julia Sand to Chester Arthur, August 15, 1882, Chester Alan Arthur Papers, Library of Congress, Washington, DC.

3. Julia Sand to Chester Arthur, August 15, 24, 1882, Arthur Papers; Reeves, "President's Dwarf," 72–83.

4. DTT, 2313–14.

5. DTT, 2313–14.

6. DTT, 2318; Lowry, "Portrait of an Age," 309.

7. DTT, 2423.

8. DTT, 2428.

9. DTT, 2428–29.

10. DTT, 2428–29.

11. DTT, 2429.

12. DTT, 2434–35.

13. DTT, 2536–37.

14. DTT, 2539.

15. DTT, 2576.

16. DTT, 2576.

17. DTT, 2649.

18. William Makepeace Thackeray, *The Works of William Makepeace Thackeray*, vol. 21 (London: Smith, Elder, 1879), 33–36.

19. DTT, 2721.

20. DTT, 2780.

21. DTT, 2780.

22. HSRE, 547–48.

23. DTT, 2870.

24. DTT, 2871.

25. DTT, 2781.

26. DTT, 2781.

27. DTT, 2871.

28. Elizabeth Moore Chapin, *American Court Gossip; or, Life at the National Capitol* (Marshalltown, IA: Chapin and Hartwell Bros., 1887), 117.

29. DTT, 3107.

30. DTT, 3107.

31. *Washington Post*, June 20, 24, 1882; Lowry, "Portrait of an Age," 311–12.

32. *Testimony of Attorney-General Brewster*, 24.

33. HSRE, 549.

34. *Testimony of Attorney-General Brewster*, 25.

35. Noel and Downing, *Court-House of the District of Columbia*, 67.

36. DTT, 3112.

37. DTT, 3121.

38. *Lancaster (PA) Intelligencer Journal*, August 14, 1882.

39. *Lancaster (PA) Intelligencer Journal*, August 14, 1882.

40. Lowry, "Portrait of an Age," 310–11; *New-York Tribune*, August 14, 1882; *Boston Globe*, August 15, 1882.

41. DTT, 3190.

42. DTT, 3196.

43. DTT, 3188.

44. DTT. 3188.

45. DTT, 3223.

46. DTT, 3235–36.

47. DTT, 3235–36.

48. Record of Jury Vote, *United States v. Stephen Dorsey et al.,* GRDOJ.

49. DTT, 3241–42.

50. DTT, 3249.

51. DTT, 3267.

52. DTT, 3267.

53. DTT, 3271; HSRE, 601.

54. Klotsche, "Star Route Frauds," 134–35.

55. *Testimony of Attorney-General Brewster,* 41; "The Star Route Cases," *Washington Law Reporter* (June 14, 1882): 371.

56. HSRE, 186, 207–8.

57. HSRE, 601.

58. HSRE, 587.

59. HSRE, 108.

60. *Chicago Daily Inter Ocean,* September 12, 1882.

61. All quoted in *Washington Evening Star,* September 16, 1882.

62. All quoted in *Washington Evening Star,* September 16, 1882.

16. INCONSISTENT AND PECULIAR

1. DTT, 3196.

2. Anonymous to Richard Merrick, September 13, 1882, GRDOJ.

3. Henry, *Captain Henry of Geauga,* 329–30.

4. *Youngstown (OH) News-Register,* June 13, 1882; Henry, *Captain Henry of Geauga,* 329–30.

5. *Youngstown (OH) News-Register,* June 13, 1882; Henry, *Captain Henry of Geauga,* 330–31.

6. Henry, *Captain Henry of Geauga,* 330–31.

7. *New York Times,* April 24, 1885; *Washington Evening Critic,* April 24, 1885.

8. Leland, "Post Office and Politics," 171.

9. Leland, "Post Office and Politics," 171–74, 189–90.

10. HSRE, 208, 295; Report of Pinkerton Agents, June 2, 1882, GRDOJ.

11. HSRE, 296.

12. DTT, 3268–70.

13. DTT, 3268–70.

14. Leland, "Post Office and Politics," 189–90.

15. DTT, 3268–70.

16. Homer Cummings and Carl McFarland, *Federal Justice: Chapters in the History of Justice and Federal Executive* (New York: Macmillan, 1957), 257–58.

17. Leland, "Post Office and Politics," 195; Cummings and McFarland, *Federal Justice,* 257–58.

18. "Summary of the Week's News," *Nation,* November 2, 1882, 370; Report of Special Investigator Henry H. Wells to the Attorney General of the United States, October 20, 1882, GRDOJ.

19. *New York Times,* September 13, 1882.

20. HSRE, 107; *New York Times,* October 28, December 14, 1882, February 24, 1883.

21. *New York Times,* December 14, 1882, February 24, 1883.

22. *New York Times,* December 13, 1881.

23. *New York Times,* April 27, 1885; *Washington Evening Star,* April 27, 1885.

24. *Washington Evening Star,* April 27, 1885.

25. Benjamin Brewster to George Bliss, September 25, 1882, reproduced in HSRE, 662.

26. HSRE, 551.

27. HSRE, 552.

28. HSRE, 643–44.

29. Leland, "Post Office and Politics," 199; *New York Times,* November 26, 1882.

30. *Cincinnati Gazette,* November 28, 1882; *New-York Tribune,* November 28, 1882; Henry, *Captain Henry of Geauga,* 332.

31. Henry, *Captain Henry of Geauga,* 332.

32. *New York Times,* November 26, 1882.

33. *Sun* (New York City), November 27, 1882.

34. *New York Times,* November 27, 1882; Robert Green Ingersoll to Henry H. Wells, October 13, 1882, GRDOJ.

35. *Cleveland Daily Herald,* December 2, 1882.

36. Orvin Larson, *American Infidel: Robert G. Ingersoll, a Biography* (New York: Citadel, 1962), 178.

37. William H. Pruden III, "William Wallace Wilshire (1830–1888)," Encyclopedia of Arkansas, last updated September 29, 2021, encyclopediaofarkansas.net/entries/william-wallace-wilshire-4666/.

38. 2DT, 6.

39. Benjamin Brewster to Chester Arthur, November 24, 1882, quoted in 2DT, 11.

40. 2DT, 89–93; *New York World,* quoted ibid., 94.

41. *Washington Evening Star,* November 27, 1882; *Milwaukee Daily Sentinel,* December 1, 1882; *St. Louis Globe-Democrat,* December 3, 1882.

42. George Bliss to William Lawrence, November 12, 1882, reproduced in HSRE, 323.

43. George Bliss to Richard Merrick, November 6, 1882, reproduced in HSRE, 668.

44. William Ker to Benjamin Brewster, December 19, 1883, reproduced in HSRE, 912.

45. 2DT, 345, 351.

46. 2DT, 354–55.

47. Leland, "Post Office and Politics," 206–8.

48. *New York Times,* November 10, 1882.

49. *Civil Service Record,* November 1882, 41.

50. Dorman B. Eaton, "Assassination and the Spoils System," *Princeton Review* 2 (July–December 1881): 145–71.

51. Leland, "Post Office and Politics," 209–10.

52. Reeves, *Gentleman Boss,* 323.

53. *Chicago Tribune,* December 7, 1882; *New York Times,* December 5, 1882.

54. Leland, "Post Office and Politics," 210.

55. Reeves, *Gentleman Boss,* 323.

56. Doenecke, *Presidencies of James A. Garfield and Chester A. Arthur*, 101–2.

57. Sean M. Theriault, "Patronage, the Pendleton Act, and the Power of the People," *Journal of Politics* 65, no. 1 (2003): 50–68; Ari Hoogenboom, "The Pendleton Act and the Civil Service," *American Historical Review* 64, no. 2 (1959): 301–18.

58. David Henry Montgomery, *The Student's American History* (Boston: Ginn, 1897), 501.

17. SUCKLED IN FALSEHOOD

1. 2DT, 891.

2. Leland, "Post Office and Politics," 216; *New York Times*, January 26, 1882.

3. Leland, "Post Office and Politics," 216; *New York Times*, January 26, 31, 1883; Paine, *In One Man's Life*, 151–52.

4. Edward Taylor to Brewster Cameron, July 29, 1882, GRDOJ; F. H. Fall to Brewster Cameron, July 12, 1882, ibid.

5. 2DT, 2202, 2212.

6. 2DT, 2202; Lowry, "Portrait of an Age," 331–33; *Bangor (ME) Daily Whig and Courier*, February 19, 1883.

7. 2DT, 2251–54, 2263–65, 2268–73, 2280–98; Lowry, "Portrait of an Age," 332–34.

8. 2DT, 5652.

9. *St. Louis Globe-Democrat*, February 20, 1883.

10. *New York Times*, February 17, 1883.

11. *New York Times*, February 27, 1883.

12. *New York Times*, March 9, 1883.

13. Affidavit of Charles Cake, March 15, 1883, GRDOJ.

14. *St. Louis Globe-Democrat*, March 27, 1883.

15. 2DT, 3695–96.

16. 2DT, 3696.

17. 2DT, 3697.

18. 2DT, 3702.

19. 2DT, 3702–4.

20. 2DT, 3813.

21. Lowry, "Portrait of an Age," 343–44.

22. Leland, "Post Office and Politics," 221; *New York Times*, March 15, 1883.

23. 2DT, 3384.

24. 2DT, 3386–88.

25. *Indianapolis Journal*, March 15, 1883.

26. *St. Paul (MN) Daily Globe*, March 16, 1883.

27. 2DT, 3415–18.

28. 2DT, 3480.

29. *Middletown (DE) Transcript*, March 16, 1883.

30. 2DT, 5769.

31. 2DT, 5481.

32. *New York Times,* 15 June 1883.

33. 2DT, 5872.

34. *St. Louis Globe-Democrat,* June 14, 1883.

35. *Philadelphia North American,* June 14, 1883.

36. *St. Louis Globe-Democrat,* June 14, 1883.

37. *New York Times,* March 8, 1883.

38. *New-York Tribune,* June 15, 1883.

39. *New-York Tribune,* June 15, 1883.

40. *New-York Tribune,* June 15, 1883.

41. *New-York Tribune,* June 15, 1883.

42. *New-York Tribune,* June 15, 1883.

43. *New-York Tribune,* June 15, 1883.

44. Bradley, *Stories and Speeches,* 101–2.

45. *New-York Tribune,* June 15, 1883.

46. *New-York Tribune,* June 15, 1883.

47. *Washington Evening Critic,* June 16, 1883.

48. *New-York Tribune,* June 15, 1883.

49. *Baltimore American, Boston Herald, Buffalo (NY) Express,* and *New York Evening Post,* all quoted in *Washington Evening Star,* June 16, 1883; *New York World,* quoted in *National Republican* (Washington), June 16, 1883.

50. *New York Mail and Express* and *Columbus (OH) Daily Times,* quoted in *Washington Evening Star,* June 16, 1883.

51. *New-York Tribune,* June 15, 1883.

52. *New-York Tribune,* June 15, 1883.

53. Lowry, "Portrait of an Age," 346.

54. Leland, "Post Office and Politics," 200–205; Affidavit of James Nelson, March 18, 1884, GRDOJ.

55. Leland, "Post Office and Politics," 200–205, 222.

56. Henry A. Harman, "Is the Jury System a Failure?," *American Law Register* 31, no. 2 (1883): 81–84; Robert Y. Hayne, "Shall the Jury System Be Abolished?," *North American Review* 139, no. 335 (1884): 348–55.

57. "A Meeting," *Puck,* July 25, 1883, 328.

18. YES, THE STAR ROUTE BUSINESS KILLED GARFIELD!

1. HSRE, 97–98; *New York Times,* March 12, 1884.

2. HSRE, 14–15.

3. Norton, *Stalwarts,* iii–iv. Norton is often referenced by the surname of her husband at the time of her brother's trial, George Scoville.

4. Norton, *Stalwarts,* 230–31.

5. HSRE, 19–20.

6. HSRE, 19–20; Klotsche, "Star Route Cases," 407–18.

7. *Boston Daily Advertiser,* February 17, 1882; Klotsche, "Star Route Cases," 407–18.

8. *Philadelphia North American,* July 20, September 21, October 17, 1882.

9. HSRE, 348.

10. Patrick Henry Woodward to Chester A. Arthur, February 8, 1883, reproduced in HSRE, 348.

11. Patrick Henry Woodward to Benjamin Brewster, February 11, 1883, reproduced in HSRE, 348.

12. HSRE, 348.

13. *Testimony of Attorney-General Brewster,* 27.

14. Lowry, "Portrait of an Age," 352.

15. Klotsche, "Star Route Cases," 407–18; Benjamin Brewster to George Bliss, June 4, 1883, reproduced in HSRE, 291; *New York Times,* July 24, 1883; Walter Gresham to Benjamin Brewster, June 19, 1883, GRDOJ.

16. George Bliss to Benjamin Brewster, December 21, 1883, reproduced in HSRE, 953.

17. Klotsche, "Star Route Cases," 407–18; W. O. Bradley to Benjamin Brewster, June 24, 1884, GRDOJ.

18. Lowry, "Portrait of an Age, 286–87; *Chicago Daily Inter Ocean,* January 9. 1882.

19. *Chicago Daily Inter Ocean,* January 9, 1882.

20. HSRE, 119.

21. United States v. Cosgrove, 26 F. 908 (D.Kan. 1886); United States v. Voorhees, 135 U.S. 550 (1890); Howe, *Chester A. Arthur,* 191–92; *St. Paul (MN) Daily Globe,* June 5, 1885.

22. *Proceedings in the Case of The United States vs. William Pitt Kellogg, Charged with Receiving a Bribe while United States Senator,* in the Supreme Court of the District of Columbia, Andrew Wylie, Justice (Washington, DC: Government Printing Office, 1884), 158–59.

23. HSRE, 527–28; Edmund Burke, *Thoughts on the Present Discontent, and Speeches* (London: Cassell, 1892), 114.

24. For more detailed accounts of Arthur's final years, see, among others, Reeves, *Gentleman Boss,* and Karabell, *Chester Alan Arthur.*

25. Robert Beauvais, "The Dorsey Mansion—A New Mexico Registered Cultural Property," *New Mexico Architecture* 14, no. 6 (November–December 1972): 12–23.

26. *New York Times,* November 22, 1884; Miguel Antonio Oterero, *My Life on the Frontier, 1864–1882* (New York: Press of the Pioneers, 1935), 240.

27. Oterero, *My Life on the Frontier,* 240.

28. George W. Julian, *Later Speeches on Political Questions, with Select Controversial Papers* (Indianapolis: Carlon and Hollenbeck, 1889), 298.

29. Lowry, "Portrait of an Age," 398; *New York Times,* March 21, 1916; *Los Angeles Times,* March 21, 1916.

30. Herndon, *Centennial History of Arkansas,* 743.

31. *Middlebury (VT) Register,* August 19, 1901.

32. *New York Times,* April 24, 1904.

33. "Looking Back," theesotericcuriosa.blogspot.com/2010/06/looking-back-reminiscing -about-house-of.html.

34. *New York Times,* September 3, 1897.

35. F. E. Jackson, ed., *The Makers of the Panama Canal, 1911* [New York: F. E. Jackson and Son, ca. 1911], 134.

36. Carpenter, *Carp's Washington,* 34.

37. Savidge, *Life of Benjamin Harris Brewster,* 260.

38. Susan Jacoby, *The Great Agnostic: Robert Ingersoll and American Freethought* (New Haven, CT: Yale University Press, 2014); Robert Green Ingersoll, *What's God Got to Do with It? Robert Ingersoll on Free Thought, Honest Talk, and the Separation of Church and State* (Lebanon, NH: Steerforth, 2005).

39. *Boston Globe,* July 11, 1886.

40. *Chicago Daily Inter Ocean,* March 26, 1899; Gibson, *Political Crime,* 1.

41. *Washington Evening Star,* April 17, 1901.

42. Henry, *Captain Henry of Geauga,* 333.

19. THE STANDARD OF PUBLIC MORALS HAS BEEN ELEVATED

1. Charles W. Calhoun, "Major Party Conflict in the Gilded Age: A Hundred Years of Interpretation," *OAH Magazine of History* 13, no. 4 (Summer 1999): 5–10.

2. Charles W. Calhoun, *The Gilded Age: Perspectives on the Origins of Modern America* (Lanham, MD: Rowman and Littlefield, 2007), 239–60; Worth Robert Miller, "The Lost World of Gilded Age Politics," *Journal of the Gilded Age and Progressive Era* 1, no. 1 (January 2002): 49–67.

3. Katy J. Harriger, *The Special Prosecutor in American Politics,* 2nd ed. (Lawrence: University Press of Kansas, 2000).

4. *Meriden (CT) Journal,* September 5, 1917; HSRE, 349; Woodward, *Secret Service of the Post Office Department,* 582–84.

5. HSRE, 349.

6. Josephson, *Politicos,* 325.

7. Blevins, *Paper Trails,* 160–61; Office of the Inspector General, United States Postal Service, "Management and Oversight of Highway Contract Routes," audit report NL-AR-16-006 (Arlington, VA: Office of the Inspector General, USPS, September 30, 2016), www.oversight.gov/sites /default/files/oig-reports/NL-AR-16-006.pdf.

8. U.S. Department of Transportation, Office of the Inspector General, "Colorado Delivery Service Owners Indicted for Falsifying Driver Logs and Major Fraud against the U.S.," Investigations, March 24, 2010, www.oig.dot.gov/library-item/29828; Department of Justice, U.S. Attorney's Office, Southern District of Florida, "Trucking Company Vice President Pleads Guilty to Orchestrating United States Postal Service Contract Fraud," June 12, 2019, www.justice.gov /usao-sdfl/pr/trucking-company-vice-president-pleads-guilty-orchestrating-united-states-postal.

9. U.S. Attorney's Office, Southern District of Florida, "Trucking Company Vice President Pleads Guilty."

BIBLIOGRAPHY

TRIAL TRANSCRIPTS

Proceedings in the Case of The United States v. William Pitt Kellogg, Charged with Receiving a Bribe while United States Senator, in the Supreme Court of the District of Columbia, Andrew Wylie, Justice. Washington, DC: Government Printing Office, 1884.

Proceedings of the Second Trial of the Case of The United States v. John W. Dorsey, John R. Miner, John M. Peck, Stephen W. Dorsey, Harvey M. Vaile, Montfort C. Rerdell and Thomas J. Brady, in the Supreme Court of the District of Columbia, Andrew Wylie, Justice. Washington, DC: Government Printing Office, 1883.

Proceedings in the Trial of the Case of The United States v. John W. Dorsey, John R. Miner, John M. Peck, Stephen W. Dorsey, Harvey M. Vaile, Montfort C. Rerdell, Thomas J. Brady, and William H. Turner for Conspiracy, in the Supreme Court of the District of Columbia, Andrew Wylie, Justice. Washington, DC: Government Printing Office, 1882.

Report of the Proceedings in the Case of The United States v. Charles J. Guiteau, in the Supreme Court of the District of Columbia, Walter Cox, Justice. Washington, DC: Government Printing Office, 1882.

GOVERNMENT DOCUMENTS

Annual Report of the Postmaster General of the United States for the Fiscal Year Ended June 30, 1881. Washington, DC: Government Printing Office, 1881.

General Records of the Department of Justice, 1849–1989. Record Group 60, National Archives and Records Administration, College Park, MD.

"Management of the Post-Office Department." In *Reports of Committees of the House of Representatives for the First Session of the Forty-Fourth Congress, 1875–1876.* Washington, DC: Government Printing Office, 1876.

Miscellaneous Documents of the House of Representatives for First Session of the 48th Congress, 1883–1885. Testimony Relating to Expenditures in the Department of Justice, Star Route Cases. Washington, DC: Government Printing Office, 1884.

Miscellaneous Documents of the House of Representatives for Second Session of the 46th Congress, 1879–1880. Vol. 3. Washington, DC: Government Printing Office, 1880.

Office of the Inspector General, United States Postal Service. "Management and Oversight of Highway Contract Routes." Audit report NL-AR-16-006, Arlington, VA: Office of the Inspector General, USPS, September 30, 2016. https://www.oversight.gov /sites/default/files/oig-reports/NL-AR-16-006.pdf.

———. "Rural and Urban Origins." Report RISC-WP-19-007. August 26, 2019.

"Status and Performance of the United States Postal Service." In *Hearings before the Subcommittee on Postal Service of the Committee on Post Office and Civil Service, House of Representatives, Ninety-Second Congress, 2nd Session.* Washington, DC: Government Printing Office, 1972.

Testimony of Attorney-General Brewster, together with the Letters and Documents Furnished to the Committee of the House of Representatives Appointed to Inquire into the Expenditures of Department of Justice. Washington, DC: Government Printing Office, 1884.

"Testimony Taken before the Committee on the Post-Office and Post-Roads, in Relation to Mail Contracts." In *Reports of Committees of the House of Representatives for the First Session of the Forty-Fourth Congress, 1875–1876.* Washington, DC: Government Printing Office, 1876.

US House of Representatives. *Presidential Election Investigation, Testimony Taken by the Select Committee on Alleged Frauds in the Presidential Election of 1876.* Vol. 2, *Testimony Relating to Florida,* 45th Cong., 3rd sess., H. Misc. Doc. 31, pt. 2. Washington, DC: Government Printing Office, 1879.

War of the Rebellion: A Compilation of the Official Records of the Union and Confederate Armies. Ser. 1, vol. 31, pt. 1. Washington, DC: Government Printing Office, 1890.

MAGAZINE ARTICLES

Ames, Mary Clemmer. "A Woman's Letter from Washington." *Independent,* July 2, 1874, 13.

Andrews, E. Benjamin. "A History of the Last Quarter-Century." *Scribner's Magazine,* September 1895, 288.

Connery, T. B. "Secret History of the Garfield-Conkling Tragedy." *Cosmopolitan,* June 1897, 145–62.

Cooper, Gary (as told to Marc Crawford). "Stagecoach Mary: A Gun-Toting Black Woman Delivered the U.S. Mail in Montana." *Ebony,* October 1, 1959, 97–100.

Hyman, Stanley Edgar. "Comment." *New Yorker,* December 24, 1943, 13.

James, Thomas L. "Development of the Overland Mail Service." *Cosmopolitan*, April 1896, 603–11.

"A Meeting." *Puck*, July 25, 1883, 328.

"ROUTES: CASE I CASE II CASE III CASE IV." *Puck*, May 25, 1881, 199.

"Summary of the Week's News." *Nation*. November 2, 1882, 370.

"The Week." *Nation*. December 8, 1881, 441.

"The Week." *Nation*. May 19, 1881, 341–43.

LEGAL AND SCHOLARLY ARTICLES

Ball, Larry D. "'Just and Right in Every Particular': U.S. Marshal Zan Tidball and the Politics of Frontier Law Enforcement." *Journal of Arizona History* 34, no. 2 (1993): 177–200.

Beauvais, Robert. "The Dorsey Mansion—A New Mexico Registered Cultural Property." *New Mexico Architecture* 14, no. 6 (November–December 1972): 12–23.

Berthoff, Warner, and David Bonnell Green. "Henry Adams and Wayne MacVeagh." *Pennsylvania Magazine of History and Biography* 80, no. 4 (1956): 493–512.

Calhoun, Charles W. "Major Party Conflict in the Gilded Age: A Hundred Years of Interpretation." *OAH Magazine of History* 13, no. 4 (Summer 1999): 5–10.

Cassidy, Lewis. "The Elder Brewster of Pennsylvania." *Dickinson Law Review* 41, no. 2 (1936): 103–14.

Clark, James C. "The Murder of President James A. Garfield." *Prologue* 24 (Summer 1992): 129–39.

Dennis, William H. "In Memoriam—Hugh Thomas Taggart, Esq." *Records of the Columbia Historical Society* 18 (1915): 252–62.

Eaton, Dorman. "Assassination and the Spoils System." *Princeton Review* 2 (July–December 1881): 145–71.

Eaton, Dorothy S. "Manuscripts." *Quarterly Journal of Current Acquisitions* 16, no. 3 (1959): 133–51.

Harman, Henry A. "Is the Jury System a Failure?" *American Law Register* 31, no. 2 (1883): 81–84.

Hayne, Robert Y. "Shall the Jury System Be Abolished?" *North American Review* 139, no. 335 (1884): 348–55.

Holliday, Joseph E. "Daniel D. Pratt: Senator and Commissioner." *Indiana Magazine of History* 58, no. 1 (1962): 17–51.

Hoogenboom, Ari. "The Pendleton Act and the Civil Service." *American Historical Review* 64, no. 2 (1959): 301–18.

"In Memoriam: Justice Andrew Wylie." *Washington Law Reporter* (January 6, 1905): 803–6.

Kelley, Brooks M. "Simon Cameron and the Senatorial Nomination of 1867." *Pennsylvania Magazine of History and Biography* 87, no. 4 (1963): 375–92.

Klotsche, J. Martin. "The Star Route Cases." *Mississippi Valley Historical Review* 22, no. 3 (1935): 407–18.

Lowry, Sharon K. "Mirrors and Blue Smoke: Stephen Dorsey and the Santa Fe Ring in the 1880s." *New Mexico Historical Review* 59, no. 4 (1984): 395–407.

Miller, Worth Robert. "The Lost World of Gilded Age Politics." *Journal of the Gilded Age and Progressive Era* 1, no. 1 (January 2002): 49–67.

Mitchell, Stewart. "The Man Who Murdered Garfield." *Proceedings of the Massachusetts Historical Society* 67 (1941): 452–89.

Mowry, Duane. "Political Letters of the Post-Bellum Days: From the Doolittle Correspondence with Thomas A. Hendricks." *Indiana Quarterly Magazine of History* 5, no. 4 (1909): 171–80.

Peskin, Allan. "Who Were the Stalwarts? Who Were Their Rivals? Republican Factions in the Gilded Age." *Political Science Quarterly* 99, no. 4 (1984): 703–16.

Reeves, Thomas C. "The President's Dwarf: The Letters of Julia Sand to Chester A. Arthur." *New York History* 52, no. 1 (1971): 72–83.

Semmes, Ryan P. "From Pea Ridge to the Potomac: Lemon G. Hine and the 44th Illinois Regiment, 1861–1862." *Journal of the Illinois State Historical Society* 104, no. 1/2 (2011): 115–39.

Smith, Paul Tincher. "Indiana's Last October Campaign." *Indiana Magazine of History* 19, no. 4 (1923): 332–45.

"The Star Route Cases." *Washington Law Reporter* (June 14, 1882): 371.

Taylor, Morris F. "Stephen W. Dorsey, Speculator-Cattleman." *New Mexico Historical Review* 49, no. 1 (1974): 27–48.

Theriault, Sean M. "Patronage, the Pendleton Act, and the Power of the People." *Journal of Politics* 65, no. 1 (2003): 50–68.

BOOKS

Ackerman, Kenneth. *Dark Horse: The Surprise Election and Political Murder of President James A. Garfield.* New York: Carroll and Graf, 2003.

Anderson, Carl. *As I Remember It: Reminiscences.* Spencer, IN: Farm Bureau Printing, 1943.

Arrington, Benjamin T. *The Last Lincoln Republican: The Presidential Election of 1880.* Lawrence: University Press of Kansas, 2020.

Baldwin, Frederick C. *Biography of the Bar of Orleans County, Vermont.* Montpelier: Vermont Watchman and State Journal, 1884.

Berger, Meyer. *The Story of the New York Times: The First 100 Years, 1851–1951.* New York: Arno, 1970.

Biographical Directory of the American Congress, 1774–1961. Washington, DC: Government Printing Office, 1961,

A Biographical History of Eminent and Self-Made Men of the State of Indiana. Vol. 1. Cincinnati: Western Biographical, 1880

Blevins, Cameron. *Paper Trails: The U.S. Post and the Making of the American West.* New York: Oxford University Press, 2021.

Bradley, William O. *Stories and Speeches of William O. Bradley.* Lexington, KY: Transylvania Printing, 1916.

Brandt, Nat. *The Town That Started the Civil War.* Syracuse, NY: Syracuse University Press, 1990.

Broxmeyer, Jeffrey. *Electoral Capitalism: The Party System in New York's Gilded Age.* Philadelphia: University of Pennsylvania Press, 2020.

Burke, Edmund. *Thoughts on the Present Discontent, and Speeches.* London: Cassell, 1892.

Byron, George Gordon. *Childe Harold's Pilgrimage, a Romaunt: And Other Poems.* London: John Murray, 1815.

Calhoun, Charles W. *The Gilded Age: Perspectives on the Origins of Modern America.* Lanham, MD: Rowman and Littlefield, 2007.

Caperton, Tomas J. *Rogue! Being an Account of the Life and High Times of Stephen W. Dorsey, United States Senator and New Mexico Cattle Baron.* Santa Fe: Museum of New Mexico, 1978.

Carpenter, Frank G. *Carp's Washington.* New York: McGraw-Hill, 1960.

Cater, Harold Dean, ed. *Henry Adams and His Friends: A Collection of His Unpublished Letters.* Boston: Houghton Mifflin, 1947.

Chambers, Julius. *The Book of New York: Forty Years' Recollections of the American Metropolis.* New York: Book of New York, 1912.

Chapin, Elizabeth Moore. *American Court Gossip; or, Life at the National Capitol.* Marshalltown, IA: Chapin and Hartwell Bros., 1887.

Clark, James C. *The Murder of James A. Garfield: The President's Last Days and the Trial and Execution of His Assassin.* New York: McFarland, 1993.

Cohen, Jared. *Accidental Presidents: Eight Men Who Changed America.* New York: Simon and Schuster, 2019.

Cortissoz, Royal. *The Life of Whitelaw Reid.* New York: Charles Scribner's Sons, 1921.

Crane, John H. *More about the Washington Tammany.* Washington, DC, 1873.

———. *The Washington Ring.* Washington, DC, 1872.

Crook, William H. *Through Five Administrations.* New York: Harper and Brothers, 1910.

Cummings, Homer, and Carl McFarland. *Federal Justice: Chapters in the History of Justice and Federal Executive.* New York: Macmillan, 1957.

Curtis, George Ticknor. *Constitutional History of the United States: From Their Declaration of Independence to the Close of Their Civil War.* Vol. 2. New York: Harper and Brothers, 1896.

Cushing, Marshall. *The Story of Our Post Office: The Greatest Government Department in All Its Phases.* Boston: A. M. Thayer, 1892.

Democratic National Committee. *The Campaign Text Book: Why the People Want Change.* New York: Democratic National Committee, 1876.

———. *The Campaign Text Book: Why the People Want Change.* New York: Democratic National Committee, 1880.

Dillard, Tom. *Statesmen, Scoundrels, and Eccentrics: A Gallery of Amazing Arkansans.* Fayetteville: University of Arkansas Press, 2010.

Doenecke, Justus. *The Presidencies of James A. Garfield and Chester A. Arthur.* Lawrence: University Press of Kansas, 1981.

Donovan, John Wesley. *Trial Practice and Trial Lawyers.* St. Louis: W. H. Stevenson, 1883.

Douglas, Benjamin. *History of the Lawyers of Wayne County, Ohio, from 1812 to 1900.* Wooster, OH: Clapper Printing, 1900.

Fiske, Stephen. *Off-hand Portraits of Prominent New Yorkers.* New York: G. R. Lockwood and Son, 1884.

Ford, Worthington Chauncy, ed. *Letters of Henry Adams (1858–1891).* Boston: Houghton Mifflin, 1930.

Fowler, Dorothy Ganfield. *The Cabinet Politician: The Postmasters General, 1829–1909.* New York: Columbia University Press, 1943.

Fuller, Wayne E. *RFD: The Changing Face of Rural America.* Bloomington: Indiana University Press, 1964.

Gallagher, Winifred. *How the Post Office Created America: A History.* New York: Penguin Press, 2016.

Garfield, James A. *The Diary of James A. Garfield.* Vol. 4, *1878–1881.* East Lansing: Michigan State University Press, 1981.

Gibson, Albert M. *A Political Crime: The History of the Great Fraud.* New York: W. S. Gottsberger, 1885.

Grana, Mari. *On the Fringes of Power: The Life and Turbulent Career of Stephen Wallace Dorsey.* Lanham, MD: Rowman and Littlefield, 2015.

Greenberger, Scott. *The Unexpected President: The Life and Times of Chester A. Arthur.* Boston: Da Capo, 2019.

Guiteau, Charles J. *The Truth and the Removal.* Washington, DC: Charles J. Guiteau, 1882.

Haimbaugh, Frank D., ed. *History of Delaware County, Indiana.* Vol. 1. Indianapolis: Historical Publishing, 1924.

Harding, Warren G. *The Railways and Prosperity: Address by Warren G. Harding, at the Annual Dinner of the Railway Business Association.* New York: Railway Business Association, 1914.

Harriger, Katy J. *The Special Prosecutor in American Politics.* 2nd ed. Lawrence: University Press of Kansas, 2000.

Hayes, Rutherford Birchard. *Diary and Letters of Rutherford Birchard Hayes, Nineteenth President of the United States.* Vol. 4. Columbus: Ohio State Archeological and Historical Society, 1925.

Helm, Thomas B. *History of Delaware County, Indiana.* Chicago: Kingman Brothers, 1881.

Henry, Frederick A. *Captain Henry of Geauga, a Family Chronicle.* Cleveland: Gates, 1942.

Herndon, Dallas T., ed. *Centennial History of Arkansas.* Vol. 1. Chicago: S. J. Clarke, 1922.

Hofstadter, Richard. *The American Political Tradition and the Men Who Made It.* New York: Vintage Books, 1959.

Hoogenboom, Ari. *Outlawing the Spoils: A History of the Civil Service Reform Movement, 1865–1883.* Urbana: University of Illinois Press, 1961.

Howe, George Frederick. *Chester A. Arthur: A Quarter-Century of Machine Politics.* New York: Dodd, Mead, 1934.

Ingersoll, Robert Green. *Political Speeches of Robert G. Ingersoll.* New York: C. P. Farrell, 1914.

———. *What's God Got to Do with It? Robert Ingersoll on Free Thought, Honest Talk, and the Separation of Church and State.* Lebanon, NH: Steerforth, 2005.

———. *The Works of Robert G. Ingersoll.* Vol. 6. New York: Dresden, 1901.

Jackson, F. E., ed. *The Makers of the Panama Canal, 1911.* [New York: F. E. Jackson and Son, ca. 1911].

Jacoby, Susan. *The Great Agnostic: Robert Ingersoll and American Freethought.* New Haven, CT: Yale University Press, 2014.

Johnson, Robert Underwood. *Remembered Yesterdays.* Boston: Little, Brown, 1923.

Jordan, David M. *Roscoe Conkling of New York: Voice in the Senate.* Ithaca, NY: Cornell University Press, 1971.

Josephson, Matthew. *The Politicos: 1865–1896.* New York: Harcourt, Brace, 1938.

Joyce, John A. *Jewels of Memory.* Washington, DC: Gibson Brothers, 1896.

Julian, George W. *Later Speeches on Political Questions, with Select Controversial Papers.* Indianapolis: Carlon and Hollenbeck, 1889.

Kirk, Rollin H. *Many Secrets Revealed; or, Ten Years behind the Scenes in Washington City.* Washington, DC, 1885.

Lamkin, Uel W. *History of Henry County, Missouri.* Philadelphia: Historical Publishing, 1919.

Larson, Orvin. *American Infidel: Robert G. Ingersoll, A Biography.* New York: Citadel, 1962.

Leonard, Devin. *Neither Snow nor Rain: A History of the United States Postal Service.* New York: Grove, 2017.

Locke, David Ross. *The Nasby Letters*. Toledo, OH: Toledo Blade, 1893.

MacVeagh, Isaac Wayne. *Law And Democracy: An Address Delivered before the Graduating Classes at the Sixty-Second Anniversary of the Yale Law School, on June 29th, 1886*. New Haven, CT: Law Department of Yale College, 1886.

Makris, John N. *The Silent Investigators: The Great Untold Story of the United States Postal Inspection Service*. New York: E. P. Dutton, 1959.

"Major Simpleton." *Civil-Service Reform; or, The Postmaster's Revenge*. New York: Metropolitan, 1882.

Marcus, Robert D. *Grand Old Party: Political Structure in the Gilded Age, 1880–1896*. New York: Oxford University Press, 1971.

Menke, Richard. *Literature, Print Culture, and Media Technologies, 1880–1900: Many Inventions*. Cambridge: Cambridge University Press, 2019.

Millard, Candice. *Destiny of the Republic: A Tale of Madness, Medicine, and the Murder of a President*. New York: Doubleday, 2011.

Montgomery, David Henry. *The Student's American History*. Boston: Ginn, 1897.

Morgan, H. Wayne. *From Hayes to McKinley: National Party Politics, 1877–1896*. Syracuse, NY: Syracuse University Press, 1969.

Morris, Roy, Jr. *Fraud of the Century: Rutherford B. Hayes, Samuel Tilden, and the Stolen Election of 1876*. New York: Simon and Schuster, 2003.

Noel, Regis, and Margaret Brent Downing. *The Court-House of the District of Columbia*. Washington, DC: Judd and Detweiler, 1919.

Norris, James D., and Arthur H. Shaffer, eds. *Politics and Patronage in the Gilded Age: The Correspondence of James A. Garfield and Charles E. Henry*. Madison: State Historical Society of Wisconsin, 1970.

Norton, Frances Marie. *The Stalwarts; or, Who Were to Blame?* Chicago: Frances Marie Norton, 1888.

Norwood, Elias. *Norwood's Political Poems for the Poor Man's Rights*. Portland, ME, 1884.

Oterero, Miguel Antonio. *My Life on the Frontier, 1864–1882*. New York, Press of the Pioneers, 1935.

Paine, Albert Bigelow. *In One Man's Life, Being Chapters from the Personal & Business Career of Theodore N. Vail*. New York: Harper and Brothers, 1921.

Paxson, Frederic Logan. *Recent History of the United States*. Boston: Houghton Mifflin, 1922.

Peskin, Allan. *Garfield*. Kent, OH: Kent State University Press, 1978.

Reeves, Thomas C. *Gentleman Boss: The Life of Chester Alan Arthur*. New York: Knopf, 1975.

Reid, Brian Holden. *The Scourge of War: The Life of William Tecumseh Sherman*. New York: Oxford University Press, 2020.

Reynolds, John S. *Reconstruction in South Carolina, 1865–1877*. Columbia, SC: State Company, 1905.

Richardson, Leon Burr. *William E. Chandler, Republican*. New York: Dodd, Mead, 1940.

Rosenberg, Charles. *The Trial of the Assassin Guiteau: Psychiatry and Law in the Gilded Age*. Chicago: University of Chicago Press, 1968.

Savidge, Eugene Coleman. *Life of Benjamin Harris Brewster, with Discourses and Addresses*. Philadelphia: J. B. Lippincott, 1891.

Simon, John Y., ed. *The Papers of Ulysses S. Grant*. Vol. 22: *June 1, 1871–January 31, 1872*. Carbondale: Southern Illinois University Press, 1998.

Smith, Horace. *Roscoe's Digest of the Law of Evidence in Criminal Cases*. Philadelphia: T. and J. Johnson, 1874.

Smith, Theodore Clarke. *The Life and Letters of James Abram Garfield*. 2 vols. New Haven, CT: Yale University Press, 1925.

Stanwood, Edward. *James Gillespie Blaine*. Boston: Houghton Mifflin, 1908.

Summers, Mark Wahlgren. *The Era of Good Stealings*. New York: Oxford University Press, 2003.

———. *Rum, Romanism, & Rebellion: The Making of a President, 1884*. Chapel Hill: University of North Carolina Press, 2000.

Thackeray, William Makepeace. *The Works of William Makepeace Thackeray*. Vol. 21. London: Smith, Elder, 1879.

Thomas, Harrison Cook. *The Return of the Democratic Party to Power in 1884*. New York: Columbia University Press, 1919.

Thompson, George H. *Arkansas and Reconstruction: The Influence of Geography, Economics, and Personality*. Port Washington, NY: Kennikat, 1976.

Thoron, Ward, ed. *The Letters of Mrs. Henry Adams, 1865–1883*. Boston: Little, Brown, 1936.

Townsend, George Washington. *Our Martyred President: Memorial Life of William McKinley*. Philadelphia: Memorial, 1901.

Traubel, Horace. *With Walt Whitman in Camden*. Vol. 8. Oregon House, CA: W. L. Bentley, 1996.

Ullery, Jacob G. *Men of Vermont: An Illustrated Biographical History of Vermonters and Sons of Vermont*. Brattleboro, VT: Transcript, 1894.

Van Riper, Paul P. *History of the United States Civil Service*. Evanston, IL: Row, Peterson, 1958.

Whyte, James H. *The Uncivil War: Washington during the Reconstruction, 1865–1878*. New York: Twayne, 1958.

Woodward, Patrick Henry. *The Secret Service of the Post Office Department*. Hartford, CT: Winter, 1886.

THESES AND DISSERTATIONS

Broxmeyer, Jeffrey. "Politics as a Sphere of Wealth Accumulation: Cases of Gilded Age New York, 1855–1888." Ph.D. dissertation, City University of New York–Graduate Center, 2014.

Klotsche, Johannes Martin. "The Star Route Frauds." Ph.D. dissertation, University of Wisconsin–Madison, 1931.

LaFollette, Robert Russell. "History of Campaign Funds from 1876 to 1892." Master of Arts thesis, University of Wisconsin-Madison, 1917.

Leland, Earl. "The Post Office and Politics, 1876–1884: The Star Route Frauds." Ph.D. dissertation, University of Chicago, 1964.

Lowry, Sharon K. "Portrait of an Age: The Political Career of Stephen W. Dorsey, 1868–1889." Ph.D. dissertation, North Texas State University, 1980.

Shortridge, Annalee. "The Defeat of the Republicans in 1882." Master of Arts thesis, University of Wisconsin–Madison, 1923.

Trowbridge, Myrtle. "The Garfield Administration and the Star Route Prosecutions." Master of Arts thesis, University of Wisconsin–Madison, 1918.

ONLINE PUBLICATIONS

Arthur, Chester A. "First Annual Message," December 6, 1881. American Presidency Project. www.presidency.ucsb.edu/node/203844.

Basham, Charlie. "A Muddy Confederate Flag and the Foiled Plot." *Mountain Democrat* (Placerville, CA), April 14, 2015. www.mtdemocrat.com/prospecting/a-muddy-confederate-flag-and-the-foiled-plot/.

Carpenter, Daniel. "American Democracy Is in the Mail." Boston Review, September 10, 2020. bostonreview.net/articles/daniel-carpenter-american-democracy-mail/.

"A History of Corruption in the United States." Harvard Law Today, September 23, 2020. today.law.harvard.edu/a-history-of-corruption-in-the-united-states/.

"Isaac Wayne MacVeagh, 1881." Chester A. Arthur—Administration, U.S. Presidents. Miller Center, University of Virginia. millercenter.org/president/arthur/essays/macveagh-1881-attorney-general.

Kentucky Historical Society. "Richard B. Carpenter, Jr." Civil War Governors of Kentucky Digital Documentary Edition. discovery.civilwargovernors.org/document/N00005226.

"The Life and Legend of Mary Fields." Women's History Matters, April 8, 2014. montanawomenshistory.org/the-life-and-legend-of-mary-fields/.

"Looking Back: Reminiscing about the 'House of Gold!'" Esoteric Curiosa, June 22, 2010, theesotericcuriosa.blogspot.com/2010/06/looking-back-reminiscing-about-house-of.html.

McDaniel, W. Caleb. "In 1870, Henrietta Wood Sued for Reparations—and Won." *Smithsonian Magazine*, September 2019. www.smithsonianmag.com/history/henrietta-wood-sued-reparations-won-180972845/.

Moneyhon, Carl H. "Brooks-Baxter War." Encyclopedia of Arkansas, last updated January 10, 2019. encyclopediaofarkansas.net/entries/brooks-baxter-war-2276/.

———. "Convict Lease System." Encyclopedia of Arkansas, last updated December 22, 2020. encyclopediaofarkansas.net/entries/convict-lease-system-4153/.

Pruden, William H., III. "William Wallace Wilshire (1830–1888)." Encyclopedia of Arkansas, last updated September 29, 2021. encyclopediaofarkansas.net/entries /william-wallace-wilshire-4666/.

Sturrock, Staci. "Palm Beach County's Secret Post Office Murals Are a Delight." *Palm Beach Post*, September 23, 2016. www.palmbeachpost.com/story/lifestyle/2016/09 /23/palm-beach-county-s-secret/7010275007/.

Watson, Elbert L. "George Spencer." Encyclopedia of Alabama, November 18, 2010. encyclopediaofalabama.org/article/h-2975.

NEWSPAPERS

Alexandria (VA) Gazette

Ann Arbor (MI) Argus

Arkansas Gazette (Little Rock)

Bangor (ME) Daily Whig and Courier

Boston Globe

Boston Daily Advertiser

Chicago Daily Inter Ocean

Chicago Daily Tribune

Chicago Times

Cincinnati Enquirer

Cleveland Daily Herald

Concord (NH) Independent Statesman

Fayetteville (NC) Observer

Georgia Weekly Telegraph and Georgia Journal & Messenger (Macon)

Galveston (TX) Daily News

Concord (NH) Independent Statesman

Indiana State Sentinel (Indianapolis)

Indianapolis Sentinel

Lancaster (PA) Intelligencer Journal

Meriden (CT) Journal

Frank Leslie's Illustrated Newspaper

Little Rock (AR) Morning Republican

Lowell (MA) Daily Citizen

Middletown (DE) Transcript
Milwaukee Daily Sentinel
National Republican (Washington)
New Haven (CT) Register
New Mississippian (Jackson)
New York Herald
New York Times
New-York Tribune
New York Truth
Philadelphia North American
Rensselaer (IN) Union
St. Louis Globe-Democrat
St. Paul (MN) Daily Globe
San Francisco Daily Evening Bulletin
Silver World (Lake City, CO)
Sun (New York City)
Terre Haute (IN) Weekly Gazette
Washington Daily Patriot
Washington Evening Critic
Washington Evening Star
Washington Post
Wisconsin State Register (Portage)

INDEX

Adairville, Utah Territory, 169

Adams, Henry, xii, 60, 88, 123, 163

Adams, Marian, 88, 163

Alexandria, Virginia, 183

Alturas, California, 222

Aesop's Fables, 236

American Law Register, The, 285

Ames, Mary Clemmer, 28

Ames, Oakes, 66

Anderson, Carl, 4

Arkansas Central Railway, 26, 27, 28, 37

Arlington National Cemetery, 297

Arthur, Chester A., xi, xiii, xiv, 49, 52–53, 56, 57, 118, 119, 120, 123, 126–27, 138–42, 145, 148–49, 151–56, 163–66, 170, 176–77, 184, 218, 230–31, 233, 235–37, 240, 242, 243, 252, 254, 259–62, 265–68, 290, 295, 301, 303

Astor, John Jacob, III, 52

Atlanta Constitution, 248

Babcock, Orville, 76

Baker City, Oregon, 168, 223

Barlow, Bradley, 7, 23, 134

Báez, Buenaventura, 11

Baltimore American, 249, 283

Barnum, William Henry, 24–25, 35

Baxter, Elisha, 27

Beecher, Henry Ward, 27–28, 32

Blackburn, Joseph, 43–44

Blaine, James G., 12, 28–29, 52–53, 54, 55, 59–60, 119, 154, 187, 295, 297–98

Blevins, Cameron, 3, 4

Bliss, George, 22, 124, 126, 130–35, 137, 140, 142–45, 147, 150, 154, 155, 156, 157, 158–59, 164–66, 170, 172, 174–80, 182, 186–87, 189, 190–92, 194, 195, 201–2, 204, 207–10, 212–13, 217, 235–37, 240, 242, 244, 247, 251–53, 257–60, 263–64, 270, 278, 283, 286, 290–92, 297

Blount, James Henderson, 44

Booth, John Wilkes, 10, 303

Boone, Albert, xvi, 30–31, 33, 34, 39, 41, 89, 135, 229, 269, 293

Bosler, James, xvi, 42, 93, 135, 180, 273, 292

Boston Daily Advertiser, 214

Boston Globe, 243

Bowen, Sayles, 79

Bowen, Henry, 254–55, 257

Bowen, Thomas, 26

Boynton, Henry Van Ness, 79–80

Brady, John, 9

Brady, Thomas J., xii, xv, 9–16, 17, 19, 35–36, 39, 41, 42–47, 51, 54, 63, 73–75, 82, 84–87, 89–91, 94–95, 121–22, 124, 131–32, 134, 135, 141, 144, 146, 157, 158, 160–65, 167–69,

Henderson, John, 75

Hendricks, Thomas, 53

Henkle, Solomon, 205

Henry, Charles, 78–79, 244, 251–52, 259, 260, 299

Henry, Frederick, 299–300

Highway Contract Routes, 304–5

Hine, Lemon Galpin, 38–39, 186, 189, 194–95, 196, 223–24, 261

Hiram College, 78

Holman, William, 253

Howe, Timothy, 188

Hubbell, Jay, 161–62

Iddings, Charles, 290

Independence, Missouri, xv, 40, 272

Indiana State Sentinel, 11, 160

Ingersoll, Robert Green, 72, 78, 87, 93, 146–47, 157–58, 182, 186–89, 193, 196, 198, 200, 208, 221–22, 238–39, 260–61, 270, 272, 274–76, 279, 282–83, 285, 291, 296, 298

James, Thomas, xii, 55–64, 66–75, 81, 88–94, 117, 127, 130, 140–41, 162–63, 188, 211, 216–18, 219, 222–23, 229, 242, 288, 290, 293, 303

Jeannette (vessel), 274

Jefferson, Thomas, 1–2

Jewell, Marshall, 22, 48, 65

Johnson, Robert Underwood, 151–53

Jones, George, 74

Jones, John P., 24–25, 30

Josephson, Matthew, 304

Judas Iscariot, 285

Julian, California, 223

Julian, George W., 296

Kearney, Nebraska, 199

Kellogg, William Pitt, 68, 211, 294

Kennedy, P. A., 203

Kent, Nebraska, 199

Ker, William, 124, 127–29, 131–32, 155–56, 172–75, 176, 180, 186–87, 204, 206–8, 231–32, 237, 240–41, 255, 258, 263, 286, 290, 302

Key, David, 196

Key, Philip Barton, 151

Kirby, Thomas, 196

Klotsche, J. Martin, 35

Knox, Henry, 61, 242

Lapham, Elbridge, 57

Lawrence, William, 262

Lilley, Fred, 178, 273

Lilley, William, 158, 178, 273

Lincoln, Abraham, 9–10, 39, 174, 183, 237, 303

Locke, David Ross, 50

Lodge, Henry Cabot, 153

Los Pinos, Colorado, 190

Lowry, Sharon K., 7

Luttrell, John King, 21

MacVeagh, Isaac Wayne, xii, 59–61, 66–69, 71–73, 75–81, 87–95, 123–25, 127, 130, 137–38, 141–42, 149, 150–54, 156, 163–64, 173, 181, 199–200, 201, 211, 215, 216, 218, 219, 229, 242, 262, 286, 298, 301, 302

Martin, Thomas, 189

McClure, "Poker Jack," 29

McDevitt, Thomas, 290–91

McDonough, George, 144

McKibbin, Joseph, 17–23

McLean, Charles, 61

McSweeney, John, 29, 187, 189, 195–97, 204–5, 210, 214, 228–29, 234, 236–37, 261

Merrick, Mary Virginia, 298

Merrick, Richard, 174–75, 180, 184–87, 199–200, 202, 204–9, 225–29, 237–38, 244, 246–47, 255, 258–59, 263, 272, 274–75, 278–79, 283, 286, 290, 297–98, 302

Miller, George, 258, 273

Miller, Olive, 129

Miller, Samuel, 129

www.ingramcontent.com/pod-product-compliance
Lightning Source LLC
Chambersburg PA
CBHW020446100426
42812CB00036B/3467/J